The Complete Customer Relationship Management Handbook

Peter Flory

DIRECTORY OF SOCIAL CHANGE

Published by the Directory of Social Change (Registered Charity no. 800517 in England and Wales)
Head office: 24 Stephenson Way, London NW1 2DP
Northern office: Federation House, Hope Street, Liverpool L1 9BW
Tel: 08450 77 77 07

Visit www.dsc.org.uk to find out more about our books, subscription funding websites and training events. You can also sign up for e-newsletters so that you're always the first to hear about what's new.

The publisher welcomes suggestions and comments that will help to inform and improve future versions of this and all of our titles. Please give us your feedback by emailing publications@dsc.org.uk.

ISBN 978 1 906294 72 4

British Library Cataloguing in Publication Data
A catalogue record for this book is available from the British Library

Cover and text design by Kate Bass
Typeset by Marlinzo Services, Frome
Printed and bound by Page Bros, Norwich

MIX
Paper from
responsible sources
FSC
www.fsc.org
FSC® C023114

Contents

About the author

Dr Peter Flory is an independent information technology consultant working in the not-for-profit sector. He describes himself as an information systems professional who, many years ago, learnt how to communicate with 'real people' as well as 'techies'. His first degree is in mathematics and he is a Chartered Engineer and a Chartered IT Professional. In later years he obtained an MSc in Information Systems Management and he has a PhD on the subject of CRM.

Peter has been in the IT (or ICT, whichever you prefer) industry for more than 45 years (yes – 45 years!); the last half of that time was solely in the not-for-profit sector. He spent the first 16 years in the traditional IT areas of programming, systems analysis, project management and general management before joining a London firm of management consultants as an IT specialist where he became a bridge between real people and the techies.

In 1989 he decided to become completely independent and formed Athena Consultants to provide the highest level of independent, honest and ethical consultancy services to a wide range of clients. Almost immediately he took a decision to concentrate his efforts on the not-for-profit sector and since 1990 he has worked solely in this sector. He assists clients with the complete IT life cycle: IT strategy development, requirements specification, invitation to tender procedures, project management, quality assurance, implementation support and operational reviews.

Peter also lectures extensively on CRM and IT strategy and is a research fellow at Brunel University. This book draws heavily on his PhD research and on his more than 20 years of experience as a consultant to the not-for-profit sector.

Acknowledgements

I would like to thank the following authors and publishers for their permission to reproduce text extracts: Ken Burnett, Mike Hudson, Richard J. Schonberger, The Association for Computing Machinery, Emerald Group Publishing, IEEE Publishing, and Taylor & Francis. Thank you also to Bruce Ratner and Mike Hudson for their permission to reproduce diagrams.

I would also like to thank the following friends and colleagues who contributed case studies which help bring to life what can be a somewhat tedious subject at times: Peter Maple of London South Bank University; Phil Durbin of The Salvation Army; Scott Logie of the St. Ives Group; Aaron Woods of the British Red Cross Society; Paul Hughes of the Stroke Association.

Thanks go to Ivan Wainewright who helped me bring the list of suppliers in Chapter 21 up to date. (We both recognise that, because things move so fast in this industry, by the time you read this book the list will be out of date, but we hope it will still be useful.)

Many thanks also to John Bird formerly of the Access Group and Aaron Woods of the British Red Cross Society who reviewed the text, found typos and offered many helpful suggestions (most of which found their way into the final copy).

And last but definitely not least, special thanks to my wife Sandra, who once again has had to put up with me locking myself away writing in the study for hour after hour, day after day, week after week.

About the Directory of Social Change

The Directory of Social Change (DSC) has a vision of an independent voluntary sector at the heart of social change. The activities of independent charities, voluntary organisations and community groups are fundamental to achieve social change. We exist to help these organisations and the people who support them to achieve their goals.

We do this by:

- providing practical tools that organisations and activists need, including online and printed publications, training courses, and conferences on a huge range of topics;
- acting as a 'concerned citizen' in public policy debates, often on behalf of smaller charities, voluntary organisations and community groups;
- leading campaigns and stimulating debate on key policy issues that affect those groups;
- carrying out research and providing information to influence policymakers.

DSC is the leading provider of information and training for the voluntary sector and publishes an extensive range of guides and handbooks covering subjects such as fundraising, management, communication, finance and law. We have a range of subscription-based websites containing a wealth of information on funding from trusts, companies and government sources. We run more than 300 training courses each year, including bespoke in-house training provided at the client's location. DSC conferences, many of which run on an annual basis, include the Charity Management Conference, the Charity Accountants' Conference and the Charity Law Conference. DSC's major annual event is Charityfair, which provides low-cost training on a wide variety of subjects.

For details of all our activities, and to order publications and book courses, go to www.dsc.org.uk, call 08450 777707 or email publications@dsc.org.uk.

Foreword

A book with the word 'complete', or even 'compleat', in the title is inevitably a hostage to fortune. Scientifically, a body of knowledge is never complete – or it is only until something new is discovered. For example, the seminal work by Isaak Walton, *The Compleat Angler*, was dedicated to the Art and Spirit of Fishing, and was first published in 1653 but added to in subsequent editions over the next 25 years, all in the spirit of science and art. Hopefully we can look forward to Peter regularly updating his book on the art and spirit of CRM as technology and our wish to take full advantage of it continue to develop at a rapid pace. I can visualise Peter, like Isaak on the river bank, seeking the ideal specimen with hook and line. In Peter's case it's the perfect CRM solution.

Peter's had a lot of experience of implementing or advising on CRM systems in the not-for-profit sector. I have turned to him myself for CRM project support when I was the IT director at The Salvation Army. The role of independent adviser is a crucial one, as the motives and biases of IT Directors tend to be regarded with some suspicion within charities when there's a project affecting some aspect of the organisation through the use of technology. Peter never disappointed with his advice and his clarity and now some of his knowledge and experience are available without even requiring him to be present!

The history section of this comprehensive book is fascinating to some of us who lived through the period in which computers, organisations and individuals have developed significantly but separately. This book makes us appreciate the ongoing difficulties that organisations, even quite small ones, continue to have in operating departmentally in silos rather than working together cooperatively. The essence of CRM systems is to break down those barriers.

Early on in the book he makes it clear that CRM is not only for computer geeks, though IT directors and managers in the charity sector are frequently given the lead responsibility for system selection. But responsibility is not just for those making the IT aspect of the organisation work. Failure to appreciate and act upon this means that the organisation gets what the IT department wants or what the IT department thinks you want, and not what the business wants or needs.

Peter makes it clear that getting a CRM system right doesn't guarantee an effective new business system, because the quality of the people in the organisation and their willingness to work together are a critical part of any CRM system. The book demonstrates how complex a CRM system is for not-for-profit organisations. Peter rigorously takes us through the different views and purposes of a CRM system and all aspects of their selection and implementation.

Peter addresses the central notion of 'customer' in CRM in the not-for-profit sector very well indeed. From an IT perspective, the general way of referring to those who use the services provided was and still is a 'user'. Not only does this hint at the lack of imagination popularly deemed to be a characteristic of people working in IT, it also means that IT may share with the illegal drug industry a peculiar disinterest in the effects of its products on customers!

It is clear, from the thorough nature of the book, that there are intensively logical and complex aspects of CRM that make IT professionals not just useful but essential to ensuring that any new CRM system serves the required purposes. Those who don't naturally work in the logical, rational way so beloved of IT professionals, may wish to skim-read the more difficult technical sections, but I recommend that they read them all: they will provide themselves with a language to converse with IT people and gain a deeper understanding of what they really want from a CRM system.

Similarly, I believe that more technically interested people should concentrate on the many sections with more business language in them. It's a great way to absorb what is important to the not-for-profit organisation – a shortcut to understanding business needs and appreciating the value of different commercial offerings.

The latter parts of the book focus on planning, procuring and implementing a CRM system, and offer some excellent vignettes and examples to expose common pitfalls. Some terrific checklists enable avid readers to keep themselves on the right track.

I am convinced that reading, understanding and applying the knowledge in this book can reduce the many costly and painful mistakes made by not-for-profit organisations in their quest to improve their interactions with customers.

Good Fishing!

David Clayden
Former Director of Strategic Information for The Salvation
Army (UK and Ireland) and Non-executive Director of the Society
for IT Management (Socitm)

Part one:

What is CRM?

1 Introduction

1.1 ABOUT THIS BOOK

Customer relationship management (CRM) was originally developed in the commercial world in the 1990s, but did not become well established in the not-for-profit sector for almost ten years. With this background in mind, this book describes what CRM is, where it came from and how it is applied in the not-for-profit sector. It outlines CRM strategy considerations, what is required of CRM systems and how to choose and implement these systems. It also provides hints and tips on the effective usage of CRM in practice.

The book is divided into seven parts. This first part, 'What is CRM?', introduces the subject and describes:

- the historical background and how CRM developed, including the role of relationship marketing;
- how it is applied to the not-for-profit sector, i.e. some of the similarities to and the differences from 'traditional' (or commercial) CRM;
- the difficult question of 'Who is the customer?'

The second part, 'CRM strategy', describes the eight major principles underlying CRM, the '360 degree view' and other common CRM concepts, issues to consider when developing a CRM strategy, and how to manage a CRM project.

The third part, 'CRM systems architecture', moves on to the information technology systems required to support the implementation of a CRM strategy. It outlines the different ways of looking at CRM, how these views relate to each other, and how various IT systems are linked together to provide support for the CRM strategy.

The fourth part, 'CRM systems requirements and functionality', explains what is needed by the three main types of CRM system, namely collaborative CRM, operational CRM and analytical CRM, all three of which combine to create a complete CRM systems solution.

The fifth part, 'Setting up your CRM project', describes the stages of a complete CRM implementation project from beginning to end and the management issues that will need to be faced and overcome to achieve a successful outcome.

The sixth part, 'CRM systems procurement', outlines the problems faced by a prospective CRM systems purchaser, how to go about purchasing CRM systems and introduces some of the main CRM system suppliers.

The seventh part, 'Implementing and using CRM', describes how to go about the process of implementing CRM systems, the tasks involved, the management of the project, what to do when it all starts to go wrong, and more things to do when it is all up and running. It concludes with hints and tips when using CRM and, finally, a look into the future direction of CRM.

1.2 BACK TO BASICS

Before examining CRM in any depth, it is important to establish where it belongs in terms of organisational thinking. Many people place CRM firmly at the door of the IT (or ICT, information and communications technology, in today's terms) department and associate it simply with their 'database', but this is only one part of the story. Most readers will be familiar with figure 1.1 or some variation of it. It has been a mainstay of management philosophy for decades.

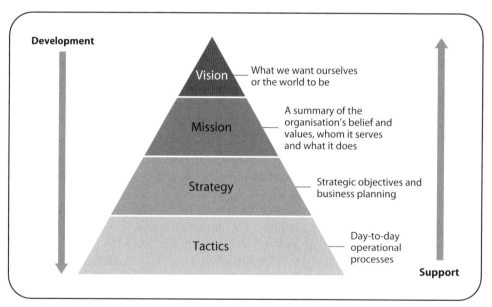

Fig. 1.1 Organisational pyramid

IT systems and databases are firmly rooted in 'tactics'. CRM belongs higher up the pyramid, as shown in figure 1.2. The first thing to get clear is that CRM is not a computer system. CRM is not a database. It is not the responsibility of the IT Manager. CRM is a business strategy. In fact, it is more than that: it is a complete organisational philosophy and a whole way of thinking and working. It is all encompassing and relevant to the entire organisation. It's about (in equal measure) people, processes and technology. It is about the ways in which you interact with your 'customers' – however you define them – and the aim of everyone in the organisation, whatever their job function, must be to keep the customer satisfied, otherwise you will soon have no organisation.

Thus, CRM is about you and everyone else in your organisation, what you do, how you do it and the tools you use (and the database is just one tool). To dispel another myth immediately, when CRM implementations fail, the failure is almost always people and/or process-related (more on this in section 8.4). The technology rarely fails, and when it does, it is the easiest part to get right.

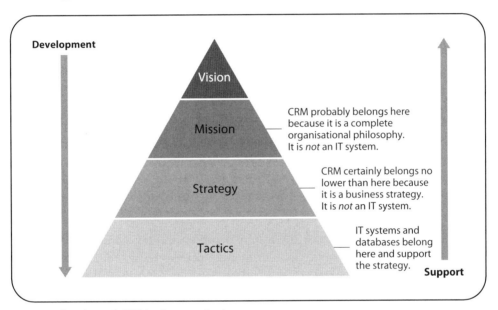

Fig. 1.2 The place of CRM in the organisation

1.3 **CRM OVERVIEW**

In a competitive world where a customer can change their allegiance quickly and easily, anything that provides facilities to attract customers and keep them loyal to the brand will help to assure the success of the business. CRM is a business strategy that incorporates such facilities.

What exactly is CRM? A number of common sayings will serve to introduce the subject:

● 'The customer is king.'
● 'The customer is always right.'
● 'Keep the customer satisfied.'
● 'Treat your customer as a person not a number.'
● 'Customers are our business, without them we have no business.'

- 'Your best future customers are your current customers.'
- 'Look after your customers and the £££s will look after themselves.'

CRM is not rocket science; it is common sense. Look after your current customers, keep them coming back for more and get them to tell all their friends about you because they have had such a good experience with you. That is CRM.

So, it is all about keeping customers satisfied, but what do customers actually want from you? Some years ago, manufacturing systems guru, Richard J. Schonberger, identified the four basic customer needs as quality, speed, flexibility and value, about which he says that 'all customers want ever better quality, ever quicker response, ever greater flexibility and ever higher value' (Schonberger, 1996, p. 31). What has changed in the meantime? Absolutely nothing! Customers want the best quality at the lowest cost, in the quickest time and they want the ability to change their requirements at any time.

There is, however, something to add to Schonberger's list and that is *customers want recognition and to be treated as individuals*. We can all relate to the cry 'I am not a number!' Customers are people. Even when dealing with organisations such as a corporate sponsor or a grant-giving trust, you are still dealing with people. People have feelings and want to be treated with respect. If you ignore them or you are rude to them, they are unlikely to remain as customers for very long.

There are many definitions of CRM, some of which will be examined in Chapter 3. However, a very simple definition was provided by the research and consultancy company Ovum, as described by Bradshaw and Brash (2001, p. 520): 'CRM is a management approach that enables organisations to identify, attract and increase retention of profitable customers, by managing relationships with them.' One of the key words in this definition is 'profitable'. This introduces the major objective of CRM: to make more money, i.e. to be more profitable, and this is to be achieved by managing the relationships with customers.

The definition of CRM above gives rise to a number of questions:

- How do you identify potential customers?
- How do you attract new customers?
- How do you retain existing customers?
- How do you upgrade existing customers?
- What is meant by managing relationships with customers?
- Is it just about making money?
- And, most importantly for the not-for-profit sector, who exactly is the customer?

These and many other questions will be addressed in this book.

2 CRM: An historical perspective

2.1 A BRIEF HISTORY

Where did CRM originate from and how did it develop? A brief summary is provided below and the major elements are discussed in the rest of this chapter.

2.1.1 1960s and 1970s: consumer marketing

> **Marketing mix** describes the choices that an organisation must make in the process of getting services or products to market, i.e. the organisation's 'offering'.

This was the time long before CRM and it was the heyday of mass marketing to large groups of individuals. There was little personalisation and brand awareness was everything. To quote common buzzwords, it was very 'product-centric' rather than being 'customer-centric'.

This approach is referred to as consumer marketing or transaction marketing and continues today as part of the overall **marketing mix**, but in the 1960s and 1970s it was *the* way to attract and sell to customers.

2.1.2 1983: relationship marketing

By the 1980s much more emphasis was being placed on maintaining and enhancing relationships with existing customers. Leonard Berry, marketing guru, published a seminal academic paper entitled simply *Relationship Marketing* in 1983, but the concepts expressed in it are much older and the origins can be traced back to the 1970s. It revolved around the concept of putting the customer at the centre of marketing thinking rather than products; hence the phrase 'customer-centric'.

2.1.3 1986: ACT!

> **Contact management** describes the sort of data to be recorded about contacts and basic functions to be performed for all types of contacts managed by the system, such as adding, amending and deleting contacts and managing duplicate records.

ACT! (which is still around today, re-branded as Act!) was the first general-purpose, inexpensive **contact management** software to be developed. This was in the days of green writing on black screens. Contact management systems allowed people to keep track of their contacts/customers and their interactions with these customers. It wasn't what we know of today as a CRM system, but it was the start. This was the first step in computerising relationships, as opposed to pencil and paper, and gave people the power to start implementing relationship marketing principles on a large scale.

2.1.4   1988: database marketing

The first definitions of database marketing appear in 1988 and revolve around large organisations with very large numbers of customers that could be segmented in a number of relatively simple ways and targeted with products and services especially suited to that group or segment.

2.1.5   Early 1990s: sales force automation

Contact management software soon began to be expanded into other areas for managing the sales process and to contact management the functions of lead management (the processing of sales enquiries), opportunity management (collaborative working to identify sales opportunities) and deal tracking (following the processes related to a sale) were added, which together constituted another buzz-phrase, sales force automation.

2.1.6   1995: customer relationship management

The term CRM was first coined by the Gartner company or by Tom Siebel (the jury is still out, but the author's money is on Tom Siebel) in 1995. Several terms including CIS (customer information system) and CIM (customer information management) were around for several years, but CRM won out in the end.

2.1.7   1997: data-driven marketing

As computerised system facilities developed, huge amounts of data were being generated and computer systems started to be developed that utilised **data warehouse** techniques. This marked the beginning of the use of sophisticated metrics which analysed customer behaviour and, indeed, the start of predictions of future customer behaviour.

A **data warehouse** is a central repository of data collected from many sources which is specifically designed for effective and efficient reporting and analysis.

2.1.8 1998: marketing, sales and service

The scope of CRM systems expanded to become a more complete customer-centred solution. After-sales service facilities were added to systems which had originally just focused on the sales process (with a bit of marketing thrown in).

2.1.9 1999: mobile CRM, eCRM and Salesforce

SaaS (also referred to as on-demand software) is a service which allows users to get software delivered via the Internet, rather than installing it on a local, office-based machine or needing updates and security patches to be done in-house (see also 21.2.2).

The first handheld device linked to a back-office CRM system was developed by Siebel all the way back in 1999. Also at this time, the Internet and the concept of outsourcing started to become important. Salesforce, the company and the CRM system that bears its name, arrived on the scene and it was provided on a Software as a Service (**SaaS**) basis. The term eCRM (electronic CRM or e-commerce CRM) started to appear, and indeed still does appear in some literature, but it is now largely redundant as almost everything in the computing world is 'e' based.

2.1.10 2002: Microsoft Dynamics CRM

Microsoft entered the CRM market (but it took them nearly ten years to get it right).

2.1.11 2004: SugarCRM

The first **open-source** CRM system, SugarCRM, appeared. It opened the way for even the smallest organisation to take advantage of the automation of CRM processes (if they had some level of technical expertise to configure the system to their requirements).

Open-source software allows the user access to the program's source code and can be freely redistributed and modified without any fee incurred. See opensource.org for a full definition.

2.1.12 2010: social CRM

This is the latest iteration of CRM, which integrates traditional CRM systems with social media such as Facebook, Twitter and LinkedIn.

2.2 **RELATIONSHIP MARKETING**

This is the first element of the brief history that is fundamental to the development of CRM. After the mass-marketing days of the 1960s and 1970s, in the early 1980s Leonard Berry and many other academics and marketing people started to seriously consider the question of retaining existing customers as opposed to attracting new ones. They reasoned that retaining an existing customer costs a great deal less than attracting a new one. This gave rise to the concept of relationship marketing. This differed from transaction or consumer marketing, which relates to single short-term communication exchanges. Relationship marketing relates to linked communication exchanges over a period of time that usually involve both financial and personal elements.

As Berry (2002) points out, relationship marketing is about retaining existing customers and making them 'loyal', as opposed to attracting new customers with no experience of the vendor and their products and services, which was the predominant aim of marketing before the 1980s. He sets out five relationship marketing strategies, namely:

1. **'Core service':** a base upon which other services can be added and sold to existing customers.
2. **'Relationship customisation':** identifying individual customer needs and offering them tailored products or services to meet that need.
3. **'Service augmentation':** adds extra services to the standard offering, services that are unlikely to be offered by the competition (the origin for the later buzzword 'cross-selling').
4. **'Relationship pricing':** offering special deals for existing customers.
5. **'Internal marketing':** this is all about attracting, retaining and motivating staff so that they provide customers with a better service (something a lot of people forget about).

When Berry reviewed his original 1983 paper in 2002, he placed less emphasis on service augmentation and relationship pricing but added 'service quality' and 'trust' to the equation. Thus we have five elements that form a basis for the later development of CRM:

1. Provision of a core service offering.
2. Provision of a high-quality offering.
3. The development of individual relationships.
4. The creation of customer loyalty (with the aim of creating 'lifetime customers').
5. Marketing to staff to keep them satisfied.

A key quote from Leonard Berry is:

> *Relationship marketing at its best is a philosophy, not just a strategy, a way of thinking about customers, marketing and value-creation, not just a set of techniques, tools, and tactics. Relationship marketing is holistic, a sum of integrated parts that drive a firm's marketing competencies.*
>
> Berry 2002, p. 73

Other writers stress the concept of one-to-one marketing and the fact that 'people sell to people'. So, although in many instances organisations might buy the products and services, it is people who make the decisions; thus the importance of personal relationships in marketing, sales and service functions.

A much-quoted concept in marketing is targeting 'the right message, at the right customers, at the right time via the right channels'. This also implies one-to-one marketing and treating people as individuals. It is vitally important to treat people with respect, but relationship marketing goes much further than this. You need to understand the customer, their motivations and their needs, and then you have to respond appropriately in order to provide the customer with the best experience possible.

2.3 THE BIRTH OF CRM

The second major element for discussion is CRM itself. The origins of CRM lie in relationship marketing and consequently can be traced back to 1983. The brief history outlined – relationship marketing in 1983, contact management software in 1986, database marketing in 1988 and sales force automation in 1990 – eventually combined and culminated in 1995 as customer relationship management.

Arguments about who originated the term are of little consequence. The point is that it appeared in 1995 as an overall organisational concept and has continually developed and become increasingly functional ever since.

The link between relationship marketing and CRM was expressed neatly by Evert Gummesson when he described CRM as:

> *Applying the values and strategies of relationship marketing in practice, with particular emphasis of the customer-supplier relationship, largely but not solely dependent on information technology.*
>
> Gummesson 2002, p. 587

This statement indicates that the power of the computer makes the implementation of some of the relationship marketing principles achievable.

When considering the subject of computer systems, the forerunners of today's personal computers (PCs) and laptops were developed in the mid-1970s, and in 1981 the first IBM PC was released. The entry of the computing giant IBM into the desktop computer market started a rush of IBM-compatible machines produced by many companies. This, and the adoption by IBM (and all the others) of an operating system from Microsoft, was the start of the standardisation of computing and its take-up by the mass market, i.e. by people like you and me.

This timescale overlapped completely with the thinking of marketing gurus such as Leonard Berry. Consequently, the development of relationship marketing theory and mass market computer systems that could support those theories went hand in hand. Before this time, all sorts of sales and marketing systems had been developed, but they were mainly the preserve of very large companies with huge mainframe computers and enormous computing budgets and were completely inaccessible to most of the workers at the coalface of sales and marketing.

The first major development in CRM was the formalisation of the very highest level of subject breakdown, namely, marketing, sales and service. This gave people a simple starting point in understanding CRM and it reflected both the sequence of operations (you market, you sell and then you service) and the breakdown of staff into separate, and separately functioning, departments (the marketing department, sales department and the service department). They may have operated independently before; for example sales force automation helped the sales department in the selling process, but when the customer called to complain about something, the service department knew nothing of the history of the sale. CRM made both departments realise that they needed to work together and know what the other was doing for the maximum benefit of both the company and the customer.

2.4   CRM AND THE NOT-FOR-PROFIT SECTOR

2.4.1   The CRM forerunners in the not-for-profit sector

In the 1970s, computers were large and expensive. Even a so-called mini-computer with five terminals would cost you £40,000. If not-for-profit organisations wished to record details of customers and their purchases or donations, their only options were as follows:

- **To write their own systems** (or have them written by a software house). This was very expensive and only the largest organisations could afford it.
- **To use a computer bureau.** This became very popular. The system development costs were borne by the bureau which operated large mainframe computers (usually IBM) and processed organisations' income records. Each

organisation paid on a per-transaction basis, so they had no large development costs. Later in the 1980s, these bureaux began to develop communications links so that the organisation could enter its own transactions if it wanted to. The biggest of these bureaux serving the sector was Southwark Computer Services, which still exists today under its new name of Acxiom.

- **To use manual recording methods.** This was the preferred option for most organisations, and involved paper or cardboard record cards and hand calculations.

By the early 1980s, a small number of packaged systems had appeared. CMG (Computer Management Group), Minerva Computer Systems and Care Business Solutions were early pioneers (which have now either gone or merged into AdvancedNFP which is part of the Advanced Computer Software Group). Unfortunately, these systems were large, cumbersome and expensive such that they could only be afforded by the very big not-for-profit organisations. At this time, 1981, the PC was beginning life, but it took a long time before sector-specific packages were developed. A system called Donorbase appeared in 1983, and although it has long since disappeared, it really started a revolution. It cost much less than its predecessors and brought early CRM-type facilities (in this case, focused on fundraising) within the reach of much smaller organisations.

> A **transaction processing** system is a back-office system that processes transactions one at a time, such as individual income items.

All the systems of the 1970s and 1980s had a number of things in common. They were 'green screen' (because the screen was usually black with green characters displayed on it), character-based (letters, digits and symbols – no pictures) and they were pure **transaction processing** systems. The emphasis was on automating the boring tasks of recording income and adding it up. The sophisticated analysis, customer profiling and **segmentation** that we take for granted today was not even a dream.

Around 1990 everything changed. The PC had become widespread and many new products appeared that were developed for PC networks. They still had the look and feel of the old systems but they were a little more sophisticated, easier to use and usually under the

> **Segmentation** is the process of querying the database to extract the groupings of customers as identified by analytics and research. Once a group of customers is selected as having satisfied a set of criteria, it is marked as belonging to that segment. (See also 16.3.5 and 'Selection and segmentation' within 15.3.2.)

control of the users (rather than the IT department) because they, and their associated hardware (the PC), were much more affordable.

The two major products to hit the market in 1990 were The Raiser's Edge and Alms. The Raiser's Edge arrived from the USA where it had been very successful for several years. It was very comprehensive with 40 main menu functions and, at £6,000, was affordable to a huge number of not-for-profit organisations, particularly charities, at which it was primarily focused. It embodied the then popular concept of 'WYSIWYG' (what you see is what you get), which meant that it was very rigid in the way that it worked, but it did most of the things that fundraisers wanted it to do. It came with around 100 standard reports and it was like a breath of fresh air. It soon became very popular and this popularity continues to this day.

Alms was developed in the UK. It covered the same basic functional areas as The Raiser's Edge (and some additional areas such as grant-making) but it was designed to be very flexible and easily tailored to any not-for-profit organisation's needs. It too became popular. There were others around but these two stood out above them all.

Then in the mid-1990s came the Windows phenomenon. The package suppliers had to redevelop their systems completely in order to take advantage of the new facilities and to keep up with the expectations of the general public. As the decade progressed, the systems gradually became more and more sophisticated. Words like segmentation, Pareto analysis and RFV (recency, frequency, value) analysis became commonplace (see 4.5.3). We were moving from transaction processing systems to information processing systems (i.e. more analytical systems).

2.4.2   The arrival of CRM and its adoption by the not-for-profit sector

As noted, CRM as a term arrived in the commercial world in 1995. It took around five years to find its way into the sector and then only in the membership arena where the operations were far more 'commercial' than those in the charity, arts, community, etc. parts of the sector. It may have arrived but the term was not widely known or accepted. In fact, confusion abounded for some time because there was already a well-established practice, **'cause-related marketing'**, which was known as CRM in this sector. (Indeed, this alternate meaning is still commonly used in the sector, but customer relationship

Cause-related marketing is where businesses link with not-for-profit organisations to help market a product or service, the desired effect being to increase both corporate credibility and customer loyalty while raising funds for a cause. One of the best-known examples is Tesco's Computers for Schools.

management is now the more dominant term.) Then in 2003 it began to change and change quickly as a commercial CRM system supplier, Ascent Technology (now part of Ciber UK), contracted to add fundraising functionality to their commercial CRM system for the charity Christian Aid.

Up until 2003, the sector had been served almost exclusively by system suppliers specific to the sector providing what they variously called contact databases, fundraising databases, membership databases or grants databases to manage what could be considered to be the organisations' customers. They were not and are still not, in the vast majority of cases, known as customers. However, in the case of charities and membership organisations, they were the people and organisations providing the money for the organisation and, in the case of grant-making organisations, they were the people and organisations to whom the grant-making organisation provided money.

Many of the systems contained some elements of CRM functionality but they were not known as such. These systems were known, and in some cases are still known, as packaged systems within the sector and not-for-profit organisations usually refer to them simply as 'the database'. More formally, they are commercial off-the-shelf (COTS) software systems. There are literally dozens of these systems available in the sector's marketplace and a survey by the author in 2009 of 150 not-for-profit organisations identified just two where the organisation had developed a bespoke system. In every other case the organisation had selected one or more COTS systems from one or more of the many suppliers.

Since 2003, a huge amount of interest in CRM has been generated in the sector. Several commercial CRM suppliers have attempted to break into the sector (these have been largely unsuccessful) and the most traditional not-for-profit system suppliers have tried to rebrand themselves as CRM suppliers (also largely unsuccessfully), sometimes simply tacking on the letters 'CRM' to their existing product name. The managing director of one major not-for-profit systems supplier when he first heard about CRM said: 'That's what we have been doing for years!' He was partly right, but overall there has been and continues to be, a large amount of confusion as to what CRM actually means to this particular sector of society. There is no agreement as to what constitutes a customer, let alone any standard definitions or statements of functionality of a not-for-profit CRM system. Both issues are addressed by this book.

2.5 CRM TODAY

These days almost everything is available over the Internet and people do almost everything using it, from looking up information, ordering products, sitting at desks with PCs and watching programmes on TVs to chatting to friends, working on the train with laptops, and walking down the road with smartphones. It is all 'web this' and 'web that' and even CRM systems are said to be 'web-enabled'. Some systems even come with a built-in content management system (CMS) with which you can build websites. This allows you to have a complete website and CRM database all in one (see section 14.6).

The words 'Internet' and 'Web' are often used interchangeably. Perhaps a word of explanation wouldn't go amiss here. Who knows the difference between the 'Internet' and the 'World Wide Web'? The Internet is a world-wide system of interconnected computer networks. Hence the name: Internet. It is the physical computers, wires, wireless transmitters and receivers, and all the clever deep-down techie software that makes it all work. The Internet carries services such as email, ecommerce and the World Wide Web. On the other hand, the World Wide Web (WWW or W3), commonly known simply as 'the Web', is an Internet-based technology. That means that it is a service carried by the Internet and it consists of a system of interlinked documents. These documents, known as web pages, can contain text, audio, pictures, video and 'hyperlinks' which are links to other documents (i.e. web pages). So, you can think of the Internet as the suitcase, and the web as the clothes, suntan oil, etc. that you pack inside to take on holiday.

Today, all CRM systems (or at least all those worth considering) allow customers a variety of 'self-service' functions provided via the Internet. Typically, customers can (all provided via the Internet):

- purchase products (including, for the not-for-profit sector, making donations, renewing memberships, booking training courses and other events);
- view their own records and amend details such as their address or their communication preferences;
- find and download product and service information;
- communicate directly with organisation staff via email, telephone or online chat.

If your organisation does not provide such services, then many potential customers and even some current customers, particularly the younger ones, are likely to switch their allegiance to another organisation that does. Part of the reason for this is the expectation that you should be keeping up with changes in technology, and the other part is the expectation that information and functionality should be available 24/7 (24 hours a day, 7 days a week).

In terms of CRM systems functionality, social CRM is the fastest growing area of CRM at the time of writing. There are two main aspects to it. The first is for the company or organisation to monitor social media websites for mentions of their organisation and/or products and services. Such monitoring allows marketers, sales staff and service staff unprecedented and immediate access to what the general public thinks of them and their products and services (i.e. market intelligence). They can then act accordingly to dispel myths and correct any real problems identified. The second aspect of social CRM is to engage directly with customers (and potential customers) in online communities via the social media websites. This gets messages across quickly and builds trust and loyalty by interacting with customers in their own space.

So, that is an overview of the history of CRM. The next chapter starts to examine exactly what CRM is, starting with a definition, or more exactly, a series of definitions. The fact that there are so many definitions is testament to the complexity of CRM and its level of maturity as an accepted organisational concept.

3 Traditional CRM

3.1 DEFINITIONS

Everyone has their own definition of CRM, and a few of the more formal ones are given below before a more comprehensive, yet straightforward, one is proposed.

> *CRM is an integrated sales, marketing, and service strategy that precludes lone showmanship and that depends on coordinated enterprise-wide actions.*
>
> Kalakota and Robinson 2001, p. 172

> *CRM is a young offspring (of relationship marketing) which I define as applying the values and strategies of relationship marketing in practice, with particular emphasis of the customer-supplier relationship, largely but not solely dependent on information technology.*
>
> Gummesson 2002, p. 587

> *CRM is an approach or business strategy providing seamless integration of every area of business that touches the customer namely marketing, sales, customer service and sales force automation through integration of people, process, and technology.*
>
> Pan and Lee 2003, p. 96

> *We define CRM as an interactive approach that achieves an optimum balance between corporate investments and the satisfaction of customer needs in order to generate maximum profits.*
>
> Geib et al 2005, p. 2

> *CRM encompasses all the processes that increase the revenues, goodwill and profitability of the business via the acquisition, gratification and retention of customers by providing each customer with 'customised' products and solutions that best fit their needs and criteria.'*
>
> Pant and Wagner 2006, p. 346

> *CRM is a data-driven strategy that utilizes organisational knowledge and technology in order to enable pro-active and profitable long-term relationships with customers.*
>
> Cunningham and Song 2007, p. 97

From the definitions above, the key elements of CRM appear to be:

- be profitable and make more money;
- get new customers and retain existing ones;
- give customers what they want;
- all parts of the organisation must work together;
- it needs the application of technology to be effective.

Most of the definitions mention giving customers what they want but none of them actually mention *being nice to customers*, which would seem to be a key element if you want them to keep coming back for more. So if we add this to the list above, a more simple definition of traditional CRM incorporating all of these elements is proposed:

> *CRM is the process of making more money by attracting and keeping customers, being nice to them and giving them what they want, all by coordinated company-wide actions, supported by technology.*

Naturally, in order to succeed in your enterprise you need to attract new customers, retain existing customers, be nice to customers and give them what they want. The aim is to keep them coming back for more, and all people in the organisation need to work together to achieve this objective. It is common sense, isn't it? So, rather than 'customer relationship management', traditional CRM could be 'common-sense realisation of money', as the main objective is to *make more money*.

3.2   CUSTOMERS AND OTHER STAKEHOLDERS

In a commercial environment, the concepts of a customer and a prospective customer are clear. They are the people who buy or might buy the products and services on offer. In terms of making more money, there are other stakeholders to be considered, not just customers. These include shareholders, partners, suppliers, lenders, the press and agencies. Shareholders own the company and can influence the running of it. The performance of partners and suppliers will affect the performance of the company. Lenders can impose conditions on the company that can affect its performance. The portrayal of the company to the public by the press will have a direct influence on the company's sales. And, finally, the performance of agencies, primarily advertising agencies, will also have a direct impact on its sales.

The degree to which the relationships with these stakeholders can be managed to make more money depends on the power they have over the company. Typically, a bank or lender will have a high level of power and a low level of interest, whereas a supplier will have a high level of interest but a much lower level of power. In other words, CRM could also be considered to be about managing relationships with people who are not customers in the true sense of the word 'customer', because the way the relationships with these other stakeholders is managed will have an effect on the performance of the company. This is an important issue which will be explored in section 4.3: who is 'the customer' in the not-for-profit sector?

3.3 THE APPLICATION OF TECHNOLOGY FOR EFFECTIVE CRM

3.3.1 First-level functional breakdown of CRM

When considering what functions would make up an **information system** to support the concept of CRM, Harej and Horvat (2004), Kalakota and Robinson (2001) and many other authors, subdivide CRM functions into marketing, sales and service. They give the major elements of a CRM system as:

> An organisation's overall **information system** comprises a collection of equipment and computerised information-processing systems which support the activities and management of an organisation. This includes hardware and software, such as donor or member relationship management software.

- **Marketing functions** consisting of customer acquisition, segmentation and retention, campaign management, marketing content management, marketing analysis and effectiveness programs, and continuity and loyalty programs.
- **Sales functions** consisting of contact management, contract management, opportunity management, order management, and sales and revenue forecasting.
- **Service functions** consisting of inquiry and service request resolution, service delivery, and customer satisfaction measurement.

(Note that the functions listed here that are relevant to the not-for-profit sector will be discussed in more detail elsewhere in the book.) Related to these general areas, Anderson (2001), Fjermestad and Romano (2003), Pan and Lee (2003) and many others, stress the importance of *communications and channels*, i.e. managing the actual communication with the customer in whatever medium is used, including web, telephone, email, SMS, direct mail, fax, interactive television, personal contact, shops and agents.

Bradshaw and Brash (2001), Lee et al (2007) and others add the subject of customer analysis or analytics (consisting of data warehousing (see 2.1.7) and establishing patterns in customer data) into the mix at the same level as marketing, sales and service. Analytics needs to be expanded to include reporting, as every system needs a variety of standard reports for day-to-day management that do not involve complex data analysis.

Also considered at the same level of importance by Anderson (2001), Goldenberg (2006) and others is systems integration, because CRM systems need to integrate with other related systems such as manufacturing, fulfilment, logistics, billing and financial accounting.

Thus it seems reasonable to subdivide the complete CRM systems area into the major areas of:

- marketing;
- sales;
- communications and channels;
- service;
- reporting and analytics;
- integration.

However, when considering a description of the functional requirements for a CRM system, there are two major areas missing from this high-level breakdown; these are environment and administration, and contact management. The environment and administration area describes the basic ground rules under which the system operates, for example:

- the operating environment (this includes servers, networks, databases, communications, other systems software and the graphical computer desktop environment);
- usability features (functions that make the system easier to use);
- accessibility (from where and how all people access the systems, including assistive technologies that help people with disabilities);
- general system administration.

Without these functions there is no system. They cannot be taken for granted. The final highest level of functional breakdown is shown in table 3.1.

Functional area	Description
Environment and administration	The operating environment, usability features, accessibility and general system administration.
Contact management	The data to be recorded about contacts and basic functions to be performed for all types of contacts.
Marketing	Customer acquisition, segmentation and retention, campaign management, marketing content management, marketing analysis and effectiveness programs, continuity and loyalty programs.
Sales	Contact management, contract management, opportunity management, order management, sales and revenue forecasting.
Communications and channels	Managing the actual communication with the customer in any given medium.
Service	Inquiry and service request resolution, service delivery, and customer satisfaction measurement.
Reporting and analytics	Day-to-day reporting, data warehousing, online analytical processing and data mining, establishing patterns in customer behaviour.
Integration	Linking with back-office functions such as manufacturing, fulfilment, billing and logistics.

Table 3.1 Major functional areas of CRM

3.3.2 Second-level functional breakdown of CRM

Beyond the most general groupings of functionality, there is no consistency in the further breakdown of CRM functionality in the published literature on the subject. In addition, an examination of a number of leading commercial CRM systems also showed no consistency in terms of a further functional breakdown. However, these systems did provide information that has been aggregated in order to identify a second level of functional breakdown, as shown in table 3.2. This table gives us a starting point for the consideration of CRM systems functionality in the not-for-profit sector, which is the subject of Part 4. All terms that are elaborated on in other parts of the book have the main relevant sections listed next to them.

Environment and administration	Communications and channels
■ Document management (15.2.3) ■ Data cleaning (15.2.3) ■ Data import and export (15.2.3) ■ Security (7.7.2)	■ Multi-channel communication (Chapter 14)
Contact management	*Service*
■ Lead/prospect management (15.4.1) ■ Customer management (15.3.1) ■ Partner management (15.3.1) ■ Relationship management (15.3.1)	■ Case management (15.5.2) ■ Service scheduling (15.5.1) ■ Workflow management (15.2.1) ■ Knowledge base management (15.5.1) ■ History tracking or logging (15.5.1)
Marketing	*Reporting and analytics*
■ Segmentation (15.3.2) ■ Campaign management (15.3.2) ■ Event management (15.4.4)	■ Standard reporting (16.2.1) ■ Custom reporting (15.2.2) ■ Analytics (Chapter 16)
Sales	*Systems integration*
■ Lead management (15.4.1) ■ Account management (15.4.1) ■ Territory management (15.4.1) ■ Call scripting (15.4.1) ■ Forecasting (15.3.2/16.5) ■ Product catalogue and pricing (15.4.1) ■ Quotes and orders ■ Contract management (15.4.1) ■ Sales force automation (15.4.1)	■ Integration with Microsoft Office, finance systems, and other related systems (15.6)

Table 3.2 Second-level functions of commercial CRM systems

3.4 **TRADITIONAL CRM SUMMARY**

This chapter first looked at a number of definitions of traditional CRM and identified its key objective, which is to make more money by actively managing relationships with customers. It then discussed who the customers are, before moving on to attempt a first- and second-level breakdown of the functions of an information system that can support the CRM objective and strategy. The next chapter discusses the nature of the not-for-profit sector and the customers it serves, before describing how CRM can be applied to that sector.

4 CRM in the not-for-profit sector

4.1 WHAT IS THE NOT-FOR-PROFIT SECTOR?

It is important first to define what is meant by the not-for-profit sector, the audience for this book. At a high level of abstraction, society is divided into the private sector, the public sector and the third sector (see figure 4.1).

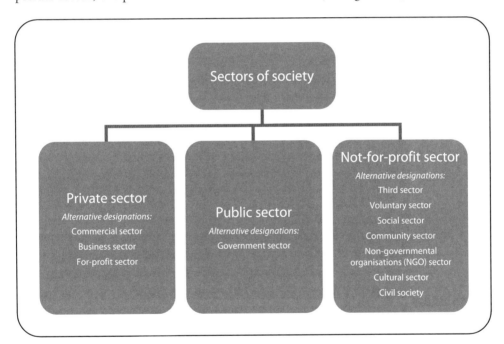

Fig. 4.1 Sectors of society

As can be seen from figure 4.1, the not-for-profit sector has many different designations, each of which indicates the focus of different organisations within it. The designations 'third sector' and 'civil society' have been favoured by successive governments but 'third sector' is non-descriptive and means little or nothing to people outside the sector (and even to many people within the sector) and the meaning of 'civil society' is far too broad to be useful. Consequently, a more meaningful term, the 'not-for-profit sector', is the term used in this book to cover all organisations that belong to this sector, as shown in figure 4.1. In other words, all of those organisations which do not have shareholders who take profits out of the organisation (i.e. the private sector), and which are not completely funded by the government (i.e. the public sector).

The subject of 'mission' is the key difference between commercial and not-for-profit organisations. Whereas a commercial organisation's prime motivation is to make profits for shareholders, a not-for-profit organisation's prime motivation is to serve some useful social purpose. This purpose could be related to health, education, vocation, entertainment, the environment, religion, community, in fact almost anything that has a positive impact on people or the planet. This does not mean that the economic profit-making motive does not exist, but it is not the prime motivation and all profits are reinvested in the organisation or spent directly on the cause itself, whatever that may be.

Olson et al. (2005) describe the three key 'orientations' of not-for-profit organisations: economic, mission-related and operational. The economic and operational orientations differ little from those in for-profit organisations. In the economic aspect they need to generate income, control costs and create jobs. In the operational aspect they need to be efficient, effective, well-managed and up to date, for example in their use of information systems. It is in the mission-related orientation that the not-for-profit organisation differs from the for-profit organisation. Olson et al. quote Quarter and Richmond (2001) who state that 'nonprofits are organized around a social mission' (Olson et al. 2005, p. 127).

This use of the word 'social' appears in other references (see Hudson below). Olson et al. say that whereas the prime motive for the for-profit organisation is economic, the prime motive for the not-for-profit organisation is mission, which links the organisation to 'society at large'. However, this does not adequately differentiate for-profit from not-for-profit, as for-profit organisations can also be said to be linked to society at large and as regards 'mission', most for-profit organisations have a 'mission statement'. The word 'mission' is too all-embracing and the word 'social' is too vague, and neither word helps to describe adequately what the not-for-profit sector does and why it exists. The word 'societal' would be better, but it still remains vague.

Mike Hudson in his excellent book, *Managing Without Profit: Leadership, management and governance of third sector organisations*, defines the not-for-profit sector as encompassing:

> *Organisations whose primary objectives are social rather than economic. The core of the sector includes charities, religious organisations, arts organisations, community organisations, campaigning organisations, trade unions and other not-for-profit organisations.*

> Hudson 2009, p. xvi

This is an extensive and diverse group, but the definition, as it is deliberately limited to a few examples of the core of the sector, does not mention other cultural organisations outside the arts, such as museums, zoos and wildlife centres, or educational establishments, hospitals and hospices, housing associations, sports clubs, trade associations, professional associations and other membership bodies all of which are significant groupings within Hudson's other not-for-profit organisations, which will have specific requirements related to CRM. Hudson's general definition of not-for-profit organisations is:

All organisations that:

1. *exist primarily for a **social purpose** rather than having a profit-making objective;*
2. *are **independent of the state** because they are governed by an independent group of people, and are not part of a government or local or health authority;*
3. ***re-invest their financial surpluses** in the services they offer or the organisation itself.*

Hudson 2009, p. 9

The first point needs to be extended or the definition of 'social purposes' expanded to include educational, vocational, entertainment, health, housing, environmental, sporting, and even political purposes, because all of these satisfy points 2 and 3. In addition, the phrase 'profit-making objective' needs to be extended to say 'profit-making objective for the benefit of shareholders', because a key objective of a not-for-profit organisation is to be as cost-effective as possible and make as much surplus or profit as possible, since the more profit they make, the more money they will have to spend on their cause, whatever it may be. So they do exist for a social purpose, but they have a significant profit-making objective as well. Admittedly this somewhat goes against the grain of using the term not-for-profit in this book, but as mentioned before, terms such as third sector are rather meaningless.

All not-for-profit organisations need to generate income in order to carry out their mission and as such they tend to fall into one of two general groups: fundraising organisations and membership organisations. This is reflected in the major system suppliers to the market which tend to specialise in fundraising-based contact management (or CRM) systems or membership-based contact management (or CRM) systems, although many not-for-profit organisations both fundraise and run membership schemes so they need elements of both. There are far fewer system suppliers which provide software systems that are dedicated to the service provision side of the not-for-profit organisations, such as systems to manage projects or systems to administer the grant-making process, but these are relatively few in number compared with fundraising and membership.

4.2   DOES CRM APPLY TO THE NOT-FOR-PROFIT SECTOR?

As CRM is defined to be a business strategy or even an organisational philosophy, the first question to ask is 'does it apply to the not-for-profit sector?' To answer this, Becky Slack, writing about 'high value donors' in *Professional Fundraising* magazine discusses how important it is for a charity to maximise the potential of supporters currently on their database, because of the high cost of recruiting new supporters (customers). CRM is seen as a way to achieve this. She also quotes Tony Elischer, a well-known charity fundraising consultant, as saying that:

> *they (potential high value donors) investigate and research which charities to support, and as such require more detailed involvement and feedback.*
>
> Slack 2007, p. 23

This is related specifically to charities, but it can be extended to other not-for-profit organisations such as membership bodies which want to attract new members and then retain them for as long as possible. Thus it is clear that the key elements of CRM, which were identified in Chapter 3 for traditional (i.e. commercial) CRM as shown below, apply equally to the not-for-profit sector.

1. Be profitable and make more money.
2. Get new customers and retain existing ones.
3. Give customers what they want.
4. All parts of the organisation must work together.
5. CRM needs the application of technology to be effective.

Thus a CRM strategy is as essential to the success of a not-for-profit organisation as it is to a profit-making business. Every not-for-profit organisation needs a CRM strategy and cannot operate effectively without it.

4.3 WHO IS THE NOT-FOR-PROFIT SECTOR CUSTOMER?

When attempting to apply CRM to not-for-profit organisations, the first question to resolve is 'Who exactly *is* the customer?' In order to answer this, it is necessary to examine the interactions that take place between the organisation and its environment. Mike Hudson has a simple diagram that provides a useful starting point (see figure 4.2).

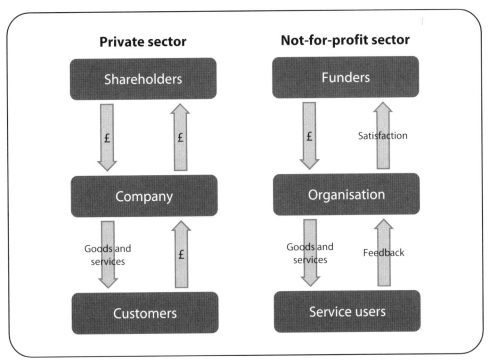

Fig. 4.2 The nature of transactions in the private and not-for-profit sectors (adapted from Hudson 2009, p. 15)

This shows that in the private sector, shareholders provide funds in the form of working capital and receive financial returns in the form of dividends, and customers receive goods and services and provide the vast majority of the income to the company. In the not-for-profit sector, however, funders (consisting of individual donors, members, companies, trusts, statutory bodies, etc.) provide all of the income, for which they get nothing in return other than a good feeling (although corporate bodies will often receive brand awareness and public relations exposure which could eventually lead to increased income) and service users (beneficiaries) receive goods and services about which they give feedback to the organisation. Thus, according to the diagram in figure 4.2, it would appear that service users of the not-for-profit organisation equate to the customers of the private company. However, it would be more correct for the not-for-profit element of this diagram to be reversed (see figure 4.3).

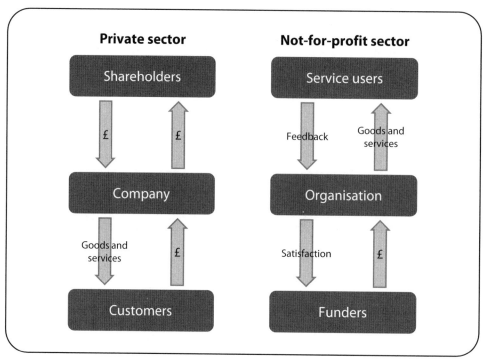

Fig. 4.3 Alternative view of transactions in the private and not-for-profit sectors

This is more realistic because it equates shareholders with service users and customers with funders. Shareholders want something out of the company (dividends) and service users want something out of the organisation (goods or services). Customers provide the bulk of the income of the company and funders provide the bulk of the income of the organisation. Both customers for the company and funders for the organisation have to be kept happy to ensure the continued prosperity of both.

However, in not-for-profit organisations it is not that simple. Some funders are also service users and vice versa. For example, a member of a professional body pays membership fees and receives benefits in return; a person living in sheltered accommodation may pay a proportion of the costs associated with the service they receive, which effectively makes them like customers in the private sector model. In addition, funders will give feedback on what the organisation is doing and service users will obtain satisfaction from the service they receive, so consequently the not-for-profit element of the diagram should appear as in figure 4.4. This means that the definition of customer in the not-for-profit sector must include all funders and all service users.

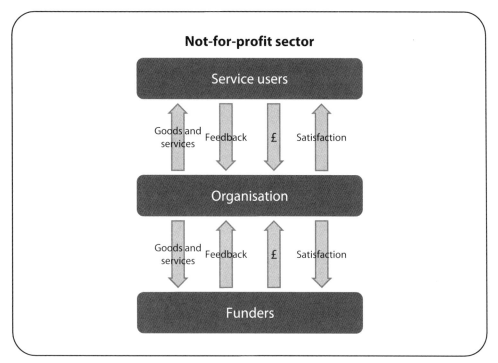

Fig. 4.4 Extended not-for-profit organisation transaction diagram

However, even this does not cover the full breadth of customers for a not-for-profit organisation, as there are large groups of people (and organisations) that come under the heading of 'volunteers' who provide goods and services to the organisation for no charge (as shown in figure 4.5). Note that the diagram shows money flowing from the organisation to the volunteer. This is simply to represent the case where a volunteer is paid expenses.

This volunteer group includes:

● the organisation's trustees or members of various committees;
● people who provide some of the organisation's services at no charge;
● supporters such as celebrities, advocates and former service recipients who help to publicise the organisation;
● sponsors who give goods and time rather than money such as a company providing an event venue or paying for the printing of marketing material.

Consequently, the term 'customer' in the not-for-profit sector must include donors, members, supporters, volunteers and sponsors, which is a much broader remit than that of the private sector.

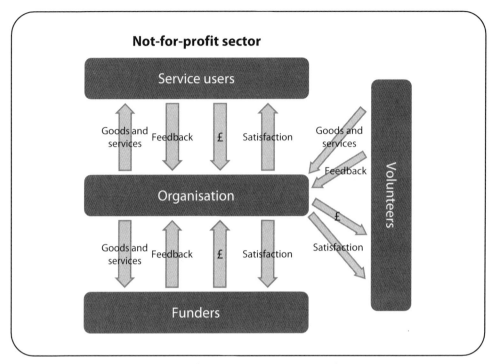

Fig. 4.5 Further extended not-for-profit organisation transaction diagram

There is yet another group of people and organisations with which the not-for-profit organisation needs to manage relationships, and these are suppliers or service providers. In some instances, these are simple providers of goods or services to the not-for-profit organisation itself, but they can also provide goods and services (particularly services such as health care) directly to the organisation's beneficiaries or service users. Commercial organisations also have suppliers but these are, on the whole, excluded from consideration within CRM, as they are primarily suppliers which provide goods and services for their own benefit and they have little or no commitment to the objectives of their own customers. In not-for-profit organisations, each organisation has a closer association with their suppliers, as these suppliers often exhibit a level of commitment to the cause of the not-for-profit organisation and work with the not-for-profit organisation for mutual benefit. Consequently, the final not-for-profit organisation transaction diagram is as shown in figure 4.6.

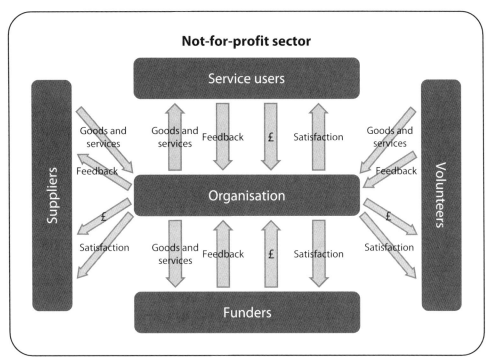

Fig. 4.6 Final not-for-profit organisation transaction diagram

In a commercial organisation, in terms of CRM, 'customers' are customers and prospective customers, and even if you extend the definition of 'customer' you only add in shareholders, staff, partners, suppliers, lenders, press and agencies. However, the 'customers' of a not-for-profit organisation are much more diverse. Table 4.1 overleaf gives a (possibly) complete list of not-for-profit 'customers'.

4.4 THE MULTI-ROLE CUSTOMER

To further complicate the picture shown in figure 4.6, just as earlier it was pointed out that a funder could also be a service user, a supplier can also be a funder giving money or goods, or can also be a volunteer giving time. Any individual or company or organisation might fall into two, three or even all four of the stakeholder groups, either simultaneously or consecutively over time. Indeed, a key driver of many not-for-profit organisations is to increase engagement through the use of CRM to position a single stakeholder into as many of these categorisations as possible. For example, a funder could be a service user who also volunteers and, through their knowledge in a given field, is also a supplier (such as a trainer). The result is a complex web of individuals and organisations, and this highlights a fundamental concept of CRM: *one object – many roles*, where the object is an individual or an organisation. This means that global categorisations such as funders, service users, suppliers and volunteers are somewhat inappropriate, as is a strict hierarchy of customers or concepts.

However, this does not affect the requirements for information systems to support the CRM strategy that will be discussed later, as different requirements for different types of customers can be identified quite easily.

For many organisations, this multi-faceted relationship is something which is very commonplace. One of the reasons for needing a relationship management strategy (in the global sense, incorporating people and processes, not just in the sense of technology) is to develop these multi-role relationships. Another is to be able to identify and manage them. This in turn leads to a need for technology to support the strategy, and hence to a need for CRM systems, and then for these systems to cater for all the types of customer (and any more you can think of) listed in table 4.1.

Academics	Event attendees	Project workers
Agencies	Families	Prospects
Alumni	Funders	Religious establishments
Areas/branches/regions	Government departments	Service departments/units
Associates	Health establishments	Service users
Beneficiaries	Health professionals	Special interest groups
Celebrities	Individuals	Sponsors
Clients	Influencers	Staff
Collectors	Legators	Students
Committee members	Lenders	Subsidiaries
Community organisations	Media	Suppliers
Companies	Members	Supporters
Customers	Customers who have opted-out	Support groups
Detractors	Organisations	Teams
Departments	Politicians	Trusts
Donors	Partners	Trustees
Educational establishments	Projects	Volunteers

Table 4.1 Types of not-for-profit customer

In terms of finally identifying customers and their relationships with the organisation, having complicated Mike Hudson's original picture, we can simplify it right down again, as shown in figure 4.7. This effectively shows that a not-for-profit organisation's customers are every person and every organisation which they come into contact with, plus even more nebulous things such as the projects they are involved with and the services they perform. All of these could be said to have 'contact points' with which the organisations' staff can interact. Consequently we can talk about contacts and contact points. Note also that in every case the interactions of goods and services, and money and satisfaction can be two-way.

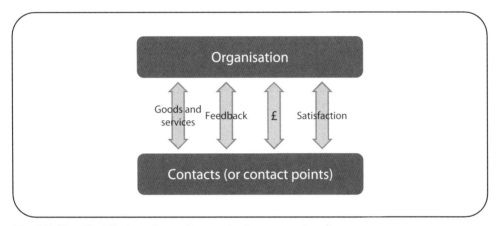

Fig. 4.7 Simplified final not-for-profit organisation transaction diagram

4.5   **NOT-FOR-PROFIT CRM CONCEPTS**

The major objective of a commercial CRM strategy is to make more money, and providing a better service is a means towards achieving that objective. In the not-for-profit sector, however, the major objective is to make more money *and* provide a better service; i.e., the provision of a better service is an objective in its own right.

There may not be a wealth of literature about not-for-profit CRM but there is a lot of literature about concepts within the sector that in fact add up to a body of information about CRM. This literature also directly covers many of the subjects that are grouped together under the heading of CRM in the commercial sector. These are: relationship management in general, marketing, sales, service and analytics. So, from an overall strategic point of view, the two sectors are broadly similar. In order to highlight the differences it is necessary to drill down to a greater level of detail.

4.5.1 **Relationship fundraising**

The central word of CRM, and the concept around which everything is based, is the word 'relationship'. In relation to charities, Ken Burnett, guru of the fundraising world, states in his book (simply entitled *Relationship Fundraising*):

> *Relationship fundraising is not just a series of isolated incidents, it is a total philosophy. It deals with every aspect of donor contact, channeling that contact toward building a lifelong relationship and ensuring that the relationship is as fruitful as possible for both parties.*
>
> Burnett 2002, p. 40

Spot the difference between this and some of the commercial CRM definitions. There really isn't any! This is apparent immediately from looking at the front cover of the book, because not only is the word 'relationship' used but also the subtitle is *A Donor-Based Approach to the Business of Raising Money*. The first edition of Ken's book was published in 1992, so the concepts of relationship marketing that underlie CRM go back at least that far in the not-for-profit sector (and probably a lot further).

This relationship concept is also central to membership organisations. As Liz Hill and Brian Whitehead say in *The Complete Membership Handbook*:

> *Those who join a membership scheme show a commitment to an organisation beyond that of simply being a 'customer'. These people reveal themselves to be willing to demonstrate their sympathies for an activity or cause and to build a relationship with an organisation that supports this activity or cause.*
>
> Hill and Whitehead 2004, p. 6

4.5.2 **Marketing, sales and service**

Thus, the management of relationships with customers, however you define them, is a crucial element in the success of a not-for-profit organisation.

There are three themes that come up time and time again in the commercial CRM literature. These are marketing, sales and service. These themes are voiced regularly in the not-for-profit sector, although not usually under the umbrella of CRM. The first of these, marketing, is very important for all not-for-profit organisations. When exploring membership organisations, Hill and Whitehead (2004) discuss 'aggressive marketing' as a method of continually attracting new members. They examine the issues of branding, provision of benefits, identifying target markets, advertising, mailing, telemarketing, advocacy, personal approaches, incentives such as gift membership, and events such as open days.

With charities, Peter Maple argues that:

> For individual charities marketing is, however, essential: to differentiate one charity from another and to help identify and sell the unique proposition of any organisation.
>
> Maple 2003, p. 12

He goes on to discuss the Five P's of marketing, product, price, promotion, place and position, and how they relate to charities, before considering branding, research and different marketing media. Burnett (2002) also rates marketing as vital to charities primarily because of the huge choice of organisations to support.

In the same way as marketing leads to sales with commercial CRM, *sales*, or trading, as it is usually referred to in the not-for-profit sector, is another function mentioned by Hill and Whitehead (2004) in relation to membership organisations. This trading can encompass both products and services. Alan Lawrie (2007) mentions trading, such as shops, in relation to charities as well. In membership organisations, providing memberships is a sales function and in a charity context, soliciting donations can also be considered as a sales function.

When it comes to *service*, Teresa Lloyd states:

> Donors want recognition for the interest, concern and passion that motivates them, and that they assume they share with trustees and staff of the recipient organisation (and in some sectors with the ultimate beneficiaries).
>
> Lloyd 2006, p. 52

She goes on to quote some charity donors:

> 'I want a personal letter of thanks, that's all' and 'I would give 10 out of 10 to an organisation which came back after a year and asked for 30 minutes of my time to explain what had happened to the money and project and what was achieved.'
>
> Lloyd 2006, p. 55

This is a theme echoed by Burnett (2002) where he devotes a whole chapter to keeping in touch with donors. He discusses advertising, mailings (particularly thank-you letters), telephone calls and even personal visits, and he says that 'Customer service is another area where first-class training is paramount' (Burnett 2002, p. 210), thus emphasising its importance. 'Aftercare' is a subject addressed by Redmond Mullin (2002, pp. 63–65) when he says that supporters want to know what the organisation is doing with their money and explains how organisations must keep up with their supporters' changing needs over time. Mike Hudson makes the point that it is not just charities where the funders want to know how their money has been spent but this also applies to all not-for-profit organisations, for example:

> *Parents want to know how schools are performing, tenants want to know how quickly housing repairs are done, members expect organisations to report on what has been achieved with the subscriptions.*
>
> Hudson 2009, p. 218

With regard to membership organisations, Hill and Whitehead (2004) stress the need for excellent customer service in order to retain members and even mention such commercial concepts of 'up-selling' (obtaining more income of the same type as received before from the customer) and 'cross-selling' (soliciting income of different types from the customer) when this customer service is done well. The same tactics of up-selling and cross-selling employed by commercial organisations are used by many not-for-profit organisations. Just as Amazon provides recommendations to a customer of books they might like to purchase based on their purchase history, a not-for-profit organisation can use the same tactics both to up-sell and cross-sell, as well as promoting its cause or non-financial mission. For example, a member books onto an event and subsequently receives recommendations of other events they might like to attend or products they might like to purchase (exactly equivalent to commercial up-selling and cross-selling). They can also receive recommendations on non-commercial items related to the cause, such as white papers, discussions and policy work. It is still reliant on the same concept of targeting and personalisation based on past activity and profiling, but the resultant action is often non-commercial. However, as with the commercial sector, the aim is to engage and retain customers by demonstrating relevance.

4.5.3 Analytics: Pareto analysis and RFV

Analytics is another much-discussed subject in commercial CRM literature. This subject is also prominent in not-for-profit literature. Burnett (2002) and Flory (2001) discuss two techniques in particular: Pareto analysis and RFV (or RFM), which are particularly relevant to the charity section of the not-for-profit sector.

Pareto analysis is the 80:20 rule of business which states that 80% of your income comes from 20% of your customers, although Burnett (2002, p. 75) mentions how in some organisations the ratio can be as high as 95:5. For charities, read 'donor' for 'customer'.

RFV, recency, frequency, value (or RFM as it is sometimes known: recency, frequency, monetary value), is a process of allocating donors to a number of bands in terms of when they last donated, how many times they have donated and how much they have donated.

Pareto is a simple analysis of the most valuable donors in monetary terms, whereas RFV can be a simple single value calculation based on the position of the donor in the various bands as described by Burnett (2002) or a more complex three-dimensional analysis of donors and their giving patterns as described by Flory (2001). For more on Pareto analysis and RFV, see 16.3.

These types of analysis, and others, are useful guides for the generation of future fundraising campaigns. However, there are rare exceptions. An example of this is the annual Children in Need appeal where such analysis is of no value because their major income source is one huge campaign per year where no potential customer selection process is required and where the vast majority of donations are effectively, if not in reality, anonymous. Although complex data analysis is less of an issue in membership-based organisations, Hill and Whitehead (2004) list a number of analysis-type reports under their heading of marketing effectiveness, including proportion of members who move up and down between membership tiers, average length of membership and average lifetime value (see 16.5.2). For more on the general subject of analytics, see Chapter 16.

4.6   NOT-FOR-PROFIT CRM DEFINITIONS

The not-for-profit sector, with its 50 plus types of customer, is far more complex than the commercial sector with its eight or nine types of customer. In terms of CRM, many not-for-profit organisations focus just on the income-generating types of customer where the parallels with commercial CRM are the greatest. This is evidenced by many of the information systems sold in the sector's marketplace and known variously as: donor relationship management, member relationship management and supporter relationship management. However, ideally, all of the not-for-profit customers listed earlier in this chapter must be catered for within a complete CRM system for the sector. The vast majority of the data held for each type of customer is of the same sort (whether a company, funder or supplier, for example). However, each customer type has some data items that are unique to their group. Similarly, most of the functionality needed for each of these types of customer is the same for all of them. Likewise, however, every customer type has some functionality which is specific to that group.

Considering the diversity of 'customers', it is reasonable to question the applicability of the term 'CRM' and its relevance to the sector, and in particular the word 'customer'. The terms 'SRM' (supporter relationship management) in the charity sphere and 'MRM' (member relationship management) in the membership sphere, are now becoming more common, but these are not generic enough for the sector as a whole. Many alternative terms have been proposed and rejected. So, it could be argued, as CRM is such a widespread term in general, it is pragmatic to use it within the not-for-profit sector but to use the word 'contact' rather than 'customer' when spelling it out in full. Even this has its problems, however, as the definition of 'contact' has to be extended to cater for projects and services that are managed by not-for-profit organisations and is further confused by the fact that the projects themselves have contacts in the true sense of the word 'contact': i.e. contact people.

In the final analysis, it is likely that CRM will remain 'customer relationship management' (one large not-for-profit organisation has already taken to calling every contact of their organisation a customer no matter what their role is in relation to the organisation). This is unless the Microsoft coined term of xRM, which stands for 'anything Relationship Management', gains wide industry acceptance. Consequently, the word 'customer' will be used as a generic term for contacts and entities of every type throughout the rest of this book.

In order to arrive at an overarching definition of CRM in the not-for-profit sector, the marketing, sales and service considerations identified in Chapter 3 need to be augmented by the major differences between the for-profit and the not-for-profit sectors. These are the much greater importance of 'mission' and the extended concept of who the customer in the not-for-profit sector. In terms of mission, the not-for-profit organisation's prime motivation is to serve a useful social purpose rather than just to make money. In terms of customers, they are many and varied. They fall into one (or more) of four broad groups: funders, service users, volunteers and suppliers, each of which requires many similar general CRM processes and each of which equally requires many different processes. The organisation must target the right products and services at the right customers, and provide them with choices and a high-quality and efficient service.

In considering the interactions between the not-for-profit organisation and its different types of customers, it is useful to look back at the final transaction diagram (figure 4.6) which shows the complex flow of goods (products) and services, feedback, money and satisfaction and clearly indicates the increased complexity from the commercial CRM model.

When considering a definition of not-for-profit CRM, it is helpful to look at some of the definitions given earlier for commercial CRM to see the level to which they could be applied to this sector. One of the more extensive definitions from Chapter 3 was as follows:

> *CRM (Customer Relationship Management) encompasses all the processes that increase the revenues, goodwill and profitability of the business via the acquisition, gratification and retention of customers by providing each customer with 'customised' products and solutions that best fit their needs and criteria.*

Pant and Wagner 2006, p. 346

A more simple definition was proposed in Chapter 3 as follows:

CRM is the process of making more money by attracting and keeping customers, being nice to them and giving them what they want, all by coordinated company-wide actions, supported by technology.

These definitions hold true for the sector given the following considerations:

- The concept of profitability is accepted by not-for-profit organisations. The designation of 'not-for-profit' is misleading because one objective is to make as much 'profit' or surplus as possible in order to be able to spend more on the beneficiaries or on the cause in general.
- The definition of 'customer' is extended to cover all types of individual or organisation with which the not-for-profit organisation has a relationship, whether they be income-generating (funders), expenditure consuming (service users), assistance providing (volunteers), or product or service providing (suppliers).
- The definition of products is extended to cover emotional gratification and support as well as physical products and services.
- The words 'high-quality' are added before 'customised products and services' to indicate that not only is the customer getting what they want but also is getting the best that the organisation can provide.

Thus, at the highest level of abstraction, as shown by the definition above, not-for-profit CRM is little different from commercial CRM. So, taking the points above into consideration (and borrowing a few words and phrases from Pant and Wagner (2006)) the following overarching definition of not-for-profit CRM is proposed.

Not-for-profit sector CRM encompasses all the processes (manual and computerised) that enable the organisation to fulfil its social mission by acquiring and retaining customers (funders, service users, volunteers and suppliers alike) and facilitating a two-way exchange of high-quality customised products and services that best fit their needs and criteria, in return for compensation which may or may not be financial and which may or not be tangible, by coordinated organisation-wide actions, supported by technology.

This is an all-encompassing definition and is a bit convoluted, so to put it in more simple terms:

Not-for-profit sector CRM is the process of doing good by attracting and keeping customers (i.e. everyone you come into contact with), being nice to them and giving them what they want, by all of the organisation's people working together, assisted by technology. (Money comes into it but only as a means to an end).

And finally, as Chapter 3 stated, traditional CRM could be said to stand for 'common-sense realisation of money' because the main objective is to make more money. In this way, not-for-profit CRM could be said to stand for 'common-sense realisation of mission', because the main objective of a not-for-profit organisation is to make a difference (to society or the planet).

4.7 NOT-FOR-PROFIT SECTOR CRM SUMMARY

This chapter first examined the nature of the not-for-profit sector, identifying the fundamental fact that the concept of 'mission' is more important than money. As traditional CRM is all about making more money, it then considered if CRM could be applied to the sector and, if so, then who the customers of the sector would be. Over 50 different types of customer were identified compared with about eight in the commercial sector. The chapter established that CRM can be applied to the sector but that its scope needs to be expanded to cater for all the different types of not-for-profit customer, many of whom have multiple roles.

The chapter then examined some literature specific to the not-for-profit sector, identifying some typical CRM concepts within it before proposing two definitions of not-for-profit CRM: one all-encompassing and another less complex (i.e. one a bit academic and one a bit more understandable!). The next chapter moves on to the consideration of general CRM strategy (applicable to both commercial and not-for-profit sectors) including principles, concepts and strategy issues.

Part two:
CRM strategy

5 The eight principles of CRM

5.1 INTRODUCTION

In CRM circles there is much talk about such concepts as the '360 degree view' or the 'single customer view', 'understanding customers,' the 'customer journey', and the 'customer experience' (all of which are outlined in detail in Chapter 6). However, working from the various definitions of CRM, it is important to consider principles at a more basic level first, before combining them to describe those higher-level concepts.

So, what are the basic principles that allow an organisation to attract new and retain existing customers, and give them what they want by finding out as much as possible about them, all by coordinated organisation-wide actions? The eight basic principles that underlie this, and therefore CRM, are as follows:

1. **Inclusiveness:** recording every interaction with the customer from every source and communications channel.
2. **Visibility:** making the interactions available to all staff so that everyone can see who is talking to whom and about what.
3. **Integration:** linking all of the organisation's systems together. This means computer systems and procedural systems.
4. **Relationships:** the essential and complex subject of maintaining a mutually beneficial dialogue with customers.
5. **Quality:** the provision of the highest quality of products and services to the customer.
6. **Knowledge:** This is acquiring as much information as possible about customers from facts about them to their opinions, likes and dislikes.
7. **Analysis:** analysing the information gathered to predict customer behaviour and identify how to attract new customers.
8. **Planning:** deciding what actions to carry out following the analysis. This includes campaign planning, execution and monitoring.

5.2 INCLUSIVENESS

The principle of inclusiveness involves capturing information about customer interactions from every possible communications channel, whether this is face to face, by mail, telephone or email, or via the organisation's website. In today's wired, and increasingly wireless, world this includes all multimedia technologies. People now interact with organisations and with their CRM systems via telephone and VoIP (Voice over Internet Protocol), SMS (Short Message Service) texting and MMS (Multimedia Messaging Service) with pictures and video clips, directly on the organisation's website and via social networking websites such as Facebook and Twitter. This capturing of customer interactions from every possible channel leads on to the need to integrate and distribute the data throughout the enterprise to everyone who could conceivably have an interaction with the customers.

Ideally you should capture *every* single interaction with each customer; but how practical is it and how desirable is it? This will inevitably result in a huge amount of data, a large proportion of which will be completely useless, for example an email reply that simply states 'Thanks' or 'OK'. Perhaps just the significant interactions should be captured. But how do you tell what is significant and what is not? Some interactions might be insignificant to one member of staff but significant to another. Trying to define rules of what is and is not significant that will be acceptable to all staff is an unenviable task. In addition, there is the question of whether the absence of a response to a communication is in fact an interaction in its own right? And if so, how do you record it?

5.3 VISIBILITY

The principle of visibility involves the opening up of information and procedure silos within the organisation so that, potentially, all of the organisation's interactions with their customers are visible to all employees, no matter their job function. Once again the question needs to asked, 'how practical and desirable is it?' Perhaps all data should be visible only to people who can demonstrate the need to know such data. Visibility opens up huge issues of company politics and confidentiality; these issues must be tackled head on. A real-life conversation which happened in one not-for-profit organisation went as follows:

- Person from department X: 'There is no reason for anyone in Department Y to see *my* data relating to customers.'
- Person from Department Y: 'Why not? There might be something relevant there, and besides, we all work for the same organisation!'

Many people think that they are protecting 'their' data, but in reality other departments are likely to have been in contact with the same customers. You just can't see it, or control it, without CRM.

On a more practical note, staff in different job functions will often want the same data presented in different ways. This, in turn, raises problems of interpretation and of systems implementation.

5.4 **INTEGRATION**

The principle of integration involves linking all of the organisation's customer-related systems together. In terms of computer systems, this is often referred to as 'end-to-end computing'. However, in this context, it means procedural systems as well as computing systems. A common theme throughout this book is that it is all about people, processes *and* technology. But, how do you integrate people? How do you eliminate the 'left hand not knowing what the right hand is doing' scenario?

5.5 **RELATIONSHIPS**

The concept of relationships is complex. The not-for-profit CRM system suppliers usually see it as simple linkages between records, usually between customer records but sometimes between records of different types, whereas the not-for-profit organisations have a much broader definition. This definition encompasses a more all-embracing concept of a relationship between the customer and the organisation which cannot be easily translated into simple links between information systems records. There are three major considerations under the heading of relationships. First are the relationships or linkages between customers themselves, for example who knows whom, a company and its subsidiaries, or a company and various contacts within the company. These are easily recorded if known. Then there are the relationships between staff and the customers they deal with. These too are easily recorded.

A completely different type of relationship, and a far more complex one in its nature from the previous two, is the relationship between the organisation as a whole and the customer. This relies heavily on market intelligence and understanding customers' needs and motivations. Why do they support the organisation? What do they want from the organisation? For example, do they want regular information updates? What level and type of interaction do they want with the organisation? For instance, some are happy to receive telephone calls and some only want email communication. What will convince them to support the organisation further?

Other issues include how to obtain more income of the same type as received before from the customer (up-selling), how to obtain income of different types from the customer (cross-selling), how to construct marketing campaigns to up-sell and cross-sell, what information and analysis is required to construct the campaigns, what the different communication channels are by which the customer can be engaged or targeted, how to provide customers with exactly what they want, and how to predict the customer's next actions (the customer journey). All of these issues, and more, have to be considered in order to build a beneficial relationship with the customer. The aim of this relationship building is to achieve mutual benefit; the customer gets what they want and the organisation gets what it wants.

Consequently, the principle of relationships involves having communication exchanges (or dialogues) with customers that are:

- **personal**, that is, no more 'Dear Supporter' or 'Dear Member' (or the proverbial 'segment of one', in that each message is appropriately tailored to every customer);
- **long-lasting and linked**, i.e. they extend over a considerable period of time and the dialogue shows that the organisation knows the history of the customer's interactions;
- **profitable**, both for the organisation *and* for the customer;
- **two-way**, in that you have to show that you listen to your customers;
- **flexible**, i.e. cognisant of the customer's changing needs over time, resulting in flexibility of systems and procedures to react appropriately to these needs.

From the organisation's perspective you want to develop a closer relationship with the customer, but you do have to ask the following question: 'Does the customer actually want a closer relationship with the organisation or do they just want to be left alone?' Some will want a closer relationship and others won't. It is important to identify and respect the customer's wishes. The key to a successful customer relationship is that it is driven by the customer, but managed by the organisation. The customer comes first and they must feel that they are in charge of the relationship.

5.6 QUALITY

The principle of quality involves giving the customer the highest level of products and services possible. Service quality is arguably more important than product quality. The aim is to be better than your competitors in every way (you do have competitors, don't you?) In addition you should never be satisfied with the current standards and should strive for continual improvement in quality. Another key requirement is that an objective of lowering costs must not compromise the quality of products, services or responses. In fact speed of response is a key factor on which customers will judge an organisation.

5.7 KNOWLEDGE

The principle of knowledge involves the acquisition of information about the customers. Who are they? What sort of people are they? What do they want? When do they want it? How do they want it? And, conversely, what do they not want? What do they like and dislike? What are their motivations? What are their attitudes and opinions? And how do you codify all this information so that you can sort it, segment your customer base using it and communicate with customers in an appropriate and the most productive way?

Customer needs and motivations is a highly complex area because customers make both **high- and low-involvement** decisions which often require different actions by the supplier. In addition, customers' needs and motivations change over time and suppliers need to recognise this.

> **High-involvement** is when the customer investigates competitive products before purchasing and **low-involvement** is when the customer simply accepts what is offered.

5.8 ANALYSIS

The principle of analysis involves analysing the knowledge gained, along with the history of the customer's previous interactions with the organisation in order to offer the customer specific products and services that they are likely to buy and which show the best financial return for the organisation.

The word 'analysis' means different things to different people. It can be an extremely sophisticated and complex subject (see Chapter 16). It covers a very wide area from simple things such as how the current campaign is doing to more sophisticated things like:

- Pareto (the 80:20 rule);
- RFV (recency, frequency, value);
- identifying profitable and less profitable customers;
- return on investment (ROI), i.e. profitability of campaigns;
- a customer's propensity to spend; and even
- predicting a customer's future lifetime value to the organisation (see 16.5.2).

Note that a difference can be drawn between analysis and analytics. Analysis is the reporting of figures using simple mathematical operators and formulae such as sums, averages and budget versus actual variance, as described in more detail under 15.2.2. Analytics, on the other hand, is the gaining of insight into given data by means of complex statistical analysis and pattern identification utilising modelling, forecasting and 'What if?' techniques in order to assist in decision making (see 16.5.10).

5.9 **PLANNING**

The principle of planning involves deciding what actions to carry out following the analysis. Once information has been gathered and analysed, the process of planning can commence. This will include campaign planning, development of the campaign message, segmentation and selection of customers to target in the campaign, types of approach to make to customers, timescales for the campaign and how to monitor its success or failure. This can be summed up as the four M's: the message, the media, the manner and the masses.

6 Common CRM concepts

6.1 COMBINING PRINCIPLES

In the previous chapter, the concepts of the '360 degree view' or the 'single customer view', 'understanding customers', the 'customer journey', and the 'customer experience', were introduced. In order to build on these concepts, the eight principles on which CRM is based can be combined in a number of ways, as shown in figure 6.1 and described in the sections that follow.

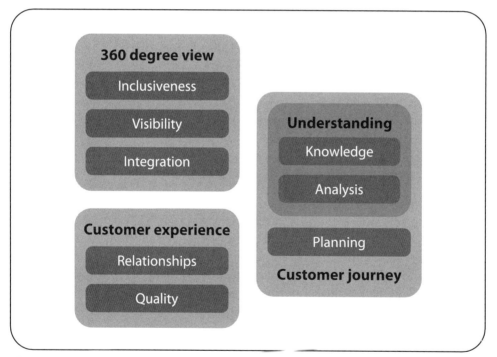

Fig. 6.1 Combining the eight principles

6.2 THE 360 DEGREE VIEW

Many CRM proponents mention the 360 degree view. This is the cornerstone of customer relationship management. The 360 degree view of a customer is, in effect, the first three principles discussed in Chapter 5, namely, inclusiveness, visibility and integration considered together. To provide the 360 degree view of a customer and their interactions with the organisation, it is essential first to capture all the data, and then make it accessible to all staff. To achieve this, all systems (procedural and computing) need to be linked together, as inevitably different data will be gathered by different people and recorded in different systems. This brings up the subject of 'data silos', i.e. similar customer-related data residing in different places and in different formats. These formats are typically CRM systems, ad hoc Access databases, Excel spreadsheets, Word address lists, etc. All of these data silos are usually incompatible with each other and each one is usually accessible to one and only one department. A survey of not-for-profit organisations by the author in 2009 showed that on average organisations had between 8 and 12 such data repositories. One extreme example showed an organisation to have more than 2000!

The 360 degree view demands that all data related to a customer should be accessible and able to be viewed together in one place. It must show who has been and who is currently engaged with the customer, and also why they were, or are, engaged with the customer. The 360 degree view enables the organisation to:

- analyse the data gathered in order to up-sell and cross-sell;
- know who to target in different campaigns;
- forecast a customer's future actions;
- manage financial requests;
- map out a complete customer journey (see 6.5);
- manage and manipulate these customer journeys;
- know where anyone is in their journey at any point in time;
- improve customer service (much more of all this later).

The 360 degree view is not without its problems, as there will inevitably be differences of opinion as to who can talk to whom about what (and often the loudest voice in the organisation wins). Another perceived problem is whether it is necessary to capture *every single interaction* a customer has with the organisation due to the enormous amount of data generated, much of which has little or no value or whether only *relevant interactions* need to be captured. If the decision is made to omit some data, who makes the decision on what is and is not valuable? This is the subject of *big data* which is a hot topic at the present moment.

The 360 degree view does not presuppose that all of the data has to be held in one place, but it must be capable of being viewed together in one place. In addition, multiple views are required. For example, senior management might want only a very high-level summary of a customer's interactions plus an indication of which departments are interacting with the customer, whereas an individual department will require the detail of each interaction.

6.3 'THE SINGLE CUSTOMER VIEW'

The 'single customer view' (or in some cases, the 'single supporter view') is characterised by the phrase 'one instance of the truth'. This means that customer data is always consistent wherever it is held. Centralising all of an organisation's customers in a single system is the preferred method of providing a single customer view, although this is not always practical or even desirable in some cases. This single customer view is often equated to the 360 degree view, but there are in fact subtle differences. The single customer view demands one instance of the truth, whereas the 360 degree view can contain multiple instances of the truth (such as different name formats, different addresses, and different preferences), as long as all of these data sets can be viewed together in one place. Another subtlety is that the single customer view could actually be a subset of the 360 degree view, as the data held in the single customer view need not necessarily be complete, whereas by definition the data in the 360 degree view is complete (or at least complete from the organisation's point of view: it is everything the organisation knows about the customer irrespective of where that data is stored).

Holding one central master record on each customer has numerous benefits:

- data is held once;
- data is entered once;
- data is updated once;
- there are no integration issues with one database communicating with another to keep records synchronised when an update is made on one;
- data is always up to date, as the first person to be notified of a change of customer details, such as a change of address, makes the change on the database.

Furthermore, this single instance of the truth makes it easier to comply with the Data Protection Act and reduces costs by decreasing the number of maintenance tasks and lessening the amount of staff time needed.

6.4 UNDERSTANDING CUSTOMERS

In order to understand customers and determine their propensity to buy your products and services you need to combine the principles of knowledge and analysis (see 5.7 and 5.8). You need to gather as much information about your customers (and prospective customers) as possible, always being wary of the Data Protection Act, and then analyse it to determine their value to you as an organisation. However, this is fraught with issues. What really motivates people to support your organisation and how do you record these qualitative issues? What information should you gather? What will be useful and what won't? How do you keep it up to date? How do you analyse it? What tools do you need?

What are you going to do with it? What choices should you offer your customer? This last question leads on to the next subject of the 'customer journey'.

6.5 THE CUSTOMER JOURNEY

The 'customer journey', sometimes known as the 'customer engagement cycle', is the combination of the principles of knowledge and analysis (5.7 and 5.8) – which, when combined, will provide you with an understanding of your customers – along with the principle of planning (5.9). The journey, which is also known as the 'purchase funnel' in commercial CRM terms, is characterised by the old acronym of AIDA (awareness, interest, desire, action), where the action is usually the purchase of a product or service.

The customer journey has two distinct aspects, firstly, the journey that the customer has been on in their time with the organisation to date, and secondly, the journey the organisation wishes them to undertake in the future. Customer journeys can become much more complex in the not-for-profit sector than the private sector because there are far more possibilities than just buying products and services, such as donating money, giving time, attending an event, providing a service and becoming an advocate. For more on the customer journey, see 7.5.6.

6.6 THE CUSTOMER EXPERIENCE

The customer experience, which is sometimes abbreviated to CX, is the totality of the interactions between the customer and the supplier. In terms of our eight principles outlined in Chapter 5, it covers relationships and quality (see 5.5 and 5.6). It means thinking about the interactions from the customer's point of view, with the objective of giving the customer the best possible products, and especially service, and an effective, quick and pleasant experience so that they keep returning to purchase more products and/or services. It can encompass actual or implied customer service-level agreements, such as answer the telephone within three rings, always be polite and send a thank-you email immediately an online donation is received.

7 CRM strategy issues

7.1 STRATEGIC PRINCIPLES

A strategy is an integrated set of plans in order to achieve a stated objective. Some common questions asked for the development of any strategy are:

- Where are we now?
- Where do we want to be?
- What is happening in the marketplace?
- What are our options?
- How do we get there?

Any strategy starts with an examination of where the organisation is at the current moment in time in relation to the subject under consideration: whether it is an overall organisation strategy, an IT strategy, a fundraising or membership strategy or a CRM strategy. In CRM terms, this involves documenting things such as:

- the types and levels of income streams you have;
- the ways in which you currently communicate with customers;
- the customer service levels you achieve;
- the methods you use to attract new customers;
- the range of products and services you offer;
- the staff you have who interface with customers;
- the systems (procedural and computerised) that you use;
- your customers' and the general public's perception of your organisation.

From there you move on to considering the ways in which you wish to change those things. This sounds easy on the face of it, because anyone can do unconstrained blue-sky thinking. But within an organisation, it always turns out to be quite complicated because there will always be assumptions, constraints, practicalities, issues and risks to take into consideration, many of which will be specific to your particular organisation. There are various devices to assist in this phase of the strategy including SWOT analysis (strengths, weaknesses, opportunities and threats), the BCG (Boston Consulting Group) Matrix, Michael Porter's Five Forces Model, the McKinsey 7-S Framework, Critical Sets, Michael Porter's Value Chain, the Cost Benefit Matrix, and the rest. And remember, once you have decided what changes you want to make (i.e. where you want to be) you should always define measurable targets (i.e. your critical success factors). For example, 'reduce customer attrition by X%', or 'convert Y customers to direct debits in the next three years'.

At the same time, you should be considering what is going on in relation to CRM in the big wide world. What are other organisations similar to yours doing? What are the trends? What are other organisations about to do? Ten years ago, the big buzz was linking the back-office CRM systems to the Internet and giving customers the ability to buy or donate or support, and access or modify their own details online. At the time of writing, the big buzz is connecting the CRM systems to social networking media: Facebook, Twitter and the like. At this point in your strategy deliberations, you can start considering options for achieving the goals set out in the 'Where do we want to be?' section. These might (and usually do) include:

- a new CRM system or systems, for which there is a bewildering choice (see Part 6 'CRM systems procurement');
- the location of systems (in-house, hosted, SaaS);
- streamlined office procedures;
- greater use of analytical techniques;
- various types and levels of systems integration, where the CRM system needs to integrate with other systems such as finance, the website, social media, stock control, address management: the potential list is huge (see 10.6 and 15.6);
- staff structure changes;
- and many more.

Then comes the analysis of options, option selection and the development of an implementation plan. Analysing options is a difficult task in itself. For each option, you have to consider:

- the advantages and disadvantages;
- the level to which each supports the organisation's mission;
- the impact on staff, procedures and the organisation as a whole;
- competing departmental priorities;
- integration with other systems;
- future-proofing (ensuring that customer data will be accessible and usable as far as possible in the future);
- expected benefits;
- the vexed issue of cost.

Once an option has been selected and accepted by everyone, an implementation plan (sometimes known as a migration plan) must be developed. As with every plan of every type, this one must contain assumptions and constraints, structure, activities, end products, resources and timescales (see chapters 18 and 23).

Remember that in order for a strategy to be effective, it must have objectives that are:

- **clear and concise** so that everyone at all levels of the organisation can understand them, with no room for misinterpretation;
- **consistent with the mission** (otherwise why are we here?);
- **consistent within themselves**, which is not always easy to achieve because of competing priorities within different departments;
- **acceptable by everyone** because the greater the level of consensus, the greater the chance of success;
- **a basis for action** so that people can easily understand exactly what is required of them;
- **achievable**, because too many people exaggerate the expected benefits in order to impress the board and get their backing: be realistic in setting targets;
- **measurable** so that you can review the project later and have a firm basis for declaring it a success (or challenged, or a failure!);
- **flexible**, as it won't happen overnight and things can change rapidly.

7.2 DEVELOPING A CRM STRATEGY

In order to develop a CRM strategy, by drawing on the definitions of not-for-profit CRM, you will need to determine what you are going to do in order to:

- acquire new customers;
- retain existing customers;
- find out more about them;
- keep them happy;
- provide them with what they want;
- get them to buy or give more;
- treat them like individuals;
- maintain and improve the quality of your products and services;
- measure your effectiveness.

And on this last point, what are you going to measure? What are your key performance indicators (KPIs) or, if you prefer, your critical success factors (CSFs)? First, you will need to have a current measure of all of the issues listed above (and any others you can think of), and then you will need to agree on targets for each of them. Four KPIs you might like to start with are as follows:

1. **Customer satisfaction index:** for this you will need to do regular surveys of customers.
2. **Customer retention rate:** the opposite of the often mentioned 'attrition' that you are trying to minimise.
3. **Net income per customer:** a measure of customer profitability.
4. **Customer acquisition rate:** monitoring your ability to attract new customers.

Here are some other questions you will need to consider in your strategy:

- What is your case for support?
- How will you raise your organisation's profile?
- What communication channels will you use to interact with your customers?
- How will you segment them and target them?
- How often will you communicate with them?
- What devices will you use? For example, letters, free gifts, special offers?
- How close to the cutting edge of technology do you want to be?
- How will you motivate your staff to perform well?
- How will you protect your customer data?
- The list goes on and on and on . . . .

7.3   IMPLEMENTING A CRM STRATEGY

When it comes to implementing a strategy of any sort, most strategists, academics and authors produce a cycle of some sort. In *Fundraising Strategy*, Redmond Mullin proposes a simple 4-step cycle, as shown in figure 7.1, and states that 'strategy for most organisations is a continuous developing process; as one cycle ends, it feeds and boosts the next' (Mullin 2002, p. 65). Note that although this is in a book on fundraising, it is a general strategic cycle that is equally applicable to any type of not-for-profit organisation.

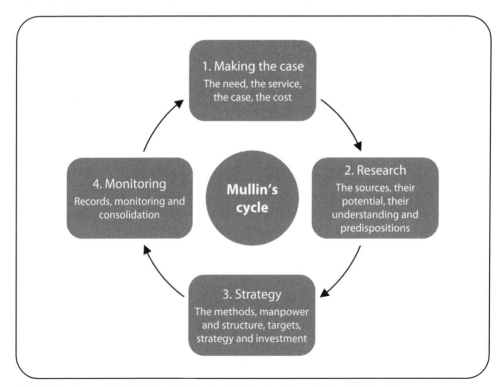

Fig. 7.1 Redmond Mullin's Fundraising Cycle (adapted from Mullin 2002, p. 65)

Making the case is very much the heart of the entire strategy. It is what you want to achieve; in other words, it is deeply tied in to your organisation's mission. Research is analysis of customers and their likelihood to buy, donate or support. Strategy is the planning of the activities to be conducted. Monitoring is the carrying out of the activities and the recording of their results. What appears to be missing is any specific reference to analysis and review of the results of the activities to feed back into the next planning phase, although this could be implied in both monitoring and research.

Peter Maple in *Marketing Strategy* proposes several cycles, one of which is a 7-step cycle he describes as 'A shortened marketing planning process', as shown in figure 7.2. In a similar way to Mullin's Cycle, the key elements of this one are research, planning, implementing (i.e. carrying out the planned activities), and reviewing (which will incorporate analysis).

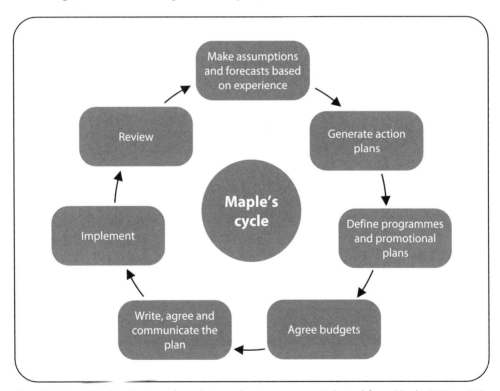

Fig. 7.2 Peter Maple's shortened marketing planning process (adapted from Maple 2003, p. 54)

The author has his own cycle for the implementation of IT strategy which has been used for many years, as shown in figure 7.3. Once again the key elements are planning, development (as opposed to research in the others; it is an IT cycle after all), implementing and reviewing.

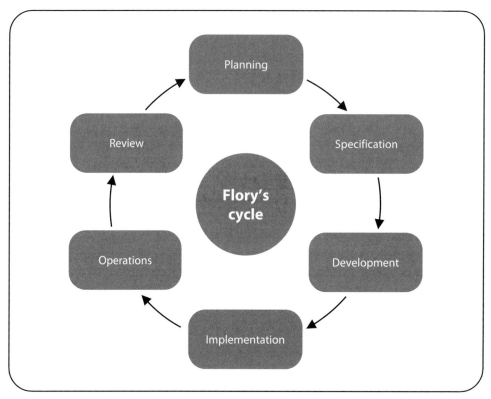

Fig. 7.3 Peter Flory's IT strategy implementation cycle

All of these cycles have four things in common; they all include:

1. researching opportunities or possibilities;
2. the planning of activities (to different degrees);
3. the conducting of activities; and
4. reviewing the activities.

If we combine this with the traditional highest level breakdown of CRM, i.e. marketing, sales and service, we can easily arrive at the cycle as shown in figure 7.4. Note that in this diagram:

- implementing is replaced with the three functional areas of marketing, sales and service;
- research is subsumed under marketing;
- review is equated with analysis, which should perhaps be styled as analysis/ review.

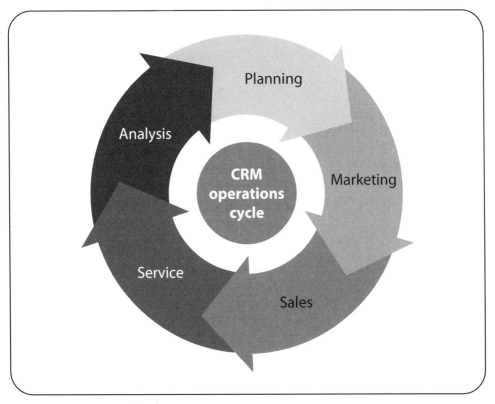

Fig. 7.4 CRM operational cycle

In order to put some of this into context, see the following real-life case study which illustrates the full cycle of analysis, planning, marketing, sales and service, and then back to analysis, planning, marketing, etc. This is CRM in action.

Case Study: Crisis UK Major Gift Campaign

In July 2002, David Gilmour made an inspirational gift of £3.6 million to Crisis. That was the catalyst that enabled the successful US concept 'Common Ground', of providing a holistic 24/7 support and housing programme for single homeless people, to be anglicised and for it to take root in London. Crisis attempted to build an ambitious £60 million capital campaign, called Urban Village, around this gift. The strategy was, in the end, not successful. This was mainly because, although most of the money was raised (in pledges) and a suitable site was found, the planners' political knees buckled and the urban regeneration proposals were turned down. After such a bruising, the charity withdrew from any further attempts to provide such holistic solutions. During the five years this project was being attempted, little other major gift strategic work was undertaken. Nevertheless, individual high-value supporters were giving around £200,000 a year.

In 2007, whilst I was still the Urban Village Appeal Director, with the help of a researcher, I undertook a detailed re-analysis of the Crisis supporter list (a Raiser's Edge database of around 80,000 verifiable names). Of these, around 650 were identifiable, contactable supporters who had given on multiple occasions and had made at least one gift of £1,000 or more. Research identified a further 600 supporters as having the potential to upgrade, having made gifts in excess of £500. Whilst the accuracy of some of the recorded data was questionable, the fact that the database had verifiable gifts and contact information going back to the early 1980s meant that the researchers could be confident of the potential value of such supporters and the likely support, given the right 'case for support'. Further wealth screening, using information provided by Factary, helped assure the team that it had a list of actual givers with a net worth in excess of £1 billion.

One of the other items felt to be very important in terms of communications continuity was the whole story of the Urban Village, which higher-value supporters had been exposed to during the project development. The concept of 'Urban Investors' was proposed by me as being something that many of these high-value givers could and would identify with. The idea of launching an 'investment' vehicle with regular reports on social return on investment (SROI) was developed using focus groups of supporters and a steering group of high-value givers.

The Urban Investor programme was successfully launched in 2009/10 with a prospectus that had the same look and feel as a new share offering, thanks to pro bono help from Slaughter and May. Independent economic analyst, Oxford Economics, worked with Crisis to track the value of each £1 spent in Skylight centres (education, training and employment centres for homeless and vulnerably housed people) and predicted that the saving to the taxpayer would be an average of £3.92 per £1. The *Financial Times* covered the story, and a significant number of investors applied.

To date, the charity continues to report regularly to its Urban Investors about the rate of SROI that the charity is achieving against its agreed performance benchmarks. It has subsequently successfully rolled out a 'mid-value' offering to a wider number of its direct-mail-responsive supporters, a programme which by July 2013 had raised over £1 million.

Peter Maple, Director of Charity Fundraising Courses at LSBU

7.4 ORGANISATIONAL ISSUES

7.4.1 Organisational strategy

The first point of consideration is the fact that *CRM is a strategy and not a system.* CRM is achieved through a combination of information systems and people (and the processes which those people use). The major message in this section is that although CRM is a strategy and not a system, it must not be implemented for its own sake. It must support the organisation's overall strategy. For example, if an element of the organisation's strategy is to recruit more members, then CRM can assist with this objective. If another element is to influence government policy, then CRM can assist with managing the lobbying of policy makers. Although most organisations see CRM as supporting various elements of the organisation's overall business strategy, some incorporate a relationship management strategy as a distinct element of this overall strategy.

Therefore, CRM can be implemented for its own sake, as it is seen as a prime contributor to the success of the organisation.

7.4.2 Departmental strategy

Problems start to arise when CRM is implemented organisation-wide. This is because different departments have diverse needs that can often be satisfied by specific sections of CRM, and they usually have different perspectives on which needs are common throughout the whole organisation. This interplay of departmental strategies needs to be managed from the top of the organisation and compromises made where appropriate. With an organisation-wide CRM strategy in place, individual departments often lose control of what they do. An example is where a fundraising department sends a supporter six appeal mailings in a year, the events department sends the same supporter six event invites in a year, and the press department also sends the same supporter six newsletters in a year. After putting an organisation-wide CRM policy in place, it dictates that no supporter should receive more than one communication per month, so something has to give!

It is a common practice for CRM to be implemented in one specific department to solve problems in that department or in support of that department's strategy. Conflicts inevitably occur when CRM is subsequently rolled out to other departments. The key to success appears to be to start at the top of the organisation and define what senior management wants to see and build downwards, rather than start at the bottom with individual departmental requirements and build up.

7.4.3 Perceived benefits

For CRM to provide direct benefits to an organisation, the CRM system has to be cost-effective. It must either increase income or reduce cost by reducing time, effort and money spent on administrative tasks. This leads to a debate on what to measure, when to measure it, what level of improvement is considered a success and whether it is possible to forecast future income (and expenditure) and identify future trends. In terms of indirect benefits, CRM systems must make the work of the organisation's staff easier and more rewarding by automating mundane tasks, guiding the user through a complex series of tasks, providing relevant information in an easily digestible manner and generally being attractive to use.

So, a CRM system should provide benefits to the organisation, but which parts of the organisation? Ideally, it should provide benefits to the *whole* organisation, which means that it should manage the relationships of *all* the customers listed in table 4.1. That is, every person and organisation which encounters or has any contact with the organisation (the jargon for this is 'touch point' and can also be seen as a communication channel – see 7.5.4). However, some customers are seen as not providing a benefit, direct or indirect, to the organisation, so should they be included? For example, those who fit into the category of 'detractors': people who are negative towards the organisation in one way or another. The answer is probably 'yes' because there would be benefit to the organisation if a better relationship with these people led to a change in their views. There is also a cost saving if the organisation knows who not to market to.

Pragmatism often dictates that CRM is applied only to high-value front-line business departments such as the fundraising department in a charity or the membership department in a professional association. It is often seen as too complex and cumbersome for some tasks and even some whole departments within organisations. For example, although full event-management facilities are an integral part of any CRM system, the person organising an annual dinner might find it quicker and easier to manage the event with a spreadsheet. However, this must be weighed against the organisational benefit of having relationship information recorded centrally. When a partial CRM implementation is undertaken, say, for one department, it is often the case that its usage will spread through a process of organisational osmosis. You might implement a CRM strategy in one department but it will start to touch others through ongoing integration and data usage issues. For example, a fundraising department sets up a system to feed information about volunteers' activities and expenses from the volunteer database. At first the volunteering department is not taken in by its initial design and doesn't use the system. Later, however, when the volunteers start to see the benefits of having quicker access to more data and easier ways of reporting, the department implements the system fully itself.

The benefits of CRM must be two-way: both the customers and the organisation must benefit. This should be in terms of quality of service, such as giving quicker responses, more relevant communications and a more personal service, with no mailings that are headed 'Dear Supporter' or 'Dear Member'. Communications that recognise who the customer is and what they have done in the past are essential. Giving the customer more control over their interactions with the organisation, for example self-service facilities on the website, should lead to greater customer loyalty.

7.5 CUSTOMER ISSUES

7.5.1 Who is the customer?

Over 50 possible types of customer were identified in table 4.1 and a not-for-profit organisation implementing a CRM strategy must decide first which customers it wishes to manage with the strategy and how it would like to manage them. It is easy to say that CRM applies to every possible person and organisation that comes into contact with the not-for-profit organisation, but political and practical issues sometimes dictate otherwise.

Some organisations see CRM as mainly applicable to the commercial sector and only related to the generation of income, and so they reason it should cover funders only. Others see the generation of income and the distribution of that income as so tightly linked that CRM must cover both. Some organisations exclude suppliers from consideration as, in their organisations, these are seen to be the province of the finance department and catered for by purchase ledger systems. Other organisations insist that volunteers should be managed within a separate system. There appear to be two reasons for these different approaches:

- The relative maturity of organisations with regard to their strategic thinking and their use of information systems, with the more mature adopting a more global view of customers.
- Organisational politics and a lack of strategic direction related to CRM as a whole.

The key issue is that a fundamental objective of CRM is to serve the *whole* organisation. Therefore, the ideal situation is if *all* customers of *all types* are contained within a single system. In addition, it is usually the case that there is a significant overlap in terms of the customers of different departments within the not-for-profit organisation. In the author's experience, this overlap is of the order of 5% to 25%, but in one extreme case, one organisation identified that 60% of the individuals on their beneficiaries database were also on their fundraising database.

7.5.2 Campaign development (or marketing)

The first point to mention in this section is that some not-for-profit organisations still have a reluctance to consider their supporters as customers and have a great reluctance to use the term 'marketing'. However, they are still happy to discuss 'campaign development' which is a significant element of marketing. There are five main areas of consideration in campaign development, namely:

1. Information
2. Analytics
3. Targeting
4. Selection and segmentation
5. Campaign monitoring (which feeds back into information)

Information

Information is essential for effective marketing. The information (or, more accurately, the data) gathered is of three types: transactional, communications and general.

- **Transactional** data includes details on what the customer has bought from, given to, done for, and received from the organisation.
- **Communications** data includes details of any communications to or from the customer that are not money or support-related, such as appeal mailings to customers, letters from customers, telephone calls to or from customers, etc.
- **General** information includes everything you know about the customer from where they live to their likes and dislikes.

Analytics

The objective of analysing the data in the CRM system is to obtain insight into customer behaviour in order to develop better marketing campaigns. Simple analytics include Pareto analysis, and RFV analysis, which puts customers into various groupings depending upon their past behaviour. This can inform future marketing campaigns.

Going further than this, analytics can be employed to identify trends and patterns in existing data so that campaigns can be constructed which will provide a better return on investment. Only a few of the largest organisations go even further and experiment with predictive analytics. This involves taking data from the CRM system, adding other external sources of data and using modelling techniques to predict the outcomes of different marketing strategies and campaigns. This whole area is complex and specialist and some people question whether analytics belongs in CRM at all or should be considered a subject of its own. Much more on this subject is to be found in Chapter 16.

Targeting

Targeting is the process of deciding whom to market to, based on the results of the analytics. An enormous number of factors may be taken into account. A few simple examples are:

- the customer's past support pattern;
- whether it is an international, national, regional or local campaign;
- the type of campaign;
- whether the customer has supported that type of campaign before;
- the customer's expressed interests;
- the customer's age;
- the customer's location;

- the customer's social demographic classification;
- the customer's household income.

The last two are examples of demographic profiling that can be obtained from specialist agencies and applied to the organisation's database. Targeting also applies to non-financial areas of the organisation's operations. For example, the analytics could identify potential volunteers or show groups of customers who could potentially, but who do not currently, benefit from the organisation's services.

Selection and segmentation

Once it has been decided whom to target, the appropriate group or groups of customers have to be selected from the database so that communication with them can be conducted. This is a complex task. It is not unknown for the selection of a single group of customers to have more than 40 criteria; i.e., more than 40 conditions that have to be tested on their data. For instance, here is a simple example of some criteria or conditions: 'select all people who are over 65 years of age, who have a direct debit and who did not respond to the Christmas mailing'. Organisations can have many groups in a single campaign, all receiving slightly different messages. The author's experience has shown that it is not uncommon to have as many as 60 groups, and one organisation had more than 120.

The words 'selection' and 'segmentation' are often used interchangeably, but technically there is a difference. Selection is querying the database and selecting records with matching criteria and is usually for a single immediate purpose such as a mailing. Segmentation goes further and implies that the group of customers selected will be permanently (or semi-permanently) identified as belonging to that group and treated in the same manner all the time or until such time as they move to a different group (or segment). (See also 15.3.2.)

Campaign monitoring

The focus of this is on analysing the results of the campaign to measure how well it did and if it met its objectives. These results are then fed back as information in order to refine the development of future campaigns.

7.5.3 **Up-selling and cross-selling**

Up-selling and cross-selling are key elements of commercial CRM and apply equally to not-for-profit organisations. Amongst the objectives of not-for-profit organisations is to sell more to their existing customer base. For example, an organisation may seek more donations from existing donors or invite members to upgrade their membership. It might also sell other products to its existing customer base such as getting someone who has bought a charity T-shirt but has never donated money to donate, and vice versa, or a member who has never bought a publication to buy one. Similarly, it may target someone who has been to an event run by the organisation but who has never donated or is not a member, to donate or join. This demands a single system or integrated systems, whereas in the past the typical not-for-profit organisation had disparate non-integrated systems, where, for example, the event management system ran on a simple Access database, or even on a spreadsheet, and was not linked in any way to the main fundraising or membership system.

Selling more of the same to a customer is not a problem. What may be a problem is cross-selling when different departments are attempting to sell different products to the same customer, because it raises major management issues such as:

- Who manages the complete relationship?
- Who owns the data?
- Who communicates with the customer and when?
- Who resolves problems raised by the customer?

Some larger not-for-profit organisations have an account manager system, where one individual in the organisation is personally responsible for the interactions with any given customer. However, it is often the case that a whole department is responsible for a single customer, such as the major donor department, so cross-selling from the events department can still give rise to problems. For instance, the events department may invite someone to speak at an event without consulting the major donor department, when this person also happens to be a major donor to the organisation.

7.5.4 Communication channels (or touch points)

The key requirement here is that the CRM system must be all-pervasive and gather information from every single touch point. This is every point at which a person or organisation encounters or has any contact with the organisation, and includes the organisation's website (and social networking presence), telephone, fax, direct mail, email, SMS messaging, event attendance and face-to-face meetings. The purist view is that data must be gathered from all these points and every single interaction should be captured, as it may aid in the understanding of the customer and enable better targeting. However, the more you collect, the more complex your operations become and the greater the demand and reliance on a specialist data analysis team. Practicality dictates that only those touch points and interactions which support the organisation's objectives and are, or may be, beneficial to the organisation are worth recording. For example, is it practical or desirable to capture what the customer says about the organisation on a social networking website?

The issue of what to record (activity and communication tracking) is one which is taken to different levels at different organisations. For example, some organisations are happy to records mailings (or emailings) sent to customers and their responses (or lack of response), whereas others record emails opened, clickthroughs and web pages visited.

The issues of the website as a communication medium and the integration of the website and the back-office CRM database are seen as increasingly important. The ability for customers to donate or join online, change their personal details, buy products and book events online, and have the results fed directly into the main CRM system, is becoming mainstream these days. There are even organisations using handheld devices at events to record not just attendance, but also personal data on customers.

7.5.5 Customer experience and choice

It is beneficial for an organisation to know as much as possible about a customer in order to provide the customer with a better service, and as such, a better experience when dealing with the organisation. Conversely, it is also beneficial for the organisation if the customer is provided with choices so that they feel they are in charge of the relationship rather than the organisation. This starts with asking the customer when they want to hear from the organisation, about what and via which communication channel. For example, 'I want to receive only one appeal per year at Christmas. I want no product catalogues, no event invitations, and I would like a quarterly email newsletter that gives me an update on which programmes you are spending my money.'

In some circumstances, the customer experience is formalised to the extent that the customer is offered a service-level agreement, for example, 'We will only contact you in global emergencies; we will respond to your written queries within 24 hours, your telephone queries within five minutes and we will spend no more than 5% of our total income on administration.' These customer-focused service-level agreements must be monitored and reports fed back to the customer.

The customer experience can be enhanced by communications that are tailored to the needs and interests of each customer: the personalised interface. This started many years ago when data drawn from the customer's record was mail-merged for the purpose of mass mailings. Today, this personalised interface has been extended to the website so that each customer sees a different screen when they log on to the organisation's website, which shows them only the information that they want to see. For example, this could contain an update on a service delivery programme in which the customer has expressed an interest, plus notification of new products related to those they have already purchased, plus advance notice with early-booking discounts of upcoming events in the same stream as those previously attended by the customer.

7.5.6 **The customer journey**

This is often described as the supporter journey, or the donor journey, depending on the type of not-for-profit organisation. There is much debate in the sector about customer journeys at the present time and there is no agreed definition as to what it really is. Marketers often use a customer engagement cycle called AIDA (awareness, interest, desire, action – see 9.2), or a variation of it such as awareness, consideration, enquiry, purchase and retention which show the stages of the customer journey.

Many years ago in the charity section of the not-for-profit sector, people talked about the donor ladder or pyramid. This started with a single donation, progressed through stages of repeat donation, regular donation and ended at some later time with the donor becoming an advocate or leaving a legacy bequest. The objective of the fundraiser was to push people up the ladder. This still works for many organisations, but many others have decided that this is far too simplistic and something more was needed, especially as giving donations was just one, albeit the most important, form of supporting the organisation. One organisation attempted to chart possible customer journeys from their first contact with the organisation, through their taking up of different products, and right up to the point of advocacy. The organisation gave up when it had 65 branches in the tree with even more backward loops.

In CRM, everyone is familiar with the expression: 'Your best future customer is your current customer'. This idea leads to the concepts of 'up-selling' (getting customers to increase their purchases or donations), and 'cross-selling' (getting customers to purchase other products or services, such as getting members or donors to attend events). The big problem is working out the best time to attempt to up-sell or cross-sell.

Many organisations nowadays are developing a small number of preferred journeys and are attempting to balance the opposing concepts of trying to push people along predetermined paths on the one hand and giving the customer the choice to determine their own path on the other. The key to all of this is knowing where the supporter has been in the past in terms of their journey with the organisation and knowing where the organisation would like them to go next. For example, if someone has had a standing order of five pounds per month for three years and gives an additional gift at Christmas, then attempt to get them to increase their standing order and/or increase the size of their

Christmas gift. Or if a member of five years regularly buys publications but does not attend any training events, then attempt to get them interested in the training programme.

7.6 STAFF ISSUES

An often-forgotten factor in the implementation of CRM is the organisation's staff. They are just as important as the customers because it is they who create and manage the customer relationships. They will be nervous about any changes to their working practices and worried about their jobs (the fear factor). They are likely to have a tendency to do the minimum amount possible to assist the introduction of new systems and processes. The whole concept of visibility, as described in 5.3, will be alien to them as they will have been used to working in their own particular part of the organisation. Suddenly it will be as if the walls have been removed and their actions are now visible to everyone. This requires a fundamental shift in attitudes and working practices. The concept of cross-departmental working is likely to be particularly hard to come to terms with and will lead to confusion, with people feeling that they are serving more than one master. In extreme cases, this could involve the concept of 'matrix management', which is particularly hard to control effectively.

In addition, staff will be brought into closer contact with customers, which could also necessitate a change in attitudes and working practices. In short, people's lives will change considerably and they will need huge amounts of training and support. They must be treated with extreme care and respect because, without their wholehearted support, the project will fail. This is a hugely complex area and probably worth a book in its own right!

7.7 CONFIDENTIALITY, SECURITY AND COMPLIANCE

7.7.1 Confidentiality and record ownership

Confidentiality and ownership of data is seen as the big problem with CRM systems that capture every single interaction with the customer. This is particularly the case in the larger not-for-profit organisations where individual staff members and even complete departments manage different activities with one subset of the organisation's customers (for example, a major donor department, a corporate fundraising department, a trust fundraising department and a membership department all contacting the same customers with different information). People can be swamped with data, not all of which is relevant to them.

One question is, 'Does everyone need to see everything or just enough to do their jobs?' For example, does a person who organises conferences need (or want) to see details of a supporter's web purchases? A second question is, 'Is some information sensitive such that it should be kept within the confines of one particular department?' This includes celebrity addresses or beneficiary case notes. A third question is 'Should parts of records, or even some complete customer records, be 'owned' by specific departments and ownership passed to other departments under specified circumstances?' The major problem with this is the left hand not knowing what the right hand is doing. A corporate policy, therefore, needs to be in place to define who can access what data, who can modify what data and who can communicate with which customers.

There are three possible approaches to the subject of who sees what data and who can add and amend what data. The first is total openness of data with restrictions only on who can add and amend records. An interesting observation is that many smaller organisations have a policy of complete openness, stating that 'we all work for the same organisation'. One comment the author has heard regularly, however, is 'we want the chief executive to be able to see what is going on but we don't want him pressing the wrong keys and messing things up!'

The second approach is records being 'owned' by different departments and restrictions placed not only on who can add and amend records, but also on who can view certain customer records or parts of records. There is always much debate on what should be restricted and why, and what is and is not confidential. A common problem is individual departments' reluctance to give up 'their' customers during CRM systems implementation. The reason given for this is always that they are afraid that other departments will send inappropriate communications to their customers. This is particularly the case with the distinction between income-generating customers and service-consuming customers. In some organisations there are separate CRM systems for income generation and for service provision but there is a level of integration between them, so that although there is some level of record duplication between systems, everyone can see who is communicating with whom. In addition, the ownership issue can sometimes be a big problem in large not-for-profit organisations that have complex, overlapping audience-based, product-based and geography-based 'sales' (income-generating) teams.

The third approach is one where a policy decision is taken to keep income-generation systems and service-provision systems completely separate. This results in two CRM systems with a very large overlap in functionality and with an unknown level of customer record duplication between systems because there is no integration between the systems at all.

One very large not-for-profit organisation analysed these options at length and decided on a policy of openness (except for very sensitive information) but reporting on any abuse of trust. To implement an ownership model based on staff teams, times of year, communications channel, customer's preferences, etc.

which was reviewed whenever anything changed, was deemed to be just not practical.

There are some exceptions to the single view philosophy; for example, NSPCC has two separate databases because it needs to keep its funders and beneficiaries completely separate. But these are extremely rare.

7.7.2 Security

The issues that will be considered under security are:

- 1, 2 or 3 circles?
- In-house v. hosting v. SaaS
- Data corruption or loss, backups and disaster plans

1, 2 or 3 circles?

In terms of security, the consideration of 1, 2 or 3 circles (collaborative, operational or analytical CRM systems – see 10.2) comes down to a question of whether one has a web database and a main database or just one database. (The third circle, the analytics database, is a different issue.)

Some suppliers provide a single database solution (a CRM and CMS database all in one) and some can only operate with the concept of two databases. Some not-for-profit organisations want the separation of their main database from the web database to protect against the fear of their website being hacked which could lead to wholesale corruption or destruction of data, depending on the malevolence of the hackers.

This leads to the softer data corruption issues such as the much vaunted 'Mickey Mouse' syndrome. This is where a customer, given access to their own record, changes their name to Mickey Mouse and their address to Disneyland. It seems unlikely, however, that this has ever happened. If it were to happen, then obviously it would signal that the customer doesn't want to be on your database and you are well rid of them! This sort of thing, and other issues where customers make genuine mistakes, leads many people to request a 'gatekeeper' function where changes made by customers can be viewed and accepted or rejected before being applied to the main database.

In-house versus hosting versus SaaS

The question of the location of systems – in-house versus hosting (i.e. hosted externally at a data centre) versus SaaS (see 2.1.9) – nowadays is a case of personal preference plus practicality and economics. Gone are the days when people were neurotic about where their data was stored and insisted on keeping it in the UK, and usually keeping it in-house. Of course you still have to be aware of UK and EU legislation, but questions such as, 'Is hosted or SaaS data more or less secure than in-house?' have largely been resolved in favour of, yes, it is more secure than in-house (and it's a lot less hassle too).

Data corruption or loss, backups and disaster plans

The issues of data corruption or loss, backups and disaster recovery plans are essential subjects for in-house operations but are largely irrelevant to hosted and SaaS operations where they are someone else's problem. The major issue facing organisations today is one of mobile devices containing valuable data.

People carry laptops everywhere (and leave them in cars and on trains), they store huge amounts of data on mobile devices like smart phones and, as for memory sticks, they are just so easy to lose. Organisations have to decide what data can be stored on these devices and how to protect that data and associated system login details and passwords. Encryption might seem like the answer but what can be encrypted could potentially be decrypted. It can be a serious problem.

7.7.3 **Compliance**

Issues to be considered under compliance are legal obligations and codes of practice. The issues are complex and important. Every not-for-profit organisation needs someone who understands the implications of all the laws, codes of good practice and the general guidance outlined below.

The main legal obligations are administered by the Information Commissioner's Office. These are the Data Protection Act with its eight basic principles, which has been in force for many years and with which everyone should be familiar; the Freedom of Information Act which might in certain circumstances apply to your CRM systems; and the hugely complex Privacy and Electronic Communications Regulations (including European Union regulations). Just to indicate the complexity of the latter, the Information Commissioner's Office publishes guidance for these regulations under the following headings:

- Rules on marketing: Key definitions, Automated calls, Telephone marketing, Fax marketing, Electronic mail, Viral marketing, Appending email addresses/ mobile numbers, Loyalty schemes, Pan European marketing, Marketing to more than one medium;
- Other rules: Security of services, Security breaches, Cookies, Traffic data, Location data, Itemised bills, Calling or connected line identification (CLI), Directories of subscribers, Contracts, National security, and Legal requirements.

ICO 2012

Then there is the Financial Services and Markets Act 2000 which is administered by the Financial Conduct Authority (FCA), which itself is a not-for-profit organisation. This is all about the Banking Conduct Regime and Payment Services Regulations and covers such things as direct debits, money transfers and credit card transactions.

For a large part of the sector there is the Charity Commission to consider. The Commission publishes regulations and guidance for charities. The regulations mainly cover the administration of charities, but the guidance covers the day-to-day operations of the organisation that are all part and parcel of CRM. There are, in fact, numerous other regulatory bodies for other parts of the overall sector, especially for trade associations, and each not-for-profit organisation needs to search for all the different bodies that might have power to determine how they conduct their business. It is not an easy task and is time-consuming, but essential.

And, finally, both the Direct Marketing Association and the Institute of Fundraising publish codes of practice by which all not-for-profit organisations should abide. They do not have the force of the law behind them, but they are there for a reason. They are codes of good/reasonable/fair practice that should be followed by all well-meaning organisations.

Consequently, anyone managing the implementation of CRM within their organisation needs to be familiar with and be aware of everything coming out of the:

- Information Commissioner's Office;
- Financial Conduct Authority;
- Charity Commission;
- Institute of Fundraising;
- Direct Marketing Association;
- and possibly many others!

7.8 SYSTEMS AND DATA ISSUES

7.8.1 Functionality

When considering functionality you need to think through the following questions:

- What do you need to achieve your strategic objectives?
- Do you need 1, 2 or 3 circles? (See section 10.2.)
- What do you really need to run your business?
- What other systems do you need to integrate with?
- The big question of the moment: how will you integrate with social media? (See section 14.5.)

Great care needs to be taken in the selection and construction of a complete CRM solution because not-for-profit organisations usually want all or most of the functionality described in Part 4, but very few system providers can supply all the requested functionality in one product, or even a family of products. The only conclusion which can be drawn is that most not-for-profit organisations will have to deal with a number of system suppliers in order to obtain all the required functionality. Furthermore, systems providers will have to decide where their respective key strengths lie and provide suggestions (and integration facilities) as to how their customers and prospective customers can obtain functionality that they themselves cannot provide.

Smaller organisations tend to want, and are often able to obtain, a single system that carries out all of their required CRM functionality, primarily because their needs are not overly complex. However, even the larger organisations often also want to minimise the number of systems they utilise because, as one large organisation representative put it:

> *The complexity is in the scope of the processes, so if people want multiple systems they are actually indicating they need more resources, and using 'different systems' as the tool to achieve this. I think it is a false economy, since you then need multiple contracts, separate support staff, etc.*

This is an area that needs very careful investigation because the 'best of breed' systems (i.e. those systems that have been proven to be the best of their kind) tend to be more sophisticated and functionally rich than the facilities provided within most CRM systems in those specific areas. The question that should always be asked by not-for-profit organisations for each of these areas where best of breed systems exist, is 'Could we operate effectively with the facilities within our main CRM system such that we do not really need an additional best of breed system, or not?'

7.8.2 System flexibility and extensibility

There should be facilities in the system's software that allow changes to be made in-house, from the simple adding of new data fields to any existing **data table** to the ability to add complete new modules (i.e. new software or add-ons) when, for example, new methods of fundraising or new types of membership are developed. To maintain the 360 degree view of the customer, it is necessary to develop and integrate new functionality with the existing system quickly as the business changes. Some not-for-profit organisations desire to have these

A **data table** is a visual display of named rows and columns that organises the information contained within a computer's database. (See also figure 10.2.)

facilities available to users (staff), or at least to selected users who have the technical skills to use these facilities effectively (rather than having to go back to the system supplier for such changes and additions). However, this can have negative ramifications because installed systems can rapidly diverge from the standard, making supplier upgrades problematic. Careful management control is required.

Almost all not-for-profit organisations want to have facilities where they themselves, rather than the supplier, can extend the breadth of data stored by the system and even extend the functionality of the system. Consequently, suppliers feel duty bound to provide such facilities. However, this can give rise to problems, as expressed by one systems provider:

> The front end should use generic-enough data tables to render this unnecessary for existing objects or processes in the system, save for the odd extra field here and there. It is only when building entirely new (organisation-specific) processes that new work should be done, and then with the database provider. When the customer does their own development, support and training become harder, as does upgradability, and organisations become reliant on key individuals in their IT department – they would never have purchased the system from a one-man band. Suppliers say yes to this because it is technically possible, and because customers ask for it, but it doesn't make it right!

A member of one not-for-profit organisation also commented on the flexibility issue:

> We spent a lot of time and money adding specific functionality to the system just for us and tailoring existing functionality to operate in the way we wanted it to, only to find 12 months later that the supplier had added that specific functionality into the standard product and upon using it, almost all of our changes to the existing functionality were less efficient than those of the standard product. I wish we hadn't bothered!

However, a member of another not-for-profit organisation said:

> We re-engineered their Gift Aid functions because we thought they were inadequate and we did it better. As a result, the supplier then incorporated our functionality into the standard product.

System flexibility is always required because, as one member of a not-for-profit organisation put it:

> Requirements are dynamic – the set of CRM requirements for not-for-profits, I would argue, are larger than those for a generic commercial CRM, they also extend continually with the introduction of new media and communication/interaction methods. Can the requirements ever be 'complete', therefore?' The

key would appear to be having a responsive supplier who keeps up with the latest technology, the latest CRM trends and who is always thinking ahead such that 'they put the functionality in the product' before you actually need it.

Case study: is flexibility a good thing?

A common theme in all the CRM systems I have been involved with has been the level of flexibility required in the system to be able to run the particular organisation's (allegedly unique) business processes. In my experience, this flexibility pays off at the initial configuration stage of the CRM system to ensure all the business processes can be set up to run as efficiently as possible with little or (ideally) no bespoke software development. Once live, however, overly flexible software can become an Achilles' heel.

For example, when introducing payroll giving for the first time, a particular charity extended its CRM software to handle the new business process using the built-in flexibility. The level of flexibility available meant this new process could be created by the (non-technical) business process administrator (BPA). When the charity introduced a second payroll giving agency, a completely separate set of business processes were created, as the BPA wasn't able to extend the original processes. This poor design only came to light much later when consolidated payroll giving information was requested. Separate processes had to be run for each agency and the data manually combined to provide the necessary information, a process that was inefficient, prone to errors and was a major stumbling block to introducing a third agency. Implementing best of breed payroll giving business processes, engineered to a tightly defined set of comprehensive requirements, would have paid off. Once configured, there should have been no need for flexibility, even when the charity added new agencies or stopped dealing with certain agencies.

In another example, by careful analysis of the direct debit processes, one organisation reduced its processing times from days to hours by introducing a best of breed system. With no flexibility, one cannot make changes (such as reducing bloated business processes) without careful analysis of benefits versus costs. Only if deemed as commercially or operationally advantageous, is any improvement designed into the best of breed processes at a future release; there is then no need to pay for unnecessary flexibility. The back-office systems can still be designed to minimise processing time and the number of staff required to run them, thereby increasing the total disposable income of the charity.

However, there is the ongoing pressure to gain a competitive edge in attracting and retaining supporters. Fundraisers are constantly dreaming up new and exciting ways to raise money. This is in stark contrast to the business processes (many common to all charities) that are well-established and do not need continual changes. So fundraisers depend on flexibility to be first to market and maximise income opportunities. Charity CRM vendors are slow to respond to such changes in my experience. So *tight* integration of the CRM system with more agile (perhaps even in-house developed) applications, ideally through web services, is a good way to provide the responsiveness demanded by fundraisers rather than necessarily building flexibility into the CRM system itself.

Phil Durbin, Secretary of the Charity IT Leaders (formerly CCitDG) and Head of Corporate Systems (The Salvation Army)

7.8.3 **System deployment and hosting**

With regard to SaaS (see 2.1.9) and external database hosting, some organisations are adamant that they want complete control over their data and that the CRM database must be hosted in-house. These organisations quote security and accessibility concerns as the reasons for this. Other organisations take the opposite approach and insist that the CRM database is hosted externally. They cite reduced costs and reduced organisational complexity as the reasons for this. Although this issue can arouse strong feelings one way or the other, it is a matter of implementation choice for each organisation because almost all CRM systems can now be deployed locally or remotely.

7.8.4 **Configuration**

All CRM system offerings will have a standard way of displaying data and a standard way of carrying out each function. In addition they may include functions and data that are not relevant to some not-for-profit organisations. Consequently, some level of configuration will always be required for each organisation implementing a CRM system. Some of the questions and considerations that come up under this heading are as follows:

- Everyone wants their own way of doing things and their own screen designs, but the question has to be posed, *why*? Surely all organisations are carrying out the same basic functions and there is a best way, isn't there? Is it just a case of familiarity with current practices or are there genuine reasons for doing things in different ways?
- The suppliers which have many, sometimes several hundred, customers have more experience than each individual not-for-profit organisation, don't they? They should have been able to develop best practice, therefore. However, aren't most of them techies with no real-world experience?
- If organisations adopt standard ways, this may save them a lot of money.

The debate will undoubtedly continue, as people in different organisations often think that their way of doing things is the best and most effective. This debate will go on until there are recognised industry-standard best-practice processes for every CRM process, and at present there appears to be no move in this direction.

7.8.5 **Efficiency**

A key objective of every CRM system implementation is improvements in efficiency, which in turn reduces costs. These are obtained not only by automation but also by speeding up, consolidating and streamlining processes (i.e. identifying better ways of doing things).

7.8.6 **Automation**

The more processes that can be automated, the more time staff have to spend on relationship building with their customers. Workflows should be defined wherever possible so that tasks in a sequence are initiated automatically. For instance, the receipt of a grant application from an organisation's website:

- creates the applicant record in the system;
- triggers an email to the Grants Manager to allocate referees;
- emails the application to the referees;
- when all references are received, puts the application onto the agenda for the next grants committee meeting; and then
- prints an acceptance or rejection letter when the committee result is entered.

It is worth noting that automation does not mean the entire process has to be done by magic with no user intervention. Turning a 10-step process into a 3-step process counts as automation in the eyes of most users and achieves the objective effectively.

7.8.7 **Standardisation**

If CRM is being implemented organisation-wide, then standard processes need to be defined so that data is recorded in the same way, and common processes are carried out in the same way, throughout the whole organisation. This demands significant management effort to agree in the first place and even more effort to enforce.

7.8.8 **Support**

The effective use of the system will come from comprehensive training and even more comprehensive documentation both online and in paper form. Immediate access to technical support is also essential to resolve any operational problems and keep staff motivated.

7.8.9 **Data considerations**

Some questions that require answers under this heading are:

- What data do you need to record?
- What data might be useful?
- What are you going to do with it?
- Who can see what?
- Who can use it and when?
- Who manages or is responsible for it?
- Who keeps it up to date?
- How do you keep it up to date?
- How long do you keep it?
- Where do you keep it?

7.8.10   Data storage

The issues here revolve around what is stored, where it is stored and the costs versus the benefits of storing the data. A prime example is the data related to major donors to a charity. The charity staff will interact with the donor in a very personal manner, so a CRM system will be invaluable in keeping track of and managing the relationship. A huge amount of data on the donor will be collected, such as press cuttings where the donor is mentioned. But does all this data need to be stored in a CRM system? In terms of where the data is stored, does all the **base data** relating to the different types of customer need to be in one system, or is a series of linked systems the best solution? (This is another example of the crossover of discussions between strategy and technology.)

> **Base data** is simply the basic information which has been collected on any given person or thing, such as a donor's name and donation amount in this instance. **Summary data** is an aggregation of this individual-record data or base data.

Another aspect is **summary data** for management reporting or analytical purposes: is this best stored with the base data or in a specialist system? On this last point, with the larger not-for-profit organisations it is clear that the only practical solution for conducting sophisticated analytic processing is to store data in a specialist system in order to avoid unacceptable performance and **table locking** issues.

> A **table lock** is a way of restricting access to individual records or even to complete tables of records, to ensure that database rows (within data tables) are not inadvertently overwritten.

7.8.11   Data control

Issues related to the usage and control of data include its source, accuracy, currency, relevance, legality and quality.

- **Source:** it is important to know where data came from in the first instance and how it got into the system; i.e. who entered it and why? This is to identify where inaccurate data came from, who made mistakes with the data entry and, more importantly, which are the best sources of data.
- **Accuracy:** data must be as accurate as possible. For example, it is unacceptable and shows a lack of care if a mailing is sent to someone with their name spelt incorrectly. Such things detract immediately from the organisation's relationship with the customer.
- **Currency:** data must be kept continually up to date. For example, if someone says don't send me any more direct mail or emails then their record must be updated immediately or the relationship will suffer.

- **Relevance:** there is a temptation to record everything that is known about a customer *just in case* it may come in useful in the future. Firstly, it goes against one of the principles of the Data Protection Act and secondly this is wasteful of space and people's time maintaining the data. The opposite side of relevance is data that is required to service the customer effectively. It is important to capture data that is considered mandatory and which will actually be used for marketing purposes or needed to service customer requests.
- **Legality:** it is essential to comply with all relevant government legislation regarding the holding of data. One aspect of the Data Protection Act has already been mentioned and there are many other principles of the Act to uphold. There is also other legislation to consider such as Privacy and Electronic Communications Regulations and PCI DSS (Payment Card Industry Data Security Standards).
- **Quality:** this is more than just data accuracy. A big issue for all not-for-profit organisations is the identification and handling of duplicate records. Some of these will contain the same data and some will contain conflicting data. Other quality issues centre on standards for what data is entered, for example not putting commas in addresses or other fields that might be exported, or making sure that people input data such as gender codes, honours and qualifications consistently. These sorts of examples and many more must be strictly controlled.

7.8.12 Reporting

The issue of standard day-to-day reporting is relatively straightforward. It is not difficult to compile a list or choose from a system supplier's ready-made list. However, the non-technical person's lament, heard at every single not-for-profit organisation, is 'Why can't I get the reports I want out of the database?' The answer is simple. The underlying structure of the data in a database that is used to record transactions, look up an individual customer or campaign or transaction record, and to run simple reports such as campaign totals to date by day, week, month, etc., is completely different from the structure of the data required to provide complex analysis of huge amounts of data in a reasonable timeframe (for more on this see 10.5).

Creation, maintenance and use of an analysis (or analytics or marketing) database which is built using data warehousing (see 2.1.7) techniques is a specialist task. Users of these databases need to be part data manipulator and part statistician. In the main, they treat their subject as a dark art and talk about such technical things as ETL (extract, transform and load), i.e. the way they get the transactional data into their analytics database, OLAP (online analytical processing), data modelling and data cubes (see 16.4 and 16.5). A rule of thumb for the CRM manager who does not understand these things is: if any individual report you request takes more than half a day to develop and more than two hours to run, then you need an analytics database and a specialist to operate it.

8 CRM management

8.1 ROLES AND RESPONSIBILITIES

A CRM project involves a lot of people, all with different roles and responsibilities. This takes a lot of coordination and serves to indicate the scale of a CRM undertaking. These roles and responsibilities must be defined, allocated and continually monitored. The following text outlines the essential roles of the individuals and groups of people required to make the implementation of CRM a success.

8.1.1 Project sponsor

The drive for CRM must come from the top of the organisation, whether CRM is a strategy in its own right or a support to an element of the organisational strategy. The highest level of the organisation must approve and legitimise the organisational and procedural changes needed to implement a CRM strategy, and this must form part of the overall strategy.

If CRM is being implemented widely within the organisation, then decisions on how it is used, where it is used, what data is recorded, who can have access to what data, who can communicate with which customers and when, are the responsibility of and have to be approved by the highest management level of the organisation, and this means the chief executive (or at the very least someone who has organisation-wide responsibilities *and* authority). Actual decisions and recommendations will often be made at lower management levels, however. This means that in order to achieve a successful CRM implementation, the project sponsor should really be the chief executive and thus take overall responsibility for the project.

8.1.2 Project board

The project sponsor will chair the project board (or steering committee, whichever terminology you prefer). The job of the project board is to take overall control of the project. The members of the board are the people who take important decisions, commit resources (staff and money) and sign-off various project stages. Traditionally, a project board has three elements: **executive**, **senior-user** and **senior-technical**, often represented by one person each.

The **executive** representative is responsible for the overall business management related to the project (this usually means they are responsible for money). The **senior-user** representative(s) represent(s) the management and staff who actually do the day-to-day work of the organisation related to CRM, and the **senior-technical** representative speaks for the people responsible for the technical implementation elements of the project.

Therefore, along with the project sponsor, a project board will usually consist of four people. However, as CRM is an organisation-wide project, there will often be more than one user representative (three is a practical limit if you don't want to get involved in protracted decision-making).

In addition, in a very large project you might even have an optional implementation panel group that sits below the board. This includes senior people from other areas of the organisation who might not have staff using the system, but whose processes may be altered because of it or they might have data used by it or produced by it.

8.1.3 Project manager

The next most important role after the project sponsor is the implementation project manager. This is the person who has a working knowledge of all parts of the organisation, develops the plans, monitors progress and makes sure that things get done. This is a full-time job and not a part-time role (as many people seem to think they can get away with)! Ideally, it should be someone from within the organisation, but this is not always possible and a professional project manager is sometimes hired for the duration of the implementation.

8.1.4 Project team

The project manager manages the project team (or teams, each with a team leader, in a very big project). The project team carries out the tasks associated with the project. The make-up of the project team will vary according to the size of the organisation, the complexity of the project and the availability of people. It could be one or two full-time people or it could be several part-time people combining their day jobs with their project tasks. In larger organisations, there will also be departmental project representatives who are responsible for coordinating the activities and responses from other members of their respective departments and who represent their departments in meetings and planning sessions. This will be not only the marketing, sales and service departments, or various sub-divisions of them, but also the IT and the finance departments.

8.1.5 **System users**

There will always be system users to consider. These are the people who will use the system or systems on a day-to-day basis. Most of the project team will be drawn from these people. However, *all* users need to be involved all the way through the project from its inception, and many will have particular responsibilities in the specification of requirements, the testing of the system(s) and the development of new clerical procedures. However, you need to take care to ensure that the right people carry out appropriate activities; you don't want every single person in the organisation reviewing system specifications and feeding back test results. The project board and project team members need to accept their responsibilities and liaise with everyday users as appropriate.

8.1.6 **Supplier staff**

Beyond your own organisation there are people from the supplier organisation or organisations involved in the project who are vital to its success (or otherwise). They will have their account manager (equivalent to your project sponsor), their own project manager who plans things and sees that things get done from their side of the fence, and finally there are supplier staff who do all the techie work.

8.2 **CHANGE MANAGEMENT**

8.2.1 **Systems and procedures changes**

A common feature of all organisations is people's natural resistance to change. The first lesson is don't change for the sake of it just because CRM is flavour of the month or the organisation down the road has done it. Change has to be justified. Once it has been justified and set in motion it must be managed. A CRM programme will demand changes to established procedures and ways of working. People need to be convinced that there is a better way of working. Comprehensive training and good revised documentation are key to the acceptance and implementation of new methods, as is, wherever possible, the involvement of users in the configuration of new processes relating to the system. Different areas of the organisation will move at different speeds, so a step-by step approach is better than a big-bang approach.

Once an organisation has embarked on a CRM programme, change management is a continual process because the marketplace changes, customers change, ways of generating income change, and services to beneficiaries change. This raises an often-forgotten area: ongoing and refresher training. Many organisations only train their staff when a new system is implemented. New joiners have no formal training and have to pick it up from old hands. This is a recipe for chaos and for a database full of data of dubious quality (and most organisations have just that)!

8.2.2 **The changing role of the employee**

It is one thing to change procedures that the organisation's staff carry out; in fact, irrespective of what was stated above, it is relatively easy to change the way that people do things. What is not easy to change is people's hearts and minds. And they do have to change, and change significantly, if the implementation of CRM within the organisation is to be a success. Firstly, people can no longer hide within their own department or job function; their actions will now be visible to the whole organisation. This generates fear, fear that their mistakes will be visible to all, fear that everyone else is judging them, fear that others might think they can do the job better, fear that they might be responsible for losing customers, and ultimately, fear for their very job. It is an important management task to alleviate this fear and instigate an environment of cooperation, cross-departmental working and joint responsibility; in other words, an environment of 'we are all in this together, folks'. This is easier said than done.

Staff also have to get used to a much closer relationship with customers. No longer are they faceless beings who can be fobbed off with inanities if they write or telephone to complain. They are people who can now tell their story to the world via social networking sites and a poor response to a service call can soon spiral out of control. More care, diplomacy and patience are required. Even office-based staff now need significant people skills.

8.3 **OTHER MANAGEMENT ISSUES**

Any change programme is about people, processes and technology, with an accent on the people. Your organisation needs to clarify who is responsible for various aspects of the CRM programme. Who defines the requirements? Who defines the standards? Who manages the implementation (resources, costs, timescales)? Who manages the cultural changes brought about by the implementation of the system? Who manages the system when it is operational? Who controls the quality of the data and the quality of the usage of the system? Who provides support? Who resolves departmental conflicts? Who ensures fair play so that the strongest voice doesn't monopolise the system? Does a CRM system change the dynamics of management itself because it straddles the whole organisation? These are all management issues that have to be resolved with the introduction of CRM within an organisation.

8.4 WHY MOST CRM IMPLEMENTATIONS FAIL

8.4.1 CRM project success rates

It is a very sad fact that most CRM implementations fail. The Standish Group publish their *Chaos Report* every year which charts the success (or otherwise) rates of IT projects. The comparative figures for 1995 and 2011 are shown in figure 8.1. This shows that project success rates were 16% in 1995 and had improved to 37% in 2011. This might seem to be encouraging, as things are definitely moving in the right direction, *but* it still means that you are almost twice as likely to fail (either entirely or in part) as to succeed. Note that the Standish Group define 'failure' as the fact that the project was abandoned and never implemented and they define 'challenged' as the project cost more than expected, took longer than expected or did not meet all of its functional objectives. Therefore, in terms of whether or not it eventually achieves its objectives, the picture is undoubtedly somewhat better. However, it is also worth noting that some other organisations which produce these sorts of statistics put the failure rate of CRM projects in particular as high as 80%!

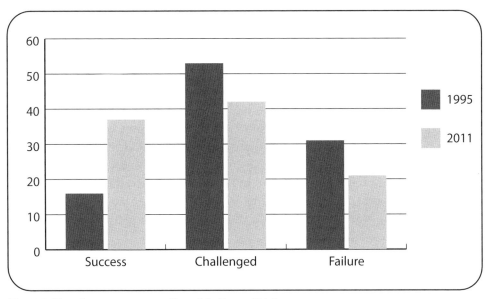

Fig. 8.1 IT project success rates (Standish Group 2011)

8.4.2 Reasons for failure

A significant number of system implementation failures are due to problems during the selection process which result in an inappropriate system being implemented. Examples of these failures are given in section 22.4 This section in this chapter deals with problems encountered during the implementation process. Some of what follows will not make pleasant reading, but all the reasons described are real and the examples given are drawn from real-life case histories.

New systems implementations are complex, confusing and painful, and PAINFUL sums up the major reasons why projects fail: Politics, Arrogance, Incompetence, Nearsightedness, Fear, Unfamiliarity and Lethargy.

Politics

Internal organisational politics, in-fighting and empire building are responsible for many system failures. Some people never agree, they are fiercely protective of their own patch ('my' customers, 'my' data), they don't want to lose status and reduce their headcount, they don't want other people to have what they have, the list goes on. One example of a failed, or at least challenged, project was where one department refused to let other departments have access to 'their' customers. They were allowed to get away with it because of the high status of the director in charge of the department and a single customer view (see 6.3) was never achieved. Another case was where a CRM system was implemented to solve pressing problems in one particular department and when it was rolled out to other departments it was found that the entire system table (see under 15.1.2) structure was inappropriate for the rest of the organisation, but the first department shouted loudest and got the system in first.

Arrogance

This is where certain people think they know best and/or bully the rest of the staff into accepting their views. One example was where the staff chose System X but the director chose System Y because it was 'more whizzy, more clever, more modern looking' and bullied the staff into accepting it. Half of the staff refused to use the system. Another similar case concerns a chief executive who chose a system for his staff and it did not have much of the functionality required by the staff. When concerns were pointed out to him, his response was 'It's a good system; make it work'. They didn't; they created workarounds (temporary solutions) in Access and Excel.

Incompetence

Examples abound of people being out of their depth and making huge mistakes in selection especially but also in implementation. One case concerns a project manager whose previous experience was in insurance; he knew nothing of the not-for-profit sector and the resulting implementation was chaotic. There was one crisis after another. Another case concerns the organisation which had three CRM systems in five years. The first two implementations were led by trustees with little or no knowledge of IT and little or no knowledge of the day-to-day processes of the charity. For the third and successful system, a third trustee acted as a proper project sponsor and left all the detailed work to the staff and an independent consultant. Another case concerns a chief executive who wanted to sue his CRM supplier because the system was late, over-budget and didn't have all the functionality he expected. Unfortunately he hadn't produced a detailed requirements specification and didn't have a leg to stand on, legally speaking.

Nearsightedness

CRM is an organisation-wide operation. Too many people only consider its effect on their own little part of the organisation and do not see the big picture. Consequently, they do things like only entering data needed by their department and ignoring other information they might possess that could be of interest to other people in the organisation. One specific example of nearsightedness concerns a department which found that the CRM system was much more cumbersome and slower to use than their previous spreadsheet, so they continued to use their spreadsheet. The result was that no single customer view was created. Another concerns a department which refused to change its working methods and hired additional staff to handle the 'extra' workload the system put on them. In fact, these staff were printing and filing documents that would never be looked at.

Fear

This is a very big problem which generally manifests itself in terms of non-cooperation, resulting in a delayed or over-budget project. Staff are 'too busy' to do testing or to attend training. They are asked to do something and they do it reluctantly or half-heartedly, if at all. In one extreme case, staff at a large organisation were so paranoid at the thought of changes to the way they did things that they insisted on modifications to the system which ended up costing the organisation a six-figure sum.

Unfamiliarity

There are two aspects to unfamiliarity. One is moving from a system that has been used for many years to something which is new and different. This is related to Fear above. The second is not being familiar with the full functionality of the system being implemented. There are numerous examples of consultants being asked to help an organisation to choose a new system 'because it doesn't do X or it doesn't do Y', only to find that upon investigation, it does do X and Y. They just didn't know about it or hadn't kept up with the latest version of their software.

Lethargy

Lastly is lethargy. Some, possibly many, people are inherently lazy and will do the minimum they can get away with in all situations. This can have disastrous effects during testing if shortcuts are taken because problems often manifest themselves during live operations. One example of this was where the staff of one organisation were asked to do one hour's testing per day for a month. They didn't, they asked the project manager to do it for them. The result was a system that did not meet their expectations and was eventually abandoned.

8.4.3   Failure mitigation

So what can you do to stop things going wrong? The first thing you need to do is to recognise the early warning signs. For this you need a detailed project plan with defined roles and responsibilities, allocated tasks, resources and timescales, and you need to monitor this plan continually. There is more on this subject in section 23.1.

8.5   CRM STRATEGY SUMMARY

This part of the book, chapters 5, 6, 7 and 8, looked at the eight basic principles that underlie CRM, some of the common concepts which people talk about all the time, such as the 360 degree view of the customer and the customer experience, some of the issues involved in defining an overall organisational CRM strategy, and finally, some of the challenges faced by management teams when they decide to implement CRM in their organisation.

The next part of the book examines the architecture of the information systems required to assist the implementation of the CRM strategy because, as we learnt earlier, you cannot do this effectively without the application of technology.

Part three:

CRM systems

architecture

9 The operational view

Before considering the technical architecture of CRM systems, it is important to consider the day-to-day operations of staff within an organisation that are related to CRM – i.e. the operations that the systems are there to support – and also to consider the reactions of customers to the organisation's marketing messages.

9.1 THE ORGANISATION'S PERSPECTIVE

Figure 9.1 shows an operational cycle at the highest possible level of abstraction (as previously shown in figure 7.4). This shows the cycle where planning a campaign of an approach (or approaches) to customers (or potential customers) is followed by:

- the actual making of the approaches;
- making a sale (or sales);
- servicing the sales;
- an analysis of how the campaign performed, the results of which are fed back into the planning of the next campaign.

This is a somewhat simplistic view, but it is the cycle that people follow, and often within larger organisations there are separate departments for planning, marketing, sales, service and analysis. In smaller organisations these are often not completely separate departments, but there will at least be separate job functions for the five sets of activities. Consequently, this is the first point to start the consideration of the structure (i.e. the technical architecture) and the functionality (i.e. the requirements) of a CRM system or systems.

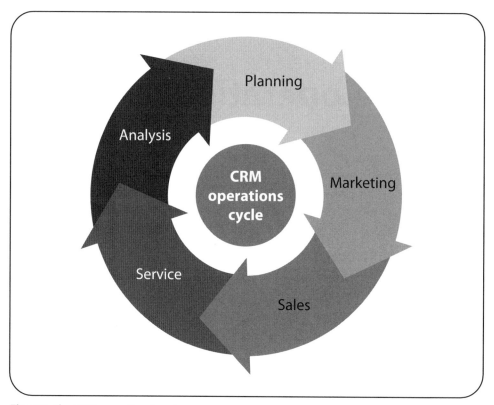

Fig. 9.1 The CRM operational cycle

9.2 **THE CUSTOMER'S PERSPECTIVE**

The organisation's operational cycle needs to be considered alongside the customer lifecycle, as shown in figure 9.2. This is the AIDA cycle (awareness, interest, desire, action) with the following practicalities of life added:

- losing the customer (defection);
- keeping the customer (retention), which in turn leads back to interest;
- the customer becoming inactive (dormancy); and
- awakening the customer's interest again (reactivation), which in turn leads back to interest.

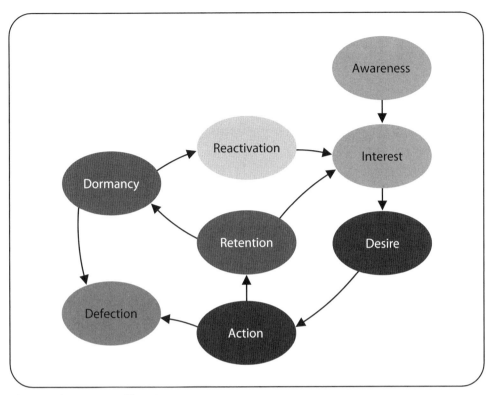

Fig. 9.2 The customer lifecycle

9.3 MERGING THE TWO PERSPECTIVES

Merging the two cycles can be accomplished as shown in figure 9.3. (Don't you just love it when academics and consultants come up with incomprehensible diagrams?) This shows that:

- awareness and interest are generated by marketing;
- desire and action are generated by sales;
- retention and dormancy by service;
- defection by sales and service; and
- reactivation by planning.

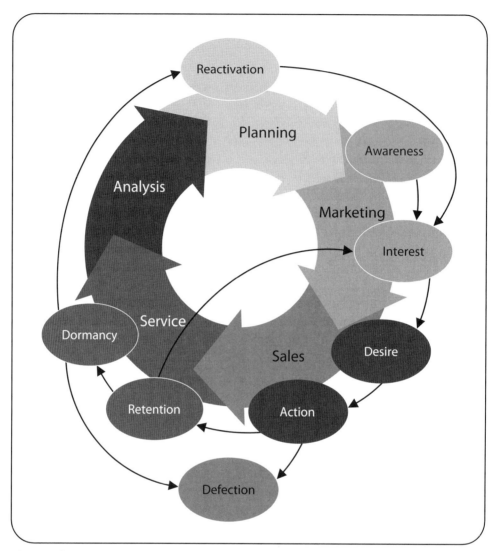

Fig. 9.3 The CRM operational cycle plus the customer lifecycle

From this global view of how organisations operate and how customers react, we need to move on to consideration of the information systems needed to support those activities.

10 The systems view

10.1 REASONS FOR CONSIDERING SYSTEMS ARCHITECTURE

Before delving into the detail of CRM systems requirements, it is important to spend a short time considering the overarching information systems architecture. This means considering the following questions:

- What are the building blocks of a complete CRM solution?
- Is there a single system solution?
- Is there such a thing as '*a* CRM system', i.e. a single system that can do everything required?
- If the answer to the last question is 'no' (and it is), then what elements do we need in order to create a complete solution?

As an aside, be very sceptical about information system suppliers claiming that they have a complete CRM system and quiz them very carefully about what their system can and cannot do. There is more on this later (see Chapter 22 in particular).

The reasons for considering not-for-profit CRM systems architecture are threefold: 1) the very large size or scope of a system (or systems) to cater for all the identified requirements; 2) the desire for flexibility of data storage and functionality; and 3) the desire to make the most effective use of what is seen as specialist or best of breed software systems.

10.1.1 Size and scope

Within a CRM system there are a huge number of functional requirements and a number of fundamental differences between the ideal technical solutions for many of these requirements. Added to these are the differences in the requirements themselves that cater for the needs of so many different types of customer. This leads many people to conclude that one system cannot do everything. Indeed, the bigger the system is, the more complex it is and the more difficult to manage. This in turn makes it more likely that the system will become inefficient and will fail to meet all needs. Consequently, there is a desire in some organisations to split the complete not-for-profit CRM functionality over multiple installed systems.

10.1.2   **Flexibility**

Having the flexibility to be able to add to and modify both the database design and the system functionality is seen as a key issue because not-for-profit organisational strategies frequently change. For example, a charity may start a completely new method of fundraising, or a membership body may devise a completely new form of membership. In both of these cases, the originally implemented CRM system may not have been designed to support these new developments.

It must be possible to integrate new ideas easily and cost-effectively at any stage of the system's lifetime. It should even be possible to swap parts of the system's software with new versions when different or better ways of doing things are devised. The best systems are the ones where the building blocks (i.e. the raw code, or new software/add-ons) can be changed easily. An example of when this flexibility was needed happened some years ago when the government changed Deeds of Covenant into Gift Aid. Such changes lead to a desire to have a system or systems that have as many components as possible.

The debate in this area is related to where the flexibility lies. Should it be available to the not-for-profit organisations themselves or should it remain with the system suppliers? The answer will vary from not-for-profit organisation to the next.

10.1.3   **Best of breed software**

This subject comes under the category of 'Why reinvent the wheel?' There are many functional areas, large and small, within a total CRM solution where ready-made and proven systems exist in the marketplace, so it is a waste of time and money for a CRM supplier to redevelop the systems themselves. (See also 10.6.)

10.2   **'THE THREE CIRCLES'**

CRM systems architecture is usually described as consisting of 'collaborative CRM systems', 'operational CRM systems' and 'analytical CRM systems', which is often shown as three circles (see figure 10.1):

- **Collaborative CRM** handles the interactions with the customer from whatever communication channel or touch point they may come (face-to-face, letter, fax, telephone, email, web, etc.).
- **Operational CRM** manages the automation of traditional marketing, sales and service functions, i.e. the actions that give rise to the customer interactions and the actions arising from the customer interactions.

- **Analytical CRM** consists of data warehousing (see 2.1.7), online analytical processing (OLAP) and data mining, in order to arrive at a better understanding of customers and their behaviour that can be fed back into the marketing department. (For information on OLAP, see 16.4.1 and for data mining see 'Analytics and data mining' under 15.3.2.)

What is being described here is that collaborative CRM is truly customer-facing, as it handles the communication with the customer; operational CRM handles the back-office functionality required for or arising from the customer interaction; and analytical CRM is understanding customer behaviour in order to inform future communications with the customer better.

Note that there is a bit of a problem with the terminology here. The words 'collaborative', 'operational' and 'analytical' are adjectives describing a type of CRM system, whereas what is being described are three different sets of functions (or systems) that together make up a complete CRM system. Consequently, the terminology should be either, collaborative CRM functions, operational CRM functions and analytical CRM functions, or, CRM collaborative systems, CRM operational systems and CRM analytical systems. (But perhaps this is being a little picky.) We will stick with the simpler terminology for the sake of brevity.

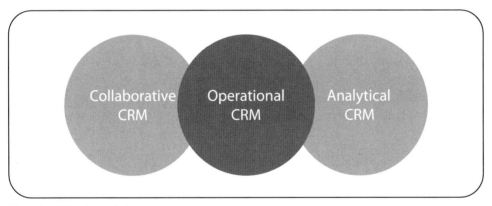

Fig. 10.1 The three circles

Other ways of thinking about the three circles are:

- Customer facing – Back office – Specialist; *or*
- Communications – Nuts and bolts – Clever stuff.

It should be noted that the three circles overlap. In particular, operational CRM, which historically came first, almost always has some level of direct customer interaction, for example direct mail functions, and some level of data analysis over and above day-to-day reporting (more on this subject in Chapter 16).

10.3 COLLABORATIVE CRM

Collaborative CRM is the interface between the organisation and the customer: the customer-facing part. It handles the interactions with the customer from whatever communication channel or touch point they may come (face-to-face, letter, fax, telephone, email, web, etc.). The main focus of collaborative CRM is on web communications where many organisations often require a database which is separate from their day-to-day, back-office database for security and performance reasons. In addition, performance issues dictate that it is often more efficient for the production of traditional mailings to export the data required (for any given mailing) in one system. A separate system is then used to sort, segment and merge the data with different output devices and collate it for sending to customers. Likewise, bulk emailing is usually more efficient when the data is exported to a specialist system. (For more on collaborative CRM, see Chapter 14.)

10.4 OPERATIONAL CRM

Operational CRM, or the back-office system, manages the automation of traditional marketing, sales and service functions; i.e. the actions that give rise to the customer interactions and the actions arising from the customer interactions. There is always some element of overlap between operational and collaborative and between operational and analytical. The main reasons for this overlap are:

- operational came first, i.e. before the Internet and World Wide Web revolution; and
- many smaller organisations do not require complex web interactions (although this is changing rapidly with even the smallest organisation now wanting to do everything possible on the Web) and they do not require, or see the need for, sophisticated data analysis (although this too will change in time).

10.5 ANALYTICAL CRM

Analytical CRM consists of analysing the data collected and created by the collaborative and the operational systems in order to arrive at a better understanding of customers and their behaviour that can be fed back into the marketing function. This is usually implemented as a separate system and a separate database.

The question as to why analytical CRM is a separate entity and usually a completely separate database relates to the underlying structure of the data required to produce the analysis requested in a 'reasonable' time; i.e. in minutes rather than hours, or hours rather than days. *This is important* and is where so many people go wrong. This is what so many people don't understand: you *cannot* perform complex analytics on a typical operational CRM database. They are completely different things.

A typical CRM database is structured as shown in figure 10.2 (and this is an extremely simple one with only 26 data tables; some systems available in the marketplace have up to 800). Although this is a very simple CRM database, it is still a spider's web of linkages between tables. Imagine what the picture must look like for a database that contains 800 tables. Database suppliers and database administrators understand this type of structure. Database administrators spend their time creating complex SQL (Structured Query Language) statements joining lots of tables in order to produce some of the reports and analyses requested of them.

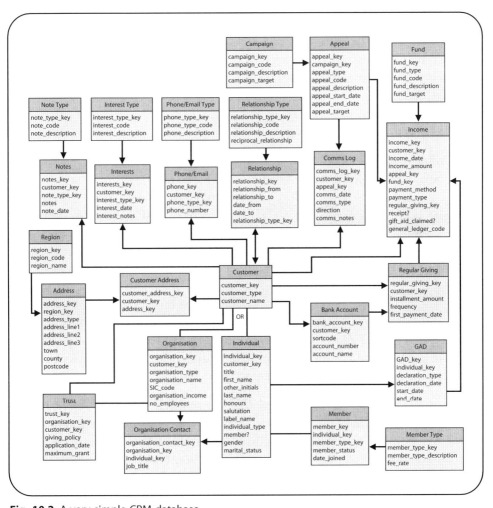

Fig. 10.2 A very simple CRM database

The problem comes when a staff member asks for a report which requires data selected from one table which is sorted and selected via data in two, three or more other tables which are linked to it. This requires complex programming and time-consuming processing.

A typical analytics database is structured as shown in figure 10.3 (and this is an extremely simple one with only one '**fact table**' and six '**dimension tables**'). This overly simple data warehouse picture is just to show the concept of one single fact table surrounded by a number of dimension tables. In this instance, the data that is to be reported on, such as income items, is in the fact table and all the data items from the two, three or more tables for sorting and selecting are gathered together into a single one of the dimension tables, thus rendering the report easy and quick to produce.

> A **fact table** contains the data you are interested in and therefore the data to be analysed, such as income items. It is the central table in the visual plan of the database (known as snowflake and star schemas). **Dimension tables** contain the various combinations of keys (see figure 10.3) which you can summarise and use to report on the data.

The problem here is that such analytics systems are expensive and a time-consuming. A complex process known as ETL (extract, transform and load) is required to take data from the operational CRM system to create the analytics database (usually known as a data warehouse, although technically it is a **data mart**) in the first instance. This process is then also needed to keep it continually up to date. Another general point in this area is that, while complex database architecture allows very clever stuff to be drawn out, it is also very easy to make a mistake that means information disappears or is double counted, without it being obvious that it has happened.

> A **data mart** is a small data warehouse containing data from one specific organisational area, such as a fundraising or membership department.

The example in figure 10.3 is a very simple star schema. A real data warehouse is likely to be a snowflake or a starflake schema and also contain multiple fact tables, lightly summarised data, highly summarised data and metadata. Don't worry if you don't understand the previous sentence. It just goes to show that we are dealing with a highly complex and specialist area. None of your typical database administrators understand this and you wouldn't really expect them to do so, would you? This is a specialist subject. It is complex and time-consuming to develop and get right, and demands a special sort of brain to comprehend it. The main reasons for getting involved in it and for understanding the basics are because a data warehouse can produce in minutes what takes hours (or even days) from the main (i.e. operational) CRM database. It can produce results that are literally not possible from an operational CRM system. To try and run it on an operational system would render it unusable due to blocking (i.e. users are unable to access customer records because the analytics or reporting programme blocks access to the records until it has completed its own task).

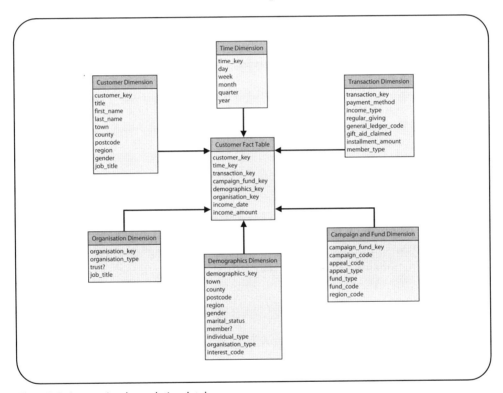

Fig. 10.3 A very simple analytics database

10.6 **BEST OF BREED SOFTWARE**

10.6.1 **Standard software**

There are a number of functional areas required as a part of the overall CRM picture where specialist software already exists, so it is unnecessary and wasteful of time and money for CRM system suppliers to develop these themselves. Simple examples are:

- word processing, spreadsheet and other office software, typically Microsoft Office but there are increasing numbers of open-source (see 2.1.11) and cloud-based alternatives (see 21.2.2);
- address management software that provides complete addresses from the entry of a postcode and a house number and keeps all addresses standardised and up to date;
- bulk emailing software;
- banking and credit card payment software.

A more complex example is the use of sophisticated statistical analysis software which only operates effectively on data warehouse-type data structures. These are completely different from the data structures in a typical transaction-based (i.e. operational) CRM system.

10.6.2 **Specialist software**

There are a number of less generalised, but nevertheless important, functional areas where many potential system solutions exist that could be incorporated within the CRM solution set or where CRM suppliers might consider developing their own functionality. These are related to specific functional areas which can be complete systems in their own right. Examples of such areas are:

- sales order processing;
- stock control;
- legacy administration;
- event management;
- project management.

It is usually the case that these best of breed specialist systems will have a greater depth of functionality than anything developed by the CRM system suppliers, but depending upon the particular not-for-profit organisation, this depth of functionality is not always required. It is also sometimes the case that the best of breed systems, although more sophisticated in general terms, do not always cater for some of the special requirements of the not-for-profit sector.

10.6.3 Typical best of breed software

Table 10.1 gives a list of standard and specialist software systems that are often incorporated within complete not-for-profit CRM solutions.

Software systems	Purpose or function
Office software	Word processing, mail merge, spreadsheets, email, calendar and tasks (usually Microsoft Office).
Bulk email processing	Sending bulk emails and collecting statistics on receipts, opens and links clicked.
Address management	Fast data entry and accurate addressing.
Geographic mapping	Visual representations of customer locations.
CTI: computer telephony integration	Linking the database to the telephone system for auto-dial and 'screen popping' (automatically displaying the customer's record on screen when the customer telephones the organisation).
EPOS: electronic point of sale	Managing income from shops.
Banking and payment systems	Validating bank accounts, managing credit and debit card payments, collecting direct debit payments.
Financial accounting	Usually the nominal ledger that receives a summary of CRM income.
Report writing	Creating and modifying analytical reports.
Sales order processing	Selling and invoicing products and services.
Stock control	Ensuring that product stock is always available.
Sales ledger	Managing the invoices and payments received.
Legacy administration	Managing the process of receiving notification of a bequest through to the receipt of the money (or sale of assets). *Cont.*

Media customer management	Keeping up to date with people in the media and their positions and movements using online systems.
Raffle management	Monitoring ticket sellers, ticket distribution and winners.
Lottery management	Monitoring players, collectors, rounds, payments, selecting winners and printing cheques.
Event and conference management	Managing all aspects of setting up and running events of all types (including subsidiary systems such as table planning software).
Survey software	Defining, distributing, collecting results, and analysing results of surveys.
Call centre management	Information and helpline management, including call monitoring and outcome recording.
Case management	Managing all aspects of support for beneficiaries, including document management, calendar functions, professional links and progress.
Grant-making	Maintaining grant programmes, tracking applications for grants and making payments once grants have been awarded.
Project management	Monitoring project dates, activities, resources, costs and progress.
Volunteer management	Monitoring skills, training, availability, scheduling, activities, time recording and payments to volunteers.

Table 10.1 Best of breed software

11 The functional (or requirements) view

11.1 FUNCTIONALITY VERSUS REQUIREMENTS

The terms 'functionality' and 'requirements' are often used interchangeably. This is not strictly correct because there are functional and non-functional requirements. Functional requirements are those actions performed by a system that can be clearly defined and easily tested such that the answer is a definite 'yes' the system does it, or 'no' the system does not do it. Non-functional requirements, on the other hand, are global qualities of a system that are loosely defined and not easily tested, or where the results of the testing are open to interpretation. Examples of such qualities (often referred to as '-ilities') are flexibility, maintainability, usability, etc. As well as being loosely defined, they can conflict with each other, are difficult to define, design, implement and test, and often contribute to system failure. A classic example is a system attribute proposed by most end users that 'the system must be easy to use'. However, such requirements are very important to the operation of any system and must be considered seriously.

11.2 COMMERCIAL CRM FUNCTIONALITY VERSUS NOT-FOR-PROFIT CRM FUNCTIONALITY

In table 3.1, eight high-level functional groupings of CRM were identified as:

- environment and administration;
- contact management;
- marketing;
- sales;
- communications and channels;
- service;
- reporting and analytics;
- integration.

These functional groupings were broken down to a second level for commercial CRM systems as shown in table 3.2. Most (if not all) of these functional areas apply to the not-for-profit sector, albeit some such as partner management, lead management and territory management find little usage in the sector. More importantly, however, is the fact that the not-for-profit sector requires a number of additional functional areas, as shown in table 11.1. These have to be fitted into the structure or added to it somewhere in order to arrive at a complete functional breakdown for not-for-profit CRM.

Functional area	
Other functional areas	
Stock control	Ballots and elections
Fundraising	Legacy administration
Fund management	Finance
Project management	Fulfilment
Membership management	Alumni tracking
Publications and subscriptions	Volunteer management
Committee management	Sponsorship
Education and examinations	Grant-making
Surveys	

Table 11.1 Additional functional areas of not-for-profit CRM systems

The items in table 11.1 can be consolidated into higher level groups as shown in table 11.2.

Functional area	
Other functional areas	*Consolidated area*
Stock control	Sales
Fundraising	Fundraising
Fund management	Beneficiary services
Project management	Beneficiary services
Membership management	Membership management
Publications and subscriptions	Membership management
Committee management	Customer management
Education and examinations	Membership management
Surveys	Services (traditional)
Ballots and elections	Membership management
Legacy administration	Fundraising
Finance	Financial management
Fulfilment	Financial management
Alumni tracking	Customer management
Volunteer management	Customer management
Sponsorship	Fundraising
Grant-making	Beneficiary services

Table 11.2 Consolidation of additional functional areas

11.3 TOP-LEVEL FUNCTIONAL BREAKDOWN

Most general CRM literature, as discussed in Chapter 3, almost always starts with just the major groups of marketing, sales and service. To this should be added 1) a non-functional requirements group, 2) a general group to cover functionality that is applicable to the entire system, and 3) an integration group that describes the links with other systems. As the highest level of functional breakdown, it is logical to start with this. It gives an initial breakdown from which we can start to build a full functional description of what a not-for-profit CRM system should actually do and how it should perform. Thus, at the highest level of functional breakdown we have:

- non-functional requirements;
- general functionality;
- marketing-related functionality;
- sales-related functionality;
- service-related functionality;
- systems integration.

These six major groups can be further subdivided as shown in table 11.3. This gives us a structure that is logical and recognisable to the majority of not-for-profit organisations and to not-for-profit information system suppliers. This then provides the starting point for discussion of lower-level functionality in a manner that everyone can relate to, as described in Part 4.

Note that this functionality is primarily related to operational CRM which is the bulk of any complete CRM solution. Requirements for collaborative CRM and analytical CRM are more fluid and will be considered separately in Part 4.

Non-functional requirements	Sales-related functionality
Technical issues	Sales
Configuration and customisation	Fundraising
Security	Membership management
Audit trail	Event management
Compliance	Financial management
Documentation and help	
General functionality	*Service-related functionality*
Business rules processing	Service
Query reporting and analysis (QRA)	Beneficiary services
Data management	
Database administrator functions	
Marketing-related functionality	*Systems integration*
Customer management	Other types of CRM
Marketing	Standard systems
Communications	Optional systems
Channels	

Table 11.3 First- and second-level functional breakdown

The major differences between this table and table 3.2 (and hence the differences between the for-profit and not-for-profit sectors) are as follows:

- A non-functional requirements section has been added.
- Marketing, sales and service have become super-groups named marketing-related, sales-related and service-related in order to incorporate not-for-profit specific areas.
- The environment and administration section has been renamed general functionality.
- Reporting and analytics have been split up. Reporting is within QRA (under general functionality) and analytics has been incorporated into marketing (under marketing-related functionality).

- The marketing section has been expanded to incorporate customer management, and analytics (as noted).
- The sales section has been expanded to incorporate fundraising, membership management, and event management (moved from marketing), all of which are different methods of generating income, plus financial management. Financial management is in this group because it is an essential element of sales, and the finance-related processes in the not-for-profit sector are far more complex than those required for commercial organisations.
- The service section has been expanded to incorporate beneficiary services alongside traditional service functions.

Note that in Chapter 2 event management was recorded under the major heading of marketing because in a commercial environment the main objective of it is to raise awareness of the organisation and its aims and objectives. This is true to some extent in the not-for-profit sector, as the various different types of events run by organisations in the sector are primarily run for the benefit of the organisations' customers, be this educational, general interest or social. However, in many cases, the organisations receive considerable financial benefit by way of attendance fees.

It should be noted that within not-for-profit organisations, some events are purely for income-generating purposes, so although the customer obtains some benefit, such as a dinner, the main benefit is financial for the organisation. As with fundraising and membership, event management is a very large functional area in its own right, as is witnessed by the fact that many not-for-profit organisations have events and conferences departments. Consequently, the section has moved from marketing to the sales-related super-group.

12 Systems versus functions

So how does the systems view of CRM – collaborative, operational and analytical CRM (along with all the associated best of breed software) – relate to the functional (requirements) view of CRM (namely, non-functional requirements, general functionality, marketing-related functionality, sales-related functionality, service-related functionality and systems integration)?

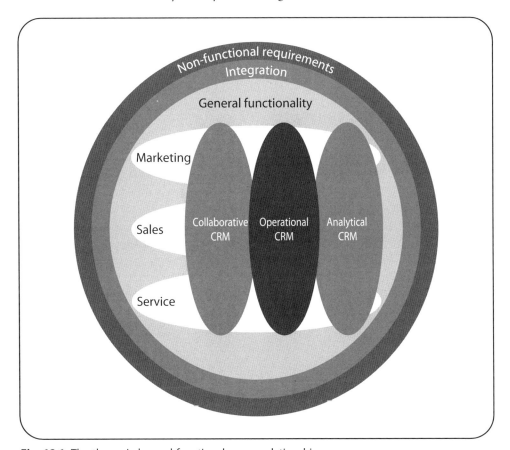

Fig. 12.1 The three circles and functional group relationships

Basically, they can be considered as two different ways of looking at the same thing. See figure 12.1 for this in diagrammatic form. This shows that marketing, sales and service are all crossed by collaborative, operational and analytical. The operations of marketing, sales and service all require communication with customers at various stages, so collaborative CRM crosses all areas. Likewise, operational CRM contains functionality from each of marketing, sales and service, and analytical CRM uses data provided by each of marketing, sales, and service. Surrounding these specific areas of functionality is general functionality, such as workflow processing, which is relevant to all areas of functionality, whether considered from a marketing, sales and service perspective or from a collaborative, operational and analytical perspective. Finally, surrounding the entire system and relevant to all functionality, however described or defined, are the non-functional requirements to which the system as a whole must adhere.

13 Typical architectural scenarios

13.1 ARCHITECTURAL OPTIONS

System architecture (the system's structure or design) is considered at two levels: the high-level architecture which is characterised by differences in the basic design of the database to enable it to operate efficiently, and lower-level architecture which is characterised by the fact that there are many options to satisfy the requirements.

13.1.1 High-level architecture

The discussion at the highest level of abstraction revolves around three circles (see figure 13.1). These circles correspond to what was described in Chapter 10 as operational CRM, analytical CRM and collaborative CRM.

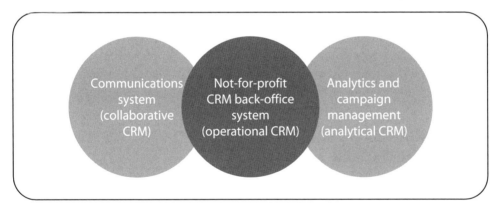

Fig. 13.1 The three circles

One circle (not-for-profit CRM back-office system): this represents a single system which carries out all the CRM functionality required by the organisation. This base system is primarily a transaction-processing back-office system, but it will have limited web functionality and limited analysis and campaign management functionality. This functionality is limited to the extent that it is considered sufficient by many smaller not-for-profit organisations or organisations whose needs in these areas are not complex, but it is not considered sufficient by the larger organisations. This circle is, in essence, what has been referred to in section 10.2 as operational CRM.

Two circles, option A (not-for-profit CRM back-office system + analytics and campaign management): this represents the situation where the single system is complemented by the addition of a specialist analytics and campaign management system (based on data warehousing principles) and the majority of the marketing functionality is carried out by this system rather than the base system. This second circle is what has been referred to as analytical CRM.

Two circles, option B (not-for-profit CRM back-office system + communications system (primarily a web database)): this represents the situation where the single system is complemented by the addition of a communications system which handles some of the communications with the customers (usually just the web-based communications).

Three circles (not-for-profit CRM back-office system + analytics and campaign management + communications system): this is when the two systems in option A above are further complemented by a communications system that handles all the communication with the customers, much of which may be web-based. This third circle is what has been referred to as collaborative CRM.

13.1.2 Lower-level architecture

These are individual functions or complete functional areas where there is specialist or best of breed software that could be incorporated within the overall system, but where most not-for-profit CRM system suppliers have some level of functionality that they themselves have developed. These represent the items listed under the heading of best of breed software in section 10.6.

13.2 ORGANISATIONAL APPROACHES TO CRM SYSTEMS ARCHITECTURE

The level to which not-for-profit organisations adopt any of the system architecture options depends upon their size and complexity. It is useful to consider not-for-profit organisations to be divided into:

• large organisations (annual income in excess of £50 million);
• medium-sized organisations (annual income £10 million to £50 million);
• small organisations (annual income less than £10 million).

When considering an organisation's approach to CRM architecture, this division does not always apply, as some small organisations have very complex requirements and some large organisations have simple requirements; but, in general, it is found that size and complexity of requirements do tend to go together.

In terms of the high-level architecture of 1, 2 or 3 circles:

- Small organisations usually adopt the single-circle approach because their campaigns tend to be simple enough not to need the sophistication of a specialist analytics and campaign management system. Also, the number of customers with whom they communicate is usually small enough (a few thousand) that they do not need specialist systems to accommodate these communications.
- The larger the organisation, the more likely they are to adopt the two-circle approach because they will have upwards of 100,000 customers and upwards of 1,000,000 transaction records. (The very largest have several million customers and hundreds of millions of transactions.)
- Only the very largest organisations can contemplate the true three-circle approach and, to date, only a few organisations have been identified which have successfully implemented it or which are attempting to implement it. However, it should be noted that the majority of organisations now adopt a simplified version of the third circle, i.e. a separate system that handles web-based communications with customers (with other types of communications handled by the back-office system, i.e. the first circle).

In terms of the lower-level architecture:

- Small organisations usually adopt very few of the specialist or best of breed systems and these are office software (always), address management (sometimes), banking and payment systems (usually), and the rest seldom, if ever.
- The larger and the more departmentalised the organisation is, the more likely they are to adopt more of the systems. It depends also on the numbers involved. For example, an organisation receiving several hundred legacy bequests per year is more likely to adopt a legacy administration system, an organisation with 1,000 volunteers is more likely to adopt a volunteer management system, an organisation selling hundreds of products per day is more likely to adopt sales order processing and stock control systems, and the organisation specialising in making hundreds of small grants a year is more likely to adopt a grants management system.

The subject of systems architecture arises from a consideration of how the functionality described in Chapter 11 is to be provided. The question that many not-for-profit organisations ask is 'Can we get all this from a single system?' The answer is 'yes' if the organisation is very small and its requirements are not very sophisticated, but in the vast majority of cases the answer is 'no'. The reasons for this are: most available not-for-profit CRM systems provide only simplistic functionality in many areas where specialist systems exist in the marketplace, and the database design of CRM systems is not compatible with the design required for complex statistical analysis. Consequently, not-for-profit CRM is normally implemented as a series of linked systems.

A typical scenario for small and medium-sized organisations is shown in figure 13.2 below. This shows the main structural elements as two of the major elements outlined in Chapter 2, namely:

- collaborative CRM functions (shown here as 'web database');
- operational CRM functions (shown as 'not-for-profit CRM back-office system').

In addition, there are a small number of other functional areas that are often handled via integration with best of breed systems.

The one major difference here from what is described in Chapter 10 (and shown in figure 13.1) is that the collaborative CRM element is restricted to web-based functionality. Collaborative CRM as previously described covers all methods of interaction with the customer such as direct mail, email and telephone, which in this scenario are handled by the back-office system.

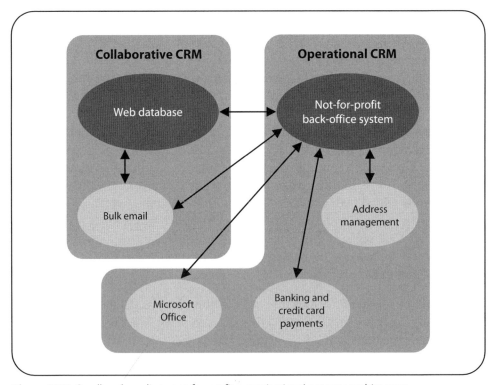

Figure 13.2 Small and medium not-for-profit organisations' systems architecture

A typical scenario for large not-for-profit organisations is as shown in figure 13.3. This shows all three of the main structural elements as outlined in Chapter 10, namely:

- collaborative CRM functions (again shown here as 'web database');
- operational CRM functions (shown as 'not-for-profit CRM back-office system');
- analytical CRM functions (shown as 'analytics and campaign management').

In addition, there are a larger number of other functional areas that are often handled via integration with best of breed systems.

Once again the one major difference here from what is described in Chapter 10 (and shown in figure 13.1) is the restriction of the collaborative CRM element to web-based functionality.

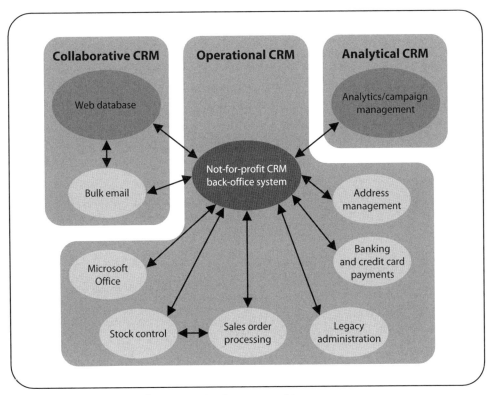

Fig. 13.3 Large not-for-profit organisations' systems architecture

Part four:

CRM systems requirements and functionality

14 Collaborative CRM

As outlined in Chapter 10, collaborative CRM is the interface between the organisation and the customer, i.e. the customer-facing part. It handles the interactions with the customer from whatever communication channel or touch point they may come (whether face to face, by mail, telephone or email, or via the organisation's website).

So, if it is all about communications and channels, then why is it called 'collaborative' CRM? The collaboration referred to was traditionally between the different departments of the organisation. Each department collects and records data on its individual interactions with each customer and then makes that data visible to all other departments. Consequently, a customer expressing an interest in a specific product as a result of the marketing department's activity is instantly visible to the sales department; a complaint to the service department is instantly visible to the marketing department and to the sales person who sold the product, and so on. This information-sharing between departments should lead to each department having a more complete picture of the customers and a better understanding of them. The theory is that this will lead to improvements in the quality of service to the customers, such as faster response times, consistency of approach, and an image of the organisation as a single entity, all of which lead to increased customer satisfaction and, consequently, greater customer loyalty.

Lately, the definition of 'collaboration' has been extended to cover not only different departments of the organisation, but also collaboration between the organisation and its customers. This has been driven by the increasing use of social media by both the organisation and its customers.

Collaborative CRM theoretically covers *all* types of communication with customers, but in practice (from a technical point of view in terms of a collaborative system's functionality) it is often restricted to communications via the Internet in the broadest terms, which includes single and bulk emailing, communication via the organisation's website, and social media interaction. (The other types of interaction are usually managed by the operational CRM system).

14.1 CUSTOMER COMMUNICATIONS

This section outlines the 'preparatory functions', i.e. the standard processes or the basic automated work which can be done for the following types of customer communications:

- single ad hoc communications;
- simple mail merge;
- complex mail merge;
- conditional processing;
- communication logging.

14.1.1 Single ad hoc communications

There are numerous times when you need to communicate with a single customer. What is required are functions to speed and smooth the process. For example, if the communication is by letter then the systems must produce a skeleton letter with name and address, salutation and signatory at a single click of the mouse. Likewise, if by email, a skeleton email with salutation and signatory. If by telephone, then one click of the mouse dials the customer's number (see section on computer telephony integration within 15.6.2).

14.1.2 Simple mail merge (or file creation)

The simplest mail merge is the production of a file or files of names and addresses (and a very few other data fields such as the campaign code) for transmission to a mailing house which will send out the organisation's letters, magazines or other physical media. Similarly, this can be done for the production of labels for attaching to standard mail packs. Another function under this heading is the creation of a telephone list in preparation for a telesales operation.

14.1.3 Complex mail merge (or file creation)

Complex mail merges include within each communication, in addition to names and addresses, basic text for letter, email or SMS creation, numerous data fields from the customer record and various other items, or even entire paragraphs of information (such as project descriptions), which are dependent upon the values of various data fields from the customer record.

14.1.4 **Conditional processing**

There are a number of standard processes that can be carried out once the customers have been selected and the communication media (files, letters and emails) prepared for transmission. These include maintenance of communication preferences, selective sending and communication checking:

- **Communication preferences:** these can range from a simple set of flags or indicators (such as: do not mail, do not telephone, Christmas appeal only) to a matrix of communication indicators of 'channel' (contact me by mail, email, telephone, etc.) versus 'product' (I would like to receive appeal mailings, newsletters, annual review, etc.) and, in some cases, even 'channel' versus 'product' versus 'date range' (I only want one appeal per year, by email at Christmas).

- **Selective sending:** these are optional processes that may or may not be relevant depending on the particular campaign. They include: sending only one communication per household (sometimes with the added complication of joint salutations) or one per organisation, no matter how many customers are registered at that address; not sending the communication if the customer has already received a specified number of communications this year; and a 'one-in-N' facility with 'roll-out', for example send the communication to every tenth contact and then send it to the rest at a later date if the one-in-ten responses were deemed to be worthwhile.

- **Communication checking:** this is the process of including certain special customer records in every single communication selection in order to check that the communication was sent, was accurate and how long it took to arrive. Such customers are called 'seeds' or 'sleepers' and would usually be members of staff. There is a variation on this theme called 'dummies' where specific and easily identifiable customer records are included in every reciprocal list, which is a list that has been swapped with another organisation (see 'Reciprocal processing and rented lists' under 15.2.3), to check that the other organisation obeys the rules and doesn't communicate with your customers too many times.

14.1.5 **Communication logging**

All communications sent to customers, ad hoc and bulk, should be logged so that a full record is readily available showing what they have been sent and when. These were traditionally called 'mailing histories' when most of the marketing campaigns were conducted using the ordinary postal system, what we now affectionately (or disparagingly?) call 'snail mail'. The principle is now applied to all communications irrespective of the channel. A key requirement is the ability to link a customer's communication log record to the actual text that was sent.

All communications from the customer should also be logged, for example scanning an incoming letter, linking an incoming email, recording the results details of a telephone conversation. Also, the results of other interactions such as face-to-face meetings should be recorded.

14.2 **TRADITIONAL CHANNELS**

These are the different media by which the communication with the customers is made. This can be in bulk (i.e. using mail-merging) or singly for one-to-one contacts. They include traditional or direct mail (or snail mail if you like!), email, telephone (a list and a script), fax and SMS texts. Other channels which are related to marketing campaigns but do not require selections and mail merges are:

- personal approaches (usually known as 'face to face') which are of two types:
  - planned where the person being approached is known
  - unplanned such as approaching the public in the street;
- DRTV (direct response television) i.e. television advertising;
- inserts (usually in magazines) and other advertising, all of which request people to respond in a variety of ways.

14.3 **THE ORGANISATION'S WEBSITE**

14.3.1 **Customer self-service**

Communication via the organisation's website is becoming increasingly important (if not essential) to every not-for-profit organisation. The communication process begins with a customer arriving at the organisation's website. Customers can arrive at the website directly from their own searches or by clicking a hyperlink sent to them in a marketing campaign email. Once they are at your website, customers want to able to carry out all data entry functions themselves via the website that would previously have been requested via mail, email or telephone and entered by the organisation's own staff. This is commonly referred to as 'customer self-service' (see table 14.1). This, as well as benefiting the customer because they can do it themselves and the process is immediate, has significant benefits for the organisation. There is less paper, less data entry for staff and a higher probability of greater data accuracy, as customers are more likely to ensure that their data is correct.

Registering as a customer (of any type)
Amending personal details such as address changes, interest indicators, communication indicators
Making donations: one-off by credit card
Setting up a regular payment by direct debit
Making Gift Aid declarations
Membership sign-up and renewal
Subscription sign-up and renewal
Searching membership directories
Entering CPD (continuing professional development) details (see CPD under 15.4.3)
Purchasing products including product search function and stock control
Booking onto events
Responding to surveys
Requesting downloadable or printed information
Requesting contact or service from the organisation
Applying for grants
Applying for a job
Volunteering
Participating in web forums or discussion groups
Complaints or positive feedback

Table 14.1 Customer self-service functions

14.3.2 **Web activity monitoring and statistics**

Once customers and prospective customers arrive at the organisation's website, it is essential to track where they go and how long they stay there. A system such as Google Analytics can provide a host of information about how your website is performing and how people are using it, but only in general terms. It can tell you which pages are most popular. It can tell you how many visitors are new versus how many are returning visitors. It can tell you where visitors came from so you can monitor the success (or otherwise) of online campaigns. The list is almost endless. However, what it cannot do is tell you about individual customers' activities. For that you need visitors to log in, i.e. identify themselves, as they would have to in order to carry out any of the functions listed above, whereupon you can monitor their activity and download individual statistics into their CRM records. By monitoring and then analysing the customer's web activity such as pages viewed, clickthroughs, site stickiness (how much time a visitor spends on the site), etc., you can produce tailored web pages for each customer based on their personal profile and activity. Also remember that if you want to go down this route, you need to give customers an incentive to log in – the information and functionality behind the log in has to be worth the effort.

14.4 **OTHER WEBSITES**

Customers can support not-for-profit organisations via third-party websites, Just Giving and Virgin Money Giving being the most popular examples. (This applies primarily to charities). On these websites, supporters of the charity set up their own pages where friends and family can sponsor them to undertake an activity (such as running a marathon or carrying out an individual challenge – in fact, just about anything) in support of their nominated charity. The sponsor money is collected online, or by text message, by the third party and sent to the charity. The third party also claims any Gift Aid applicable from HMRC on behalf of the charity. Details of the money collected is usually transferred to the charity via a data export by the third party and a data import by the charity into its CRM system, although lately some suppliers have started to use an API (application programming interface) supplied by the third party to access the details directly.

14.5 **SOCIAL MEDIA**

The big buzz of the moment is social media and social networking. The major social networking sites are Twitter, Facebook and LinkedIn (there are others, but these are the main sites used by the general public at the time of writing). Every not-for-profit organisation needs a presence in these media and they need to monitor what people are saying about their organisations and their work. CRM suppliers are still coming to terms with how to interact with social networking (and some still don't do it at all). This interaction is possible at a number of levels. The simplest level is to record a customer's social networking site links so that, for example, with one click you can have direct access to a customer's Facebook page or LinkedIn profile, etc. The next level is to be able to have a direct feed from social networking sites into a window in your CRM system, for example Twitter tweets that mention your organisation or mission. (This might look clever but it does not add a great deal of value to your CRM system because you get masses of irrelevant data to sift through and you seldom, if ever, get anything useful from your own customers.)

The really useful functionality is to have a service that monitors customers' and your own social networking sites, extracts profile data that customers make public, plus appropriate feeds and messages and then filters them and records selected ones against customers, organisations, campaigns, events, funds, etc. in the CRM system as appropriate. Some filtering rules can be defined and applied automatically by the system, but manual filtering is also required to identify and delete unhelpful and spurious data. (Note that some social networking sites such as LinkedIn don't allow you to import data from its site and Facebook states that you must make every effort to make sure any data you have imported is kept up to date.)

The other side of social media is for the organisation to send out information on these networking sites as a part of its marketing mix, and to respond to requests and comments from customers, prospective customers and the general public. It is becoming essential for every not-for-profit organisation to transmit its messages in this way, for example by making regular tweets about their work. However, this raises a host of potential problems and needs very careful management. While there are a limited number of national and European laws and regulations which have ramifications for information systems of which you have to be aware and act accordingly (see 15.1.5), the number of potential laws and regulations of which you have to be aware with social media is vast. There are libel laws, harassment laws, misrepresentation laws, fraud laws, privacy laws, obscenity laws, copyright laws; the list goes on and on. It is a minefield and, as a social media population, we have barely taken the first step in terms of finding out how laws may be broken. Time will most likely throw up some surprises, so tread carefully!

In addition to these general marketing activities, with some social networking sites, such as Twitter, it is possible to send direct messages from the CRM system, providing yet another campaigning channel.

A recent development in the social media sphere is true collaboration between the organisation and its customers by the use of wikis (websites that allow a community of users to add and edit content collaboratively). Knowledge bases are increasingly implemented in the form of a wiki. If service-oriented wikis are opened up to the organisation's customers, they can add value to the store of knowledge, including the best way to use products, what to do when things go wrong, and suggestions for product and service improvements. If implemented, this needs careful monitoring and moderation by the organisation.

Much of this is still developing or yet to come, but it is an area which is evolving all the time.

14.6 WEBSITE DEVELOPMENT VERSUS INTEGRATION

Traditionally, website development and operational CRM development have grown up as two very distinct areas of technology that are serviced by very different suppliers. This is because web development is primarily design-led, whereas CRM needs to be functionality-led. These are very different skills. Just because they both involve software doesn't mean that a full public-facing website necessarily should be part of the same product as CRM. This is still true in the majority of cases, which means that integration of some form is required between the website and the CRM database. However, a slowly increasing number of suppliers are crossing over and moving into the other area, i.e. website developers developing CRM functionality, and operational CRM developers developing web development facilities (i.e. content management systems (CMSs)).

14.6.1 Integration

Integration between operational CRM and the website is achieved in four different ways (with an increasing level of complexity):

- **Import and export of data files:** the export of data files from the back-office CRM database and import of those files to a web database, plus the export of files of data entered on the web and import of those files into the back-office CRM database. This process is long-winded and tedious and is usually at least 24 hours out of date.
- **Web modules (usually supplied by the back-office CRM database supplier):** the CRM supplier develops and hosts web pages that the web developer links to from the organisation's website. This is currently the most prevalent method of integration.
- **API (application programming interface) supplied by database supplier:** this is used by the web developer to extract data from the database in a controlled manner and put data into the database, again in a controlled manner.
- **Direct access (by the web developer) into the database:** this is the situation where the web developer has direct access to the underlying data files and tables of the operational CRM system and controls what data is extracted and input. This is not advisable as an outside agency will be modifying your data and you will not be in control of it.

14.6.2 CRM and CMS all in one

Those who require an all-in-one CRM and CMS system need to ask what a CMS (or website development facility) needs to allow for the operations listed in table 14.1 and all the other functionality required. This is a specialist area and it is not the purpose of this book to delve into too much detail on the subject. Consequently, an overview of only some of the major functionality of a CMS is given below for those who wish to go down the route of a combined system i.e. combining collaborative CRM and operational CRM in one: the two circles.

- **Core functionality:** the ability for the not-for-profit organisation to create, delete, edit and organise web pages.
- **Templates:** the ability to maintain multiple page templates.
- **Page editor:** the provision of a WYSIWYG (what you see is what you get) page editor that can add or change existing data, documents, icons, menus, templates.
- **Page organisation:** the ability to structure pages in a hierarchy (or tree structure).
- **Attached files:** the ability to attach files of any type to any content item on a page.
- **Images:** the ability to edit images (photographs, drawing files of any type, etc.).
- **Design versus content:** the page design and page content should be maintained separately for easy maintenance of either.
- **Navigation:** the ability to modify website navigation.
- **Search:** the provision of a search function over all website content.
- **Extended search:** the standard search function should cover attached files as well as page content.
- **Forums, communities, etc:** the functionality to include chat, forums, an image gallery, a video gallery, comments and ratings on the website.
- **Forms, etc:** the ability to post forms and collect responses (and export responses to Excel).
- **Permissions:** the provision of varying security permissions – people are allowed different levels of access to specified functionality and given designations such as 'editor' (allowed full access), and 'approver' (limited access).
- **Versioning:** the ability, at the lowest level, to revert to last saved version of the website, and at the highest level, to maintain multiple versions of the website that can be switched at any time.
- **Archiving:** the ability to archive old pages and documents (and retrieve them on request).
- **Multiple websites:** the ability to manage and run multiple websites from the one installation.
- **Mobile devices:** the ability to create a separate website for mobile devices.
- **Web statistics:** the ability for the not-for-profit organisation to view a selection of website visit statistics (pages visited, clickthroughs, etc.).

15 Operational CRM

Operational CRM, or the back-office system (or the transaction processing system), manages the automation of traditional marketing, sales and service functions, i.e. the actions that give rise to the customer interactions and the actions arising from the customer interactions. There is always some element of overlap between operational and collaborative, and between operational and analytical. These overlap areas, where they exist, will be highlighted in the sections that follow. These sections as defined in Chapter 11 are:

- non-functional requirements;
- general functionality;
- marketing-related functionality;
- sales-related functionality;
- service-related functionality;
- systems integration.

15.1   NON-FUNCTIONAL REQUIREMENTS

This section consists of the characteristics of the system rather than the functions that it performs. These characteristics need to be identified in conjunction with the functions. The areas to be considered under non-functional requirements were listed in Chapter 11 as:

- technical issues;
- configuration and customisation;
- security;
- audit trail;
- compliance;
- documentation and help.

15.1.1   Technical issues

The technical issues of interest to not-for-profit organisations are the operating environment, database technology, method of deployment, hosting, and support for mobile devices and for other specialist devices.

Operating environment

This specifies the server and workstation operating system under which the CRM system will operate. Most not-for-profit organisations are completely Microsoft-based and so demand systems that operate under Microsoft Windows Server with Windows on the desktop or laptop and which integrate with other Microsoft software such as Word, Excel, Microsoft Exchange, etc., but a few are system-agnostic and have no preference. This is one area that is currently changing, as more people opt for an outsourced solution (see 'Hosting' overleaf) and for open-source software.

Database technology

Many not-for-profit organisations have told the author that they are 'database agnostic': they 'don't care what it is, as long as it works'. Some not-for-profit organisations, however, express a definite preference for Microsoft technology, usually SQL Server or Access. However, for the majority of organisations Access is seen as too lightweight in terms of the number of users that it can support effectively and is only suitable for very small organisations with limited functional requirements. A very small (but growing) number of not-for-profit organisations express a preference for open-source technology (see 2.1.11).

A **thick client** is a networked computer with most resources installed locally. This is the case for most PCs which have their own hard drives, software applications, etc. A **thin client** is a system which is distributed over a network and does not have a hard drive. It is browser-based and needs to be in constant communication with the server. A **smart client** is a system that has some components and software installed but also uses resources that are distributed over a network.

Deployment

This covers the issues of **thick client** versus **thin client** versus **smart client**. Non-technical people's eyes glaze over at this point, but it does need to be considered! (The definition box may help.) The decision usually revolves around the question of remote access. If there are few remote users then a thick client system is often preferred, whereas if there are remote offices, each containing several staff, then a thin client or smart client system is preferred. There appears to be a steadily increasing move towards organisations demanding a fully web-enabled system such that every single function is available via a web browser. In the near future all systems that survive will be browser-based so that their full functionality can be delivered anywhere to any device using any technology.

Hosting

This is the question of whether an organisation wants its systems hosted externally at a data centre or running on a server in its own office. On the one hand, many organisations are reluctant to allow their data, which is a key asset of their organisation, to leave their premises. This is primarily for security reasons, but also for availability reasons, as a hosted system would be unavailable if the organisation's Internet link failed for any reason. In addition, you lose control over the host applying updates, and cannot get database administrator access for performance tuning and bulk (or global) data changes.

On the other hand, hosting is seen to have a number of advantages because technical infrastructure within the organisation is reduced – there are no servers to maintain, no regular software upgrades to do and no security backups to do. Everything is taken care of by someone else and fewer numbers of technical staff (or even none) are required.

Hosting can come in two forms. Either the organisation's servers are moved to a data centre and the systems on them are accessed via the Internet or via another wide-area networking system, or, the organisation's systems are loaded onto servers belonging to or rented by the hosting company which can be anywhere in the world, and which are accessed via the Internet. In the latter case the organisation's systems are said to be 'in the cloud'. The hosted systems themselves can be browser-based or thick client or smart client, depending on the method of access.

Mobile devices

Many people are now demanding access to their CRM systems via mobile devices, such as smart phones, when they are out of the office. This demands a completely different user interface from the one they are used to on their desktop or laptop computer because of the small screen size. Consequently, the CRM system should support these devices and provide cut-down enquiry and data display functions to provide frontline staff with up-to-the minute information, primarily on customers, campaigns and events. It is a moot point whether data entry functions need to be provided on these devices, as data entry is accomplished far easier using a full-size screen and keyboard.

Because a smart phone always knows where it is geographically, a useful function for people out and about is to be able to query the database in order to find customers within a specified radius of where they are at any given time. There is also an argument for yet another user interface for tablet-type devices whose screen size is somewhere between a standard PC's and a smart phone's.

Specialist devices

The system should support a direct interface with devices such as barcode readers, scanners, specialist label printers, screen readers and any number of other specialist input and output devices used by not-for-profit organisations.

15.1.2 **Configuration and customisation**

When a CRM system is first deployed it is rarely deployed out of the box (i.e. in its standard form). Organisations normally require the system to look the way they want it to look and to operate in a way that suits their business processes in the best manner. This configuration and customisation needs to be carried out in such a way not to compromise future upgrades to the standard system. In addition to the original deployment, the configuration and customisation facilities need to be available during the lifetime of the system, as business needs change over time. The requirements here are in eight categories (which are explained below):

- the handling of multiple organisations in a single database;
- deploying the system in multiple languages;
- the user interface;
- data validation;
- initial data values;
- maintenance of system tables;
- additional data items;
- system extensions.

Multiple organisations

Some organisations manage the CRM functions for other organisations as well as their own. The traditional method of meeting this need is to have multiple copies of the system – one for each organisation. The more sophisticated systems will have functionality to handle multiple organisations within a single database. This demands facilities to keep the data separate and to be able to extract and remove a single organisation's data if required.

Multiple languages

Some international not-for-profit organisations require for the system to be translated into different foreign languages, although this is neither a common requirement nor a common offering by system suppliers.

User interface

At the highest level, organisations will have a preference for the look and feel of the system, such as a Microsoft appearance or a website appearance, data field colour preferences, amount of data on each screen, keyboard equivalents for mouse operations, menus, tabs or buttons, etc. A major requirement is to have a screen designer so that the organisation, or its individual departments, can see only the data fields they want to see on each screen. In other words, standard fields within the system that are not required are hidden and they can see the required data fields grouped on screens in the way they prefer them to be grouped.

Accessibility is a key issue here: a modern CRM solution must allow text, tabs, tool tips, etc., to be interpreted by **screen readers** or improved visibility modes while still allowing the CRM system to be functional.

> **Screen readers** are software applications that enable people with visual impairments to use computers or smart phones. They interpret what is being displayed on the screen and then relay the information to the user via sound or Braille.

Data validation

Data validation is where data is checked for accuracy as it is entered into the system by comparing it against system tables (see overleaf) or checking that it is within specified parameters. Some data fields will be:

- mandatory (if the user doesn't fill in a mandatory field they will not be allowed to go any further in the process until it has been entered);
- validated by having standard individual field types (such as date, currency or number, so if letters were put in a number field this would not be valid);
- validated by user-definable rules (for example, date of birth cannot be greater than 120 years ago or less than 18 years ago);
- validated by other fields (for instance, if Title is Mr then Gender must be Male);
- checked for consistency (for example, for to make sure that postcodes are correct).

Initial data values

This entails being able to define default values for specified data fields when new records are added and being able to define which data fields are mandatory. This means that the record cannot be created until all mandatory fields are completed. This applies not just to basic customer records but to records in any file or table within the system.

System tables

System tables display a fixed number of options to choose from, which apply across an organisation's system, using drop-down lists. The values in all of the drop-down lists within the system must be under the not-for-profit organisation's control and should have a suitable level of security, for example available only to the database administrator (see 15.1.3 below). These system tables are of two main types: tables with standard entries such as title and occupation; and tables with entries that are specific to each organisation, such as customer categories and interests.

Additional data

The system should allow the organisation to add new data fields, and even entire new data tables (see 7.8.2) that are linked to existing data tables, at any time in the life of the system. This data must be available for inclusion on user-defined screens and for searching, querying and reporting.

System extensions

Some not-for-profit organisations require, and some systems allow, the user to add their own complete sub-systems to the main system, but this is not a common requirement. Such systems allow the user to utilise the full facilities of a programming language, usually .NET languages such as C#, or SQL (Structured Query Language).

15.1.3 **Security**

Security within a CRM system goes far beyond the simple user ID and password to log on to the system. It encompasses general system controls, a complex user permissions matrix, ownership of customer records, and data encryption.

System security

This is the general security of the system in terms of (for example) user access permissions, system controls (such as undo functions and processes for confirming the validity of data entries), completeness of single and related operations (such as when deleting a redundant event record also deletes all records associated with it or ensuring that every record on a file of income items from a fulfilment house is imported into the system correctly), data integrity and system backups.

User permissions

Individual users, or groups of users, can have access restricted at a number of levels. These range from the basic ability of viewing only, adding new records and updating existing records, to the ability to access (or inability to access) complete menus, screens, parts of screens or individual data fields on screens. Typical examples include hiding celebrity addresses from all but a small number of staff, restricting who can request specified selections and reports, and who can run various processes such as record merging and record deletion.

Record ownership

Some organisations require an extension of the user permissions from a function-based level, as defined in 'User permissions' above, to defining which customer records an individual user or group of users, can view, add or amend. This could be the case where a Care department does not want other departments to know who its clients are in order to safeguard them from inappropriate or unwanted communications, and certainly wants to restrict access to sensitive and confidential data.

Data encryption

Additional safeguards on important data such as passwords, and credit card and bank details are desirable and encryption of these details gives users and customers a sense of security.

15.1.4 **Audit trail**

There are three aspects to the audit trails required within the system: a financial audit trail, a data change audit trail, and the user actions audit trail.

Financial audit trail

This is the ability to follow every financial transaction from its point of entry into the system right through to its input into the financial accounting system, and back the other way. It is particularly important when transferring summary data (see 7.8.10) to a finance system to be able to identify exactly which items made up each summary line. This is especially important if the original data entry was done in batches but the summaries are produced by nominal ledger code because what is transferred to the nominal ledger is a single record which relates to many income records in the CRM system.

Data audit trail (or audit logging)

This is capturing the date, time and user ID (of the person entering the data) of not only the entry of all new records but also every change made to every record (and the before and after images of the data field or fields). This can amount to a huge volume of data over time and periodic purging is often required.

User actions audit trail

This is capturing the date, time and user ID (of the person entering the data) of not only record changes but also what other actions the user carried out, such as selections they ran or reports they produced. This too can amount to a huge volume of data over time and periodic purging is often required.

15.1.5 **Compliance**

There are various legal requirements and codes of conduct that have to (or should) be complied with which have ramifications for information systems. The most notable of these is the Data Protection Act. Others include the Privacy and Electronic Communications Regulations, credit card regulations, the Institute of Fundraising's codes of practice, Charity Commission regulations and the Direct Marketing Association's DM Code of Practice. This is a small paragraph but it is a huge subject. Some of the regulations are complex and changes happen regularly. The recent law on the use of cookies is a prime example.

15.1.6 **Documentation and help**

This identifies the manuals, online help text and tutorials that the user expects to receive with the operational system. Some systems may contain help text behind every data field and some may even contain context-sensitive help that suggests what type of data should be entered in a field depending on the values in other data fields. Online tutorials can assist new users to become effective quickly without waiting for a formal training course (but they are no substitute for the real thing!).

The subject of error messages is also in this area. They should be in clear and consistent language rather than obscure numbers and/or incomprehensible technical language.

15.2   **GENERAL FUNCTIONALITY**

This section covers general functionality that applies to the CRM system as a whole and/or which does not come under the heading of marketing, sales or service. The areas to be considered under general functionality were listed in Chapter 11 as:

- business rules processing;
- query, reporting and analysis (QRA);
- data management;
- database administrator functions.

15.2.1   **Business rules processing**

The objective of this functionality group is to align software system processes with business processes and automate them as far as possible. There are three sub-groups outlined in this category: simple rules processing, wizards and full workflow processing.

Simple rules

These are straightforward rules of the type 'if field A is not blank then field B must be not blank also', or data entered with a future effective date, such as an address where on the effective date the system marks the current address as a previous address and puts the new address in the current address field.

Wizards

These can be used to lead the user through a complex, but single, process in a structured manner so that nothing is forgotten. A common example is setting up a new customer record where data is required to be entered on several screens. The wizard prompts the user to enter all of the relevant information on each screen.

Workflow processing

This is an extension of wizards where a sequence of tasks is set up, including sequences of tasks with decision points, each of which create a new sequence of tasks. Some of these tasks will be automated and some will depend on user action. The tasks do not have to be, and are usually not, all carried out by the same user and do not have to be all carried out on the same day (and again are usually not). Each user receives an automated notification of their next task to be carried out when it is due (and reminders if it is overdue). A typical example would be a grant application that has to be reviewed internally then sent to referees, then put to a decision-making panel, the result communicated to the applicant, a schedule of payments initiated if it is successful and, finally, review dates set.

15.2.2 **Query, reporting and analysis: QRA**

This section covers searching for individual customer records, regular and ad hoc reporting and simple data analysis (as opposed to analytics which is described under marketing (15.3.2)).

Query

Search facilities: search or query functions are of four types:

- simple, with a small number of data fields that can be used to find customer records;
- query by example, where any number of fields from the entire database can be used to find customer records. These fields can also be searched for the absence of data;
- query builders, which allow you to construct complex conditional statements using a combination of AND, OR and NOT, plus brackets. A very simple example could be, find the records of all customers who live in (Birmingham OR Manchester) AND who did NOT respond to the last appeal;
- Google-type searches, where incomplete expressions can be entered and records returned in the sequence of those most likely to fit the criteria.

A **fuzzy search** is a process which finds records that are most likely to be relevant to the key words the user has typed into the search function, even when they are misspelt, incomplete or do not exactly correspond to what the user is looking for. This includes words that sound the same but are spelt differently.

Each of the first three functions can be done with or without **fuzzy searching** (Google-type searches imply fuzzy searching).

Search responses: there is usually a standard set of data about the customer that every user wants to see when they retrieve a record (name, address, communication preferences, etc.), but equally there are different sets of data that users with different job responsibilities wish to see on the first screen returned by the system. For example, a trust fundraiser wishes to see details of the latest funding proposal put to the customer, whereas the membership manager wants to see the status of the customer's membership (and one is not necessarily interested in the other).

Reporting

The subjects in this group are list management, standard reports, parameterised reports and report writing facilities.

- **List management:** this is done using a simple list generator, usually to produce names only and a limited set of fields such as the address or telephone number. List management allows you to merge lists, export lists and input a list to a process that will carry out any number of set functions, such as set the 'Do not telephone' communication indicator for every record on the list.
- **Standard reports:** every organisation expects the system to have a number of standard out-of-the-box reports that cover everyday reporting and monitoring needs. All operational CRM systems come with a pre-written set of reports that the supplier will have developed in conjunction with other customers over a period of time. Depending on your chosen system and supplier, you might get 20 or 30 standard reports or even 200 or more with some systems. It is likely that the vast majority of a not-for-profit organisation's reporting needs will be catered for by these reports. You will also find that many of them are flexible to the extent that you can:
  - enter parameters such as a date range, area and/or region codes, or customer types, which has the effect of multiplying the number of standard reports available;
  - sort and display the data in different sequences;
  - modify the structure and format of the reports including the fields displayed to tailor them to your own needs.

There is no generally agreed 'standard set' of reports, but some readers might find the following list helpful:

- Daily detailed batch list (see 'batch function' under 15.2.3)
- Banking list
- Income summary by day, week, month and year-to-date
- Income summary by campaign, appeal or segment
- Campaign, appeal or segment analysis and return on investment
- Income summary by fund, project or sub-project
- Income summary by payment method
- Income summary by payment type
- Potential Gift Aid income for day, week, month and year-to-date
- Standing order and direct debit expected not received
- Standing order and direct debit received not expected
- High value donor report
- Pledge status report
- Cash flow report
- LYBUNT (customers from whom income was received 'Last Year But Unfortunately Not This (year)')

- SYBUNT (customers from whom income was received 'Some Year But Unfortunately Not This (year)')
- Various counts of customers by type and category, for example those who use direct debit versus non-direct debit customers
- Standing order or direct debit drop-out rates
- Members by type
- Members by status
- Subscriptions list
- Pareto analysis
- RFV analysis
- Full customer details (for Data Protection Act purposes if the customer requests it)

- **Parameterised reports:** the same report often needs to be run but with different selection criteria (parameters). For example, it could be rerun with a different date range or for a different class of customer. Thus the need for parameter-driven standard reports.
- **Report writer:** although most systems are delivered with a set of standard reports, every organisation will have its own reporting requirements which will change over time. Consequently, a report writing tool is an essential element of the CRM system. This requires a flexible report writer that can access every data field in every table in the database (and run-time calculated fields, i.e. data fields that are not in the database but which are calculated at the time you run the report) and report it in any way required. Most CRM systems will incorporate or integrate with an industry-standard report writing tool such as Crystal Reports or Microsoft Reporting Services. Crystal is almost the de facto industry standard reporting system today, particularly as it is capable of reading files or tables from all of the major database development systems, such as Access, SQL Server, and Oracle, although Microsoft Reporting Services is gaining in popularity. Many of the CRM systems provide their own standard reports in an editable format, so if you find a standard report that is *almost* what you want, then you can modify it in a couple of minutes and have the report *exactly* how you want it.

A big word of warning is required here. Writing your own reports from a CRM system is not as easy as it sounds. You may have an easy-to-use report writing system but you still have to understand the structure of the files and tables in the database in order to create reports that make sense. This is easy if all you have is a customer table, an income table and a campaign table, but what happens when your database has 600 linked tables and the data you want to report on is contained in 10 of them? Wizards (see under 15.2.1) can help to overcome this inevitable gap between users and the technology, but it is still no mean task to create the report and get it right. You may need a database expert to help you out. Of course, you may have no choice but to produce your own reports if you possess one of the flexible CRM systems and you have added lots of your own data fields or even complete new data tables.

Analysis

This is an important area where there is a great overlap between operational CRM and analytical CRM. The discussion here will be restricted to which simple analysis is realistically achievable from an operational CRM database that is primarily a transaction processing (back-office) engine as opposed to one which requires a database built on data warehousing principles (see 2.1.7), which is the subject of Chapter 16.

- **'The Balanced Scorecard':** This term is sometimes found in CRM literature. In effect it is simply a performance monitoring report. You define a number of factors to monitor, such as income this month, new sign-ups this month and number of event attendees this month, assign targets to them and alert management when actual performance falls outside specified tolerances. The balanced scorecard will often be split by staff member, for example by salesperson, fundraiser or by income-generating departments.
- **Performance measurement:** a number of real-time monitoring reports that measure response rates and return on investment are essential to know how a campaign is performing at any point in time. Also required is the ability to compare current campaigns with similar campaigns from previous years.
- **Dashboards:** these are visual overviews of CRM data using a combination of charts, graphs, lists and maps and are becoming popular as a way of instantly viewing key performance indicators (KPIs) in a graphical form. They are updated on a regular basis and show the user a snapshot in time of the status of chosen KPIs. These KPIs will vary from organisation to organisation and from department to department. A fundraising or membership department might want to see the up-to-date responses to a campaign or to measure donor or member attrition whereas a service delivery department might want to measure the number of new beneficiaries assisted.
- **Pareto analysis:** this is the 80:20 rule which states that 80% of an organisation's income comes from 20% of the customers (the same holds true in the not-for-profit sector although sometimes the figures can be as high as 95:5). See also 16.3.1.
- **RFV (recency, frequency, value) analysis** (sometimes known as RFM: recency, frequency, monetary value): this analysis method used in the commercial world is also common in charities. It is a 3D matrix of 1) the time elapsed since the customer last gave money, 2) how many times they have given and 3) how much they have given. See also 16.3.2.
- **Further analysis:** other common analysis requirements are the ability to drill down from individual or groups of Pareto or RFV segments to a greater level of detail, calculate lifetime value (see 16.5.2), and predict future cash flow.

For more on these subjects see Chapter 16.

15.2.3 **Data management**

This section covers the general processing of the following data issues: management of documents, bulk or global updating of data, cleaning data, data import and export and deleting or archiving of data.

Document management

Document management (for 'document' read 'documents, images and data files of any type') covers everything from scanning documents and linking them to customer records, such as membership applications, to the retrieval of all documents of a specified type, such as Gift Aid declarations. Other examples include the storage of general documents, such as project descriptions, the generation of web pages tailored from these documents depending on the customer's interests, and the destruction of documents after a given length of time. It also includes cataloguing, indexing and searching of these documents or files. Search facilities can include keyword searching within files or, in some cases, even searching for any word or phrase.

Global updates

This is the bulk updating of records according to specified criteria, for example increase all fees for membership type A by 5% and all fees for membership type B by 8%, or change all relevant phone numbers when a phone number prefix changes.

Data cleaning

This section is about the quality of the data in the system and the processes to keep it as accurate as possible. The areas covered are data validation and auditing, data de-duplication, and record merging.

- **Data validation and auditing**: validation is the checking of data for accuracy as it is entered into the system by comparing it against system tables or checking that it is within specified parameters. Auditing is a **batch function** which can be run at any time that does the same type of validation, often with different parameters and including consistency checks between different fields.

> A **batch function** is when a series of tasks are lined up in a queue and are executed one after the other without needing a user to set off the individual tasks.

For example, this function can check that postcodes are correct or that people applying for student membership are under a certain age. The auditing function should produce a report on the results first of all and ask the user whether they wish to proceed with the cleaning of the data.

- **De-duplication** (often simply referred to as 'de-dupe', although you won't find that word in the dictionary!): duplicate records are a common problem within not-for-profit CRM systems and a function is required to scan the database to identify possible duplicate records. The parameters for de-duplication should be under user control, as should the decision whether to delete or merge the duplicate records identified.
- **Record merging** (often referred to as 'merge-purge'): this is a complex task because if two records are found to be the same customer, there could be personal, transactional and communication data on both that have to be consolidated, and decisions are required on data that is inconsistent between the two records. Some systems work on a simple 'master-slave' principle (where the 'master' is the record you are going to keep and 'slave' is the record you are going to take bits from (to add into the master record) and then delete; once the slave data is validated it can be merged with the master) whereas others work on a more sophisticated 'what do you want to merge?' principle, where you are given choices on what should and should not be merged into the master record.

Import and export

The ability to import data into the CRM system from other sources and to export data from the CRM system for use in other systems is of vital importance to not-for-profit organisations. The major reason for this is that not-for-profit organisations often utilise the services of third-party agencies and fulfilment houses for some functions, such as large-scale capturing of donations or outbound telephone campaigns. Most of these third-party organisations will have their own information systems with which some level of integration is required. In the vast majority of cases this integration is carried out by exporting data to the third party, such as a complete file of names and addresses, and the third party imports the data.

- **Import:** any and all data in the system must be capable of being imported. There are a number of aspects to importing data. These include:
  - an initial data load when first deploying the system;
  - importing files of names and addresses received from various sources;
  - importing files of financial transactions from fulfilment agencies;
  - importing files of communication records from specialist agencies, such as those which undertake telephone fundraising on behalf of charities;
  - importing any data to update existing records, for instance the results of external demographic profiling.

  Business functions such as duplicate checking and individual field and inter-field consistency checking are essential during data import.

- **Export:** as with import, any and all data (including linked documents) must be capable of being exported. This includes:
  - files of selected names and addresses for sending to a mailing company or to a profiling company;
  - files of names, telephone numbers and other relevant data for sending to a telephone agency, for example to attempt to get lapsed members to renew their membership;
  - transactional and other relevant data for uploading to an analysis or marketing system;
  - the complete database in the event of a change of system.
- **Reciprocal processing and rented lists:** organisations sometimes swap the details of a number of their customers with another organisation or they rent a list of names and addresses (or phone numbers or email addresses). In each case the rules of the arrangement are that the reciprocal or rented customers can be communicated a specified number of times in an identified period. If they respond, they can be added to the organisation's database. If they don't respond, they have to be removed completely from the organisation's system.

Deleting and archiving

Deletion is the physical deletion of customer records (or parts of records) permanently, whereas archiving is the deletion of customer records on a temporary basis (i.e. the removal of the data to an off-line data store) along with the ability to retrieve the data if required. Deletion can also apply to files or tables related to customer records, for example a decision could be taken to delete all communication log records which are more than five years old.

15.2.4 **Database administrator functions**

Facilities are required to provide one or more persons with full control over the set-up, amendment and deletion of user IDs, passwords, system tables, user-defined screen design, wizards, workflows, job scheduling and, in many instances, record deletion, record merging, global data updates, data imports and data exports.

15.3 **MARKETING-RELATED FUNCTIONALITY**

These are the functional groups that relate to the marketing of the organisation's products and services. The areas to be considered under marketing-related functionality are as listed in Chapter 11: customer management, marketing, communications, and channels.

15.3.1 **Customer management**

This is the first group of categories that is directly related to customers. There is some debate about whether it should appear under the marketing super-group or under the general super-group, or even in a group of its own. However, it is generally considered correct to include it under marketing. This group is the cornerstone of CRM because it contains all of the functionality that must exist before the traditional elements of marketing, sales and service can be carried out. The major categories in this group to be discussed are:

- types of customer;
- name and address management;
- customers with no address;
- common data;
- unique data;
- marketing data;
- prospective support;
- individuals;
- media management;
- special customer relationships;
- volunteer management;
- organisations;
- other customer groups;
- customer relationships;
- activity and communication tracking;
- action management;
- action pledges;
- non-monetary support.

Types of customer

This simply lists all the possible types of customer with which the organisation may have a relationship (i.e. the 50 plus different types of customers listed in section 4.3). It serves solely as a checklist for each organisation to determine the boundaries of their CRM system. That is, the categories of customer that the system will manage, which in turn will determine the functionality required.

Name and address

The initial entry and later maintenance of name and address data is the starting point for CRM. Names of individuals need to be structured and titles, honours and qualifications verified, i.e. checked for accuracy (see 'Data validation' under 15.1.2). Names of organisations need to be captured along with their common abbreviations in order to make searching for them easier. In addition, one or more named contacts, and their position or job titles(s) should be maintained for each organisation entered on the database.

Addresses need to be confirmed, preferably using specialist addressing software and kept up to date when postcodes change. There must be facilities to allow multiple customers at the same address and multiple addresses for each customer, with an indication of what they are and when they are used, for example current address and previous address, or home address and term-time address. Each address should have an associated date range to indicate when it is relevant. Where the not-for-profit organisation has structured itself geographically into branches and/or areas and/or regions, then the corresponding branch/area/region should be defaulted to automatically using the postcode.

The concept of an address should be extended to capture and maintain (multiple, if necessary) telephone numbers and email addresses, plus web addresses for organisations. Systems should allow for the creation and maintenance of customer records with no mailing address, but with one or more email addresses or telephone numbers, as some customers may prefer to have email or telephone contact only.

Accuracy is all-important, especially with regard to addresses. Specialist addressing systems that link with most CRM systems help you to maintain accurate addresses. These systems utilise the Royal Mail's Postcode Address File, commonly referred to as the PAF file (even though that does mean you use the word 'file' twice). There are many levels of these systems, but the basic level inserts the whole address into your database record when you enter simply the postcode and the house number. This not only ensures accuracy and consistency of addressing but also saves data entry time. Other levels of these systems allow:

- the generation of the complete address from a partial address (useful when you have difficulty reading someone's writing);
- automatic insertion of parliamentary constituencies, NHS districts, TV region and other geographic and demographic breakdowns into contact records based on the postcode;
- the regeneration of postcodes when the Post Office recodes an area (which it does all the time). Note that if you don't do this then addresses that had correct postcodes when you entered them in the database may no longer be accurate.

Customers with no address

In today's world every not-for-profit organisation will need to hold records for customers for whom they have no postal address, for example:

- someone who communicates exclusively by email and pays or donates via the website and who has declined to give you their postal address;
- somebody who only gives you their mobile number;
- someone who uses Twitter to talk about your organisation for whom you only have their Twitter ID;
- institutions such as churches which have a physical address but not a postal address.

Common data

A large number of data items common to every type of customer record need to be maintained, including telephone numbers (mobile and fixed), email addresses and social media IDs. An important related set of data are the communication indicators which signify which types of communications the customer wishes to receive, by which method and when. These indicators can range from simple Yes/ No flags such as 'no mail', 'no telephone calls', 'Christmas catalogue only', etc., to complex three-dimensional matrices of communication type, method and timing. Each indicator should have a start date, an end date and a source code to indicate when and why it was set.

Other common data to be maintained includes any number of customer categories/profile codes, interests, types of support provided, notes and bank account details. With regard to the management of notes, all CRM systems allow you to add general notes to customer records, but there are some special requirements. These include:

- important notes that pop up on-screen like a post-it note as the record is accessed;
- date, time and user-ID 'stamping' of all notes, which means you can keep track of who is entering data and when;
- structured notes, which allow notes to be categorised;
- confidential notes which are restricted to certain users or departments.

Unique data

There are data items which are unique for almost every type of customer that have to be maintained. Some examples are:

- classes, years and qualifications obtained for alumni;
- political party, specific interests and voting patterns for politicians;
- turnover and number of employees for companies;

• giving policy and meeting dates for trusts;
• the UK Standard Industrial Classification (UK SIC) category.

The system must cater for all of these and more and have suitable screen design options for each type of customer.

Marketing data

These data items are transaction summary information for each customer, such as:

• income and expenditure to date, average income and expenditure value;
• demographics, such as age group, social demographic group, counties, constituencies, regions and LEAs (local education authorities).

Individuals

This is the maintenance of all general data related to individuals of all types. It includes such things as name (and its various elements: title, first name, last name, honours), salutation, label name (for the first line on an envelope), alternate names, National Insurance number, education history, employment history, date of birth, gender, interests and a host of other personal items.

Media

There are two aspects to this: 1) customers who are usually beneficiaries of the organisation who speak to the press about the organisation and 2) the media people themselves. In the first case media management often involves maintaining case studies related to the beneficiary. In the second case it involves what the media people write about and their relationship with the not-for-profit organisation. Both cases need security procedures so that only specified people within the organisation communicate with these people.

Special customer relationships

This is normally related to VIPs, celebrities or major (high-value) donors who support the organisation. Security procedures, as per the media, apply but also procedures to ensure they receive special treatment and are never sent 'standard' communications. For example, if they send a donation of any amount, or renew their membership, they would not get a standard receipt or thank-you letter but a personal communication from their designated contact within the organisation.

Volunteers

This can be a complex area of not only maintaining unique data items such as skills, training courses attended and availability, but also recording jobs done and time volunteered, and managing expenses and their payment. It can also include a workflow-based approval process for the requesting and recording of references, CRB (Criminal Records Bureau) checks and committee approval.

Partners

This is the management of indirect sales via partners or agents and the integration and reporting of these sales with direct sales. It also includes facilities for the partners themselves to be able to track and manage the leads and sales they are working on. It can even include an analysis of sales leads and their matching and distribution to the appropriate partner.

Organisations

This term can cover companies, grant-giving trusts, government departments, statutory bodies (such as the National Lottery and local authorities), Lions and Rotary Clubs, etc. The major functional requirement, in addition to the basic functions of name and address management, common data and unique data (outlined above), is the maintenance of multiple contacts at the organisation and the circumstances under which each contact is communicated. These organisations can be formed into hierarchies, such as when a company has many offices or branches. There is also the complication that the contact person of the organisation can be a customer in their own right with their own addresses, telephone numbers and email addresses.

Other customer groups

There are a number of other groupings of customers that need to be considered and for which there are a number of functional areas in addition to those of name and address management, common data and unique data. These groupings include joint or family customers, committees, special interest groups, support groups and regions.

- **Joint or family customers:** facilities are required to manage single, joint and family communications with appropriate salutations (for instance one mailing per family), and to be able to record and view activities for each individual or the group.
- **Committees:** the functions needed for committee management include those for maintaining records of positions and dates held, communicating with the committee as a group, managing committee meetings and diaries, recording minutes, and managing and recording ballots.

- **Special interest groups:** similar functions to committees are needed, plus the ability to access a special subset of the website which contains items relating to the interest.
- **Support groups:** again similar functions to committees are needed, plus the ability for the members of the group to share information regarding their group's activities.
- **Regions:** similar functions to committees are needed if the region (or a complete hierarchy of geographic breakdowns) has post holders such chairs, secretaries, etc., plus the ability to manage and report on income and expenditure at the regional level.

Customer relationships

This is maintaining records of the links between customers of all types, including companies and their subsidiaries, companies and their individual contacts, links between people such as family relationships and who knows whom. These links can form a hierarchy with many levels, which is best displayed as a tree structure in a form similar to Microsoft Windows Explorer (where you can open and close different levels of the hierarchy in order to see (or hide) greater levels of detail). A six-level hierarchy is quite common. It is essential to be able to move freely around the hierarchy and jump to any record within it and then return to the hierarchy. Additional functionality is usually required to maintain a history of past relationships, such as to chart an individual's career movements.

Activity and communication logging

This consists of tracking every communication with an activity undertaken by or in relation to the customer. Typical examples are records of:

- every communication sent to the customer (with a link to the Word letter or the actual email, or to their templates if it was a standard communication), when it was sent and what it was about;
- every communication from the customer (including storage and links to scanned incoming letters, emails in, etc.);
- all telephone calls, meetings, event attendances, and any other activities the customer has undertaken, promises the customer has made, etc.

These, along with financial transactions which are usually held separately, provide a full history of the customer's relationship with the organisation and can be analysed to help predict the customer's future behaviour.

Actions

Actions are activities as defined above, but they will be carried out in the future. These actions are often recorded along with the past activities, so that *all* activities, past and future, can be viewed together. Action management provides the facility to record future actions that should be undertaken and a system of reminders to the user when the actions are due, such as 'write to the customer next week reminding him about X' or a reminder for six months' time to start preparing the submission for a grant from trust Y. Typically the reminders for actions due each day should appear automatically on the due date when the user first logs on to the system that day, although the reminder list can be viewed at any time.

Action pledges

This is the ability to record when customers are willing to do something for the organisation, such as speak to the press. It also includes the ability to store and recall case studies for marketing purposes.

Non-monetary support

This is the ability to capture the ways that customers support the organisation which are not transactional but are important and valuable to the organisation. Examples include people who:

- influence others to support the organisation;
- donate their time to the organisation;
- take clothes to the organisation's charity shops;
- sponsor friends to do things for the organisation.

All of these need a value of some sort attached to them so that you can take account of them when carrying out marketing segmentations and selection.

This is a *major difference* between traditional CRM and not-for-profit CRM and many suppliers (and even many not-for-profit organisations themselves) have yet to get to grips with it and devise a realistic formula that takes account of these types of support in conjunction with pure pound notes! For example, how do you put a value on people who give no money themselves but who do collections for you, or volunteer for one day a week, or talk about your organisation in glowing terms in a variety of media? Some organisations apply an hourly rate to such things and consider it as a gift in kind.

15.3.2 **Marketing**

The major marketing functions which are outlined in this section are planning, budgeting and forecasting; prospect research; analytics and data mining; campaign management; segmentation and selection; and customer journeys.

Planning, budgeting and forecasting

The functions which are often carried out within a financial management system include:

- creating income and expenditure budgets against departments and costs centres (for example a fundraising department and within that direct marketing, trust fundraising, corporate fundraising, etc. or a membership department and within it standard memberships, special memberships, subscriptions, etc.);
- budget update and approval process;
- monthly re-forecasting.

However, income forecasting is an important function within CRM and, although projecting forward direct debit and standing order figures is simple, complete income forecasting can be complex and is better dealt with in section 16.5 'Data modelling and prediction'.

Prospect research

In charities the objective of prospect research is usually to identify potential givers of large gifts (although it could be to identify potential givers of any value of gift or even potential givers of time, i.e. volunteers). One method is to analyse the demographics of customers currently on the database, searching, for example, for specific titles, postcodes or words in an address. Other more complex techniques require the recording and analysis of large amounts of publicly available information.

In membership organisations, the objective is to identify potential new members. This could entail, for example, targeting companies in a specific business area or people with particular job titles.

Analytics and data mining

This is the area referred to as analytical CRM. However, it is included here as a fundamental element of marketing, rather than as a major group in its own right, as its results are always used to inform future marketing campaigns. Huge amounts of data, both transactional (what the customer has bought from, given to, done for, and received from the organisation) and demographic, can be extracted from the CRM database into a data warehouse or, more accurately, a data mart (see 10.5), as there is only one major source of data: the CRM system. Numerous analytical techniques and data mining tools can then be applied to the data such as analysis of variance (see 16.5.5), regression analysis (16.5.8) and chi-squared analysis (16.5.6) to arrive at suggestions for marketing campaigns. This analysis can be used to group customers together and to identify trends.

Campaign management

Once the analytics and research have identified groups of customers to be targeted, campaigns can be constructed. Campaign management consists primarily of two categories: campaign set-up and campaign monitoring.

- **Campaign set-up:** marketing campaigns are usually constructed as a multi-level hierarchy: three levels often called 'campaign', 'appeal' and 'segment' are common, but campaigns can be developed with any number of levels. Campaigns with 50 groupings of customers at the lowest level of the hierarchy are not uncommon. Data associated with any and every level of the campaign structure includes income and expenditure targets (or budgets), actual income and expenditure realised, and even the allocation of resources for the campaign, i.e. who is doing what. A diary feature related to the campaign is often included, as the set-up of every marketing campaign involves many tasks over a period of time and many people, including outside agencies such as designers and printers of marketing material.
- **Campaign monitoring:** once the campaign has commenced, for example after a mailing or emailing has gone out, real-time monitoring of responses becomes important. At a high level this is tracking the total income and expenditure against the targets, and at a lower level it is tracking any number of KPIs such as the number of responses and response rates (percentages), number of new donors or members, average income item value, and return on investment. In addition, reports are required that don't just show the latest position but which chart the progress of any of these factors over time. Being able to produce all of these statistics at any time in graphical form is also seen as an important requirement.

Selection and segmentation

Selection and segmentation is the process of querying the database to extract the groupings of customers, as identified by the analytics and research, so that they can be added to the appropriate level of the campaign hierarchy. As outlined under section 7.5.2, selection is querying the database to select records with matching criteria and is usually for a single immediate purpose such as a mailing. Segmentation has a slightly different meaning in that a group of customers, once selected as having satisfied a set of criteria, are marked as belonging to that segment. For example, all customers who have given a single gift of more that

£1,000 in the last three years are classified as major donors, and are treated in the same way and their behaviour monitored. This includes their movement between segments, because a customer can move in and out of the major donor segment.

Something that must be considered in this category is the subject of permission marketing. We are in a world now where we risk all sorts of unhelpful ramifications if we invade people's privacy and ignore their wishes. We have to obtain people's permission to send them marketing emails (otherwise known as an 'opt-in'), we must not cold call organisations whose telephone number is on the Telephone Preference Service list, we can still send snail mail to people who are registered with the Mailing Preference Service, but it is bad practice to do so, and the restrictions go on and on. This is a subject in its own right, and something that marketers need to consider seriously.

Customer (or supporter) journeys

The concept of customer journeys is a very inexact science and no two not-for-profit organisations will agree on what constitutes 'a customer journey'. In essence, it means tracking the customer's behaviour and allocating them to different campaigns depending upon their previous actions and which campaigns they have been selected for in the past. It has the dual purpose of 1) attempting to predict what customers will respond to next and allocating them to the appropriate campaign, and 2) attempting to push the customers down a particular path and encourage them to respond to what the organisation wants them to respond to, for example getting a purchaser of a single product to become a regular subscriber.

The ultimate aim of many not-for-profit organisations is to treat every customer as a segment of one; that is, appropriately tailoring each message to every customer so that the concept of a multi-customer segment disappears. However, most people consider this to be impractical in general terms and only applicable to a small set of specially selected customers such as high-value donors or celebrities.

15.3.3 Communications

Once the campaigns have been set up and the customers have been selected, the next step is to communicate with them. This section of the system includes the general communications processing functions of single ad hoc communications, simple mail merge, complex mail merge, conditional processing, and communication logging, as described in section 14.1.

15.3.4 **Channels**

The communication channels cover the different ways in which communication with customers exists. These channels are often known as 'touch points'. They are separated into traditional channels, the organisation's website, other websites and social media, as described in sections 14.2, 14.3, 14.4 and 14.5 respectively.

15.4 **SALES-RELATED FUNCTIONALITY**

These are the functional groups that relate to the selling of the organisation's products and services or other forms of income generation. The areas to be considered under sales-related functionality are sales, fundraising, membership management, event management, financial management (as listed in table 11.3).

15.4.1 **Sales**

Almost every not-for-profit organisation sells products of some sort, even if it is only charity Christmas cards. However, although the functions traditionally associated with a sales operation are used extensively by some not-for-profit organisations, they are not used at all by others which designate, say, Christmas card sales as just a special type of donation. The major sales functions (as outlined below) are product catalogue and pricing, order processing, and stock control. Other sales functions that are used by a small minority of not-for-profit organisations are grouped under the heading of 'other sales functions' and include lead management, contract management and sales force automation.

Product catalogue and pricing

The sales process starts with the production of a catalogue of products, both in printed form and available on the web. The web system requires full search facilities on multiple criteria. Also in this section of the system is the management of products and contract costs.

Order processing

The functions under this heading cover the creation of quotations and the processing of sales orders via back-office sales, telesales (including call guides) and eCommerce.

- **Quotations:** in some circumstances a quotation is produced for a customer prior to them placing an order. These quotations are monitored and followed up on a regular basis until they are translated into invoices or deemed to be dead.
- **Back-office sales:** orders placed by customers over the telephone, or received in the post or by email are entered to the system by the organisation's staff.

This requires processes to enter order details, calculate VAT and postage and packing, handle discounts, sale or return items, returns, refunds, credit notes and back orders, produce picking lists and delivery notes, and process payments (see 15.4.5).

- **Agent sales:** the sending of products to agents for them to sell on a sale or return basis. Separate stock level records need to be maintained for each agent as well as contract and fees and/or commission details.
- **Telesales (including call guides or call scripting):** requires pre-selected lists of people to phone; scripts of what to say with decision points (which help the caller to deal with many permutations of potential customer answers), depending upon the customer's responses; access to all data held about the customer, in particular, the customer's record of previous purchases; and all the processes listed under back-office sales to process orders that are given.
- **eCommerce:** a slightly modified form of all the processes listed under back-office sales that enable people to place orders themselves via the organisation's website.

Stock control

Real-time maintenance of stock levels (at multiple locations or warehouses if appropriate) may be required as orders are being taken and deliveries of stock are received. Other functions such as parts explosion (where one product contains other products which contain yet other products), automated re-order reports, suggested alternative items and stock-taking, may also be also required by some organisations.

Other sales functions

Other sales functions that are used by very few not-for-profit organisations include lead management, account management, territory management, contract management and sales force automation.

- **Lead management (or prospect management):** consists primarily of capturing customer enquiries, prioritising them and following them up in order to turn the enquirer (or prospect) into a customer proper.
- **Account management:** a set of processes to manage multiple sales and sales leads with a single customer.
- **Territory management:** the monitoring of the number of active customer accounts and prospective customers or leads, plus the sales personnel servicing them within a designated geographic area (or within some other demographic breakdown such as major accounts, lesser accounts, etc.).
- **Contract management:** contracts are sometimes made with customers of different types and the main function is recording and monitoring the terms and conditions of the contract.

- **Sales force automation:** this is actually a combination of many other sales functions including lead management, account management, territory management, order processing and tracking, and even sales forecasting. The prime functions of sales force automation, however, are tracking the stages of the sales process, managing follow-up actions and ensuring that duplication of effort by different staff members is avoided.

15.4.2　**Fundraising**

There is a strong argument for incorporating fundraising under the general heading of sales because it is a sales process in that the customer gives the organisation money and in return they receive, not a product but, the satisfaction that they have done something useful for a cause. (In addition, they sometimes receive other benefits from the organisation such as discounted entry to events.) However, fundraising is a very large and complex section of the not-for-profit CRM requirements, and so it warrants a major section of its own within an overall super-group of sales-related functions. It consists of the following functional areas: applications and pledges, donations, legacies, raffles and lotteries, and events and sponsorship.

Applications and pledges

The functions under this heading cover the process of applying for funds from various agencies or funders such as grant-giving trusts and statutory bodies, and the promises from these agencies (and individual donors) to provide funds to the organisation in the future.

- **Funding applications:** the recording and monitoring of requests for funding sent to grant-giving trusts, companies, the National Lottery and statutory bodies such as the European Union and local authorities. It incorporates the maintenance of contacts, recording of research data, recording of application details, logging of all activities related to the application (such as requests for information and feedback provided to the funder), and a diary and reminder facility.
- **Income pledges:** the recording of promises by the customer to give money to the organisation in the future: either one-off amounts or multiple payments. It incorporates the recording of amount(s) and the dates when they are due, and a reminder facility to check if the payments have been made as promised. The conditions associated with the pledge, such as the need to send annual accounts and project status reports to the funder, are also recorded.

Donations

This section covers all types of donations made to the organisation from all types of funder.

- **Ad hoc donations:** the recording of single amounts of money given by customers to the organisations. The money can come in a variety of ways, as outlined in 'Income processing' under 15.4.5. This includes any special processes needed to record and report on anonymous donations.
- **Regular (or committed) giving:** the recording and monitoring of regular financial commitments made by customers to the organisation. This includes the amounts, the payment method, the payment frequency, and financial reconciliations such as reporting on missing, incorrect or extra payments. The primary methods of payment are by direct debit or standing order (see also 15.4.5).
- **In memoriam giving:** facilities are required for managing donations given in memory of someone who died. There are two methods of recording this type of income: donor related and fund related. *Donor related*: the income is recorded against the donor and also against the deceased as a soft credit so that reports on the total amount given in memory of the deceased can be produced easily for the next of kin by viewing the deceased's record. *Fund related*: a fund (or destination code) is set up in the name of the deceased and income is recorded only against the donor and allocated to the appropriate fund so that the total given can be obtained by viewing the fund.
- **Tribute funds:** these are similar to in memoriam giving but are for long-term tributes that always necessitate a formal destination (fund) code. For example, Light up a Life community events, which are organised by hospices to allow people to celebrate the lives of loved ones, will have specific destination codes.
- **In honour gifts:** these are similar in concept to tribute funds but are a special form of time-limited dedications such as to celebrate an anniversary, wedding, birthday, etc.
- **Matched giving:** the recording and monitoring of pledges from organisations which agree to match their employees' donations to the not-for-profit organisation. There may be restrictions placed on the pledge which need to be recorded. Some organisations, for example may require an invoice showing the employees' donations before they release the promised funds.
- **Payroll giving:** the recording and monitoring of donations from individuals made from their salary before taxation, plus records for their employers and for the agencies which collect the money.
- **Standing orders from giving agencies:** the collection and management of standing orders in favour of not-for-profit organisations which are set up with organisations other than banks.

- **Static media (often simply known as collection boxes, but they can take other forms):** the recording and monitoring of static collection media, who has them, when they were sent, monies received from them and reminders when nothing has been received for a specified period.
- **Public collections:** the recording and monitoring of collectors, their rounds if appropriate (for example, for house-to-house (or door-to-door) collections), items sent to them (such as collection tins or envelopes), all money received, and reminders when no income has been received after a specified period.
- **Telephone fundraising:** this section has many similarities with telesales and call scripting in that it requires pre-selected lists of people to phone, scripts of what to say with decision points (which help the caller to deal with many permutations of potential customer answers), access to all data held about the customer, in particular, the customer's record of previous donations, and the ability to enter donations (via credit card), set up direct debits or create income pledges.
- **Gift Aid:** the recording of Gift Aid declarations made by the customer, monitoring of the donations made by the customer which qualify for Gift Aid, and the production of Gift Aid claims to HMRC at regular intervals, listing the donations made by customers and the amount of tax to be reclaimed.

Legacies

This section covers the sending and recording of legacy marketing materials to prospective legators and the administration of bequests made in favour of the organisation when the legator dies.

- **Legacy marketing:** legacy marketing could be considered to be under the general heading of marketing but there are special circumstances that warrant it being considered under the fundraising heading. It is necessary to record who has received legacy marketing material and who has pledged to remember the organisation in their will. These people are then treated personally and with extreme care by fundraising staff.
- **Legacy administration:** the average time from notification of a bequest to an organisation until the case is closed and all the money is received is usually between one and two years and can be, in extreme cases, many years. Consequently, facilities are required to manage the process, which includes records of legacy details, executors, solicitors, next of kin, type of bequest, conditions, amounts expected and received, correspondence, actions and reminders.

Raffles and lotteries

This section is the administration of raffles and lotteries run by the organisation to increase the funds of the organisation.

Raffles: the recording and monitoring of raffle ticket sellers, ticket distribution, ticket sales and winners. Ticket tracking is required, which is done by ticket numbers being recorded against sellers (usually by ticket book number). Re-order procedures and income-monitoring facilities are also required.

Lotteries: this is the recording and monitoring of lottery players, the collectors and their rounds, the lottery payments and players' 'paid-up-to dates' (i.e. the point at which a player's credit runs out), plus the selection of winning numbers and the printing of winners' cheques and winner lists. Note that this functionality requires licensing from the Gambling Commission.

Events and sponsorship

This section relates to events that are run not by an organisation but by supporters (customers) of the organisation, and to sponsorship by other supporters of both the organisation in general and the organisation's supporters and what they do.

- **Gifts in kind:** the recording of non-monetary gifts made by the customer to the organisation. These gifts will have a nominal value associated with them. It must be possible to report on the sum of the nominal values of gifts in kind along with the actual monetary gifts made in order to ascertain the true value of the customer to the organisation.
- **Corporate sponsorship:** the recording and monitoring of the sponsorship of marketing campaigns or events by organisations, usually companies. This involves maintaining lists of items that can be sponsored and their values, recording who is sponsoring what, allowing multiple sponsors per event, invoicing sponsors, recording income and gifts in kind received, and recording the benefits the sponsor receives in recognition of their sponsorship.
- **Auctions:** recording the items donated or purchased (often things like cars, holidays, dinner with a celebrity, etc.) that are to be auctioned, along with details of the date of the auction, people associated with the auction such as a celebrity auctioneer, the cost of the items, the price realised and details of the successful bidders.
- **Supporter fundraising events:** the recording and monitoring of the intention of a supporter to hold a fundraising event such as a coffee morning or bring-and-buy sale, promotional items requested and/or sent to them, income received and reminders when income has not been received after a specified time.

- **Supporter sponsorship:** the recording and monitoring of all the data and activities associated with a supporter being sponsored by other individuals (or organisations) to undertake an event such as the London Marathon. Some of the complexities to be taken into account include:
  - individuals competing as teams;
  - some sponsorship money qualifying for Gift Aid and some not,
  - some income coming from the participant and other income coming from third parties such as Just Giving;
  - some individual income items need to be split into parts such as fees (for example an entry fee) and donations;
  - some sponsors do not pay up;
  - particular events (often referred to as Challenge Events) have special requirements and entail legal obligations, expenditure, insurance and third-party organisers, for instance skydiving, mountain climbing and foreign treks.

15.4.3 Membership management

As in the area of fundraising, membership should be considered under the general heading of sales because it is a sales process in that the customer gives the organisation money and in return they get not a product but the kudos of belonging to an organisation (usually a professional body but also fundraising charities in some cases). In addition, they receive a variety of membership benefits such as specialist magazines, discounted entry to venues (museum exhibitions for instance), and discounted attendance at conferences and other events. Also as with fundraising, membership is a very large and complex section of the not-for-profit CRM requirements, and so it also warrants a major section of its own. It consists of the following functional areas: membership, subscriptions, examinations and awards, CPD (continuing professional development), elections and balloting, and member case management.

Membership

Membership management consists of processes for new memberships (joining), renewal of existing memberships, gift memberships, members' affiliations and members' directories.

- **Joining:** the processes related to joining a membership scheme include calculating fees, which can be extremely complex owing to the multiple membership types, multiple grades, multiple rates, different time periods, initial discounts, different statuses and different benefits. Some applications require a workflow process for obtaining and checking references and further information, and an internal approval process. Payments have to be checked, processed and reconciled and in many cases membership cards have to be printed and distributed.

- **Renewing:** renewing memberships involves an automated sequence of renewal and reminder notices, a lapsing process, a reinstatement process, and payment and membership card printing processes.
- **Gift membership:** sometimes a third party pays the member's fees such as a family member or an employer. This entails keeping records of the giver and the member and processes to remind the giver for renewals, or not as the case may be, and ensuring that, although no money appears against the member's record, the member is considered to be 'paid up' and receives all the usual benefits associated with their membership type and grade.
- **Affiliations:** members can be associated with branches or regions depending upon where they live and the allocation to these branches or regions should be automatically dependent upon their home or work address. The branches can be in a hierarchy, such as branch/area/region. In addition, most membership schemes have any number of special interest groups to which the member can belong. All of these may or may not involve additional fees and act as memberships within a membership, each with its own benefits.
- **Directories:** many organisations publish directories of members in printed form, interactive CD and online, some of which are available to members only and some of which are available to the general public to view and search for members.

Subscriptions

This encompasses processes for members and non-members to sign up to receive regular publications, printed or online, with varying rates, multiple copies and varying periods. Renewal and reminders, lapsing, reinstatement and payments, as per the membership processes, are required. Formal invoices are often required by subscribers.

Examinations and awards

The major requirements are for maintaining candidate and course records, and the entry of results.

- **Candidate records:** maintain records of every candidate's courses, dates, results and qualifications obtained.
- **Course records:** maintain records of courses (and modules within courses); course prerequisites; course dates and locations; examination dates and locations; other assessments (such as written papers or practical sessions); lecturers, assessors, etc.; and the candidates who are taking the courses each year.
- **Results entry:** rapid data entry of results, assessments and grades is required.

CPD (continuing professional development)

CPD is assessed in different ways by different organisations. Some use a points system with a number of points to be accumulated each year, for instance attending conference X results in 10 points (and 50 points must be accumulated every single year). Others use hours and stipulate a number of hours of specified activities to be undertaken each year. Others use a simple list of activities to be undertaken each year.

Data entry of activities undertaken is required, including the automatic updating of members' CPD records if attendances at events or conferences run by the organisation qualify for a particular number of points, hours or activities. In addition, it is acceptable in some organisations for members to update their own CPD records with activities they have undertaken.

Elections and balloting

Many membership organisations hold elections and ballots of various types, for example to elect officers such as a chair or secretary, or decide on rules and regulations of the organisation, or issues affecting the membership. Therefore, processes are required to print and distribute ballot papers and to enter and reconcile responses.

Member case management

Some professional membership organisations have procedures for managing complaints against members. This is a workflow process for stages of the case with review points, linked documents, alerts for when things are diarised to occur, records of hearing dates, witnesses, assessors and outcomes.

15.4.4 Event management

As with the areas of fundraising and membership, the set-up and running of events is a large and complex area and thus event management demands a section of its own. It appears in the sales super-group because it is a significant revenue generator for many not-for-profit organisations. There are some quite different types of events run by not-for-profit organisations such as social events, training courses and conferences, but they all require similar systems functionality to manage them.

The major functional groupings explained below are venue management, event management (including event planning, event sponsorship, invitations and bookings, reserved tickets, ticketing, seat planning, travel and accommodation, and event reporting), and abstract management.

Venue management

This consists of maintaining details of venues, their contacts and their facilities, matching these facilities against the needs of the events, booking venues and equipment, and liaising with the venue.

Event management

The activities under this heading are event planning, event sponsorship, invitations and bookings, reserved tickets, ticketing, seat planning, travel and accommodation and event reporting.

- **Event planning:** the process of constructing the event. This includes event structure, with different streams and sessions (including even managing an event within an event, such as a separately costed dinner within a three-day conference), identifying speakers and other event personnel, income and expenditure budgeting, target attendance, and pricing.
- **Event sponsorship:** there are three types of sponsorship for events: 1) the sponsor provides money to pay for items such as venue hire or printing, 2) the sponsor provides goods or services themselves free of charge, and 3) the sponsor buys something such as exhibition space at the event or advertising in the event documentation.
- **Invitations and bookings:** attendance at some events is by invitation and some by response to advertising in different forms. Where this is by invitation, invitees must be recorded to determine who responded and who did not. Bookings can be self-served, for example people booking themselves on the event via the organisation's website, or the data can be entered by staff. Bookings can be complex, for example you must be able to:
  - book a single event at a time;
  - book several events at the same time;
  - book multiple attendees at the same time (some may be named and on the database, others may be named and not on the database and others may not be named);
  - maintain waiting lists for events that are full and for sessions that are full;
  - do cancellations and transfers to other events;
  - document and allow for special requirements such as diet and disability requirements;
  - create and distribute acknowledgements and other delegate information by post or email.
- **Reserved tickets:** the ability to manage sale-or-return tickets sent to agents and other interested parties, and also complimentary tickets sent to sponsors and VIPs.

- **Ticketing:** admission to events and sessions within events is sometimes by ticket only, so tickets must be printed, distributed and monitored as delegates arrive.
- **Seat planning:** some events, such as an annual dinner, require table plans and seat allocation. Automatic system allocation, delegate self-allocation and individual allocation by staff, preferably via a drag and drop facility, along with visual seat representation is required by some organisations.
- **Travel and accommodation:** some events require the organisation to make and manage travel arrangements and accommodation arrangements for the delegates. This involves liaising with third parties such as travel companies and hotels and checking, monitoring and paying their invoices. This liaison with third parties can also be required for other things such as outings.
- **Event reporting:** this is the production of on-the-day reports (badge labels, delegate lists, session lists), and after-event reports (attendees, income and expenditure).

Abstract management

This is the process of managing abstracts of authors' papers or presentations for an event and planning the event sessions and the content. It can also be extended to cover the management of the entire session content (as opposed to just abstracts) and to the production of the event programme. Facilities are required to record details of the authors, their papers and/or presentations, reviewers and their comments, acceptance or rejection, and searching by author, subject, keyword and event.

15.4.5 Financial management

Financial management is a major functionality grouping in a not-for-profit CRM system primarily because the processing of income in the sector is complex. Some income is processed as a result of a response to an invoice but very few payments made will have been invoiced. Sophisticated input and control procedures are necessary, therefore, especially as there are so many different ways in which customers can make payments to the organisation. And it is not just income; there is also expenditure to consider.

The major functional groupings in this section are: multi-currency handling, invoicing, income processing, acknowledgements, expenditure processing, refunds reversals and transaction amendments, financial history and financial ledgers.

Multi-currency

Many not-for-profit organisations receive income in different currencies, euros and US dollars being the most common. Some organisations maintain accounts within the CRM system in multiple currencies so the system needs to be able to record income in different currencies separately. Most organisations, however, record transactions only in sterling but have to accept and process foreign currency income. There are three methods of dealing with this which depend on the individual organisation. The first is simply not to enter the income into the system until such time as it has been converted to sterling at the bank. The second is to enter it as a currency amount and then enter the sterling amount after it has been converted by the bank. The third is to maintain a currency conversion table within the system, enter the currency amount and the system converts it immediately, and has a process for dealing with the small differences that occur when the currency is converted by the bank. Whichever system is used, it is good practice to thank the customer in their own currency.

Some not-for-profit organisations also pay out money in foreign currencies, such as for the payment of grants to overseas beneficiaries, so processes are required for the converse of foreign income.

Invoicing

Some systems pass details of sales orders to a financial accounting system for the production and management of invoices, and indeed some not-for-profit organisations prefer this way of operating. However, the production and management of invoices within the CRM system is the method preferred by most organisations with invoice details passed to the sales ledger within the finance system if required. Most invoices are produced as a consequence of product sales, as defined earlier in 15.4.1. However, there are sometimes cases where invoices are required by individuals or organisations for some of the functionality in sub-sections of other major not-for-profit CRM functionality groupings, such as corporate sponsorship under fundraising, subscriptions under membership management and event attendance under event management. Consequently, invoicing appears here as a sub-section of financial management.

Income processing

This is the most complex functional grouping within the financial management section. The first sub-grouping is payment methods, which describes the different types of income. Then the sub-groups follow that encompass processes for simple income entry, simple batch income entry, entry of income via controlled batch procedures, the handling of at least seven different types of income, Gift Aid reclaims, the handling of VAT, the process of 'soft credits', standing orders and direct debits.

- **Payment methods:** this is simply a list of the types of income that can be accepted by the organisation. They are many and varied and require several procedures to process them. Income can be in the form of cash, postal orders, cheques, credit cards, debit cards, bank direct credits, standing orders, direct debits, charity cards, and charity vouchers.
- **Simple income entry:** when a small number of income items are received on a single day they can be entered to the system by searching for the customer record and entering the income details one at a time against the customer with minimal formality.
- **Simple batch income entry:** known as 'end-of-day batching'. It is the creation of a batch of income transactions, entered singly, since the last time it was requested (at the end of the day, for instance), with the system calculating the number of items and the total value.
- **Regular batch income entry:** many not-for-profit organisations, especially the larger ones, receive hundreds of income items in the mail, over the telephone, via files imported from the website, from fulfilment agencies, etc. every day. Very few of these items will have been expected; that is, very few will have been invoiced. Therefore, control procedures are required to manage the process of data entry, protect against data entry errors and to prevent fraud. These procedures consist of collecting the items into batches of usually 20 to 50 items and pre-processing them by adding the income values and producing control totals that are checked when the entry of each batch is complete. (A control total is the sum of the numbers in a specified record field of a batch of items; it allows the person entering the batch of income items, and the computer, to know how many items are in the batch and their total value so that any discrepancies from the control will be flagged up as errors.)
- **Income entry:** different processes are required for each type of income. The types include cash, cheques, credit cards, debit cards, vouchers (there can be many different types of vouchers that are sent to different agencies for encashment), standing orders, direct debits and direct bank credits.
- **Gift Aid reclaims:** some organisations post Gift Aid reclaim amounts against the donor at the time that the claim file for HMRC is generated. Other organisations hold the file of reclaim amounts in suspense and run a batch function to post these reclaim amounts against the donors when the payment is received from HMRC.
- **VAT:** when the not-for-profit organisation produces invoices for goods and services, some items attract VAT and some do not, and so procedures are required to account for VAT.
- **Soft credits:** the process of recording the same income items against more than one customer. The customer sending the money has the 'real' income recorded

against their record and the other customer has the same income recorded against their record as a 'soft credit' which is specially marked and not taken into account when reporting actual money. Some examples of soft crediting are in memoriam donations where money is given in memory of a deceased person, and gift membership where one customer pays another customer's membership fees and the second customer receives all the membership benefits as if they had personally paid for it. Special processes are required to ensure financial integrity and that income is not counted twice.

- **Manual banked direct income entry:** the entry, manually from bank statements, of *ad hoc* income received direct into the bank. The process is similar to regular batch income entry.
- **Manual standing order entry:** the entry of *regular* income received direct into the bank manually from bank statements, usually using a process of 'standing batches' where batches of income items can be reproduced each month and any necessary adjustments made for any new items or missing items.
- **Automated standing order entry:** the ability to import standing order transaction files provided by the bank and apply the transactions to the appropriate committed giving records associated with customers. Processes are required to handle missing or unexpected transactions.
- **Direct debits and credit card revolving authorities:** the ability to generate direct debit files for the bank and apply the transactions to the appropriate committed giving records associated with customers. Also, the organisation may need to be able to set up and manage paperless direct debits and apply the various feedback files provided by the bank to the database.

Acknowledgements

In almost every instance, once a financial transaction has been processed, an acknowledgement is sent to the person or organisation making the payment. This is normally in the form of a word-processed thank-you letter or a formal receipt or sometimes both. The exceptions to this rule are for regular payments, standing orders, direct debits and payroll giving, where a single acknowledgement is usually sent on the setting up of the regular commitment and then once per year. Recording of the acknowledgements against customer records is important in order to complete the relationship cycle.

Expenditure processing

Many not-for-profit organisations wish to record expenditure within their CRM system. Typical examples are payments of grants to beneficiaries or volunteers' expenses. Facilities are required to enter these transactions singly or in batches. Batches are often created automatically by a regular process that searches for all due payments. Much of the functionality is identical to income entry but instead it creates negative transactions. An additional feature may be required for grants because you need to enter the total liability for the grant (that is the total amount to be paid to the beneficiary over a period of time) to the finance system and then allocate individual instalments as they are paid, thus reducing the liability.

Refunds reversals and transaction amendments

Functions are required for:

- refunds where the money has been banked and the customer requests the return of their money;
- reversals of income where a payment fails to complete for any reason, for instance a bounced cheque or non-approved credit card transaction;
- changes to transactions after they have been entered such as where the income was allocated to the wrong customer or allocated to the wrong campaign code.

Financial history

Detailed recording of all financial transactions, including refunds and reversals, is a fundamental requirement (along with the recording of all non-financial communications) of relationship management. The details must include when, how much, why, for what purpose and in response to what campaign or other stimulus.

Financial ledgers

Most not-for-profit CRM systems have the functionality to integrate with financial accounting systems: usually the nominal ledger, but sometimes the sales and purchase ledgers as well. However, some systems incorporate the functionality associated with a traditional sales ledger to enable the full financial control of income within a single system. An even smaller number contain the functionality of purchase and nominal ledgers as well, thus obviating the need for a separate financial accounting system.

15.5 SERVICE-RELATED FUNCTIONALITY

These are the functional groups that relate to the provision of services (as opposed to products) to the organisation's customers. The section consists of general service functions (exactly as per commercial organisations) and functions related solely to the organisation's beneficiaries (i.e. the functions on which the organisation's funds are expended).

The areas to be considered under service-related functionality are service and beneficiary services, as listed in Chapter 11.

15.5.1 **Service**

The service section covers activities where the not-for-profit organisation provides a service, usually (but not always), free of charge to the customer. These services revolve mainly around the concept of a call centre or service centre, although the not-for-profit terminology is usually a helpline or an advice line. Prerequisites for managing a call centre are customer communication history logging (see below) and a computerised knowledge base. Customer complaints are often handled and recorded separately from other call centre activities. To provide more information on individual customers and to add to the knowledge base in general, surveys and questionnaires need to be managed.

Call centre (aka help line, advice line and information centre)

The prime function is to respond to telephone or email (or even printed letter) complaints or requests for information or action. This demands fast access to customer records, often via screen popping where the customer's record is automatically displayed on screen when they telephone the organisation, plus quick access to all relevant information (see 'Knowledge base' below). Also required is the ability to capture call durations and notes related to the calls and their outcomes. In addition, details of anonymous calls need to be recorded for analysis purposes (such as the average call duration or number of calls per subject). Note that screen popping may seem like a luxury to many people but it goes to the very heart of relationship management. It enables you to have immediate access to all customer information – no more asking people their name and postcode in order to find their record and no more asking people to repeat things that they have often told you before.

Complaints handling

Some organisations require the facility to record and manage complaints against the organisation separately from all other communications recording (although the actual processes are the same).

Communication history tracking or logging

The most important requirement is to have immediate access to every previous communication with the customer, whether initiated by the customer or by the organisation.

Knowledge base management

It is essential for call centre staff to have fast access to all information about the organisation itself and the processes that might be needed to answer customer queries. This entails the storage and searching of structured and unstructured information. This information is normally contained within documents such as organisational brochures, policy statements, newsletters, project reports, meeting minutes, etc.

Service scheduling

This activity is related to some product sales and to equipment loans and involves a predetermined schedule of servicing events with assigned dates, assigned service representatives, reminders, actions, and records of faults and remedies, call-backs and sign-offs on jobs.

Surveys and questionnaires

Questionnaires are an important source of information for any organisation. They are of two main types: personal information and opinions. The former are used to gather previously unknown information about customers and the latter are used to find out the customers' reactions to the organisation's activities, such as feedback on an event they attended. Care needs to be exercised with this facility. If the purpose of the survey is to gather opinions and statistics and there is no need to store the responses against individual customers then this should be kept out of the CRM system. The facility is only relevant when it is important to gather and record personal information. When used, the facilities required will enable you to:

- define questions and a new data set in the database (linked to customers) to capture the responses;
- select who will receive the questionnaire;
- publish the questionnaire (by mail or email, calling people using a telephone list, or via the website);
- capture the data responses quickly;
- analyse the results.

15.5.2 **Beneficiary services**

Beneficiary services includes all the processes that relate to just one specific group of customers: the beneficiaries of the not-for-profit organisation. This represents where the money raised is spent or distributed to, and as such is fundamentally different from the general concept of service within traditional CRM as described in Chapter 3. These subsets are fund management, case studies, grant-making, project management and sponsorship, case management, and other beneficiary services.

Fund management

Fund management within beneficiary services is comparable to campaign management within marketing. Funds in this context are designations for where income (money) will be spent. Confusion can occur between the use of the word 'funds' in this context and the use of the word funds meaning money in general and, particularly, income. Consequently other terms such as 'earmarks', 'restrictions' or 'destinations', are sometimes used.

A campaign represents the *source* of money and a fund represents the *destination* or use of the money. In most instances the objective of a campaign is to raise funds for a specific purpose, therefore the fund (destination) can be inferred from the campaign code. However, this is not always the case and the two concepts of campaigns and funds have to be managed independently. In a similar way to campaign management, fund management usually consists of a multi-level hierarchy (often funds/projects/sub-projects). Data associated with any and every level of the structure includes income and expenditure targets (or budgets), and actual income received. Expenditure made is often split over calendar or financial years.

Case studies

This is the maintenance of details of beneficiary case studies or stories that can be used to assist in marketing initiatives. These case studies will be part of the knowledge base of the organisation and will often be linked to the appropriate customers or beneficiaries who are happy to tell their own story as part of the marketing.

Grant-making

The grant-making process has three main areas of functionality: maintaining grant programmes, handling applications and making payments.

- **Maintaining grant programmes:** the setting up of basic details such as the types of grants to be made, the number of grants to be awarded, the funds from which the grants will be drawn, the amounts to be awarded and the conditions that will apply. In some cases it can be a series of linked grants where a beneficiary can apply for one grant and then on completion of certain activities apply for a different grant. In some cases it can be matched funding whereby the organisation is only matching other external funding provided by other organisations.
- **Handling applications:** this entails managing the application and an approval or rejection process. This will be a series of linked tasks (requiring a flexible 'workflow' tool) that need to be completed; for example: check application form for completeness and accuracy, send to referees for approval, put to an awards panel, communicate decision to applicant, etc.

- **Managing grants and making payments:** once an award has been made then payments are calculated and made according to a predefined schedule. Conditions often have to be met before each payment is made, such as a project report received.

Project management and sponsorship

These are processes to set up, manage and monitor projects that the organisation is carrying out or for which it is paying. This requires data to be maintained on start dates, end dates, activities, resources, costs and progress. Specific funders can often be linked to the projects. This is where a funder is paying for a particular project or element of a project and receives reports on progress, for example a developing world education project where an individual funder is paying for the primary education of an individual child. Facilities are required to allow multiple funders per project and to allow a funder to sponsor multiple projects. Other requirements are the management of and payments to third parties who may be undertaking some of the activities.

Case management

This is the management of activities related to individual beneficiaries who may be receiving a variety of support, not just financial. The main functions are: the recording of documents (incoming and outgoing) which may be confidential, such as medical records; the use of a calendar function for appointments, referrals and treatments; setting links with professional people such as doctors and social workers; and the recording of progress and outcomes. This is all the basics of standard CRM, but it is drawn together into a separate place because it is usually highly sensitive and confidential information, rather than information available for general use within the organisation.

Other beneficiary services

There are innumerable other functional areas that could be considered under the heading of beneficiary services because of the diverse nature of the not-for-profit sector. They are listed here because they are fundamentally important to the organisations that require them but they will not be described in any detail because they have a limited audience and consequently should not be considered within a generic not-for-profit CRM functionality set. Some of those areas are: coaching and umpiring, financial loans, fostering and adoption, equipment loans and distributions, holiday bookings, housing management, patient administration, wish granting, sports facilities management, time booking, and welfare control. The list is almost endless because of the diverse nature of the sector.

15.6 **SYSTEMS INTEGRATION**

When considering the best of breed software (see also 10.6), it is important that not-for-profit CRM systems have all the relevant integration facilities built in. They should ideally cater for the organisation's individual choice of such systems where there are competing products in the particular functional area. For example, it is far from ideal if an organisation already uses a particular address management system within another application but their chosen CRM supplier only provides integration with a different address management system. They will be faced with additional expenditure to get the CRM supplier to develop a new interface or alternatively purchase a second address management system. The integration of these specialist and best of breed systems with the main not-for-profit CRM system needs to be seamless from the users' point of view. They need to feel that they are using a single complete system. Compromises such as re-keying an account number or a postcode into a separate screen are unacceptable.

The areas to be considered under systems integration are: other types of CRM, standard systems and optional systems (as listed in table 11.3). This group of categories covers functionality that is not always provided directly by the CRM system itself but with which the CRM system requires links. It represents functionality that is required by the CRM system but where specialist software already exists, so integration with these systems is usually (but not always) preferred to redeveloping the facilities within the CRM system. There are three types or levels of integration. These are integration between the main database (the operational CRM system) and the following systems:

- **Other types of CRM:** websites (a subset of collaborative CRM) and analysis and marketing systems (analytical CRM).
- **Standard systems:** systems in common usage that could be considered to be standard. These are information systems areas that can be considered as well-defined domains in their own right (or as sub-domains of CRM), for example office systems (such as Microsoft Office), addressing software, and banking or card payment systems.
- **Optional systems:** systems for areas that can be considered as well-defined domains in their own right (or as sub-domains of CRM) but which many not-for-profit organisations (particularly the smaller and medium-sized organisations) often do not require at all or for which they require a lesser level of functionality than the larger organisations. (Typical examples include sales order processing and stock control, legacy administration, and event and conference management systems.) In these instances, the larger organisations will require integration with these systems and the small or medium-sized organisations will be satisfied with the basic facilities developed by CRM system suppliers.

15.6.1 **Other types of CRM**

Collaborative CRM (in reality, websites)

Integration of the CRM system with the organisation's website is of vital importance to every not-for-profit organisation in order to allow customers to carry out a variety of functions on the web such as make donations, renew their membership, buy products or book places on events. This integration can be of four different types (as described in 14.6):

- Import and export of batch data files. (This method is long-winded and tedious.)
- Provision of fixed-format web forms or modules by the database supplier that can be accessed by simple links on the existing website. These web forms are implemented utilising the organisation's website style sheets in order to give the appearance of being an integral part of the website.
- An API (application programming interface) supplied by database supplier and used by the web developer to design web forms in any way they wish and send data to and extract data from the organisation's main database.
- Direct access by the web developer into the database (technically this can be done but it is not a good idea).

A small number of not-for-profit CRM system suppliers provide a single CRM system that incorporates within it a complete CMS (content management system). This means that the organisation can not only design its own web forms related to the database but also create a complete website that incorporates the forms that feed data to the main database and accept data from the database directly (as described in 14.6).

The majority of suppliers prefer a less direct approach where they have a web database which is separate from the main organisational database. These two databases then exchange and synchronise data at regular intervals or as and when requested. Some not-for-profit organisations require the facility to check and approve (or not) the data coming from the website before allowing it to update the main database. This is commonly called a 'gatekeeper' function but is probably not necessary (see also '1, 2 or 3 circles?' under 7.7.2).

Analytical CRM (analysis, marketing and campaign management systems)

All operational CRM systems will contain some degree of data analysis and campaign management functionality, but many organisations, particularly the larger ones, require a high degree of sophistication and functionality that is the domain of specialist systems. An example would be when they require such facilities as data mining (see 'Analytics and data mining' under 15.3.2) and predictive modelling, for example to generate 'true' (i.e. sophisticated estimations of) lifetime values for customers (see 16.5.2). As the underlying data structures of analytical systems are completely different from those of operational CRM systems, integration of the two consists of exporting data from the operational CRM system, manipulating it to conform with the data structures of the analytical system and the importing it to that system. This process is known as ETL (extract, transform and load).

15.6.2 Standard systems

There are number of systems areas that can be considered to be standard containing facilities that every not-for-profit organisation needs. There are several leading suppliers which provide systems in each of these areas, rendering the development of such facilities unnecessary by the operational CRM system suppliers. Consequently, every operational CRM system should integrate all (or most) of them. These systems areas are listed below.

- **Office software** (usually Microsoft Office): integration with Microsoft Word for producing ad hoc and mail-merged letters, Microsoft Excel for reports, graphs and further data analysis, and Outlook for sending and receiving emails, and managing tasks and calendars, is essential. In theory, this could be integration with any office suite, including open-source alternatives, but the vast majority of not-for-profit organisations use Microsoft products.
- **Bulk email:** Microsoft Outlook is considered by many not-for-profit organisations to be lacking in feedback features and inadequate in performance for large numbers of emails, so integration with other third-party email management systems is preferred for the bulk emailing of several thousand and more.
- **Address management:** there is specialist software to manage addresses and the CRM system must be able to integrate with this software. Among many more facilities, when a house number and a postcode is provided to the system, this software can return a full address or determine which political constituency or NHS district an address is in. The companies providing this software supply regular updates so that the data is accurate when entered and kept accurate during its lifetime in the CRM system.
- **Geographic mapping:** linking to mapping software allows organisations to see on a map exactly where their customers are located. From there they can target their marketing campaigns geographically.
- **Telephony** (CTI: computer telephony integration): some organisations have linked, or wish to link, their CRM system to their telephone system. This allows users to click on a link and have the system dial the telephone number (auto-dial) and have the system display the caller's CRM record immediately when they telephone the organisation (screen popping).

- **EPOS** (electronic point of sale): these are specialised systems for managing traditional sales transactions from shops, which are usually based on electronic tills.
- **Banking and credit card systems:** there is specialist software for organisations to find bank addresses from sort codes, check the validity of bank account numbers, perform credit card authorisations, send data to and receive data from banks, etc.
- **Financial accounting:** a very small number of not-for-profit CRM systems provide a full set of financial ledgers (sales, purchase and nominal) within their system, whereas almost all not-for-profit organisations use one of the many industry-standard financial accounting systems such as Sage, Sun, Microsoft Great Plains and Access Accounts. Consequently, the CRM system is required to transfer details of income (and in some cases, expenditure) in detail or summary form to these systems. There are a few variations, for example where the CRM database takes the place of the sales ledger, or where purchase ledger information is fed back into the CRM system to allow for return on investment calculations to be performed for marketing campaigns.
- **Report writing:** although all CRM systems will have a set of pre-programmed standard reports, system users will always require additional reports, the need for which can arise at any time in the lifetime of the system. Consequently, facilities are required to build these reports from scratch and also to allow existing standard reports to be modified.

15.6.3 **Optional systems**

Many operational CRM systems contain functionality for some or even all of the areas listed below. However, in some systems this functionality is rather basic and many not-for-profit organisations require more sophisticated functionality. This is provided in the available best of breed software.

- **Sales order processing:** for the selling and invoicing of products and services, often where complex discount structures are involved or where bill of materials (i.e. the parts of any given product) parts explosion (where one product contains other products which contain yet other products), is required.
- **Stock control:** to monitor stock levels and to ensure that stocks of products (and parts of products) are always available.
- **Sales ledger:** managing the invoices produced by the CRM system or a separate invoicing system, monitoring payments received and chasing late payments. Some CRM systems will assume the payment is or will be received as soon as the invoice is produced whereas others require a communication from the sales ledger to tell it when the payment is received.
- **Legacy administration:** a major area within the fundraising grouping under the major heading of sales-related functionality. However, there is specialist legacy administration software which is considered to be best of breed by many

legacy managers. Consequently, some organisations wish to use it and therefore a level of integration between it and the main CRM system is required.

- **Media systems:** similar to legacy administration, there are a number of specialist systems that maintain an up-to-date database of media organisations (newspapers, magazines, radio, and television) and people within those organisations. Consequently, some organisations also wish to use one of these systems and have some level of integration with the main CRM database.
- **Raffle management:** to monitor ticket books, tickets, ticket sellers, ticket distribution and raffle winners.
- **Lottery management:** to monitor lottery players, collectors, rounds and payments, select winners and print cheques and winner lists.
- **Event and conference management:** specialist systems to manage all aspects of setting up and running events of all types.
- **Survey software:** for defining, distributing and collecting results, and analysing the results of surveys and questionnaires.
- **Call centre management:** specialist systems for information and helpline management which include call allocation to operatives, call timing, call monitoring and outcome recording.
- **Case management:** to manage all aspects of support for beneficiaries including assessment, document management, appointments, calendar functions, professional links, referrals and progress.
- **Grant-making:** specialist systems to maintain grant programmes, track applications for grants and make payments once grants have been awarded.
- **Project management:** to monitor all details and activities of projects, including project types, locations, dates, staff, activities, resources, costs and progress.
- **Volunteer management:** to monitor volunteers' skills, training, availability and activities, and payments to volunteers.
- **Other systems:** some CRM systems allow links and data exchanges with other (less often required) specialist systems that are based on customers in the broadest sense, i.e. any data based on names and addresses. Examples of such systems which are commonly seen are ticketing, patient tracking and subscriptions.

Specialist systems for people with disabilities, such as screen readers, will require integration and need to be compatible with the CRM system.

16 Analytical CRM

16.1 INTRODUCTION

The purpose of analytics is to enable the organisation to make better and more effective marketing decisions. If you can target the right message at the right customers at the right time via the right medium, then you can improve your response rates, decrease your costs and increase your return on investment.

Analytical CRM is where you turn data into knowledge. Using analytics will help you to understand your customers' behaviour better so that you can predict their future behaviour better. However, all this comes at a cost, in terms of time, money and system complexity. The ability to use analytics effectively is a specialist job and there is a lack of understanding, generally speaking, within not-for-profit management of how to use analytics to improve the business. Do not approach the subject lightly!

The point has been made before and it will be made again here because it is so important: *you cannot do serious analytics on a traditional operational CRM database* (irrespective of what any CRM database suppliers may tell you). You need a data warehouse type of data structure – a central repository of data collected from many sources which is specifically designed for effective and efficient reporting and analysis – to carry out all but the simplest of data analysis. Therefore, you need a separate analytical CRM database, more commonly known simply as a 'marketing database'.

In the world of analytics, buzzwords and phrases you might come across are: business intelligence, business insight, data mining, data modelling, customer modelling, predictive modelling, probability distributions, demographic profiling, geodemographic profiling, the list goes on. In addition, there are all the statistical tools and techniques that you might hear about, such as scatter diagrams, standard deviation, linear regression, non-linear regression, multiple regression, time series analysis, statistical decision theory, analysis of variance (ANOVA), chi-square tests, the list goes on. And, on top of all these, there are pseudo-technical terms that will be thrown at you, such as data cubes, online analytical processing (OLAP), data warehouse, data mart, extract transform and load (ETL), middleware, again the list goes on.

Do you feel daunted yet? If so, you are not alone. This really is a specialist area and it is not the purpose, or even the place, of this book to describe many of the things mentioned above in any detail. However, some of these terms have been explained in the previous chapters, and the following sections describe in the briefest possible terms some of the techniques that many not-for-profit organisations have found useful. (And in some cases this will provide a recap on terms which have already been introduced.) The purpose of this is to help you to think about what might be relevant and useful for your organisation.

The complexity of the techniques mentioned below increases with each section of the chapter. We start with the reporting of standard management information, move on to some relatively simple analysis tools and techniques, then to more sophisticated analysis, and lastly to the final goal of analytics: data modelling and prediction of future customer behaviour. It is fair to say that the majority of not-for-profit organisations have neither the volume nor the depth of data required to do the things listed below under the heading of 'More sophisticated analysis' (16.4). It is also likely that, because of capacity issues, they do not have a complete or even a realistic understanding of the subject area. In addition, an organisation needs to be careful not to over-resource or complicate this area. You might find that it is a case of the tail wagging the dog, where lots of energy goes into the analysis, which in turn pushes operational CRM changes, but it doesn't alter or improve the marketing and donations by an equivalent amount. Tread with care and take one step at a time.

16.2 MEASUREMENT AND MANAGEMENT INFORMATION

16.2.1 Standard reporting

The starting point for analytical CRM is the simple reporting of facts, such as how a campaign performed, how much money came in, when it came in and who it came from. This area was dealt with in 'Query, reporting and analysis' (15.2.2) and is mentioned here for the sake of completeness, as these facts are the raw material of analytics. Even without sophisticated analytics, valuable information can be obtained, such as which campaigns work better than others and where money would be better spent in future.

16.2.2 Pivot tables

Moving on slightly from standard reports, pivot tables are a method of summarising data in a variety of ways. The same base data (used in standard reporting), usually presented in a flat table form like a spreadsheet, can be sorted, counted, totalled and averaged on a number of variables quickly and easily using drag and drop facilities. Sophisticated users of spreadsheets will already be familiar with the technique. It is an ideal way of looking very quickly at campaign results from a number of viewpoints. For example, you might initially look at income by date, and then, at the click of a mouse, income by region, or income by payment method, mail pack or channel.

16.3 SIMPLE ANALYSIS TOOLS AND TECHNIQUES

16.3.1 Pareto analysis

Pareto analysis, which has been mentioned several times in this book, is named after Vilfredo Pareto (1848–1923). It is the old 80:20 rule, and is (or certainly should be) a standard report in any CRM system. Unfortunately, this is not always the case! This function calculates the total income from each customer, ranks the customers in order of their total income, splits the ranked customers into 'deciles' or customer groups, where each decile is 10% of the customer base, and finally reports the percentage of total organisational income associated with each decile (see a charity example in figure 16.1).

If you have a really good system, you should be able to display the report on screen and drill down on each decile to either display, report (i.e. print) or export a list of the customers in the selected decile (customer group), and further drill down to open the record of any customer in the decile. Each decile, or group, of customers can then be selected for different treatment for marketing purposes. Note that some people work on the basis of half-deciles (or semi-deciles), i.e. each half decile is 5% of the customer base, which makes 20 groups of customers rather than 10. Smaller groups can give a more detailed picture. This has to be balanced against the extra work required to manage them.

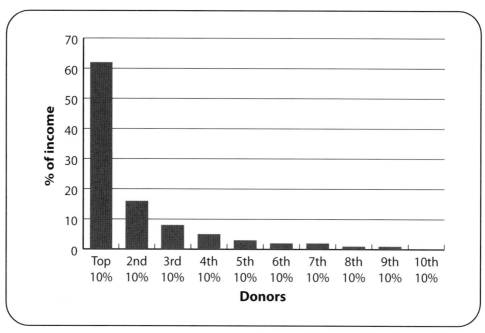

Fig. 16.1 Example Pareto analysis

16.3.2 **RFV: recency, frequency , value analysis (or RFM: recency, frequency, monetary value)**

This is a much more flexible tool than Pareto analysis. Firstly, it allocates customers to a number of bands (usually three or five) depending on the date of their last payment (recency). You can choose the time intervals.

Secondly, it allocates customers to a number of bands depending how many times they have bought from you or given to you (frequency). Note that this is not the number of times in a given period, as you might expect from the word frequency, but the total number of income items received. Again, you can choose the width of each band.

Thirdly, it allocates customers to a number of bands according to the total value of their payments to date (value). Again, you can choose the width of each band.

Figure 16.2 shows an example for a charity of the bands for recency, frequency and value taken one at a time.

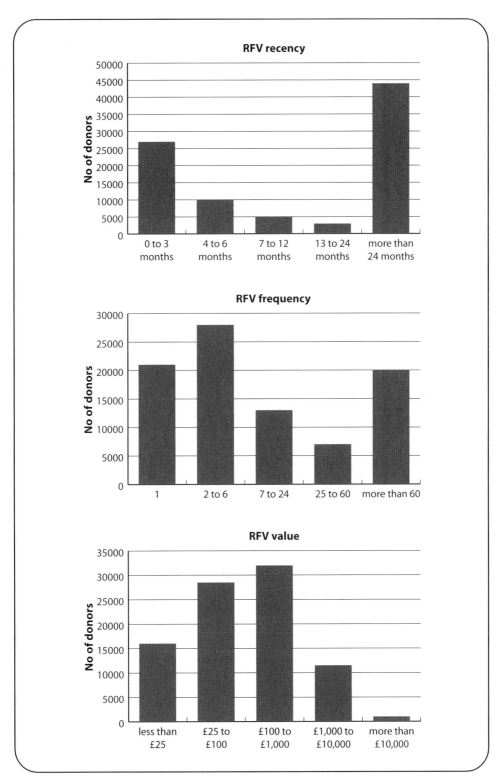

Fig. 16.2 Example single dimension RFV analysis

Once customers are allocated to a band in each of the designations, recency, frequency and value, you can examine combinations of recency, frequency and value (such as recency and frequency; recency and value; frequency and value). See figure 16.3 for an example of one combination. Note that this gives you 25 blocks or segments of data to examine. If you can cope with the concept of data in three dimensions, then you can consider recency, frequency and value all together, but you will have 125 separate blocks or segments of data to look at!

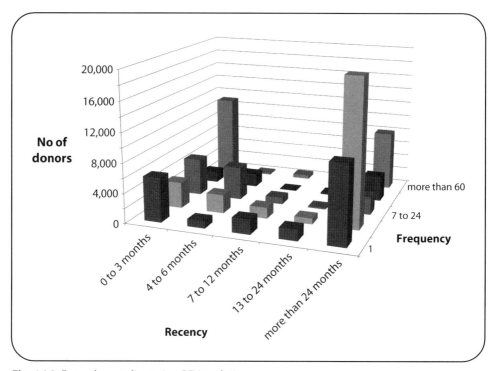

Fig. 16.3 Example two dimension RFV analysis

'Scores' can be allocated to each recency band, each frequency band and each value band so that every customer ends up with three scores which are often added together to give a total RFV value. For example, you could allocate the numbers 1 to 5 to each band depending on the importance of the band. So in the example above, for recency you could allocate 5 points to 0 to 3 months, 4 points to 4 to 6 months, 3 points to 7 to 12 months, 2 points to 13 to 24 months and 1 point to more than 24 months. Doing this your total RFV value (or score) will range from 3 to 15. This is the simplest system and you can make it far more complex if you wish. This is an advance on Pareto analysis, which simply looked at total value, because in the case of RFV you could find that a customer who bought (or gave) little and often ends up with a higher score than the person who has bought or given one single large amount. You can tailor the width of the bands and the scores in order to decide which customers are worth the most to you.

As with Pareto analysis, a good system will allow you, after creating the analysis, to drill down to the customers that are in each individual band or band combination so that you can treat the customers in each one separately.

16.3.3 Profiling

Profiling is the process of identifying the characteristics of a group of customers. For example, what is a typical person who attends events like? What are the characteristics of a committed giver? Any number of variables can be examined, such as age, gender, interests and location, in order to construct different profiles of your customers. There are numerous reasons for doing this, which include identifying:

- the similarities between customers in a specified group;
- the differences between customers in different groups;
- target groups outside the organisation's customer base in order to obtain more customers;
- who your most valuable customers are;
- why they are customers;
- those customers who are likely to remain customers and those who are likely to defect;
- the likelihood of specific groups of customers to respond to your appeals.

16.3.4 Clustering or cluster analysis

Clustering is taking a set of data and grouping values together depending on how close together they are numerically and showing them in a diagrammatic form. In simple terms, you can do things such as plotting on a map the location of people who responded to a particular campaign or plotting the location of your biggest customers. Cluster analysis can consist of simple scatter diagrams (see 16.5.7) or incredibly complex models requiring complex equations to explain them. At the more technical level there are various types of clustering models you can build such as K-means clustering, density-based clustering, and distribution-based clustering (but explaining these models is beyond the scope of this book).

16.3.5 Segmentation

Profiling and clustering leads on to segmentation where you group customers with similar characteristics together and then market to them and monitor them as a group. Note the difference between segmentation and selection (as outlined within 15.3.2): selection is merely choosing a set of customers that meet specified criteria, whereas segmentation is taking that selection and treating that set of customers as a group over a period of time.

16.4 MORE SOPHISTICATED ANALYSIS

This is where you really get to the point of needing a specialist analysis system/database/data warehouse (and specialist data analysts to make it happen and make sense of the results).

16.4.1 Data cubes

RFV is just one specialised example of a data cube (otherwise known as online analytical processing or OLAP). A data cube is just that: a cube. It is a three-dimensional array of data (see figure 16.4 for a simple representation based on recency, frequency and value where the data value in each small cube or cell is the number of customers. Note that there is such a thing as a hypercube which has more than three dimensions, but we won't go into this either: three is quite enough to manage.

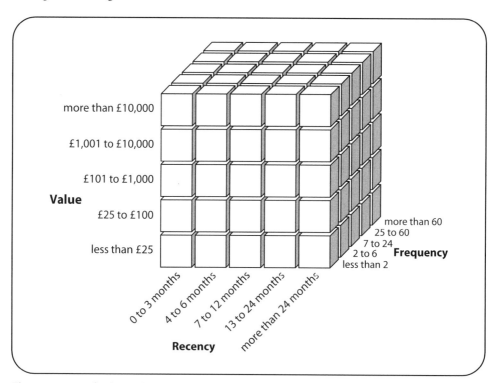

Fig. 16.4 Example data cube

A useful extension of RFV is to introduce your own variables into the mix. For example, you might replace one of the three designations, recency, frequency or value, with length of time as a customer, or with age of the customer. The latter might help you overcome one of the criticisms of RFV which is that it treats every customer as the same and takes no account of people's age or life stage (people in different age groups and at different stages of their life respond differently to marketing campaigns). The combinations you can try are almost endless.

16.4.2 Attrition analysis

Attrition rate, sometimes called 'churn', is the number of customers you lose over a given period. This needs constant monitoring. There are various formulae that can be applied to calculate attrition rates. It is easy to determine the attrition rate of monthly direct debit payers but not so easy to determine the attrition rate of ad hoc purchasers or donors. If someone hasn't bought or donated for two years, are they lost or just dormant? Here is an example formula:

attrition % = ((start position − end position)/start position) × 100

An extension of attrition rate is to predict how and when customers will be lost in the future and what effect this will have on future revenue. This leads us on to the subject of data modelling and prediction.

16.5 DATA MODELLING AND PREDICTION

16.5.1 Trend analysis

The term 'trend analysis' is often bandied about but it isn't particularly useful or precise. It is a catchy generic term for the whole subject of data modelling and prediction, for which there are many techniques, some of which will be described below in the briefest possible terms. All of the techniques take subsets of your data (usually income-related data), build pictures of it, look for patterns in it, and from that, attempt to suggest ways in which your income returns can be improved.

Note that all of these techniques need a large volume of data in order to be effective, so if you have a small database, say, fewer than 30,000 records, then you need to be very careful in interpreting the results because applying these techniques to small volumes of data can give inconsistent and misleading results.

16.5.2 Lifetime value

The first point to make here is that lifetime value does not mean the total of income to date for a customer (this is a common misconception). It means the total income to date *plus* the predicted future income from today until the point at which the customer defects, i.e. stops buying or giving, or until the customer dies. This prediction element is where it gets complicated and where specialist analysis techniques are required in order to arrive at a result that is realistic.

16.5.3 **Probability distribution**

A probability distribution is the prediction of an outcome of an event along with the probability of that outcome occurring. For example, if you spent £X on a campaign and achieved £X income, what is the probability that you will achieve twice the income if you spend twice as much? There are many types of probability distribution and they are either discrete or continuous. Discrete probability distribution concerns a countable number of values for the variable you are trying to predict. For instance, you can have 650 customers but not 650.5 customers, so the number of customers is a discrete variable. Continuous probability distribution concerns a continuous variable which can have an infinitely large number of values that are measurable, such as people's income or age. To complicate things further, there are different types of discrete probability distribution and different types of continuous distribution. This is a confusing area and is probably one to leave to the experts.

One type of probability distribution that is worth considering is the normal distribution (which is an example of a discrete probability distribution). When shown pictorially it is characterised by the bell-shaped curve (formally known as a Gaussian function) as shown in figure 16.5. In simple terms (without the clever mathematics), an example might be where the X axis represents the age of your customers, the Y axis represents the number of customers, and the area under the curve represents 100% of your customers. You can then calculate things like the mean age of your customers and the probability of any customer being in any particular age range.

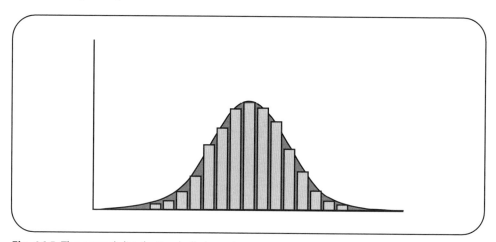

Fig. 16.5 The normal distribution bell-shaped curve

16.5.4 Chi-square tests

This is a statistical technique that tests whether variables in a set of data are independent of each other. A typical example might be testing whether putting a gift such as a free pen into an appeal mailing elicits a better response rate than no gift, or sending six different mailing packs to one individual as opposed to two. Any number of variables can be analysed.

Chi-square tests are best used to work out if something is significantly different from what you would expect. An obvious example is response rates to campaigns, but it also works well for other areas. For example, if a year's worth of marketing activity is designed to create a balance of customers, such as a balance of event participants, ad hoc donors, committed givers and so on, you can use chi-squared testing to check if what you have now is in line with expectations or if there is a significant difference.

16.5.5 Analysis of variance (ANOVA)

This is a statistical test to see if the *means* (*averages* to the layperson, although there is a difference in statistical terms that need not concern us here!) of a group of variables are the same or not. For example, it could be used to calculate whether there was a significant difference in the response rates for several different mailing packs. The layman might think that they can work out the averages and see that they are different, but to prove that the differences are *significant* requires the use of statistical equations.

16.5.6 CHAID (Chi-squared Automatic Interaction Detection)

CHAID by its very name detects the interaction between different variables in a set of data (or the relationship between the variables). Its beauty is that it can be implemented in an easily understandable graphical form – a 'decision tree' – rather than in complex equations, as is the case for chi-squared analysis. If you start your tree with the group of customers who responded to a particular campaign, you can split them into groups, say male and female, then split these two groups into other groups, such as areas of the country, and continue splitting as far as you like. Then you can easily work out which of these sub-groups had a higher (or lower) response rate than the overall response rate at the top level of the tree and tailor future campaigns accordingly. See a simple example of a CHAID tree in figure 16.6 which has been adapted from an example by statistics expert Dr Bruce Ratner. (This was not created specifically for a not-for-profit audience, but it could be directly applicable to animal welfare charities, for instance.)

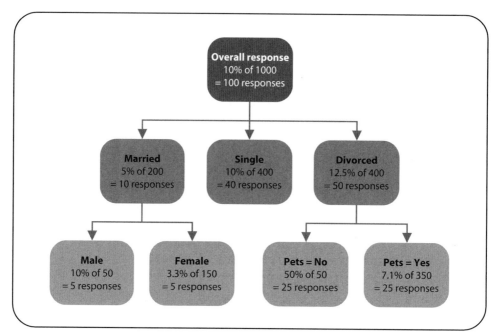

Fig. 16.6 Example CHAID tree (Ratner 2012)

From figure 16.6 you can see that the average response rate for the whole campaign was 10%, the response rate for divorced people with no pets was 50% and the response rate from married females was 3.3%. From this you can start asking questions such as 'We get the best response rate from divorced people with no pets so should we target them more often?' or 'We get a very poor response rate from married women, what are we going to do about it to improve their response rate?'. The data is there, it is up to you what you do with it.

16.5.7 Scatter diagrams, correlation and linear regression analysis

A scatter diagram is simply plotting points on a graph. These can be simple, as shown in figure 16.7, or a complex three-dimensional example, as shown in figure 16.8. From this you can start to identify groupings and relationships between the variables you have plotted. This grouping and relationship identification is called correlation and regression, the objective of which is to predict the future behaviour of your customers, such as how much an individual will give in the future based on their past performance.

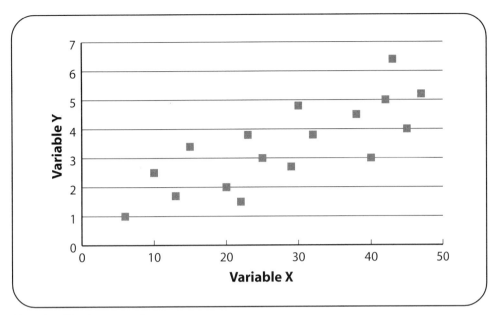

Fig. 16.7 Simple scatter diagram

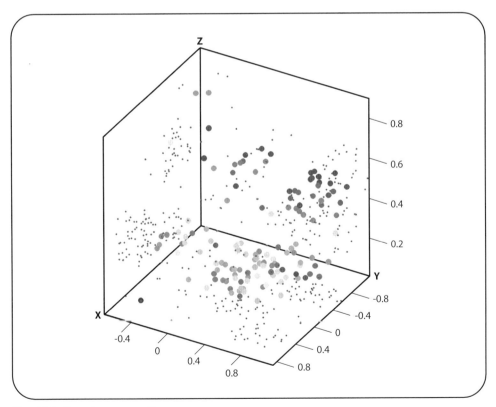

Fig. 16.8 Complex scatter diagram

Correlation and regression are not the same thing. Regression attempts to define one variable as being *dependent* on one or more other variables, whereas correlation makes no assumption of dependence between the variables (i.e. it does not presume that a change in one causes a predictable change in another) but simply tries to find the *degree of association* between the variables in question.

In figure 16.7 you can see that there is a general tendency of variable X to increase as variable Y increases. This is represented by the regression line (see figure 16.9). Some simple mathematics has been applied to the data to calculate an average line or 'line of best fit'. The general equation for this line is $x = ay + b$. From this you can predict that if you increase Y beyond 5 then you will increase X. So in the example above, if variable Y was the cost of mailing packs in £s and variable X was average donation value in £s, you can predict that if you increase the cost of the mailing pack to £7, then your average donation value should be greater than £50.

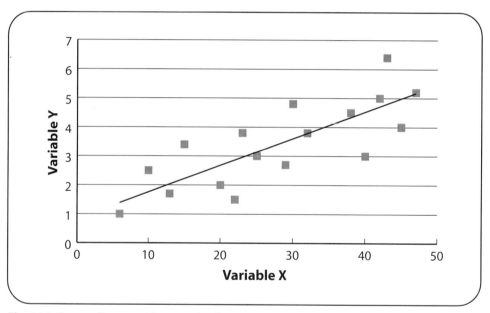

Fig. 16.9 Scatter diagram with regression line

16.5.8 **Multiple regression analysis**

Figure 16.9 shows an example of simple linear regression. This analysis is quite easy to use and very useful for predicting future behaviour if your data fits the pattern. There are such things as non-linear regression and multiple regression if the pattern of your data is more complex. For non-linear regression there are polynomial, logarithmic and power series regressions for identifying and explaining trend lines that are not straight lines. Multiple regression means adding additional variables into the mix, i.e. three-dimensional (and more) graphs. This is where things start to get very complex!

16.5.9 Time series analysis

This, as the name implies, is the study of how data changes over time. Consequently, in order to predict how data (such as income) might change in the future, first you need to provide several years of historical data in chronological order.

There are two main types of time series analysis – time series smoothing and moving averages:

- **Time series smoothing** eliminates irregular and seasonal variations (such as the big peak of charity donations at Christmas or the annual membership renewals if you are one of those organisations which renews all its memberships on a specific date) so that you can see long-term trends.
- **Moving averages** takes seasonal variations into account so that long-term trends at a more detailed level can be identified. This is directly related to regression analysis where the X axis of the graph is time and allows you to predict the outcome of individual campaigns more accurately.

Time series smoothing and moving averages predict the future and identify ways of improving your relationship with customers (and that means more income in terms of customers who are traditional sales customers, members or donors).

16.5.10 Simulations and modelling

Once you have identified correlations and carried out your regression analysis you can make models of the data where you alter one or more of the variables and see what the result would be. You can extrapolate the data in any number of ways and attempt to predict what will result in greater and better responses to campaigns. Here we get into the area of scenario planning and 'what if' analysis. For example, what would happen if you altered the media mix of your next campaign? Take care, however; this is definitely not an exact science.

16.6 A FINAL WORD ON ANALYTICS

Gaining a better understanding of your customers, predicting their future behaviour, increasing revenues, retaining customers and decreasing costs will make a huge difference to your organisation in the furtherance of its mission. Analytics can assist in every area.

Top tips for those starting out in the analytics arena

- **Ensure your data is clean and accurate:** for example, you will get little or no value analysing by type of campaign if all records that are more than three years old are coded as 'conversion from old system', because the converted data has lost the required data, in this case the campaign code. Similarly, you will get little or no value analysing by project if the all the records are coded as 'general funds' or 'restricted funds' rather than with the specific project designations.

- **Ensure you have the right data:** for example you will get little value analysing by age group if only 20% of your customer records contain their birth date.

- **Derive your analytics objectives from your business objectives:** for example don't spend inordinate amounts of time profiling current customers to attract new ones of the same type if the major business objective is to maximise revenues from current customers.

- **Start simple:** start with something you can understand and relate to rather than immediately letting the experts loose to satisfy their specialist egos. Also ensure that you start with something that can produce a measurable benefit quickly. 'Quick wins' always focus the mind and improve morale. Then you can gradually increase the sophistication level of your analytics.

- **Trial and test:** don't be afraid to get an external agency to do some trials and tests for you to prove the worth of the tools and techniques before bringing the agency in house.

The very last word on analytics is that while in one way it is the end of the cycle after you have carried out lots of marketing, made many sales (or obtained lots of donations or signed up many members), conducted lots of interactions with customers, and recorded masses of data, it is in fact just the beginning of a new marketing cycle; a cycle that will hopefully prove even more successful than the previous one.

Case study: analytics is just the beginning!

Established in 1860, Battersea Dogs and Cats Home reunites lost dogs and cats with their owners or cares for them until new homes can be found, giving them shelter and the highest standards of veterinary care. The charity is heavily reliant on the generosity of its supporters who provide gifts in wills and donations.

Battersea Dogs and Cats Home appointed Response One (a data-driven marketing agency) in August 2011 and began work on an initiative to create a new customer acquisition programme. The aim of this programme was to enable the charity to use its existing insight about its most loyal supporters and translate this into a targeting strategy to find the 'right' new supporters, i.e. those who are most likely to become long-term loyal valuable supporters for the charity. The objective was to implement a robust, structured programme that would prove the effectiveness of cold recruitment.

In order to understand Battersea Dogs and Cats Home supporters and build a rich picture of the types of people who donate, fundraise, adopt dogs and make an enquiry, Response One extracted data from all the various disparate silos of data held across the organisation and built a single view upon which to profile and build targeting models. Whilst analysing the data, Response One identified a number of key challenges:

- The data held about people who had actually donated was fairly small and would not form a robust basis for all acquisition planning, but did provide a basis for profiling to help understand who Battersea Dogs and Cats Home supporters were and their characteristics.
- The data held on 'other' activities, including enquirers, was much larger; however, it held limited information, but did include name and address.

In order to extract as much insight as possible and fully use all of the existing data available to drive targeting, Response One utilised the untapped resource of approximately 200,000 individuals who had engaged with Battersea Dogs and Cats Home in the past but the reason or recency of this contact hadn't been captured. To prioritise these individuals for inclusion in the direct mail and telemarketing campaigns, Response One produced geo-demographic profiles using Experian's MOSAIC segmentation in comparison to existing Battersea Dogs and Cats Home supporters and telemarketing responders. From these profiles selected segments were contacted.

Using its charity experience gained from working across more than 60 clients Response One built a robust test plan. Based on the analysis, campaign objective and pack type it leant heavily on the charity data.

One of the key drivers of this decision was the pack itself which was incentive-led: it included labels, calendar, cards, etc. The targeting plan had to reflect the types of responders most likely to engage with such a pack and therefore approximately 60% of data selected was charity-related. This type of data tends to be from a fairly expensive data source and to offset this cost Response One balanced the plan by adding data from Reciprocate, a data consortium run by Response One for the charity sector and containing data cheaper than lifestyle lists. Response One also used models built from its insight work to identify the supporters most likely to respond. The agency's prior experience helped it to direct the targeting strategy and it also included all obvious likely influencing factors such as 'known pet owners' or 'like pets' indicators.

Response One recommended an initial test volume of 200,000 to ensure that there was enough data to be statistically valid per cell and a base large enough to build learning upon which to grow and validate results. This volume was also large enough to allow for the testing of two pack variants. The plan utilised data from more than 25 lists. The agency also implemented a geography test by selecting the preferred target list with no geographic bias and testing if the results would be geographically representative. It overlaid results to understand if there was a South East England bias in the responses to challenge the assumption that the Battersea connection would influence giving. Results proved that there was actually no difference in performance, which is helpful insight and ensured that there was nothing restricting a UK-wide rollout.

Results

The profile data was the best performing data, outperforming the charity-specific data. Two of the top five best performing lists were modelled data, which validates the strength of the model built by Response One and allows future targeting to be less reliant on charity data. This helps to further minimise data costs and improve the return on investment.

The campaign exceeded all targets, with:

- a 27% increase in response against budget;
- a 24% increase in income v. target;
- a return on investment of 0.61.

Future strategy

The campaign has been so successful that Response One will be implementing a second test using the same volume of data but further refining the list selection. The campaign has proved the effectiveness of cold recruitment and provided valuable insight into accurate and effective targeting for rollout campaigns.

'We are delighted with the results that Response One has delivered for us at Battersea. We were so pleased that we immediately started planning our next campaign building on the learning from this one.... Early indications are that this campaign is on track to outperform the last one.' Maddy Eastwood, Direct Marketing Manager Fundraising.

Scott Logie, Strategic Marketing Director, St. Ives Group

Part five:

Setting up your CRM project

17 Where do you start?

17.1 BEFORE YOU START

Now you have a good grasp of all the principles and techniques, you can look at how to set up your CRM project. Firstly, however, here is a word of warning. When implementing CRM systems, there are pitfalls at every stage. You are unlikely to get it right. You are unlikely to ever finish it. It will be the most traumatic experience of your life! This may sound dramatic, but the statistics speak for themselves: only around one in three projects are counted as completely successful (see 8.4.1). Therefore, you must do everything possible to ensure success and take it one step at a time.

There is no such thing as an 'IT' project. There are only 'business' projects. Every project of every type within your organisation will consist of approximately equal parts of people, processes and technology. People are human, not machines. Therefore they are fallible. They have frailties, issues and opinions. They need careful management. Procedures are created by people, and as such they are never perfect. System changes mean procedural changes. Technology is almost always blamed for project failures and yet machines are dumb – they just do as they are told. And, contrary to popular belief, they seldom fail. In terms of the systems that run on the machines, they simply do what human beings program them to do. Also contrary to popular belief, they are always consistent in what they do! If you get an unexpected result, there is a human being behind it somewhere.

17.2 GENERAL IMPLEMENTATION FLOW

When considering the interaction of people, processes and technology, one way of looking at the flow of a project is as shown in figure 17.1. It looks complicated, but it isn't really.

- It all starts with senior management defining the CRM strategy, which leads to the development of CRM processes.
- Upon the decision to start a CRM project, the senior management appoints a project sponsor and sets up a project board.
- The project board then gets the users involved and appoints a project manager. (Note that although the arrows in figure 17.1 could imply the beginning and

end of involvement of any given participant, this is not intended: once a person or group of people become(s) involved, they stay involved throughout the rest of the project.)

- The users, project manager and the member of the senior management team who is the project sponsor contribute to and create the project justification. This leads to the creation of a definition of requirements. The current CRM processes, confirmed by the CRM strategy, are integrated into these requirements.
- This leads to a system selection exercise (and in some cases some system design and development). The details of the current technical infrastructure within the organisation are fed into this selection exercise. At this stage the supplier(s) become involved.
- The next stage is the technical implementation of the system or systems, and this leads to the user implementation.
- Consequently the new or amended CRM processes are developed. This requires a serious amount of change management (which many people overlook) which is overseen by the business change manager.
- This eventually leads to a successful project conclusion.

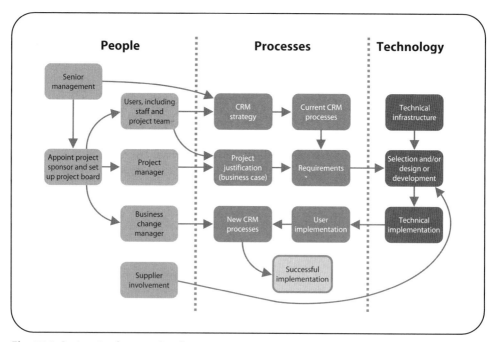

Fig. 17.1 Project implementation flow

Next we look at some of the specific issues related to people, processes and technology.

18 Management issues

18.1 PEOPLE

Although proponents for the implementation of new systems will be enthusiastic and excited about the advantages associated with the new systems (and that probably is those of you who are reading this book), they might be surprised to learn that their enthusiasm and excitement is not shared by most of the people who will be affected by the implementation of these systems. People often have a natural fear of change and consequently a natural resistance to it. Some fear that they might lose their jobs. Some fear that they won't be able to cope with the new system. Some just want what is familiar to them and do not want to learn new things. Add all of these people's fears together and you get the well-known and documented concept of 'organisational inertia'. This exits in every organisation; it is an extremely complex subject and it is difficult to overcome.

Consequently, a very large management task is required to get all staff involved in the project, feeling positive about it and working hard to make the project a success. Management must lead by example and must provide:

- a clear vision of the future (so everyone knows why it is happening);
- enthusiasm for change (so people don't feel that they are on their own);
- realistic expectations (because there will be changes);
- a description of the benefits that the system users will notice (to gain their support);
- an environment conducive to learning (so the users know that management is on their side);
- opportunities for cross-functional and cross-departmental working so people appreciate each other's challenges and issues and work together as a team;
- a listening environment and a willingness to accept staff feedback.

It is essential to have the right people doing the right jobs. You will need the following roles filled:

- **A project sponsor:** for a CRM project this *must* be the chief executive. As stated right at the beginning of this book, CRM is a complete organisational philosophy and a whole way of thinking and working. It is all encompassing and relevant to the entire organisation. Consequently, the chief executive is the only person who can allocate and approve the appropriate budget, bang heads together when necessary and lead by example. Another important aspect to the project sponsor's role is one of effective delegation and non-interference (more on this in 18.4.3).
- **Project board members:** these are chaired by the project sponsor who controls the project and make strategic decisions.
- **A project manager:** this preferably should be someone from within the organisation who knows the organisation and its people, systems and processes. However, this not always possible as people have their own day jobs, and project management is a full-time role. Whoever it is, the project manager needs to be competent, dedicated, strong-willed and a good communicator, and have an obsession with details and appropriate project experience.
- **A business change manager:** the person who is responsible for ensuring that what the project delivers is actually used and value is obtained from it. This role is part of the project team but is on a par with the project manager.
- **Project team:** usually drawn from the staff who carry out the CRM processes on a day-to-day basis. These people will carry out the project tasks.
- **Staff:** all staff who will be affected by the change of system should be involved in some manner in the entire process from beginning to end, including having involvement in the system's specification, selection, configuration and testing; receiving training in using the new system; and being involved in procedural changes and (after implementation) the operational review.
- **External support (if required):** this could be a consultant to help with the specification and system selection, a professional project manager or temporary staff to cover the jobs of existing internal staff as they are released to work on the project.

18.2 PROCESSES

System change always involves changes to processes, and indeed process changes often involve system changes. One of the major reasons for implementing new systems is to speed up or even eliminate clerical processes. This means changes to what people do on a day-to-day basis. In one large CRM implementation, 150 jobs were affected. Of these, 30 disappeared, 100 required changes and only 20 stayed the same.

Consequently, all current processes must be documented (preferably before the new system is implemented!), a review of the current processes must be undertaken and each existing process adapted, changed, eliminated or replaced in order to make the most effective use of the new system. This should involve close cooperation between the system supplier and the organisation's staff. It is not just, as some people seem to think, a case of training people in the operation of the new system. The result should be full documentation of clerical procedures related to the new system and, somewhere along the line, there should be a document that maps every process related to the old system onto the processes defined for the new system. This documentation will help people to see how the procedures have changed and will be a fundamental element in any training.

In terms of management issues, process change is so big a part of the implementation that a serious change management programme must be adopted. This is much more far-reaching than simply changing a few clerical procedures. It will also involve changes to job descriptions, and may involve redundancies and staff restructuring. This needs careful handling and is in itself reason enough for the responsibility for the project resting at the door of the chief executive.

18.3 TECHNOLOGY

As stated previously, the technology itself seldom fails. However, it is fundamentally important to get the right technology and to get the technology right. The first issue is to choose the 'right' system. This will be discussed in detail in Part 6. Don't forget when choosing systems, to consider the technical infrastructure required to operate the systems effectively.

Case studies: technology blunders

One organisation found upon implementation of its new system that it was so slow that it was impractical to use. The organisation then had to spend several thousands of pounds on a new server configuration – money that was not budgeted!

Another organisation adopted a cloud-based solution and then found that its Internet bandwidth was so low that the system was practically unusable. To make matters worse, it was impossible to obtain a faster Internet connection in their building.

207

The following points are vitally important with regard to technology:

- **Testing:** don't expect the system to just work. Test every function, run every report, try out every possible type of query. Test, test and test again. And remember to test your new clerical procedures at the same time
- **Training:** train all the staff in all the processes that they might need to use. Train them, train them and train them again. Don't expect them to pick up everything the first time around. Give them plenty of time to become familiar with the system before using it for real.
- **Change control:** if you find things that need changing, then adopt a formal change control mechanism. Don't rely on ad hoc change requests, such as asking the supplier over the telephone 'Could you just tweak this function for me?' (See also section 23.2.18.)

18.4   PROJECT MANAGEMENT

18.4.1   Formal methodologies

Some organisations will adopt formal project management methodologies such as PRINCE2 (the name is made up from PRojects IN Controlled Environments version 2) or a derivative of it, for managing large-scale implementations such as this. However, assuming you don't use such methodologies which can sometimes be overly bureaucratic and time-consuming, your project manager will (or certainly should) have created a project plan with eleven standard sections:

1. Assumptions and constraints
2. Risk assessment
3. Structure
4. Milestones
5. End products
6. Activities
7. Resources
8. Timescales
9. Monitoring mechanism
10. Controls
11. Impact analysis

For much more on planning, see Chapter 23.

Once you have set up your project (see Chapter 19) and selected your preferred system (see Chapters 21 and 22) for the implementation of the project you will have (or certainly should have) tasks or task groups for the following actions:

1. Have a kick-off meeting
2. Negotiate contracts
3. Review the project team

4. Plan the project
5. Review and implement infrastructure changes
6. Install the test system
7. Become familiar with the new system
8. Test the proof of concept
9. **Take a formal decision and sign contracts**
10. Analyse the current system
11. Extract the data from the current system(s)
12. Clean and restructure the current data
13. Undertake a process review
14. Map the current data to the new system
15. Convert the data and load it into the new system (multiple times)
16. Test the converted data (multiple times)
17. Review and implement staffing changes
18. Train those in technical and/or supervisory positions
19. Configure the system
20. Test the configuration
21. Set up standard data tables
22. Document new processes
23. Write reports
24. Define security
25. Set up users
26. Train the users
27. Undertake acceptance testing
28. **Go live**
29. Do an operational review
30. Implement remedial actions
31. **Sign off the project**
32. Further developments and system enhancements (on-going)

Each of these tasks or task areas are outlined in Chapter 23.

18.4.2 **Progress monitoring**

The key to progress monitoring is a single chart that incorporates four items: milestones, activities, resources and timescales. These are normally shown on what is known as a Gantt chart (named after Henry Gantt, 1861–1919) – a classic, perennially used tool.

You can, and probably should, use a project planning tool like Microsoft Project (which allows the project to be viewed as a Gantt chart) to produce your plan in the first instance, including expected costs. You can also use the same system to enter actual figures of time and cost and produce regular monitoring reports. However, this can be very time-consuming and many people find it satisfactory to pin up a master copy of the plan and plot progress on it with coloured pens, only redoing the plan if major rescheduling is required.

Whichever way you do things you must keep a tight check on progress, hold regular progress meetings (weekly, two-weekly or monthly – your choice) and have an escalation procedure for when things start to go off plan (and they will).

18.4.3 When things start going wrong

You will soon know when things are going wrong because one of the elements of your project plan under the heading of 'controls' is time and cost tolerances. An example of this is raising a warning if any activity is more than two weeks late starting or finishing. You then have decisions to make: can the time be recovered or will the timescale slip? Another part of the controls section will be an escalation procedure; for example, report to the project sponsor and/or the supplier account manager if the problems continue. Remedial actions will have to be defined and at some point it is likely that a decision to re-plan the project will be made.

19 The first steps

19.1 DEVELOP THE PROJECT JUSTIFICATION (BUSINESS CASE)

A business case, project justification or feasibility study – call it what you like, but make sure you produce something that clearly sets out what you want to do, why you want to do it and what you expect to get out of it. (In the following chapters it will be referred to as the business case.)

A business case outline

Your business case must include the following contents:

Background	Setting the scene, a little bit of history as to how you got to where you are at the present time
Current problems	A summary of the problems faced by the organisation that have led to the desire for new systems
New requirements	Requirements and functionality of the proposed new systems in very general terms at this stage
Options	An analysis of different solutions to the problems including computer systems and manual systems
Benefits expected	A list of the advantages you expect to obtain by implementing new systems, both tangible and intangible
Risks	Risks associated with the implementation of new systems, not forgetting the risks to the business of not doing anything
Costs	A very broad estimate at this stage but it is essential to start somewhere and continually refine it as the project progresses
Expected timescales	A list of key milestones (not a detailed project plan) and expected and hoped-for attainment dates

Producing a business case is difficult in the extreme. Do not underestimate the size of the task. You need to get board approval for the project and the board will want to see costs and benefits, and benefits preferably in terms of pound notes. That is where problems arise. Estimating costs is relatively easy; you can draw on the experience of other organisations and other implementations. However, it is not so easy to estimate cost savings or increased income resulting from the project. You are usually reduced to saying things such as 'By implementing this system we should be able to reduce our attrition rate. If we can reduce it by X% then we will increase income by £Y', or 'The provision of a 360 degree view of our customers will allow us greater cross-selling opportunities. If we can increase sales of product X by Y% we will increase income by £Z'.

Added to these things which are expected to result in cost savings or increased income are the intangibles. For example, how do you put a value on providing people with more accurate information, or providing a single customer view so that customers' interactions with you are smoother and more efficient, or even to providing faster access to customer information? Whichever way you attempt to justify your project, a leap of faith is required. Therefore, the better your arguments the better chance you have of getting board approval. And remember, you need not only to get board approval for the project, but also to get active board support if the project is to stand any chance of success.

19.2 APPOINT THE PROJECT SPONSOR AND THE PROJECT BOARD

It is essential to get the right people in the right roles, preferably starting with the chief executive for the project sponsor role. This is followed by the appointment of the project board. This consists of one or more senior managers or directors to represent the user departments, a senior manager or director to take responsibility for the technical elements of the project, and finally a senior manager or director to represent the overall interests of the business.

19.3 APPOINT THE PROJECT MANAGER AND THE PROJECT TEAM

Firstly, you need a project manager, someone who has an overview of the whole organisation and who has experience with CRM and with large-scale projects. Then you need a number of appropriate department representatives, people who will actually carry out most of the work. Make sure you get the best people possible. Do not dump it on junior staff who may have little interest in the project and even less influence on its outcome.

Make sure that all of these people have their project responsibilities defined so that everyone knows what is expected of them. Also, do not expect any of these people to undertake project activities *and* their day jobs. They must be given the time to carry out their project activities, even if it means hiring temporary staff to relieve them of some of their day-to-day activities.

Part six:

CRM systems

procurement

20 The buyer's dilemma

Firstly, a word of advice: *never, never*, be tempted to construct a system yourself with Access (or similar). You may think that you have unique requirements, but the probability of that is vanishingly small. You will almost certainly have different ways of doing things but the underlying functional requirements of a CRM system for your organisation will be the same as everyone else's (or more accurately, will be a subset of a larger standard set with which the major CRM system suppliers will be familiar). And don't be tempted to do it yourself because you have little or no money and you think a CRM system will cost a fortune. Those days are long gone. There are very good, inexpensive systems available for smaller organisations.

So, why reinvent the wheel? Packaged systems are:

- tried and tested;
- best practice (used by dozens if not hundreds of organisations);
- fully functional (with a large range of ready-made reports);
- flexible for you to tailor them to your own specific look and feel;
- up-to-date technically (new associated software systems and technologies are incorporated as soon as they are stable, for instance new versions of Microsoft Office);
- under continual development (the future functions you might need are likely to be in there before you want them).

Packaged systems have:

- support readily available;
- a wide knowledge base (with user groups you can join to exchange ideas and experiences with other people using the same system);
- a ready supply of people who have used them before so new recruits are effective more quickly with an industry-standard system they are used to;
- complex functionality which you can grow into (as you get more familiar the system, you can use more of the functionality);
- proven to be much cheaper in the long run.

From £100 to £1,000,000 there is a package (or there are packages) for you!

In the operational CRM arena, there are well over 100 products available (but about 40 worth considering and about 12 to 15 that come up all the time – affectionately known as 'the usual suspects'). IT system suppliers come and go at an alarming rate. At least one a year goes out of business and others get taken over (this can be a good or bad thing). At least one per year joins the market. The market is volatile – there are too many suppliers chasing too little business. (The market isn't as big as you might think.)

Today the CRM systems market (collaborative, operational and analytical) is more vibrant and exciting than ever before. There are more suppliers offering a greater number of products and the products themselves are becoming increasingly sophisticated and function-rich. There are literally hundreds of systems that call themselves all sorts of things from CRM Databases to Contact Databases, Fundraising Databases, Membership Databases, Grant Management Databases, Project Management Systems, Data Analysis Systems, and more. Some are better than others in one aspect or another but basically they can all do at least 80% of the functions that most not-for-profit organisations require, no matter the type of organisation (fundraising, membership, campaigning, grant-making, etc.). You are really spoilt for choice.

However, this brings its own problems – how do you choose between them? To answer this question you have to decide first of all where your organisation fits into the scheme of things. Is your organisation large with a big budget or is it small with a smaller budget? Do you have £1,000, £10,000, £100,000 or even £1,000,000 to spend? Once you know the answers to these questions then you can start looking at an appropriate sub-set of the dozens of systems on the market and you can decide how to choose between them. Here are some rules of thumb for you to decide which category you fit into:

- **Tiny:** less than £1,000 to spend and probably only a single user
- **Small:** less than £10,000 to spend and a maximum of five or six users
- **Medium:** between £10,000 and £100,000 to spend and up to 50 users
- **Large:** more than £100,000 to spend and more than 50 users

Suppliers generally specialise in systems for one of these categories and although some cover more than one category, it should help you to slim down the list.

Remember, your CRM system is the most expensive IT system you will ever have and it is likely to be budgeted to last at least seven years. You cannot afford to get it wrong!

21 Who are the suppliers?

This chapter comes with a very large caveat. In its various sections it lists names of products and suppliers and naturally there will be changes to these lists over time (additions, deletions, takeovers, etc.). However, the names are accurate at the time of going to press and it makes more sense to put them within the flow of the text rather than in an Appendix which will never be looked at!

21.1 COLLABORATIVE CRM

The first thing to realise with collaborative CRM is that there is no standard list of suppliers because, unlike operational and analytical CRM, there is no collaborative CRM system as such. Collaborative CRM is a concept rather than a system. Certainly, there is a set of functionality required as outlined in Chapter 14, but in total this is provided partly by your operational CRM systems supplier and partly by your web developers (unless you choose one of the few system suppliers that incorporates a CMS into its CRM offering, so you get CRM and website in one product). It is also provided in part by other software products used by either your operational CRM systems supplier or by your web developers. The various elements of collaborative CRM will be provided by the relevant supplier as shown below.

21.1.1 Snail mail

Letter creation and mail-merging is provided by your operational CRM system supplier, which will often also supply data exports to specialist mailing houses for bulk mailing. The mailing house will also undertake things such as de-duplication (see 'Data cleaning' under 15.2.3) and sorting your data using Mailsort software, which prepares your mailing list in order to take advantage of cheaper postage rates as outlined by Royal Mail's Mailsort discount schemes.

21.1.2 Email

Small-scale email facilities are provided either by your operational CRM system supplier or by your current web developer. Bulk emailing is provided by either of these suppliers, utilising specialist bulk emailing software such as dotMailer or MailChimp.

21.1.3 Telephone (i.e. CTI: computer telephony integration)

CTI is provided by your operational CRM system supplier and integrates directly with your particular telephone system. (Note that this integration is not possible with many older telephone systems.)

21.1.4 SMS (i.e. texting)

SMS services are provided by your operational CRM system supplier linking with specialist SMS software such as TextClever, Green Text and TextAnywhere.

21.1.5 Recording events and face-to-face encounters

The facility to record events and face-to-face encounters is provided by your operational CRM system supplier as standard data entry functions.

21.1.6 Recording other campaign media (inserts, DRTV, other advertising)

The facility to record other campaign media is provided by your operational CRM system supplier as standard data entry functions.

21.1.7 Website

This requires the services of both your operational CRM system supplier and your current web developer, with one or the other taking the lead, depending on your chosen method of providing the required facilities.

21.1.8 Social media

The facilities to interact with and download data from the various social media websites are created by your operational CRM system supplier.

21.2 **OPERATIONAL CRM**

21.2.1 **Major suppliers**

Operational CRM is the foundation of your complete CRM solution. It is the hub around which everything else revolves. It is what was simply called 'the database' in the good old days. We might pontificate about it being just a transaction processing (back-office) engine rather than an information producing engine, but the point is that the operational CRM system is the essential element upon which everything else depends. You cannot do without it and it is the thing you should get right first (before you start thinking about the clever stuff you put on either side of it).

There are literally hundreds of systems available that style themselves as CRM systems. Of these, there are more than 100 that either specialise in or have some experience of the not-for-profit sector. What follows in table 21.1 is not a list of 100 plus, but it is a representative sample of the most prominent suppliers within the not-for-profit sector at the time of writing.

In the table, (M) indicates a membership bias in the product and in the supplier's experience. That doesn't mean they do not cater for fundraising or for grant-making, because many of them do, it simply means that the majority of their clients are membership bodies and membership is where their major expertise lies. Those with an (F) tend to specialise in fundraising and, similarly, that doesn't mean they do not cater for membership or grant-making because again many of them do, it simply indicates that the majority of their not-for-profit clients are fundraising organisations.

In table 21.1 the 'product' column is the name of the software solution that the supplier provides. Where the product name is followed by a name in brackets, this indicates the underlying software system that forms the basis for the product, such as Microsoft Dynamics CRM or Salesforce. The T, S, M and L columns indicate that the product is suitable for different sized organisations as described in Chapter 20 (and reiterated in the table's key).

N.B. Almost all of the suppliers listed *will undoubtedly take issue* with the fact that their products have been designated as T, S, M or L because they will all state that they cater for the complete spectrum of not-for-profit organisations. However, not-for-profit organisations looking for a new CRM system need some way of starting to narrow down their search. The Xs in the four columns indicate the size of the majority of the not-for-profit clients each supplier works with, and consequently each supplier's major experience.

Supplier	Product		T	S	M	L
3Si	OM.net	(M)		X	X	
Access Group	thankQ	(F)		X	X	X
Advanced NFP (formerly Iris NFP)	Care NG	(F)			X	X
Advanced NFP	Donor Strategy	(F)	X	X	X	
Advanced NFP	Integra NG	(M)			X	X
Advanced NFP	Member Strategy	(M)	X	X	X	
Alfapeople	(Microsoft Dynamics CRM)	(F)		X	X	
appiChar	supporter360 (Salesforce)	(F)		X	X	
APT Solutions	Stratum	(M)			X	X
ASI Europe	iMIS	(M)			X	X
ASI Europe	ProgressCRM	(F)		X	X	X
Blackbaud Europe	The Raiser's Edge	(F)		X	X	
Blackbaud Europe	Blackbaud CRM	(F)				X
Blackbaud Europe	eTapestry	(F)	X	X		
Care Data	Donorflex	(F)		X	X	
Centrepoint Computer Services	eTarget	(M)		X	X	X
Ciber UK	(Microsoft Dynamics CRM)	(F)			X	X
Circle Interactive	(CiviCRM)	(F)		X	X	
Convio (Now owned by Blackbaud)	Luminate CRM	(F)		X	X	
Dataware	Subscriber	(M)	X	X	X	
dk Software	dk Not-for-profit	(F)	X	X		*Cont.*

Supplier	Product		T	S	M	L
DMACS	DonorPerfect	(F)		X	X	
Harlequin	Harlequin Fundraising	(F)		X	X	
ICARIS (formerly JA Computer Systems)	ICARIS	(F)	X	X		
KIS Software Solutions	KIS Contacts	(F)	X	X		
MTL Software Solutions	SoldalitaS	(M)			X	X
MTL Software Solutions	(CiviCRM)	(F)	X	X		
PremierIT	CentricCRM	(F)		X	X	
ProTech Computer Systems	Pro-8	(M)			X	X
Pythagoras	(Microsoft Dynamics CRM)	(F)		X	X	
Redbourn Business Systems	Advantage NFP Fundraiser	(F)	X	X	X	
SaturnBV	Eprisa	(F)			X	X
Tessitura Network	Tessitura Software	(F)			X	X
Third Sector Design	(CiviCRM)	(F)	X	X		
Touchstone Group	(Microsoft Dynamics CRM)	(F)		X	X	
TSG	TSG tribe	(M)		X	X	
Westbrook International	force for good (Salesforce)	(F)		X	X	

Key

T	**Tiny:** less than £1,000 to spend, often single user
S	**Small:** up to five or six users, typically Microsoft Access based
M	**Medium:** up to about 50 users, typically Microsoft SQL Server based
L	**Large:** more than 50 users, typically SQL Server or Oracle-based
(M)	With a membership leaning
(F)	With a fundraising leaning

Table 21.1 not-for-profit operational CRM suppliers

21.2.2 **Cloud-based solutions**

Firstly, let us deal with the subject of hosting. There are a few suppliers, such as SaturnBV, which specialise in hosted solutions, but most of the suppliers listed in table 21.1 will provide a hosted service if you want it. The technical manner of providing the service may vary, but the point is that if you would prefer your system to be off-site, i.e. not on your premises, then you have that option almost irrespective of the system you select.

Next, we should consider the subject of Software as a Service (SaaS). SaaS (or on-demand software) consists of applications which are hosted somewhere 'in the cloud', meaning that they are accessed via an Internet browser. In the majority of cases there is one instance of the software and it is accessed by multiple organisations, each of whose data is kept separate by the provider. This is the key difference between SaaS and a hosted solution because, although both are in the cloud, with the hosted solution you have your own copy of the software. The names you are most likely to come across in the SaaS world are:

- **CiviCRM:** open-source, small scale, and free to use. Some expenditure on configuration is required by each organisation.
- **Salesforce.com:** huge, complex and sophisticated. The first 10 licences are free and the rest come at an 80% discount for not-for-profit organisations. Quite a lot of expenditure on configuration is required by each organisation.
- There are lots of others, such as SugarCRM, vtigerCRM, SplendidCRM, CentricCRM, hipergate, to name a few!

All the above have limited specialist not-for-profit functionality compared with the market-leading products but they are improving all the time (especially CiviCRM and Salesforce) and all cost money to set up even if the licences are free. The time is coming when CiviCRM and Salesforce will be developed to such an extent, and become so popular, that some (or possibly many) of the suppliers in table 21.1 will disappear (but not for some years).

Lastly, there is Microsoft Dynamics CRM. It too has limited not-for-profit-specific functionality but an increasing number of the sector's system suppliers are using it as the basis for the development of their tailored solutions. As with CiviCRM and Salesforce, Microsoft Dynamics CRM is becoming increasingly popular, especially as the vast majority of not-for-profit organisations' IT infrastructure is still completely Microsoft-based with Microsoft Windows Server, Microsoft Windows Desktop and Microsoft Office.

21.2.3 **Tightly integrated best of breed software**

There are a number of best of breed system areas that are either incorporated completely within the operational CRM systems, i.e. they are transparent to the user, or are very tightly integrated such that the interface between the systems is seamless or nearly seamless. These system areas include office software (word processing, spreadsheets, contact management and email, etc.); address management; banking and payment software; and bulk email. In each case there are a number of options available and your chosen operational CRM system supplier may or may not provide integration facilities with them all. Consequently, it is best to take your lead from your operational CRM supplier in these areas and accept their advice. However, some of the more popular options are listed below.

- **Office software:** more than 90% of not-for-profit organisations use Microsoft Office and all operational CRM system suppliers provide tight integration with this as standard. There are a small (but growing) number of not-for-profit organisations that are opting for open-source office solutions and some suppliers offer integration with these systems as an option.
- **Address management:** some suppliers have their own address management software built in to their CRM products (such as Blackbaud) but most integrate with software from one or more of the following suppliers: AFD Software, Capscan, Experian QAS, GB Group, Hopewiser, and Postcode Anywhere.
- **Banking and payment software:** suppliers include Adflex, AFD Software, Albany Software, Experian (who acquired Eiger Systems), The Logic Group, and Mosaic Software.
- **Bulk email:** there are huge number of suppliers and services in this category but some that come up regularly are dotMailer, GraphicMail, GroupMail, MailChip, and Mailing Manager.

21.2.4 Off-line integrated best of breed software

There is such a vast array of software available in the market that can have an association with CRM that it is impossible for operational CRM system suppliers to provide links with them all. However, many systems and functions, unlike address checking and credit card validation for example, do not require immediate real-time connections with the operational CRM system. Consequently, the integration with most of these systems is via regular or ad hoc import and export functions. Some of the major areas that will require this level of integration are finance (accounting), legacy administration, sales order processing and stock control, raffles, and lotteries.

- **Finance:** very few CRM systems incorporate a full-scale accounting system these days (i.e. sales, purchase and nominal ledgers). The majority of suppliers prefer to provide export facilities in the appropriate format to (and in some cases import facilities from) the leading financial management systems such as Access Dimensions, Agresso, Exchequer, Microsoft Dynamics Great Plains, Pegasus, Sage (in all its varieties), Sun and others.
- **Legacy administration:** different operational CRM suppliers provide different levels of legacy administration functionality but the providers of fully functional legacy administration systems include Clearwater Consultancy with its product First Class, and Lawbase Legal Systems with Lawbase Legacy Administration.
- **Sales order processing and stock control:** some operational CRM suppliers provide sophisticated functionality in this area; others provide limited functionality and others no functionality. All suppliers provide import facilities that can take names and addresses and sales transactions (in detail or summary form) from sales order processing systems whether they are server-based or web-based, and conversely, they provide export facilities that can send customer details to such systems. There are far too many of such systems to list here (especially web shop systems for online sales) and none that stand out as market leaders, so each case needs to be taken separately.
- **Raffles:** a few operational CRM system suppliers have incorporated a raffle module within their system, so the majority of not-for-profit organisations that run raffles have to import data from specialist raffle systems in order to obtain the 360 degree view of the customers' interactions with the organisation. Examples of raffle system suppliers are: Rogavi and Sterling.
- **Lotteries:** to date there are only one or two operational CRM system suppliers which have incorporated a lottery module within their system so once again organisations that operate a lottery need to import data from specialist lottery systems such as Combase, Sterling, and Tower.

21.2.5 Grant-making and other specialist systems

Grant-making, along with fundraising and membership, is one of the main business areas within the not-for-profit sector and many of the suppliers listed in table 21.1 provide modules within their CRM system for the administration of the grants that their clients make to beneficiaries. However, many grant-making organisations are just that: they do little or no fundraising and have no members. These organisations have always been served by suppliers that provide specialist grants management systems (which contain many of the elements of CRM) and this continues to be the case. Some of the more well-known specialist grants suppliers are listed in table 21.2.

Supplier	Product
Bright Systems	Grant Application Processor
Buzzacot Giving Solutions	GIFTS
CC Technology	CC Grant Tracker
The Gallery Partnership	Benefactor
Lawbase Legal Systems	Lawbase Grants Administration
QAPlus	QA+PARIS
Quest Computing	AIMS Grant Management Software

Table 21.2 Grants management system suppliers

Note that there are also grants modules available for CiviCRM and Microsoft Dynamics CRM.

21.3 ANALYTICAL CRM

There are dozens (if not hundreds) of systems available that do analysis in some form or another, many of which also include segmentation, selection and marketing campaign management. Again there is a much smaller number that either specialise in or have some experience of the not-for-profit sector. Table 21.3 is a representative sample of the most prominent suppliers within the not-for-profit sector.

Supplier	Product	
Access Group	Access Insight	
Alterian	Alterian Suite	Now owned by SDL
Apteco	FastStats	Apteco own it, Tangible, Occam and many others use it
Datawatch	Monarch	
Emailvision	Smart Focus	
Google	Google Analytics	For the web
IBM	Cognos	IBM own it, COA Solutions and others use it
IBM	SPSS	IBM own it, many companies specialise in its use
Microsoft	Microsoft Analysis Services	Touchstone and many others use it
Oracle	Eloqua	
QlikView	QlikView	
SAP	Business Objects	SAP own it, COA Solutions and others use it
SAS Institute	SAS	

Table 21.3 not-for-profit analytical CRM suppliers

22 10 steps to a successful purchase

22.1 DIFFERENT SELECTION TECHNIQUES

22.1.1 Introducing the 10 steps

So, how can you choose the best system for your organisation? There is no obvious 'best' system (no matter what some of the market leaders might tell you). It really is a case of horses for courses. What suits one not-for-profit organisation does not necessarily suit the next not-for-profit organisation, even if their basic requirements are identical.

The traditional approach is still the best. Follow the 10 steps below (and don't skip any of them!). Note, however, that you will conduct these 10 steps differently and at different levels depending upon the category of organisation you fall into, i.e. Tiny, Small, Medium or Large, as described in Chapter 20.

1. **Produce a business case**	This is the project justification. Why do you want a new or different system and what will it achieve?
2. **Initial investigations**	What is on the market? What are other organisations similar to yours using?
3. **Define your requirements**	Specify these so that you know what you are looking for and to provide a basis on which to evaluate alternate solutions.
4. **Define your selection criteria**	Define these before receiving proposals from suppliers so that you can make an informed and unbiased choice.
5. **Invite proposals from suppliers**	Carry out a sequence of formal procedures so that you don't get taken in by sales talk.
6. **Analyse the proposals**	Review submissions, taking care to compare like with like. *Cont.*

7. **See demonstrations**	Does the system do what the suppliers say it will do and would you be happy using it?
8. **Take up references**	See the system in action at client sites and determine if other users are happy with it.
9. **Make the choice**	This is the big decision, and is always a combination of hard and soft factors (functional and non-functional requirements).
10. **Try before you buy**	You test-drive a car before buying it, so why not test- drive your CRM system?

22.1.2 **If you are Tiny**

First, let's reiterate a word of warning: do not be tempted to do it yourself! That is, don't try to develop the system yourself in Microsoft Access or something similar. *It is not worth the effort.* Your requirements are not unique. Someone will have done it before, and probably better than you can. It may appear to be cheaper in financial terms, but you will spend vast amounts of time reinventing a wheel that has been invented so many times before and it isn't that easy. In order to develop a really useful system you will need to have access to someone with the appropriate skills in Microsoft Access or similar, and you will need to put staff resources into getting the system developed, which can turn into several years of effort. In addition, if and when your developer moves on to another organisation you will be in big trouble with a system that is probably not documented and no-one knows how to work. It will become rapidly out of date and, eventually, it will be abandoned. Ten years or so ago this was the way for small organisations to get started with a CRM system, but times change and this approach is no longer appropriate or necessary.

At the bottom end of the market for very small not-for-profit organisations with very little money to spare there are a number of potential solutions available on the Internet ('in the cloud') that are variously called shareware, open-source or SaaS (see 21.2.2). Many of these cost nothing or almost nothing. Be very careful with these and choose carefully. Some of them are US-focused, unsuitable for UK not-for-profit organisations and you will receive no support.

There are simple systems available in the UK for as little as £100 that can be installed in-house and there are a small number of cloud-based systems that have had significant UK-specialised functionality added such as CiviCRM and Salesforce.com mentioned earlier. Salesforce.com offers the first ten licences free of charge to not-for-profit organisations and CiviCRM is open-source so it is free. Of course you will need configuration and some training to use them effectively, but for £1,000 you can get a good single-user system which has been developed in and for the UK market complete with installation and training.

So how do you choose a database if your organisation is Tiny? The suggestion is that you condense the 10 steps above into three simple ones. First, you have to do the research to find suitable suppliers. Second, you should spend half a day writing down the main functions you want in the form of a demonstration programme and finally invite several suppliers (three or four) to attend a 'beauty parade' (preferably on the same day) where they demonstrate their systems according to your programme. Then make a decision based on what you have seen.

22.1.3 **If you are Small**

If your organisation is small, then follow the 10-step procedure above but, as well as defining a demonstration programme, spend a bit more time and write out your requirements in more detail. Add in all the questions you might think of asking the supplier. For example:

- How long have you been in business?
- How many staff do you have?
- What is your annual turnover?
- What is your annual profit?
- How many customers do you have?
- Who are your customers?
- Will you give us a fixed price?
- What is the total implementation cost?
- What are the annual charges?
- What are your daily rates?

Write this up as an official 'request for information' to which the suppliers must reply in writing. Send it to the suppliers ahead of the demonstration date (along with your demonstration programme) and ask them to bring the response with them to the demonstration day. At the end of the day you can make a decision based on what you have seen and their written responses.

22.1.4　If you are Medium or Large

If your organisation comes into the medium or large categories then you will be spending significantly more money and you should be more thorough and more formal. In this case it is suggested that you conduct a full-scale invitation to tender exercise where you go through the 10 steps in detail, as described in the next section.

22.2　THE 10 STEPS

1.　The business case

This was covered in detail in Chapter 19. The purpose of repeating it here is to reiterate the point that you should not start a procurement exercise without it.

2.　Initial investigations

With more than 100 systems to choose from, this stage is vital so that you can concentrate your efforts on the systems most likely to satisfy your needs. It is worth noting that although many of the major not-for-profit CRM suppliers have been around for years (some since the mid-eighties in one form or another), other suppliers come and go with amazing rapidity. The idea of this stage is to gather as much information as you can, see what is available, see what other people are using, and come up with a shortlist of the most likely potential suppliers of your system(s).

You can find out what is available by attending conferences and exhibitions, doing web searches, participating in web forums and asking organisations similar to yours what they use. From these investigations you are likely to have identified a long list of possible suppliers, often 20 or more. You need to get this list down to manageable proportions. This can be done by defining the most important features you require and the key criteria that you want your system and its supplier to meet. Then send a brief request for information to the long list of suppliers you identified. Finally, do an initial evaluation of the responses and agree on shortlist to invite to tender, say, to three to six suppliers.

3. Define your requirements

By this time you will have seen a few systems, talked to some salespeople and heard all the hype. Now you have to define what you really want. You should adopt the traditional approach of a top-down specification. That is, start with the big issues, such as:

- What do you need to achieve your strategic objectives?
- Do you need 1, 2 or 3 circles? (See section 7.7.2.)
- What do you really need to run your business?
- What other systems do you need to integrate with?
- How will you integrate with social media?

Take the time and trouble to specify exactly what you want the system to do for you. Although most of the available systems will do the basics, there are enormous differences in what they can and cannot do (and in what they can and cannot *do well*). The level of detail you go into at this stage is up to you. It might be three pages or it might be 30 pages or more, but make sure that you specify what you want concisely (preferably in bullet point or table form) in terms of what the system should do and not how it should do it, and allocate priorities to every point on your list. Why? Because no system will do absolutely everything you want of it, so you need to know which items are absolutely essential and which items you can live without. To allocate priorities, IT people like to talk about MoSCoW rules, which stand for:

- Must have
- Should have
- Could have
- Won't have (this time around)

However, 'real' people often prefer something more familiar such as:

- Mandatory
- Desirable
- Luxury
- Future

Whatever it is that you want, write it down. Be demanding but practical. Whether it is 20 points or 2000 points, it doesn't matter; write down what is important to you. Take every point seriously, but be sensible – resist the temptation to make almost everything mandatory. Be realistic with what you can actually manage. Today's information systems contain many complex and sophisticated features, to which most people's reaction is 'That would be nice!' and then they put it down as mandatory without sitting back and thinking, 'Will I really use this feature?' Don't forget the soft features, i.e. the non-functional requirements, such as how easy it is to use!

An important point is detail, detail, detail. You will never get what you want or need if you have vague or general requirements. Resist the temptation to only define vague requirements, select a supplier and then start down the prototyping route, i.e. where you work together with the supplier to gradually build a complete system. The problem you will face is where to stop the process. You will be in danger of entering an endless prototyping route. It is important to draw a line in the sand somewhere and, let's face it, you know what you do now and you know what you would like to do in the future, so it isn't that hard to define the requirements of the 'complete' system you require from the outset, it just takes time. Of course you will never be able to define 100% of your requirements at the beginning but you can realistically expect to get to 90% or 95%, even if you do need a bit of help to get there.

Speaking of a bit of help, don't be afraid to get advice if you need it. Getting advice on requirements can be a good idea because people from other not-for-profit organisations who have done it before and 'domain experts' (consultants who really know their stuff) can often suggest useful functionality that you wouldn't have come up with on your own. So, definitely get advice, but always make your own decisions.

And finally, you can, on your own or with a little help, specify 90% or more of your requirements at the outset. However, your organisation and what it does will change over time and you need your CRM system(s) to change with it. Consequently, you need to specify some element of flexibility in the system(s) you define, so that you have some way of securing some confidence that the supplier will change and continue to develop their system(s) and keep up with the times.

4. Define your selection criteria

At the same time as defining your requirements, and definitely before the responses are received from suppliers, you should be defining exactly how you will choose between the various suppliers and their offerings. Your process will be personal to you. It might be simply the numbers of ticks or plus points that you put against each supplier. You might devise a complex scoring system with weightings for each requirement. It might be judged on price. It might be on soft issues like whether you find them believable or not or whether you feel you can work with them. Some of the criteria will be related to their written responses, others related to demonstrations, others to site visits, etc. The complete list will be a combination of factors but make sure they are clear before you start. The following list might be helpful.

Example selection criteria list

1 **Proposal criteria**
Clarity and quality of proposal
Number of requirements satisfied by standard packages
The degree of fit with the client's installed technical infrastructure

2 **Demonstration criteria**
Ease of use
How well software met requirements and its flexibility
Supplier's performance

3 **Question criteria**
Supplier's ability to answer our questions
Level of satisfaction with their responses
Supplier's attitude and level of professionalism

4 **Reference site visit criteria**
Supplier's ability to deliver on time and on budget
Supplier's level and quality of support
Level of satisfaction of users

5 **Supplier site visit criteria**
Their understanding of our specific not-for-profit area
Their motivation and team spirit
The support arrangements

6 **General supplier criteria**
Supplier's reputation and position in the market
Supplier's commitment to ongoing system developments
Reasonableness of supplier's contractual terms

7 **Implementation criteria**
General implementation approach
Data conversion approach
Quality of training

8 **Cost criteria**
Initial
Recurring
Five-year cost

5. Invite proposals from suppliers

When you have a requirements specification then prepare and distribute an invitation to tender to your shortlisted suppliers. A requirements specification, no matter how detailed, is not an invitation to tender. An invitation to tender will contain:

- a description of the selection process;
- the decision-making timescale;
- how to obtain further information;
- information about your organisation and your current systems;
- exactly how you want them to respond i.e. the format of their response;
- a request for information about the supplier:
  - How do they do business?
  - Who are their customers?
  - What is their support like?
  - How much do they cost?
  - How good is their ability to deliver?
  - And anything else you want to know about them
- the requirements specification

Send your invitation to tender to your shortlisted suppliers and give them a reasonable amount of time to respond. Four weeks is reasonable, two weeks is not. They are people with schedules and priorities too!

6. Analyse the proposals

When you receive responses from suppliers, you need to analyse them on a like-for-like basis. This is not always straightforward. Suppliers often calculate costs on different bases. They might include different things. They might have different perceptions of your requirements (which is why it is important to keep the language you use as clear and unambiguous as you can). You will have huge amounts of paper (or very large email attachments) to wade through, so it is a good idea to carry out an initial cursory review to eliminate no-hopers. There will usually be one or two who fail at a very high level and you can save a lot of time by not reading all the detail. You will then have to read the remaining proposals carefully and analyse each response against the predefined selection criteria (some of which won't be relevant at this stage). You will need a team of people analysing the proposals. You need a user perspective, a technical perspective, a finance perspective and a management perspective.

There are a myriad of things to consider but you should pay careful attention to the subjects of configuration and customisation. Firstly, be clear about the difference between the two.

Configuration is using features within the system to make it look and act in different ways for different organisations, but the underlying system remain standard and upgrades can be applied without problems. Examples of configuration are the development of workflows i.e. sequences of actions, or the modification of screen designs such as moving or hiding a field.

Customisation, on the other hand, is writing new code that is not a standard feature, i.e. it is written just for you. You should endeavour to minimise this. In fact you should aim to have no customisation at all because having it means that you have a non-standard system. This can lead to problems and added expense when the inevitable regular upgrades are released by the supplier.

Customisation is often the unnecessary answer to two things: 1) achieving 100% of the requested requirements, and 2) doing things in exactly the way you do them now. A healthy dose of realism is required here. If the system does 98% of what you want, do you really need the other 2%, or can you live without it? And, if it does what you want but in a different way, is your way significantly better or could you change your processes to fit the system? This problem tends to occur more often in large organisations where processes are likely to be more complex and ingrained in the organisation's psyche. The more these processes are ingrained, the harder they are to change. Large not-for-profit organisations with specific ways of doing things sometimes do have found better methods, but not often. Remember, many of the suppliers have worked with hundreds of not-for-profit organisations and have had years to hone their system processes to perfection. Whatever you decide, a trade-off is required between embarking on customisation and changing your processes.

So, in summary, configuration is OK but customisation is not. Note that some suppliers have what could be called a 'toolkit approach': something of a halfway house between configuration and customisation. It can be an excellent solution if you have genuine unique requirements but care is needed and you will need technical advice and guidance.

Your objective at this stage is to agree a short shortlist of proposals (usually two) that you will take to the next stage and consider further.

7. See demonstrations and real-life scenarios

Once you have agreed on your short shortlist of two (and definitely no more than three), you need to actually see the systems in operation. Get everyone who will use the system to see demonstrations of these shortlisted systems. However, do not just invite suppliers in to demonstrate their products. Prepare a list of features you want to see, and make sure that you see them! Have the demonstrations initially in your office (not the supplier's). Invite the suppliers back for a second time if you don't get to see everything in one session. Stay in control and follow your agenda, not the supplier's. Question everything, and beware of 'vapourware': the things they say it can do but which they don't show it actually doing. Having a technical person there as well as the potential users should help you see through any smoke and mirrors employed by some suppliers, that is, the things it appears to do but doesn't actually do. Also, ensure that at each session there are participants and an observer. The observer just watches all the proceedings, doesn't get involved or ask questions, but just takes it all in, reading body language and taking notes.

Once you have had initial general demonstrations, revisit the selection criteria again and determine if any supplier can be eliminated at this stage. If not then prepare for further in-depth demonstrations where you visit the suppliers in their offices. These further demonstrations should be more in terms of real-life scenarios where you and the supplier work together through typical jobs and job situations and preferably with a subset of your own data. This may involve a small outlay of money by your organisation as the supplier may have to do some configuration and data conversion, but it will be worth it in the end. You should try to carry out as many functions as possible in the allotted time; all the functions that your staff will expect to use every day.

8. Take up references

Make site visits to current customers to see the shortlisted systems being used in real life by real people (without the salespeople in attendance). Ask lots of questions about the supplier and their performance and the product and whether it matches up to their original expectations. Try to gauge the level of satisfaction of the other customers. Are they prepared to demonstrate the system to you? Ask some pointed questions: Do you have a happy relationship with the supplier? Would you buy again from the same supplier? Are you happy to recommend it to others?

Also contact the user group (if there is one) and find out the general level of experience and satisfaction, or otherwise, of the entire user population.

9. Make the choice

Revisit any of the previous points if necessary, for instance additional demonstrations with more real-life scenarios. Discuss contract terms and the implementation process with the suppliers to determine how reasonable they are and whether you can work with these people. Review your selection criteria again and make the final choice. You have your criteria, so use them! You have the results of all the previous stages. Don't forget to use your intuition, *but don't let it rule.* Involve as many people as possible in the decision-making process and, most importantly of all, obtain a consensus.

10. **Try before you buy**

By this time the supplier will be encouraging you to sign on the dotted line, but don't do it yet. You must establish what is known as 'proof of concept', i.e. a significant free trial. You would test drive a car so why not test drive an information system which will be significantly more expensive than a car? This proof of concept is whether it actually works in your office situation. It looks easy when the salesperson demonstrates it and even when you are working in conjunction with the supplier on a few real-life scenarios, but things have a habit of being different when you are left to your own devices. Test everything. Try out everything, and especially make sure you perform 'volume testing' which is done to determine what happens when the system is put under strain. So, for example, what happens when several people enter transactions at the same time, or people search for records whilst a big report is being produced or a complex selection is being carried out? A one-month free trial is reasonable. If that goes OK, then agree to sign contracts. A word of warning, however; to do a free trial properly will require time and added expenditure for training and conversion of a subset of your data. Compromises will inevitably have to be made, but do as much as is practical.

22.3 **SOME GOLDEN RULES FOR SUCCESS**

Use the following golden rules as a quick reminder during the purchasing process and as go-to guidelines to keep you on track.

- Define your objectives *and write them down*!
- Define your requirements *and allocate priorities*!
- Define your criteria *and stick to them*!
- Check suppliers carefully *and beware of salespeople*!
- Take up references *and see the system in action*!
- Plan, budget and monitor *and look ahead five years*!
- Ensure system continuity *and retain knowledge*!
- Make sure you have all the understanding you need *or use a consultant*!
- Obtain a consensus decision *and listen to your staff*!
- Try before you buy *and don't sign a contract until you are happy*!

22.4 **Those who got it wrong**

Unfortunately, not everyone selects the right system for their organisation and disappointment, frustration and wasted resources (in terms of time and money) occur all too often. What follows is a set of case studies detailing situations where the 10 steps were not followed, or were not followed properly, and bad, expensive decisions were taken.

Case studies: sticky (systems) situations

Case 1

The charity which had three different CRM systems in five years. The first involved a smoke and mirrors demonstration and an overbearing project sponsor who did not obtain consensus. The second involved a different project sponsor who did not define requirements adequately.

Case 2

The organisation which signed a fixed-price contract for a bespoke development at £24,000. Those making the decisions thought there was nothing on the market that covered everything the organisation did (but in fact there was). The organisation spent £90,000 altogether and then ended up buying one of the usual suspects in its standard form, which itself didn't cover the full range of their activities!

Case 3

The charity which fell in love with product X, was warned not to buy it, but bought it anyway. Then the product X supplier went out of business before it was fully implemented.

Case 4

The very small charity which bought product Y for £20,000 plus £3,000 annual support (because that was what the charity down the road was using). All the charity needed was product Z at £2,000 plus £750 annual support!

Case 5

The very large organisation which spent many millions on a bespoke development because the project team thought their organisation's requirements were unique. Of course they weren't and so the organisation finally bought one of the usual suspects.

Case 6

The organisation that went through the first 8 steps and then the chief executive chose the system without consulting adequately. The staff didn't agree with the choice and the system fell into disuse almost immediately!

Case 7

The organisation that went through the first 9 steps, and then on day 2 of a 30-day free trial (which the supplier agreed to with great reluctance) decided that it just wouldn't work for them. This might be seen as a success for the process, and is certainly preferable to having gone ahead without the trial, but the problems should have been picked up during the demonstration and real-life scenarios stage.

Part seven:

Implementing and using CRM

23 Implementation tasks

The sections of this chapter comprise a standard list of tasks that need to be completed for any systems-related project. It might help you get started on planning your project. Note that you will need to do many of the tasks more than once when implementing multiple linked systems and many tasks will have sub-tasks depending on the complexity of your project.

The chapter is split into three sections. The first section deals with tasks (or activities, whichever word you prefer) that need to be conducted after a supplier has (or suppliers have) been selected *but* before any contract is signed. The second section deals with tasks after contracts have been signed and up to the point of going live with the new system. The third part deals with tasks required after the system has gone live (this is a set of tasks that many people forget!).

23.1 FROM KICK-OFF TO CONTRACTS

The tasks described in this section are as follows:

- Have a kick-off meeting
- Negotiate contracts
- Plan the project
- Review the project team
- Review and implement infrastructure changes
- Install the test system
- Become familiar with the new system
- Test the proof of concept
- **Take a formal decision and sign contracts**

23.1.1 Have a kick-off meeting

Every project should commence with a kick-off meeting, preferably chaired by the project sponsor and attended by all interested parties including representatives of the chosen system supplier, where the business case will be presented and the complete project discussed in outline. Table 23.1 shows an example kick-off meeting agenda. Yours may be different but this will give you some ideas.

1	**Responsibilities**
	a. Who are the contacts for what on each side?
	b. Who is doing what?
2	**Contracts**
	a. How do we firm up the price?
	b. Process for the agreement of contractual terms
	c. When can we sign?
3	**Milestones (targets)**
	a. Key dates for client
	b. Anything to avoid (such as holidays)?
	c. Critical timings (such as a major campaign mailing to go out)
4	**Outline project plan**
	a. Client-proposed plan
	b. Supplier-proposed plan
	c. Any dependencies on other people or organisations?
5	**Proposed invoicing schedule**
6	**Installation**
	a. Trial system
	b. Training system
	c. Live system
7	**Training**
	a. Who?
	b. When?
8	**Support arrangements**
	a. On-site
	b. Remote access by client
	c. Remote access by supplier
9	**Next actions**
10	**Any other business**

Table 23.1 Sample kick-off meeting agenda

23.1.2 **Negotiate contracts**

Let us start with the first major activity that you should do once you have chosen your preferred system(s) and supplier(s): negotiating contracts. Read the contract carefully and make sure that you understand everything. If anything is unclear then insist on clarification. Don't be afraid to ask for amendments if you see something you don't like. If the supplier really wants your business, they will compromise. You know and they know that you have choices and can easily select another supplier if you cannot come to an agreement.

Involve your legal department (or your legal advisor or solicitor if you do not have any legally qualified members of staff) in the review of the contract. Keep a tight control over this activity as it can significantly delay the start of the project.

Pay particular attention to the supplier's service-level agreement. Does it make vague statements like 'using best endeavours'? What happens when the system, or a part of the system, fails? How long can you afford to be without the system? How quickly will the supplier respond? What backup and support will it provide?

And as a final thought: always try to negotiate on price. You never know, you might get a pleasant surprise!

23.1.3 **Plan the project**

The kick-off meeting discussed a plan at a very high level: main target dates, which organisation is responsible for which parts of the project, etc. This activity is detailed project planning. This is a much-neglected task from the client organisation's side. Too many not-for-profit organisations simply accept the supplier's project plan and timetable without question and then complain when something goes wrong at some later date. The organisation needs to develop its own preferred implementation plan. This very important because there will be much more to the organisation's own plan than that of the supplier. You then need to compare and contrast the relevant sections of it with the supplier's plan and work together to arrive at a compromise plan that suits you both.

Key features of a project plan

Every project plan must contain the following points:

1. **Assumptions and constraints:** for example, the system must be live before the next year's membership renewals are due or person X does not work on Fridays.
2. **Risk assessment:** what could go wrong, how these things could affect the project and the organisation as a whole, etc.
3. **Structure:** who is in charge, who reports to whom, who is involved in specific areas such as quality assurance and finance.
4. **Milestones:** significant or key review points in the project that can indicate progress, when phases are complete, etc.
5. **End products:** a list of the actual deliverables, such as the system being installed, the modifications installed and test plans written.
6. **Activities:** the actual tasks that people have to carry out.
7. **Resources:** not just the people involved but also any other resources such as equipment, desks and ancillary software.
8. **Timescales:** the proposed start and end dates of each activity.
9. **Monitoring mechanism:** progress meetings, feedback, Gantt charts, and recording actual against budgets (time and cost).
10. **Controls:** the management team with overview responsibilities, a quality-assurance team or function, published project tolerances (time and cost), checkpoint reports, and escalation procedures.
11. **Impact analysis:** how jobs will change (some might even disappear), new job descriptions, new system operating and clerical procedures. This is very important. Remember, people in general fear change. Keep people informed, involved, enthusiastic, and trained in the new processes.

If you don't have these eleven items then you don't have a proper project plan and your project is doomed from the start! Another top tip when planning is to implement the system in stages rather than in a Big Bang approach, i.e. implementing the whole system for all users and all data at once. A Big Bang approach is high-risk and there is a lot that can go wrong. A phased approach allows you to achieve a series of small wins and gradually gain in confidence with the new system.

And finally on the subject of project planning, remember the old saying that has been attributed variously to Winston Churchill, Dwight D Eisenhower and others: 'Plans are useless but planning is essential' (or invaluable or indispensable, as it is sometimes quoted). Plans don't stand still, they are living things, and they need constant monitoring, reviewing and updating.

23.1.4 Review the project team

You set up a project team prior to the procurement phase (as outlined in 19.3). This team will undergo changes as a result of the procurement and the planning exercises. The planning exercise usually uncovers the fact that more or different resources are now required from what was originally envisaged. It is normal at this stage to require different people with different skills. At this point you will also need to add people from the supplier organisation to the team: an account manager, a project manager and some technical staff. The people from the supplier side must be people with whom you feel you can work effectively and in whom you have confidence (you don't want them to be continually changing). There will be activities that will require input from both the client and the supplier such as conversion of data from old systems. This is just the sort of area where things can go wrong: diaries don't match up, people are not sure who is responsible for what, people don't know that something is ready for their input, client staff have normal day jobs to do as well as tasks on this project and things get forgotten or priorities are changed. The key to avoiding these problems is to have a careful definition of responsibilities and an allocation of tasks and then communicate, communicate, communicate.

23.1.5 Review and implement infrastructure changes

Many projects will require changes to servers and/or workstations, or a move of servers to a data centre, or even a move of systems into the cloud (see 21.2.2). These things need to be planned, executed and tested. They won't work first time!

23.1.6 Install the test system

Remember, you are going to 'try before you buy', aren't you?

23.1.7 Become familiar with the new system

Get a small group of users (including the person who will be the systems administrator) to simply play with the system with a minimum of training to get a feel of its intuitiveness and general applicability.

23.1.8 **Test the proof of concept**

This exercise is very important. It could be a very short exercise or a very long exercise depending on the complexity of your requirements. The objective is to ensure that the system will meet your needs in general terms. (This is not the same as full systems acceptance testing which comes later.) You will run as many real-life scenarios as is possible and practical in the time allowed with your own data to determine how the system performs. You will need the assistance and cooperation of the supplier with this and you should be prepared for some expenditure outside the quoted system implementation cost.

23.1.9 *Take a formal decision and sign contracts*

Only when you are happy with the proof of concept testing and you can, hand on heart, say 'yes it will work for us', should you make the formal decision to go ahead and sign the previously agreed contract with the supplier.

23.2 **FROM ANALYSIS TO GOING LIVE**

The tasks described in this section are as follows:

- Analyse the current system
- Extract the data from current system(s)
- Clean and restructure the current data
- Undertake a process review
- Map the current data to the new system
- Convert the data and load it into the new system (multiple times)
- Test the converted data (multiple times)
- Review and implement staffing changes
- Train those in technical and/or supervisory positions
- Configure the system
- Test the configuration
- Set up standard data tables
- Document new processes
- Write reports
- Define security
- Set up users
- Train the users
- Undertake acceptance testing
- **Go live**

23.2.1 Analyse the current system

You will have previously documented what functions your current system carries out along with all the additional things you want your new system to do when you defined your requirements. This analysis is primarily concerned with the data that is contained in your current system(s). You need to know what data is available, how useful it is and whether you intend to transfer it to your new system or not. Some people transfer all the historic data to their new systems, some transfer selected data and some transfer none at all, preferring to start again with a clean sheet. It is your choice.

23.2.2 Extract the data from the current system(s)

The ease or difficulty with which this can be achieved depends entirely on the system from which you are migrating. It can often be a simple data extraction via a number of CSV (comma-separated values) files but it has been known in some cases to be somewhere between complex and impossible because of the construction of the current system.

23.2.3 Clean and restructure the current data

You will inevitably have data that is inaccurate, inconsistent, out-of-date, useless and in a different form from the way you want it in the new system. Some people decide to take everything from their old systems and clean it up in their new systems because the new system has more powerful facilities to assist the process. However, don't do it! The clean-up will never happen. Instead you will start and continue using the new system with rubbish data. Take heed of an old computer science phrase: 'Garbage in, garbage out', which succinctly expresses the point that if you input invalid data the output will be similarly invalid. So make sure you clean the data and restructure it first before it gets anywhere near the new system, and start the wonderful new system with data that is accurate and relevant. Getting your data into a fit state for conversion to the new system is probably the biggest task of all, so do not underestimate it.

There will usually be multiple sources of data and each one with its idiosyncrasies. There will always be one main source of data, say an old CRM database, but most organisations have at least eight. Sorting this lot out will be a nightmare! *Do not underestimate the size of the task.* Clean your addresses. Identify and merge duplicate records. Don't convert useless data. Identify and clean inappropriate and inaccurate data. Create consistent coding structures. Make sure data is complete, – especially income data. It will take months and months, so be prepared. But if you put the effort in, it will pay dividends in the end.

23.2.4 **Undertake a process review**

New systems mean new ways of doing things and in some cases the ability to do things that were not possible previously. You start by documenting every process you currently carry out (if you don't have this already). You then need to review every process you carried out in the past and re-engineer them in order to make the most effective use of the new system.

23.2.5 **Map the current data to the new system**

The data structures, i.e. the way the data is held in files or tables in the new system, will not be exactly the same as in the old systems and you will have taken the opportunity to change things for the better anyway. Much of the data will go across exactly as it is, but quite often you will need to define a set of rules about how to convert some data items into a different format, or into multiple fields, or combined into a single field, or consolidated into summary fields, or even completely changed into something different. Consequently, it will be a significant task to decide exactly where every single item from the old system goes and how it should be treated in the new system. You will also have to give serious consideration to the subject of coding and what data is held in standard system tables. You will probably take this opportunity to rationalise some of the existing data coding which will have become complex, confusing, illogical and, in all probability, a complete mess! This will necessitate a wholesale review of coding and coding structures and the development of a set of conversion rules, some of which will inevitably be quite complex and require a significant level of testing.

23.2.6 **Convert the data and load it into the new system (multiple times)**

You have analysed it, extracted it, cleaned it and mapped it. Now you just turn the handle and import it into the new system, don't you? Unfortunately, life isn't that simple. Things can and will go wrong. Mistakes in the mapping will be made. Conversion rules won't give the correct results. Unexpected values will be found. Different people will make different assumptions. Consequently, multiple attempts to convert and load the data will be made. It is quite normal to have three attempts and you need to factor this into your project plan.

23.2.7 **Test the converted data (multiple times)**

This activity is linked to the point above and its purpose is to identify all the problems. Why is it a separate item? Because it will be carried out by different people; in this case, usually the system users who know the data well whereas the previous item requires technical people either from the supplier company or your own organisation or both. It is a good idea to make tests sequential, so that you don't keep going back to scratch and testing the same things each time. Once something is right, accept that it is right.

23.2.8 Review and implement staffing changes

The creation of new jobs, the changes in existing jobs and any redundant jobs will require the heavy involvement of your human resources department (or the person responsible for HR in your organisation).

23.2.9 Train those in technical and/or supervisory positions

Training will be in two phases. The first phase will be to train the people who will be responsible for supporting the system on a day-to-day basis and who will be responsible for such things as system security, passwords, data integrity, changes to system tables and a host of other administrative tasks. The second phase, user training, comes later.

23.2.10 Configure the system

Gone are the days of WYSIWYG (what you see is what you get) when systems weren't easily adaptable. Today's systems are so flexible that they can be extensively personalised. This is a joint exercise between the client and the supplier to determine exactly how the system will look and how it will work for each individual user or groups of users. This involves tailoring the look and feel of the system, defining who can do what and who can see what, identifying mandatory fields, defining data entry rules, defining work flows, and writing standard queries and reports.

23.2.11 Test the configuration

As with data conversion, mistakes will happen during configuration and sometimes the actual end result doesn't always match the expectation, so a specific task is required to test and sign off the configuration.

23.2.12 Set up standard data tables

There will be a large number of tables of standard data (titles, honours, job titles, marital status, etc. – the list is almost endless) to be entered or modified. Some will be pre-populated by the supplier, others will need changes to suit your organisation and others will be specific to your organisation and will need to be set up from scratch.

23.2.13 Document new processes

This naturally follows the process review mentioned earlier. This activity must be conducted in conjunction with the staff who actually do the jobs. If you do this you stand half a chance of the processes being followed and achieving accuracy and consistency of operation.

23.2.14 Write reports

Every system will come with its own set of preprogrammed reports. These will inevitably cover 90% or more of your reporting needs as they will have been designed in conjunction with many previous customers of the system. However, almost every organisation will have some reporting requirements that are unique to it and which need to be developed (and tested) before the system goes live.

23.2.15 Define security

This is setting the security rules in the system at both a macro level (for instance who can view only, who can add data and who can change data) and at a detail level (for example who can see what records (and even individual fields) and who can enter and modify what data).

23.2.16 Set up users

Individuals will need to be allocated user IDs and passwords and they will need to be put into groups for similar functions.

23.2.17 Train the users

This is the second phase of training and is for the day-to-day users of the system. This training should be carried out on a system configured for the organisation and containing the organisation's data. Standard training on sample data is far less effective. Training must be specific to the user in terms of what they need to know.

23.2.18 Undertake acceptance testing

This is vital. This is where the users find out if the system does what they expect it to do and in the way they expect it. The users must do this testing themselves and they must find (or be given) time in their busy schedules to complete the task. It is important to test as much of the system as possible; 100% is probably unrealistic, but at the very least you will want to test all the normal everyday functions. There will inevitably be problems to resolve and re-testing to carry out. Note that acceptance testing also includes testing the documentation of the new and revised clerical procedures. The key to success here is having formal test plans, test scripts (instructions for the person doing the testing), a feedback mechanism and a **change control process**.

> A **change control process** is a systematic procedure to manage the changes made to a system and ensure that they are introduced in a controlled and coordinated way. The aim of this standardised change management process is to reduce the negative impact of any changes made to an organisation's system.

23.2.19   *Go live*

Only when every test has been signed off can the system be given the go-ahead to commence live operations. It is normal to have a period of downtime whilst the live data conversion takes place, although many people try to do this over a weekend. In years gone by it was normal to have a period of 'parallel running', i.e. operating the old system and the new system at the same time to ensure that the new system produces the same results as the old one. However, this has gone out of fashion for a number of very good reasons: it means double the amount of work for staff (or even more as you have to compare and contrast the results of the two systems), and the new system usually operates in a different way from the old one, which leads to confusion. The preferred method these days is to do enhanced acceptance testing – go live with the new system and switch the old system off at the same time.

23.3   **AFTER GOING LIVE**

The tasks described in this section are as follows:

- Operational review
- Implement remedial actions
- **Sign off the project**
- Further developments and system enhancements

23.3.1   **Do an operational review**

Once the system is up and running it is not time to relax and say that the project is complete. Once people start using the system regularly and do not have recourse to their old system, things will arise that will need changing. Hopefully, if the testing has been comprehensive, there won't be any system errors as such, but there might be. The more likely issues will be relating to the conversion of the data or to the configuration of the system that were not obvious until used in practice. The system needs to operate for a period, say three months, so that the vast majority of these issues can be identified.

23.3.2 **Implement remedial actions**

Remedial actions resulting from the operational review will be a combination of system changes by the supplier, configuration changes by the supplier or the system administrator, data corrections by the supplier or the system administrator, and changes to clerical procedures by users and the system administrator.

23.3.3 *Sign off the project*

Once all remedial actions have been carried out and tested the project finally can be said to be complete and can be signed off.

23.3.4 **Further developments and system enhancements**

Even after the project sign-off it isn't the real end of the project; in fact, it will never end. The supplier will continually develop the system, adding new features, keeping up with technology changes, and making it more efficient. (Well it will if you have done your selection correctly and chosen a good supplier!) Your needs as an organisation also will develop and change over time. This may very well entail further developments from the supplier and another round of installation, testing, training, etc.

Case study: extending the reach of CRM

In early 2009 at the British Red Cross Society (BRC) we went live with a new CRM system at our head office in London. The following year a project was started to extend the system to our 50 or so regional fundraising offices across the UK.

While head-office fundraisers had been using a shared database for some decades previously, regional staff had, until then, got by on using Microsoft Access (but not consistently in all locations or in a connected way), Excel, paper cards and collective memory. Each site's data existed in isolation both from other regional sites and also from what was held at head office. While the objectives of the regional staff were shared, there were a myriad of different processes and standards in place to achieve them. To further complicate things, most of our sites shared their offices and some resources such as finance and administration with service provision staff. Regional fundraisers took their lead on finance and administration processes from the operation they were based with, and the way these operations were run could vary across the UK's 21 operational areas.

Before we could begin to think about delivering CRM functionality to these sites we had the clear challenge of standardising regional fundraising processes, and also managing the coming change in relationship with fundraising's operational colleagues. The fundraising processes also had to align with strong existing processes at head office, and the management of the change in relationship was made harder by the variance in operational delivery across areas.

The key to fixing these challenges laid in face-to-face consultation across (soon to be) end-user staff, and the creation of an implementation panel which had senior representatives from across the BRC. Around half of all regional sites were visited and an assessment made of their data, processes, IT infrastructure and appetite for change. All those we could not visit in person were asked to contribute via online surveys.

Meanwhile our implementation panel began the task of asking key questions such as how to manage shared data ownership, how to integrate financial elements, and how to get the right balance between imposing existing head-office processes and developing new ones for unique new needs. The key to this process was the use of external facilitation; we had multiple senior staff from different areas of the charity on the panel, but an outside perspective was needed to create objective shared outcomes to define our new ways of working.

With management processes agreed and wide-ranging feedback from regional staff captured, we set about defining in detail the shared new processes and began to develop the new functionality. This phase involved eight regional, three head-office and two project staff. Development was done using Agile project management methods (which help you to respond to change through an incremental, adaptive style of working) but within a more formal waterfall management framework (a sequential process). Unless you have just one stakeholder and your system will operate in glorious isolation, don't consider the Agile management approach alone.

Thirteen months after starting the project, our first region went live. We staggered the go live stages into four sets with a month between them. Each new user went live with a member of the project team spending a day onsite to help. A lot of pre-go live effort was put into communicating the new ways of working and making strong leadership from the top down very visible.

The project was a success not only for regional fundraisers but also our head-office staff, giving them further insight into existing contacts and also opening up new prospects – which of course is what CRM is all about.

Aaron Woods, Solutions Architect, British Red Cross Society

24 CRM in practice

This chapter contains a series of hints and tips regarding the effective use of CRM within any organisation. It is not enough to have an absolutely fabulous CRM system unless it is used properly. Firstly, you have to be clear about your CRM strategy and what you are trying to achieve. Then you must procure the best solution for your organisation. Remember, there is no ideal solution. You have a choice. You have to find a solution that suits you. Next you must implement your chosen solution effectively and efficiently. Remember that the success statistics are not on your side. During the implementation you must ensure that you have the most effective processes to support your strategy, and finally when it is all up and running, you must ensure that you are targeting the right messages to the right customers via the right channels at the right time.

24.1 GET THE STRATEGY RIGHT

1. Understand where you are on the scale between implementing a CRM system and a CRM strategy. A CRM system might be a relatively straightforward technology change; a CRM strategy will involve staff restructuring, fundamental change to targets and budgeting, entirely new processes, etc. Ensure your senior management team understands and supports the scale of what is being undertaken.

2. Implementing a CRM strategy is a cultural change first and foremost, and should be undertaken with a set of clear, measurable benefits defined across the board at senior level. This is not an easy task, but it is essential. Everyone involved must have a clear idea of why they doing what they are doing and must sign up to it. Implementing a new technology platform and processes is not a strategic benefit in itself.

3. Customers see the organisation as a single entity, so you must sort out political issues before you even start the implementation, particularly issues related to different departments and 'their' customers. This means that you must have all the political and strategic headaches up front before you start the procurement process. You need to agree the ownership of data and who can do what with it and when. Without this being defined, you cannot develop a new process, design a workflow or migrate any data properly and your project will be doomed to failure at worst or will be in the challenged category at best.

4. Have an outside observer take part in your senior planning and decision-making. A real CRM strategy will aim to remove silos and radically change what people believe they have ownership of. Even the most open-minded department head will have a naturally subjective defence mechanism, but an outside facilitator can help them let go of this.

5. It is pointless to have clever analytics unless the results are used to inform future campaigns and lead to an improved return on investment. This means that you need to create a tight link between analytics and marketing.

6. The organisation's strategy must include the regular monitoring of CRM system performance and a willingness to upgrade or replace hardware and systems software as required in order to maintain, or even to improve, customer service levels.

7. Determine at the outset what values you are going to attach to things like volunteering, gifts in kind, sponsorship and influence so that you can determine the 'real' total value of each customer.

8. Don't start a CRM project unless the chief executive is on board as the project sponsor (or, at the very least, someone with cross-departmental responsibility and authority).

24.2 GET THE PROCUREMENT RIGHT

1. Do not start from the perspective of asking what potential new systems are capable of. First define *how you want to work in the future*. Then start defining requirements to achieve your preferred way of working.

2. Beware of 'desirable' features. Be realistic: will you ever use them? Be even more careful of highly advanced (whizzy) features. They have a habit of clouding your judgement and can appear overly attractive and important.

3. Decide if you are happy for your processes to be defined by the system, or if a system needs to wrap around your current and future processes. The answer to this will be a critical factor in deciding what system is right for you, and also will determine how reliant you will be on third parties, and the amount of resources you will need to invest in internally.

4. Don't let potential suppliers just do a beauty parade when demonstrating their products. Challenge them to demonstrate how they would configure their system to resolve a particular business scenario that is unique to your organisation. Admittedly very little, if anything, you do is likely to be truly unique, but your way of doing it might be. Can the potential systems handle it in your way?

5. Be open-minded when viewing systems that carry out functions in a different way from yours. Seriously consider whether their way might be better than yours. Don't be afraid to change if it is.

6. Ask suppliers how fast their system will be once installed. If they respond by saying anything other than it is impossible to say without details on your

network, data volumes, etc., they are giving you a false answer. Give suppliers some guidance on the performance you expect or would like from the system.

7. Ask that any demonstration systems contain an equivalent volume of data as you have. When testing big processes such as Gift Aid reclaims and direct debit production, if possible, have the system also running multiple dummy processes to emulate your end users' general activity (commonly known as volume testing or performance testing).

24.3   GET THE IMPLEMENTATION RIGHT

1. Whatever project management methods you choose, tailor them to fit your organisation's culture and capabilities. Full-blown PRINCE2 is great if you are building the channel tunnel, and in-depth Agile project management is great if you are building a website from scratch, but a CRM system project should cherry-pick across methods the bits you need and ignore the parts which don't add any value.

2. Don't think that taking an iterative Agile approach (where you have opportunities to adapt and change direction during the process) means that you can bypass a requirements-gathering phase. If you do, a huge amount of time will be taken up later unpicking problems due to a lack of initial consultation across stakeholders.

3. Don't overload your project board with subjective senior staff; involve some people from other parts of the organisation and keep the number below six. If you have a very broad range of stakeholders that need to be represented, form an implementation panel that reports to the board.

4. Start cleaning your data in preparation for migration *now* and don't leave the building of reports to the last minute!

5. Understand that unless your organisation is very happy with its processes, the project will be 70% change management and 30% technology. Recruit your project team with the right skills to match this balance.

6. Define a set of risks and goals, and have some of these owned by staff who carry out the day-to-day work outside the implementation team. This generates a sense of organisational ownership and reduces opposition to change.

7. Don't give the job of project manager to an existing staff member to do alongside their day job. It is a full-time role.

8. However well the project has gone, there will be problems for the first three months at least. Prepare, communicate and resource accordingly.

9. If the team implementing the system will also be the ones supporting it once it is live, understand that they cannot do both jobs at once and will need support over the transfer period.

10. Run a post-project review and gather together your lessons learnt for the benefit of future projects.

24.4   GET THE PROCESSES RIGHT

1. Ensure that there are joined-up processes between departments. Remember what 'collaborative' CRM means!
2. Ensure that frontline staff enter as much data as possible, i.e. every detail they acquire that might be of benefit to someone in the organisation. It is a fact that busy customer-facing staff such as fundraisers, don't like entering data to computer systems. It is likely that they will enter the minimum amount possible and then only that which is of direct relevance to them. However, they are the ones with the most knowledge of the customer and they must be encouraged, and given every assistance, to enter as much detail as possible, detail that could be of benefit to other people in the organisation (or even to themselves at a later date).
3. Try to ensure that call centre staff have all the information, processes and even specialist staff available or on call, so that they can answer any customer query at the time of the original call. No customer likes to be told 'I'll have to get back to you on that', or 'could you hold the line please while I try to find out?', or 'Sarah isn't in today could you call back tomorrow?' or 'why don't you go to the website?' Nor do they like to be passed around from one staff member to another.
4. Ensure that call centre staff are knowledgeable, efficient and above all polite, even though they may often feel that the customer is an idiot and is wasting their time! If the customer took the trouble to call then the issue is important to them and they expect you to resolve it.
5. Stamp out the use of ad hoc databases and spreadsheets used to record and further manipulate data. If they really are providing a useful function then there is something wrong with or lacking in your CRM system. Of particular importance is getting the reports that you need (standard customer information reports and campaign monitoring reports and analyses), as this is the main area where staff often resort to doing their own thing.
6. Customers using the Internet can get bored very quickly, fail to complete transactions and move on to something else. To ensure the maximum effectiveness of your Internet processes they must:
   a) have an intuitive look and feel, i.e. they must be easy to follow (if customers get confused they will give up);
   b) require the minimum number of clicks (remember the KISS principle: Keep It Simple Stupid!);
   c) be fast (if customers have to spend several minutes waiting for something to happen, they will cancel the transaction);
   d) provide all the necessary information to enable the customer to complete the transaction (a More Info button is always a good idea).
7. Create a file of frequently asked questions (FAQs) to assist with customer service queries.

8. People expect an instant response these days, so if you tell a customer that you are going to do something, then do it immediately and record the action in your CRM system.
9. Clean your data regularly: postcode upgrades, duplicate identification and merging, missing and non-standard data, etc.

24.5 GET THE COMMUNICATIONS RIGHT

1. Maintain the customer-oriented culture rather than a product-centric culture. For example, don't think 'my job is to manage the annual dinner', think 'my job is to ensure that people attending the annual dinner have a great experience'. This is an ongoing activity to change mindsets and is not to be underestimated.
2. Ensure that your various marketing messages are consistent: the words, the format, the materials and the quality.
3. Ensure that you always provide consistent service levels: response times, attitudes and resulting actions. Obtain regular customer feedback on how you are doing.
4. Keep track of your number of attempts to up-sell and cross-sell. Don't ask too often or you might just find yourself losing more than you gain.
5. Monitor campaign performance continually. Make use of dashboards (see 'Analysis' under 15.2.2). If your campaign response rates and your campaign return on investment are not continually improving, then you are doing something wrong. You are probably not analysing your data effectively and consequently not improving your customer targeting!
6. 'Real-time' monitoring is essential for online campaigns, such as the number of tweets that mention the organisation or campaign, or the number of new Facebook friends you have gathered.
7. If, against all expectations, a campaign does really badly, find out why. Were you targeting the wrong people? Was the message unclear? Ask your customers. Do surveys.
8. Spend time analysing existing customer journeys to attempt to predict the behaviour of other customers. Decide what you are going to do in creating campaigns in terms of taking into account your customers' lifestyle versus life stage versus life cycle versus life events.

25 The future of CRM

25.1 THE MOBILE WORLD

First there were mobile phones, next there were mobile phones that could send and receive text messages and then there were mobile phones that could send and receive text messages and send and receive emails. Now there are those that can also record video, surf the Internet and upload and download text, audio, images and video. You can even make video phone calls via Skype on a mobile phone.

Mobile phones are, in fact, no longer mobile phones but mobile computers. This will continue with mobile devices becoming more and more sophisticated and with wireless Internet access becoming available everywhere. **Moore's Law**, in terms of the power of computers and their consequent miniaturisation, continues to apply. This means that while in recent years you might have replaced your desktop PC at work with a laptop that you can take home with you to work on at home, very soon you will have a single small device as powerful as that PC in your pocket all the time and you will be able to work with your CRM system, and any other software you use, literally anytime and anywhere.

Moore's Law: in the mid-1960s Gordon Moore, a co-founder of the computer chip maker Intel, said 'the number of transistors you can get on a chip is doubling approximately every 18 to 24 months'. This has been paraphrased in many ways over the years, especially these days when most people don't even know what a transistor is! The point is that computerised devices are continually getting more powerful, smaller and cheaper all the time and the sceptics who say we will soon reach the limit beyond which it is impossible to go are continually proven to be wrong.

As new technology becomes available, everyone wants it and very soon people can't believe how they ever lived without it. We became used to people using laptops on trains; now they are surfing the Internet and updating their Facebook status on the underground.

25.1.1 **The virtual office**

Much has been made in the past of the concept of working at home and the virtual office but it has only had a limited effect so far. Unless they are specifically based at home, most people who work at home only do so on average one day per week and the vast majority of workers still do not work at home at all. Now with the miniaturisation of computers and the ever-increasing bandwidth of computer communications, there is a distinct possibility that home-working will take off in a big way in the next few years. If all your systems, including your CRM systems, are in the cloud and you can access them from everywhere, why do you need to go to an office (except for the social side of course)? Even round-table meetings are likely to become a thing of the past. In the past, video-conferencing was very expensive. Now you can do it on Skype! The virtual office is set to become a reality.

25.1.2 **The future is in the cloud**

Cloud-computing is the way of the future. More and more systems are moving to the cloud. We are now seeing offices full of people with no powerful file servers in them at all, just a big data switch to connect all the staff to the Internet. This will continue. This is another nail in the coffin of the central office. SaaS systems are becoming more popular for CRM applications and traditional CRM systems suppliers are providing their systems on an in-house or a hosted basis. The days are numbered for those who do not move their systems into the cloud in the next few years.

25.2 **THE RISE AND RISE OF SOCIAL MEDIA**

Whether we like it or not, social networking is here to stay. Its use is increasing exponentially and it seems like it will continue to do so. This leads to the dual problems of information overload and sifting out relevant information from the background noise. The future will see CRM system suppliers developing more and more sophisticated social media monitoring, sorting, sifting and data extraction techniques in conjunction with, and even as an integrated part of, their CRM systems.

Intelligent agents (computer programs, not people) will trawl the Internet searching for information to add to the existing CRM data stores. Other agents will alert you when your customers do something significant such as when your customer wins the lottery or, more realistically, when someone posts a derogatory comment about your organisation, your products or your services on a public website. We are all becoming part of one giant always-active network.

Another element of social media is bringing customers and organisation staff into closer contact. So close in fact that many customers will act as if they are members of staff, effectively selling the organisation's products and services and, by virtue of their use of social media sites, providing call centre or service request responses by the fact that they are in such close and open contact with other customers. This is having a profound effect on some staff within organisations. In the past, if you were rude to one customer on the telephone, you might alienate one customer who might tell a small number of family and friends; now if you are rude to a customer on the phone, the whole world will know in about five minutes flat! The customer truly is king now.

25.3 BLURRING THE BOUNDARIES

The future will see much closer integration of collaborative, operational and analytical CRM. We already have a number of operational CRM systems that incorporate a CMS which means that the collaborative and the operational aspects can be combined in one system. Unless there is a significant change in the underlying technology of operational CRM databases, we will not see a single combined operational and analytical database. (There are people who say they have cracked the problem with something called post-relational databases, but they have yet to prove their worth.)

However, what we are seeing at the higher end of the supplier market is a number of operational CRM suppliers that have analytical CRM systems in their portfolio and so can make the transition from operational to analytical relatively seamless. (And if it is seamless, then do you really care that there are two totally different systems underneath it?) The smaller suppliers will team up with analytical CRM suppliers to provide similar facilities. We are in a world where there are APIs (application programming interfaces) for everything. Almost everything you can think of that you want integrated with CRM can be done relatively painlessly. This will continue to the extent that eventually you will not be able to distinguish one system from another: there will be total inter-connectivity.

At the moment the nirvana of a single database that can do absolutely everything seems a long way off, but who knows what tomorrow will bring? (And with total systems inter-connectivity, do we need it anyway?)

25.4 THE CHANGING MARKETPLACE

CRM system suppliers come and go at an alarming rate and others seem to continue forever. A quick check of a list of CRM suppliers from 11 years ago (not that we called them CRM suppliers 11 years ago) shows that a quarter of them are no longer in business or they have been taken over by other companies. How can you be sure that your chosen supplier will still be here in another 11 years? The short answer is that you can't. You have to look at its track record, its technology and what is happening in the marketplace. The significant trends at the moment are supplier polarisation, the maturing of Microsoft Dynamics CRM, the rise of SaaS offerings, and the emergence of app stores.

25.4.1 Supplier polarisation

A significant trend of the last few years has been the polarisation of the not-for-profit CRM systems marketplace into the big players and the small players. There are a few large companies with up to ten products in their portfolio as a result of mergers and takeovers and a decreasing number of smaller companies with a single product offering. This trend looks set to continue.

25.4.2 Microsoft Dynamics CRM (MSDCRM)

Another important trend is the coming-of-age of Microsoft Dynamics CRM. More than 90% of the not-for-profit sector still have Microsoft-based IT installations with Microsoft Windows servers, desktops and Office software (although this percentage is slowly decreasing) and for many years MSDCRM was lacking in not-for-profit specific functionality. This has changed and MSDCRM is now a viable solution for all but the most complex of not-for-profit organisations. This then is an attractive proposition for organisations that have nailed their colours firmly to the mast of Microsoft.

25.4.3 SaaS

The most important trend, however, is the rise of SaaS offerings for the not-for-profit sector, led by Salesforce and CiviCRM. Although these offerings are often touted as being free when they actually require thousands of pounds worth of configuration and implementation services, they still tend to be less expensive than their traditional rivals and they have all the advantages of being in the cloud.

25.4.4 App stores

The users of smart phones will be familiar with apps (short for applications) which can be downloaded to their phones in seconds to give them additional functionality. The same concept is now a reality for MSDCRM, Salesforce and CiviCRM. If you have one of these products and you want some additional functionality, just look in the appropriate app store and the chances are that you will find exactly what you are looking for and you can download it, install it and have it operational in a few minutes. (Of course it is not always that easy. Sometimes the apps don't work or don't do exactly what you want them to or are lacking in documentation or support, but it is more than just a theory and the facilities are improving all the time.)

25.4.5 A supplier shake-out?

The dominance of the big players, the rise of MSDCRM, the rise of SaaS solutions, and the emergence of app stores, all point to a significant supplier shake-out coming in the next few years. Smaller suppliers will need to adapt if they are to survive.

Interesting times are ahead.

Case study: the future of CRM

What I've experienced at Stroke Association

We bought Microsoft Dynamics CRM in 2007 to provide case management for our stroke survivors and their carers. This enabled our coordinators to manage their rehabilitation, communicate with their carers and record various metrics to help measure progress. With this information being recorded in one place, for the first time we were able to produce reports and statistics accurately to help shape the services that we provide and give evidence to the bodies that commission our services.

We chose MSCRM because, as well as providing what could be considered to be standard out-of-the-box CRM functions, it enabled our in-house database development team to create bespoke solutions for the Stroke Association. This platform was seen as an enabler to migrate many of our disparate databases scattered across the organisation into a single unifying structured database.

The market reports from authorities such as Gartner also indicated that MSCRM was very strategic for Microsoft and was receiving significant investment. This coupled with what were then called commercial off-the-shelf (COTS) solutions, meant that third-party software suppliers would develop software add-ons for enhancements or complete vertical solutions. However, MSCRM was still in its infancy and was certainly not being used in the charity sector, confirmation I received from the Charity Consortium IT Director's Group (CCitDG) peers I liaised with.

We migrated many business areas to MSCRM including contract management, volunteer management, stroke club management and corporate change control.

We went out to tender in 2009 to replace our ageing fundraising system. We received tenders from the main players in this vertical market and surprisingly, again due to its infancy, we received two tenders for the MSCRM platform. One of the vendors made it through to the shortlist, but was unsuccessful as the functional specifications of the product fell short compared with the significantly more mature products in this sector. Whilst it was not unsurprising that the MSCRM vendor was not selected, the compelling arguments then (and now) for MSCRM and having contacts sharing a common record base on one system, thus avoiding complicated and often expensive interface integration work, still ring true.

We made the right decision at the time, and purchased a separate fundraising system that met all of our functional needs. The native technical ability of MSCRM has been leveraged to create an interface to this fundraising system in a supported way. If we were going out to tender today, the outcome may well be different as there is a wider choice of MSCRM fundraising solutions on the market.

Where do I think CRM is going?

The app store concept is now ubiquitous for downloading software for smartphones, tablets, etc. The big players such as Microsoft and Salesforce have now created cloud-based app stores for corporate solutions and the COTS model will diminish in value as the app store gains traction. This is a good thing, as it was often difficult to find the right COTS partner. Being able to choose corporate software in this way for CRM is a game changer and will enable CIOs and business stakeholders to seek software to extend and enhance their CRM systems for their corporate needs.

I believe the number of vendors providing fundraising systems in the charity sector will diminish as Salesforce gains more customers. Its cloud-based offering with charity discounts on a per-person, per-month offering is extremely attractive. The functionality will continue to grow with clients making their own developments and community-based developers making products available from the app store. This will make salesforce.com a likely option in a tender process.

The same can be said for MSCRM. Microsoft has invested in the product heavily and its public cloud offerings for MSCRM along with its native integration with Microsoft Office make it an attractive proposition. Microsoft's push for a public cloud is also apparent with its MSCRM roadmap. Here new functionality is often released in the public cloud first before being made available for organisations to update and upgrade their private cloud MSCRM platforms.

From a charity perspective the corporate app stores for Salesforce and MSCRM are appealing. They offer an insight into the free software that is available and the chargeable software, allowing chief information officers to build a customised roadmap of where they want to take CRM. For the first time, CIOs are not tied to proprietary systems and stuck with a slow roadmap and often expensive functionality developments.

For the fundraising suppliers which go it alone and remain in the market with their proprietary offerings, I believe there will be interesting times ahead. They will need to face the difficult question of what to do with their intellectual property. They should look to safeguard this by investing in redeveloping their code to work with MSCRM and Salesforce and so extend their reach with the huge market share these platforms have. If you can't beat them join them.

Paul Hughes
Head of IT, Stroke Association

References

Anderson, W. O. (2001), 'Customer relationship management in an e-business environment', *Change Management and the New Industrial Revolution*, 7 (9), 311–316.

Berry, L.L. (2002), 'Relationship marketing of services perspectives from 1983 to 2000', *Journal of Relationship Marketing*, 1(1), 59–77.

Bradshaw, D., and C. Brash (2001), 'Managing customer relationships in the e-business world: how to personalise computer relationships for increased profitability', *International Journal of Retail and Distribution Management*, 29 (12), 520–529.

Burnett, K. (2002), *Relationship Fundraising; A Donor-Based Approach to the Business of Raising Money* (San Francisco: Jossey-Bass).

Cunningham, C. and I.-Y. Song (2007), 'A taxonomy of customer relationship management analyses for data warehousing', *Tutorials, Posters, Panels and Industrial Contributions at the 26th International Conference on Conceptual Modeling*, 83, 97–102.

Fjermestad, J., and N. C. Romano Jr (2003), 'Electronic customer relationship management: revisiting the general principles of usability and resistance – an integrative implementation framework', *Business Process Management Journal*, 9 (5), 572–591.

Flory, P. (2001), *Fundraising Databases* (London: Directory of Social Change).

Geib, M., A. Reichold, L. Kolbe and W. Brenner (2005), 'Architecture for customer relationship management approaches to financial services', *Proceedings of the 38th Hawaii International Conference on System Sciences*, 1–10.

Goldenberg, B. (2006), 'CRM: the past and the future', *CRM Magazine*, 110 (1), 18.

Gummesson, E. (2002), 'Relationship marketing and a new economy: it's time for deprogramming', *Journal of Services Marketing*, 16 (7), 585–589.

Harej, K., and R. V. Horvat (2004), 'Customer relationship management momentum for business improvement', *26th International Conference on Information Technology Interfaces*, 1, 107–111.

Hill, L. and B. Whitehead (2004), *The Complete Membership Handbook* (London: Directory of Social Change).

Hudson, M. (2009), *Managing Without Profit: Leadership, management and governance of third sector organisations* (London: Directory of Social Change).

ICO (2012), 'Guide to the Privacy and Electronic Regulations, Information Commissioner's Office', www.ico.gov.uk/for_organisations/privacy_and_electronic_communications/the_guide.aspx, accessed 23 June 2012.

Kalakota, R. and M. Robinson (2001), *e-Business 2.0 Roadmap for Success* (New Jersey: Addison-Wesley).

Lawrie, A. (2007), *The Complete Guide to Business and Strategic Planning*, (London: Directory of Social Change).

Lee, C. S., Y. C. Wang, W. M. Liu and Y. C. Lin (2007), 'CRM ontology based on CMMI project planning for business applications', *Proceedings of the Sixth International Conference on Machine Learning and Cybernetics*, 2941–2946.

Lloyd, T. (2006), *Cultural Giving: Successful donor development for arts and heritage organisations*. (London: Directory of Social Change).

Maple, P. (2003), *Marketing Strategy for Effective Fundraising* (London: Directory of Social Change).

Mullin, R. (2002), *Fundraising Strategy* (London: Directory of Social Change).

Olson, J. R., J. A. Belohlav and K. K. Boyer (2005), 'Operational, economic and mission elements in not-for-profit organizations: the case of the Chicago Symphony Orchestra', *Journal of Operations Management*, 125–142.

Pan, S. L. and J. N. Lee (2003), 'Using e-CRM for a unified view of the customer', *Communications of the ACM*, 46 (4), 95–99.

Pant, V. and W. P Wagner. (2006), 'A framework for XML-based multi-channel contact point integration', *Business Process Management Journal*, 12 (3), 344–360.

Ratner, B. (2012), 'Response CHAID tree', *CHAID: Nine Creative, Utile Applications Beyond its Original Intent*, www.geniq.net/res/CHAID-Nine-Creative-Utile-Applications.html, retrieved 16 September 2012.

Schonberger, R. J. (1996), *World Class Manufacturing: The Next Decade: Building Power, Strength and Value* (New York: The Free Press).

Slack, B. (2007), 'Quality not Quantity', *Professional Fundraising*, April ed., 22–24.

Standish Group (2011), *Chaos Report* (Boston MA: The Standish Group).

Index

PHYSICS IN ENGINEERING 16 - 19

ELECTRICITY

Gordon Raitt

Director
Physics in Engineering Project 16–19

Principal Sponsors

Royal Commission for the
Exhibition of 1851
Department of Trade
and Industry

CAMBRIDGE
UNIVERSITY PRESS

Published by the Press Syndicate of the University of Cambridge
The Pitt Building, Trumpington Street, Cambridge CB2 1RP
40 West 20th Street, New York, NY 10011–4211, USA
10 Stamford Road, Oakleigh, Victoria 3166, Australia

First published 1992

Printed in Great Britain by Scotprint Ltd, Musselburgh

A catalogue record for this book is available from the British Library

ISBN 0 521 36677 1

Contents

Preface

The main aims

The main aims of the Physics in Engineering Project: 16–19 and its books are:

- to show students ways in which the physics that they study is used in practice in industry and engineering;
- to provide numerical and other questions and problems that are based on the engineering that has been described;
- to convey a feel of what engineers do, and to interest students and staff in engineering.

The content

The basis for the selection of the physics content has been the Examination Boards' joint publication *Common Cores at Advanced Level* (GCE Boards of England, Wales and Northern Ireland, 1983), with the object of ensuring that as much of the content as possible will be applicable to most students. The selection also relates closely to the Scottish Higher Grade Physics syllabus.

Engineering examples of the physics principles can be found throughout engineering: in the aeronautical, automobile, civil, electrical, marine, mechanical and other fields. The selection has been determined mainly by the practicalities of what was accessible for visits from the work bases, and of what was amenable to development by correspondence with more distant engineering companies. Many more topics than those which appear were actually started and developed, but proved either too difficult in concepts or in presentation for this age group, or important information was ultimately not available. The ones that are printed provide a collection to act as examples.

The book is intended as a complement to the physics textbook that is in class use. It aims to show how physics that a class is studying is important in practice. The book does not set out to teach the physics, although sometimes a summary is provided.

The project

The Physics in Engineering Project: 16–19 is the follow-on to the 13–16 years School Physics in Engineering Project, with its five books published in 1987 under the series title Physics in Action. A 16–19 years follow-on was suggested at a meeting of the Physics Panel of the Industry Education Unit of the Department of Trade and Industry. The work is based on visits to manufacturing companies and to construction sites, on studies of firms' technical literature, and on correspondence with companies.

Acknowledgements

Funding was needed to enable the visits to be made to companies during their working week, to enable the extensive correspondence to be undertaken, and for the development work itself.

I am particularly grateful to The Fellowship of Engineering, London, and to the Ove Arup Partnership, Consulting Engineers, London, for their early interest in and financial support of the work; and to the Department of Trade and Industry, and the Royal Commission for the Exhibition of 1851 whose grants provided the main funding. Because the grants were on a joint funding basis, however, the work could not have been undertaken without the interest and financial support of other bodies and companies, and these are named below in the complete list of sponsors. To them I am very grateful.

APV Baker Limited
BICC plc
BOC Limited
British Steel
Department of Trade and Industry
The Electricity Council
The Fellowship of Engineering
Sir Alexander Gibb and Partners

Johnson Matthey
Kier Limited
The Mercers' Company
Ove Arup Partnership
Plessey Company
Royal Commission for the Exhibition of 1851
United Biscuits (UK) Limited
Wiggins Teape Group Limited

Several sections of the book are based on work seen in progress at EB Nitran, Transformers and Fusegear, Dundee, and I am very grateful to the staff for guidance during a succession of visits and in correspondence. I am similarly grateful to the staffs of other firms which I visited.

The staffs of companies whose work or whose products are described have kindly read sections of the draft text and have made comments on these. Staff of Dundee Institute of Technology have helped similarly with certain sections. The comments have enabled me to clarify and to improve a number of aspects, and I am very grateful to the members of the staffs.

Engineers and engineering

Throughout the years of the two projects, several features have been apparent again and again. There is an aesthetic beauty in design drawings, in machine parts, and in finished structures. Most machines operate with many physical principles and effects interacting at the same time and in complex ways. Yet machines function smoothly day after day, month after month: often unseen and unnoticed beneath their cover; the staffs have encountered and surmounted many difficulties and challenges in design and in manufacture. These staffs seem frequently to be modestly unaware of the greatness of their achievements. And British people seem sometimes not to recognise nor appreciate the vision, the imaginativeness, the skills and the achievements of those who design and those who make. Their work is a central contribution to the life and the economy of Britain and of other nations.

Gordon Raitt
St Andrews

1. *Resistance and resistors*

The nature of current and resistance

Charge flow

Figure 1.1 *A metal conductor carrying a current of 16 A. Through the cross-section S in the conductor there is a flow of 10^{20} electrons per second.*

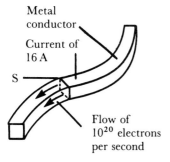

Metal conductor

Current of 16 A

S

Flow of 10^{20} electrons per second

In a liquid which conducts a current, the current consists of a flow of positive ions moving in one direction and a flow of negative ions moving in the opposite direction. In a gas discharge tube, such as a fluorescent lamp containing mercury vapour and argon gas at low pressure, the current consists of a flow of positive ions in one direction (mercury ions and argon ions), and a flow of electrons in the opposite direction.

In a vacuum tube, such as a cathode ray oscilloscope or a television tube, the current is a stream of electrons moving in the vacuum space from the cathode to the anode.

In a metal wire, the current is a flow of electrons.

Thus *an electric current consists of a flow of charge*, which may be positive or negative, or both.

The *rate at which charge flows* is the *current magnitude*, and it is measured in coulombs per second. A rate of flow of charge of one coulomb per second is a current of one amp.

Figure 1.1 shows a metal conductor carrying a current of 16 A. This consists of a flow of electrons in one direction through any cross-section in the conductor, such as at S, at a net rate of 10^{20} electrons per second.

This figure of 10^{20} electrons per second is obtained as follows. A current of 16 A is a flow of charge of 16 coulomb per second, $16\,\mathrm{C\,s^{-1}}$. The charge on an electron is $1.6 \times 10^{-19}\,\mathrm{C}$.

Number of electrons passing through section S

$$= \frac{\text{Total charge passing in 1 second}}{\text{Charge on 1 electron}}$$

$$= \frac{16\,\mathrm{C}}{1.6 \times 10^{-19}\,\mathrm{C}}$$

$$= 1 \times 10^{20}$$

Since the 16 C charge passed through S in 1 s, 10^{20} electrons passed through S in 1 s.

1.1 In a circuit, 1 million electrons pass through a section in 1 s. What is the current? (Charge on an electron $= 1.6 \times 10^{-19}\,\mathrm{C}$.)

1.2 In a circuit, 5×10^{19} electrons pass through a section in 1 s. What is the current?

Drift velocity

Figure 1.2 *The same conductor as is shown in Figure 1.1. It is made of copper, and in a 1 m length there are 1.3×10^{24} mobile electrons.*

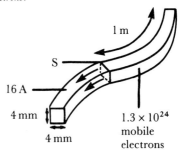

1 m

S

16 A

4 mm

4 mm

1.3×10^{24} mobile electrons

In vacuum tubes, such as cathode ray oscilloscopes and X-ray tubes, electrons approach the anode at speeds of about 30 000 kilometres per second $(3 \times 10^7 \, \text{m s}^{-1})$. This is within an order of magnitude of the speed of light $(3 \times 10^8 \, \text{m s}^{-1})$.

Let us find a value for the average speed at which electrons move, as a current, along a metallic conductor. Figure 1.2 shows a copper conductor of square cross-section 4 mm × 4 mm. Electrons are passing through the section S towards the front face, constituting a current.

In copper, each atom of copper provides one mobile electron which is able to convey charge and form a current. In a 1 m length of copper of 4 mm × 4 mm cross-section there are 1.3×10^{24} atoms of copper, and thus there are also 1.3×10^{24} mobile electrons.

The current in the conductor is 16 A, as in Figure 1.1; and a flow of 10^{20} electrons per second is needed through section S. 1.3×10^{24} electrons are contained in 1 m of the conductor. Therefore 10^{20} electrons are contained in

$$\frac{10^{20} \times 1 \, \text{m}}{1.3 \times 10^{24}} = 8 \times 10^{-5} \, \text{m} = 0.08 \, \text{mm}$$

This length of free electron 'gas' column has to move through section S in 1 s; thus the speed of the free electron 'gas' column is 0.08 mm per second. This is about 5 mm per minute. This speed contrasts markedly with the 30 000 km per second of electrons in vacuum tubes.

In a vacuum tube the electric field accelerates the electrons, and there is nothing between the cathode and the anode with which an electron can collide. The electrons thus reach very high speeds. In the 1 m length of copper conductor there are 1.3×10^{24} copper atoms with which an electron that started from the far end could collide. In a metallic conductor, the conduction electrons experience repeated collisions with metal atoms, and these collisions prevent the electrons from being accelerated to any high speed. The collisions cause a random movement of electrons, and on this is superimposed a general drift towards the positive terminal in the circuit.

In spite of the low drift velocity, of only a few millimetres per minute, metallic conductors can carry large currents because the number of mobile electrons is so very large.

Electric field strength, current and resistivity

Figure 1.3 *A metal conductor being continuously charged by a generator. The electric field causes a drift of electrons and a current.*

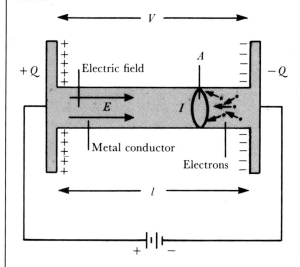

Figure 1.3 shows a metallic conductor. It is being continuously charged by a battery; thus one end is charged positive with respect to the other end, which is negative. This charge separation sets up an *electric field* in the conductor. In this electric field, electrons experience a force due to the interaction between their charge and the field; and electrons are forced along the conductor. This forms a current in the conductor.

An increase in the strength of the electric field would be expected to increase the rate of flow of electrons, and thus to increase the current, and this is so. The current, I, through a fixed cross-section area, A, of the conductor is proportional to the electric field strength, E, through that area:

$$\frac{I}{A} \propto E \qquad \text{therefore } E = \text{constant} \times \frac{I}{A}$$

$$E = \rho \times \frac{I}{A}$$

Now,

Field strength = Potential gradient

$$E = \frac{V}{l}$$

Therefore

$$\frac{V}{l} = \rho \times \frac{I}{A}$$

Now, by definition, $\frac{V}{I}$ is the resistance, R, of the conductor. Rearranging the equation:

$$R = \frac{V}{I} = \rho \times \frac{l}{A} \qquad (1.1)$$

The proportionality constant, ρ, is called the *resistivity* of the material. The resistivity of a material is a characteristic of the lattice of the material and of impurities in it. Different pure metals have different resistivities; alloying alters the resistivity of a material.

Ohmic heating of a conductor

The mobile electrons which form a current in a conductor are accelerated by the electric field in the conductor; they are then slowed down or halted by collisions with atoms in the conductor lattice. *The energy lost by the electrons in collision with the lattice is gained by the lattice.* Since the electrons are then accelerated again and the process repeats, the lattice continues to gain internal energy, and *its temperature rises.*

A current in a conductor therefore results in a temperature rise in the conductor.

The energy which is imparted by the current to the conductor per second is given by:

P = charge flow per s × potential through which the charge drops
P = current × potential difference = $I \times V$
$P = IV = I^2R$

where R is the resistance of the conductor. This rise in temperature of a conductor occurs whenever a conductor carries a current. The temperature will continue to rise until the energy which is gained by

the conductor per second from the current is balanced by the energy which is lost from the conductor per second to the surroundings. *This is of great importance in electrical equipment and machinery.*

In the design of electrical equipment, one of the first stages is a calculation of the heating that will occur; this is followed by considering suitable cooling arrangements. Large electric motors and large alternators (for producing alternating current) have built-in fans for drawing cooling air over the coils. Large transformers are wound with gaps between turns in the coils, so that cooling oil may circulate around the conductor; the transformer core and coils are then placed in a tank of oil, which has 'radiator' type cooling panels exposed to the atmosphere. (See Figures 3.9 and 3.16.)

The resistance of a conductor and its temperature

The resistance of a given conductor depends upon its temperature. As the temperature is raised, the vibrations of the conductor lattice increase in magnitude, and the frequency with which a free electron experiences a collision with the lattice increases. In this way the electron drift is slowed down, and the current is decreased.

Now, $R = \frac{V}{I}$; and if for a fixed value of V the value of I has *decreased*, the value of $\frac{V}{I} = R$ has *increased*. Thus, in general, *the resistance of a conductor increases with increasing temperature.*

Resistivity

Definition and units

The resistance of a conductor is proportional to its length and inversely proportional to its cross-section area:

$$R \propto \frac{l}{A} \qquad R = \rho\frac{l}{A} \qquad \rho = \frac{RA}{l}$$

The proportionality constant is the *resistivity, ρ.* From the right-hand relationship, above, the units of resistivity are ohm metre^2 metre^{-1}, which is ohm metre (Ω m).

The resistivity of the copper which is most commonly used in wires and cables (annealed copper) is 1.72×10^{-8} Ω m, at 20 °C; and the resistivity of nickel at 20 °C is 7.00×10^{-8} Ω m. It is necessary to state the temperature since the resistivity of a material varies with its temperature.

The importance of resistivity values

The resistivity of a material is a characteristic property of the material. It depends upon the chemical composition of the material, and upon the physical treatment which the material has received. For instance, impurities and the addition of an alloying metal alter the crystal lattice structure; and heat treatment and cold working alter the grain structure. Each of these alters the resistivity.

Measurement of resistivity, and the provision of resistivity values, are very important in industry. They provide for the manufacturing company:

1. *an acceptance test* for a firm, enabling it to decide whether a material is of a suitable quality;
2. *a means of choosing* the most appropriate material for a particular need; and
3. *a means of calculating* the length and cross-section area of a conductor which would be needed to produce a particular resistance value.

Measuring resistivity in industry

From the right-hand relationship given on page 3 it is apparent that to obtain the resistivity of a sample of a material it is necessary to measure the *resistance*, *cross-section area*, and *length* of the sample. A standard method has been devised by the American Society for Testing and Materials, and the following is an extract from the instructions document:

Standard Test Method for Resistivity of Metallically Conducting Materials
Scope
This method covers the determination of electrical resistivity of metallic materials to an accuracy of 2%.

Test specimen
The test specimen shall be in the form of a wire or a strip. It shall have a length of at least 300 mm, a diameter of at least 1.3 mm if a wire (and a thickness of at least 1.3 mm if a strip), and a resistance of at least 0.001 Ω.

The diameter (or the thickness) of the specimen shall not vary along its length by more than 3%.

The specimen shall show no surface cracks or other defects observable with normal vision, and it shall be free from surface oxide.

Apparatus
(1) A means of applying terminals to the specimen.
(2) A suitable potentiometer for making resistance measurements, with an error of less than 0.5%.
(3) A means of measuring the cross-section area, with an error of less than 0.5%.
(4) A means of measuring the length, with an error of less than 0.5%.

Measurements
(1) Cross-section area In general, the diameter of a specimen of circular cross-section, or the thickness and width of a strip specimen, shall be determined by using a micrometer. A sufficient number of measurements shall be made to obtain the mean cross-section to within 0.5%.
(2) Length The length may be measured by any scale which will give an accuracy of 0.5%.

Report
The report shall contain the following entries:
(1) Code (letters or numbers) to identify the specimen.
(2) Kind of material.
(3) Temperature of surroundings.
(4) Length of specimen used.
(5) All micrometer readings, and average value.
(6) Cross-section area calculation.
(7) Method of measuring resistance.
(8) Calculation of resistance.
(9) Calculation of resistivity.

Table 1.1 summarises extracts from a determination of the resistivity of a resistance alloy.

1.3 Table 1.1 gives data which has been summarised from an industrial determination of

Table 1.1. *Summarised data from a resistivity determination*

Material Brightray B, resistance alloy (60% Ni, 16% Cr, 24% Fe)
Cast number HYE 9832; *Test number* 468 374;
Temperature 18 °C
Form Strip. Average width 51.53 mm;
Average thickness 0.585 mm

Specimen number	(1)	(2)	(3)
Specimen length (mm)	442	594	735
Specimen resistance (Ω)	0.1634	0.2196	0.2716

(From data supplied by Inco Alloys International)

resistivity for a resistance alloy. Find the resistivity of each of the three test specimens (1), (2) and (3), to three significant figures.

1.4 Measurements to determine the resistivity of an alloy, Brightray Alloy 35, gave the following results for a wire specimen, at 20 °C: *average diameter* 1.83 mm; *length* between the electrical contacts, 826 mm; *resistance*, 0.320 Ω. Find the resistivity of the alloy at 20 °C.

Table 1.2 gives the value of the resistivity, ρ, for some materials at 20 °C. Examine the table, and notice the different magnitudes of ρ for different classes of materials.

Resistance and temperature

General trends and importance

The electrical resistance of a material depends upon its temperature. The resistance of pure metals and of alloys *increases* with increasing temperature. The resistance of insulating materials *decreases* with increasing temperature. The resistance of semi-conductors and of graphite *decreases* with increasing temperature.

Electrical equipment is manufactured at room temperature, but it may operate at a temperature very different to that at which it was made, and its resistance will thus change. The copper windings of electric motors, of alternators producing ac, and of transformers all carry a current; the current raises the temperature of the windings. The windings will be made in the factory at about 20 °C, but they may

Table 1.2. *The electrical resistivity of some materials at 20 °C*

Conductors	Resistivity ($\times 10^{-8}\,\Omega$ m)	Semi-conductors	Resistivity (Ω m)	Insulators	Resistivity (Ω m)
Metal elements				*Ceramic*	
Silver	1.6	Germanium	0.6	Electrical porcelain	10^{11}
Copper (annealed)	1.7	Silicon	2300		
Aluminium (soft)	2.8			*Glass*	
Tungsten	5.6			Vitreous silica	10^{12}
Nickel (99.98% Ni)	7.5				
Nickel (commercial				*Polymers*	
grade, 99.0% Ni)	9.5			Polyvinylchloride	10^{12}
Platinum	12			Cross-linked	10^{14}
				polyethylene	
Alloys				Polyethylene (low	10^{16}
Mild steel	14			and high density)	
Ferry alloy (similar	49			Polytetrafluoro-	10^{16}
to constantan)				ethylene	
Alloy S (similar	110				
to nichrome)					
Carbon					
Graphite	3000				

Figure 1.4 *A cut-away section of a 5 kW ac generator for producing ac at 120 V. The rotor coil has a resistance of 10 Ω when cold, but 14 Ω at the hot operating temperature of 120 °C. (Source: Markon Division of Newage International Limited, Stamford.)*

operate at about 120 °C. In the course of this temperature rise, the resistance of the windings will rise by about 40%.

Figure 1.4 shows a cut-away section of the alternator for a small, portable, petrol-engine-driven generating set to provide ac. When cold and not operating, the rotor coil has a resistance of 10 Ω; when operating, the coil is at a temperature of about 120 °C and its resistance rises to about 14 Ω.

Changes in resistance of such relative magnitudes must be taken into account in the electrical design of the equipment.

Obtaining a resistance–temperature graph in industry

In the design and manufacture of electrical equipment it is essential to know how the resistances of the conductors that will be used will change with temperature, and thus tables of data which provide resistance information are needed. The information for these tables must come from experimental determinations. Standard methods for conducting the determinations have been developed. The following is an account of a method of the American Society for Testing and Materials; it is a summary made by extracting key sections of the full document.

Standard Test Method for Change of Resistance with Temperature of Metallic Materials for Electrical Heating

Scope
This method covers the determination of the change of resistance with temperature of metallic materials for electrical heating.

Test specimen and leads
The test specimen shall be prepared from material as left by the manufacturing process (e.g. actual manufactured wire), and in a form suitable for measuring its resistance in an electric furnace. When the resistance is to be measured with a Kelvin bridge or with a potentiometer, a current lead shall be welded to each end of the specimen.

Electric furnace
The furnace for heating specimens shall be of such a type that the temperature can be controlled over the range from room temperature to the maximum desired. It shall be so constructed that the specimens and the thermocouples can be maintained at a uniform and constant temperature at the desired points within the working range.

Resistance measurements
A Kelvin bridge or a potentiometer shall be used when measuring specimens having resistances less than 10 Ω. A Wheatstone bridge may be used with specimens having resistances greater than 10 Ω. The resistance of the specimen shall be measured with an accuracy of 0.1%.

Procedure
Mount the test specimen in the furnace; bring the temperature of the furnace to the maximum specified temperature, and hold at this value until the resistance of the specimen remains constant. Take measurements of temperature and resistance.

Then lower the temperature of the furnace in steps of approximately 100 K. Take measurements at each point when temperature and resistance have become stationary.

Determine the temperature by means of calibrated thermocouples, in conjunction with a potentiometer, of such construction as to ensure an accuracy corresponding to a temperature uncertainty not exceeding 10 K.

Resistance–temperature curve

Plot a curve of resistance against temperature.

Singular points

If there are indications that the curve is not smooth at any point, carry the specimen through the temperature cycle again, and take temperature and resistance readings at intervals of approximately 25 K in the suspected region.

Accuracy

The accuracy is estimated to be within $\pm 2\%$.

1.5 (a) With what equipment is the resistance measured, for specimens with a resistance of less than $10\,\Omega$?

(b) With what is the temperature measured?

(c) The instructions use the plural for the temperature measuring instrument. Why is more than one needed? (Clue: re-read the section on the 'Electric Furnace'.)

(d) If the upper temperature was about $1000\,^\circ$C, about how many points would there be on the graph?

(e) If one point appears to be off a smooth curve, what steps must be taken?

The temperature coefficient of resistance

1.6 Plotting a resistance–temperature curve

Table 1.3. *The resistance of a wire specimen of an alloy, Brightray Alloy 35, at temperatures from $20\,^\circ$C to $1000\,^\circ$C (the dimensions of the wire were given in Question 1.4)*

Temperature (°C)	20	100	200	300	400	500
Resistance ($\times 10^{-3}\,\Omega$)	320	333	344	354	363	371

Temperature (°C)	600	700	800	900	1000
Resistance ($\times 10^{-3}\,\Omega$)	377	383	388	393	397

(a) Plot a resistance–temperature graph.

(b) Is the graph linear?

(c) Where is the rate of change of resistance with temperature greatest: at the lowest temperatures or at the highest temperatures?

1.7 Obtaining the rate of change of resistance with temperature

From the graph obtained in Question 1.6:

(a) (i) Obtain the change in resistance between $50\,^\circ$C and $250\,^\circ$C. (ii) Find the mean rate of change of resistance between these two temperatures, in $\Omega\,\mathrm{K}^{-1}$.

(b) (i) Obtain the change in resistance between $750\,^\circ$C and $950\,^\circ$C. (ii) Find the mean rate of change of resistance between these two temperature, in $\Omega\mathrm{K}^{-1}$.

Keep your graph and calculations for the next questions, Questions 1.8 and 1.9.

1.8 Obtaining the fractional change in resistance with temperature

(a) What is the resistance of the test specimen in Question 1.7 at $50\,^\circ$C?

(b) What would be the resistance of a specimen of the same type of wire but twice the length, at $50\,^\circ$C?

(c) What is the fractional change in resistance for the specimen in Question 1.7 between $50\,^\circ$C and $250\,^\circ$C; that is, $(R_{250}-R_{50})/R_{50}$?

(d) What is the fractional change in resistance for the double length specimen over the same temperature change?

(e) What is the advantage of working in fractional resistance changes?

1.9 Obtaining the fractional change in resistance per unit temperature change

Obtain a value for the fractional change in resistance per unit temperature change in the range $50\,^\circ$C to $250\,^\circ$C. That is,

$$\frac{(R_{250}-R_{50})}{R_{50}} \times \frac{1}{(250\,^\circ\mathrm{C}-50\,^\circ\mathrm{C})}$$

This is the temperature coefficient of resistance, α, over that range.

The *temperature coefficient of resistance*, α, of a material is its *fractional change in resistance per unit temperature change*.

$$\alpha = \frac{(R_2-R_1)}{R_1} \times \frac{1}{(\theta_2-\theta_1)} \qquad (1.2)$$

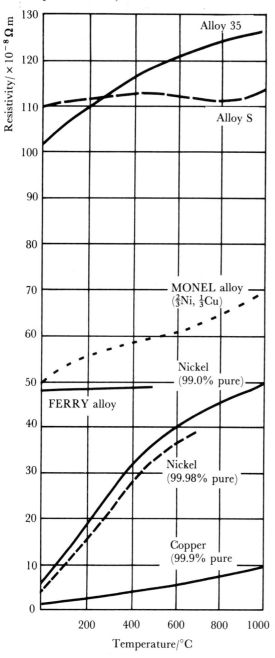

Figure 1.5 *The graphs show the changes in resistivity of some metals and alloys as their temperature changes. Ferry alloy is very similar to constantan in composition, and alloy S is very similar to nichrome. (Adapted from graphs produced by Inco Alloys International.)*

$(R_2 - R_1)/R_2$ has no units, since it is a ratio of resistances; $1/(\theta_2 - \theta_1)$ has units of K^{-1}. The units of temperature coefficient of resistance are therefore K^{-1}.

Figure 1.5 shows the change in *resistivity* of some pure metals and some alloys with temperature.

1.10 Find alloy 35 (trade name Brightray Alloy 35) and compare its curve with the others shown in Figure 1.5. Now look back to the curve which you drew of the *resistance* of a specimen of Brightray Alloy 35 against temperature (Question 1.6). Do the shapes of the two curves, *resistance against temperature* and *resistivity against temperature*, correspond closely?

For a metallic conductor, the shape of a resistance against temperature curve for a specimen and the shape of its resistivity against temperature curve are almost identical. Thus in Figure 1.5 the relative slopes and shapes of the resistivity curves for the different conductors are also the relative slopes and shapes of resistance curves against temperature.

1.11 Using the graphs given in Figure 1.5:
 (a) Which of the two metals copper and nickel has the greater rate of change of resistivity with temperature?
 (b) Which will have the greater rate of change of resistance with temperature?
 (c) Which will have the greater value of the temperature coefficient of resistance?
 (d) Consult Table 1.4 on page 9 to check your reasoning.

1.12 Of the the metals and alloys given in Figure 1.5, which will have the lowest value of α, the temperature coefficient of resistance? Check your answer by consulting Table 1.4.

A feature of the temperature coefficient, α, for many of the metal elements is that there is relatively little variation among them. A glance at Table 1.4 shows that of five very widely used metal conductors, the value of α varies only from 3.9 to 4.5 (times the common factor of $10^{-3}\,K^{-1}$). For a sixth metal, nickel, α is only slightly greater at $6.8 \times 10^{-3}\,K^{-1}$.

The importance of tables of values of α is twofold. Firstly it enables *resistances to be predicted* at

Table 1.4. *Temperature coefficient of resistance,* α

Metal elements	α at 20 °C ($\times 10^{-3}\,\mathrm{K}^{-1}$)	Uses
Nickel (99.98% pure)	6.8	Resistance thermometers
Tungsten	4.5	
Silver	4.0	
Copper	3.9	
Aluminium	3.9	
Platinum	3.9	Resistance thermometers

Alloys	Mean α 20 °C–500 °C ($\times 10^{-3}\,\mathrm{K}^{-1}$)	Uses
Monel ($\frac{2}{3}$ Ni, $\frac{1}{3}$ Cu)	0.37	
Alloy 35	0.33	
Alloy S (similar to nichrome)	0.06	Furnace elements
Ferry (similar to constantan)	0.04	Control resistors

various temperatures. Using the equation which defines α, we will rearrange it into an equation which gives a final resistance, R_2, in terms of an initial resistance, R_1.

$$\alpha = \frac{(R_2 - R_1)}{R_1} \times \frac{1}{(\theta_2 - \theta_1)} \qquad (1.2)$$

Multiplying, and then rearranging, we have

$$\alpha \times R_1 (\theta_2 - \theta_1) = R_2 - R_1$$

$$R_1 + \alpha \times R_1 (\theta_2 - \theta_1) = R_2$$

$$R_1 [1 + \alpha(\theta_2 - \theta_1)] = R_2 \qquad (1.3)$$

1.13 Resistance of hot alternator coils

Figure 1.4 shows a cut-away section of a 5 kW alternator, for producing ac at 120 V. The rotor windings when at 20 °C have a resistance of 10.0 Ω. When the alternator is working and the coil is carrying a current it is at a temperature of 120 °C. What is the resistance of the rotor coil at the working temperature? (α for copper = $3.93 \times 10^{-3}\,\mathrm{K}^{-1}$.)

1.14 Resistance of a power cable on load

Figure 1.6 shows a power cable which can carry a current of 200 A. With this current, the copper conductors may be at a temperature 90 °C. Calculate the resistance of 50.0 m of the cable at the operating temperature. The resistance per metre of the conductor at 20 °C is $0.387 \times 10^{-3}\,\Omega$; α for copper = $3.93 \times 10^{-3}\,\mathrm{K}^{-1}$. (The total length of conductor, out and back, will be 100 m.)

A second use of tables of values of α is to enable *temperatures to be determined* by measuring resistances. This is *electrical resistance thermometry*. For this, the equation which defines α needs to be rearranged so as to give a final temperature, θ_2, in terms of the other quantities.

1.15 Resistance thermometry equation

Rearrange the equation which defines α, so as to give a final temperature θ_2 in terms of the other quantities (see equation (1.2)).

1.16 Operating temperature of an inductor coil

Part of Chapter 4 describes the design and manufacture of large inductor coils for a 19 000 V power supply. Figure 4.8 shows a longitudinal section of a coil; Figure 4.15 shows three coils in position; Figure 4.16 shows the container tank, which has the coils inside immersed in cooling oil; and Figure 4.18 shows the electrical connections while the unit is under test.

The unit is designed so that, in continuous operation, with the design load current of 437 A in each coil, the mean temperature of the copper windings will be not more than 60 K above ambient temperature.

The results of the test were: ambient temperature 22 °C; resistance of one coil at ambient temperature 0.455 Ω; resistance of the same coil under steady operation conditions 0.559 Ω; temperature coefficient of resistance of the conductor copper $3.93 \times 10^{-3}\,\mathrm{K}^{-1}$.

Calculate:

(a) the mean temperature rise of the coil;
(b) the mean operating temperature of the coil. Is the coil operating within the design limit?

This method is used to obtain the mean temperature of coils in large power transformers.

1.17 The temperature of an electric lamp filament

A domestic 240 V, 60 W lamp had filament resistances of 30 Ω when cold, and 960 Ω when alight.

(a) Make an estimate of the rise in temperature of the filament. (α for tungsten at 20 °C is $4.5 \times 10^{-3}\,\mathrm{K^{-1}}$.)

(b) Approximately what is the operating temperature of the filament?

(c) State an assumption that is made in your calculation.

Ohmic heating of conductors: I^2R power losses

Inevitability of power loss, and some consequences

A current in a conductor raises the temperature of the conductor. The mobile electrons moving under the influence of the potential gradient in the conductor collide with atoms in the conductor and lose energy to them. *The internal energy of the conductor rises*, and its *temperature rises*, at the expense of the energy of the electrical system, which experiences *a power loss*.

When a conductor is carrying a current, a temperature rise and an electrical power loss will *always* occur as a consequence of the nature of an electric current. They can be reduced by good design, but they cannot be eliminated.

The temperature of the conductor will continue to rise until the rate at which energy is being *released in it* is balanced by the rate at which energy is *escaping from it* as heat. Conductors normally have to be surrounded by electrical insulation; electrical insulators are also good thermal insulators. The electrical insulation therefore acts as *thermal insulation* and *reduces the rate of loss of energy as heat*, thus causing the temperature of the conductor to rise further. Large power cables, carrying currents of

Figure 1.6 *A 415 V power cable. The copper conductors will carry a current of 200 A, and may operate at a temperature of about 90 °C.*

100 A and more, can operate with the temperature of the copper conductor being as high as 90 °C. The design of the cable for carrying a particularly large current has to take into account both the cross-section area of the conductor and the temperature which the insulation will stand safely, without suffering deterioration and breakdown.

Figure 1.6 shows a power cable which is designed to carry a continuous current of 200 A. With this current, the temperature rise of the conductor could be about 60 K; and on a very hot day with an external temperature of, say, 30 °C this gives a temperature of about 90 °C for the conductor and its adjacent insulation.

In the design of electrical machinery such as motors, alternators and transformers, a very early stage is to consider the rate of energy loss in the windings, and thus the temperature rise which may

Figure 1.7 *An air cooled cabinet for stacks of printed circuit boards. The power loss and temperature rise are such that the boards must be cooled.*

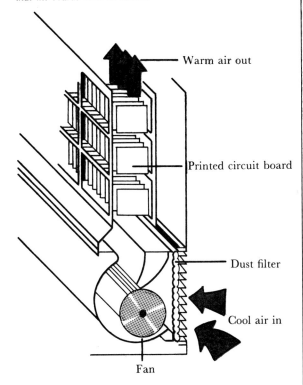

Warm air out

Printed circuit board

Dust filter

Cool air in

Fan

result. Will the insulation of the windings stand the high temperatures? How is the heat to be removed? Figure 1.4 shows a cut-away section of a 5 kW alternator. When delivering a current, the temperature of the coils is about 120 °C; and heat has to be removed at the rate of about 1000 J s^{-1} to prevent the coils from overheating. That is a power removal of about 1 kW. To achieve this, a fan draws cooling air over the coils. About 2 m^3 of air per minute is needed, and it emerges from the machine at a temperature of about 35 K higher than on entry.

The behaviour and life of electronic components is temperature-dependent. There is a limit to the temperatures at which semiconductor devices can operate without damage to the junctions. Germanium devices can operate up to a junction temperature of about 100 °C, and silicon devices up to about 175 °C.

The life expectancy of a component decreases as

its operating temperature is increased. Chemical reactions occur within some types of components, and a rise in temperature increases the rate of the reactions, thus shortening the life of the component. As an example, one manufacturer of aluminium electrolytic capacitors makes a general purpose grade for use between −40 °C and +85 °C. At an operating temperature of +40 °C the life expectancy is 100 000 hours. At the upper limit of use, 85 °C, the life expectancy is reduced to between 2000 hours and 10 000 hours.

The manufacturer states: 'Capacitor ventilation is very important, and forced cooling will greatly extend capacitor life. For example, a cooling airflow of 1 m^3 s^{-1} will double the operational life of a capacitor compared with still air.'

As a consequence of the currents which they carry, all the components on a circuit board experience a rise in temperature, and heat must be allowed to escape or must be removed if the components are not to suffer reduced life or actual damage.

Power calculations in electric circuits

Power is the rate of doing work, $P = work\,done/time\,taken$; power is also the rate of change of energy, $P = energy\,change/time\,taken$. The unit of power is therefore J s^{-1}; and 1 J s^{-1} = 1 W.

The power used by a circuit is:

Power used by a circuit
 = Potential difference across the ends of the circuit × Current through the circuit
$P = V \times I$

Since the resistance of a circuit is given by $R = \dfrac{V}{I}$,

$$P = VI = I^2R = \frac{V^2}{R}$$

Power losses in power cables

Table 1.5 shows the upper temperature at which a conductor may operate continuously when it is insulated by different types of insulation. Above

Table 1.5. *Conductor upper temperature limits for cable insulation of different types (for continuous operation)*

Type of insulation	Maximum conductor temperature (°C)
Paper (impregnated)	65
Polyvinylchloride (PVC)	70
Cross-linked polyethylene (XLPE)	90

Table 1.6. *The current carrying capacities of cables with two copper conductors, each with 50 mm² cross-section area: one cable with PVC insulation, the other with XLPE insulation (cables are supported in free air).*

Insulation	Max. conductor temperature (°C)	Current carrying capacity in free air (A)
PVC	70	190
XLPE	90	230

these temperatures, the insulation begins to deteriorate; and after a long period the insulation could fail.

Since the temperature of a conductor depends upon the rate at which electrical energy is being converted to internal energy, it depends upon the current in the conductor. The current carrying capacity of a conductor thus depends upon the insulation which surrounds it. This is shown by the figures given in Table 1.6, taken from cable manufacturers' data tables, for copper conductors with a cross-section area of 50 mm².

From Table 1.6 it can be seen that the cable with 50 mm² conductors insulated with cross-linked polyethylene is able to carry a current about 20% greater than that insulated with polyvinylchloride, because it can operate at a higher temperature.

1.18 Examine Table 1.7 and consider any point of interest.

Table 1.7. *Current ratings for two-core, copper conductor, XLPE insulated, armoured cable, supported in free air; at the maximum conductor temperature of 90 °C*

Conductor cross-section area (mm²)	16	25	50	70	95
Maximum sustained current (A)	115	150	230	290	350

(*Source:* BICC Limited)

Figure 1.8 *A transformer supplying power to a machine.*

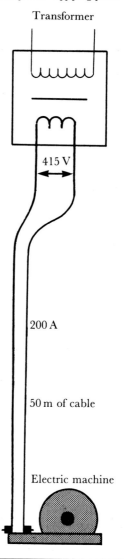

Transformer

415 V

200 A

50 m of cable

Electric machine

1.19 The transformer shown in Figure 1.8 is supplying power along a cable 50 m in length. The cable has 50 mm² copper conductors, XLPE insulated, and the total resistance of the conductors (out and back, 100 m) is 0.0493 Ω at an operating temperature of almost 90 °C. The machine takes a current of 200 A.
  (a) What is the total power that the transformer is supplying (to the machine and cable)?
  (b) What is the power loss in the cable?
  (c) Express the power loss in the cable as a percentage of the total power supplied.

1.20 Consider the effect of replacing the 50 mm² conductors in Question 1.19 by a cable with 70 mm² conductors. The machine still needs a current of 200 A. The resistance of the 70 mm² conductors at their hot operating temperature is 0.0342 Ω.
  (a) What is the power loss in the cable?
  (b) What is this power loss as a percentage of the total power supplied?
  (c) How do the losses compare, in the two cables?

It is frequently the case that engineers have to decide upon conductor size not on the basis of the maximum sustained current needed, but on a short circuit current that might occur. During a short circuit there is a sudden rise of current to a value that might be 20 times that of the sustained current. This may last for a period of between 0.2 s and 3 s until the circuit breaker operates. Since the electrical energy loss in the conductor is proportional to the square of the current, the conductor rise in internal energy and temperature can be great.

Since the time involved is short and cooling follows rapidly, the conductor insulation can withstand higher temperatures than can be allowed for sustained operation. Table 1.8 gives some examples.

Table 1.8. *Short circuit temperature limits for conductor insulation (short time duration)*

Insulation type	PVC	Paper	XLPE
Maximum conductor temperature (°C)	150	250	250

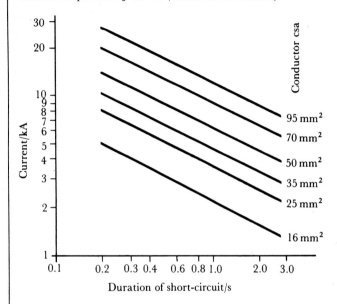

Figure 1.9 *Short circuit ratings for cables with copper conductors and XLPE insulation. It is based on maximum conductor temperatures of 250 °C. (Source: BICC Limited.)*

Figure 1.9 shows the maximum short circuit current that various sized cables can withstand, in relation to the time lapse before the circuit breaker disconnects the fault.

1.21 An electrical system has circuit breakers which will disconnect the circuit in 0.4 s. A fault current of 5000 A could be expected. What is the smallest conductor size that would be acceptable?

Printed circuit board track resistance, and power loss

Figures 1.10 and 1.11 give data for printed circuit boards with tracks of standard thickness of copper.

1.22 A particular circuit board is made with copper tracks of 70 μm thickness. Some of these are 1.0 mm in width. Using the graphs shown in Figures 1.10 and 1.11:
  (a) What is the maximum current that the tracks can carry without exceeding a 20 K temperature rise?

Figure 1.10 *Graphs for copper tracks on printed circuit boards. The track thicknesses are 35 μm (0.035 mm) and 70 μm (0.070 mm). For different track widths the curves show the maximum current that can be carried without exceeding a 10 K or a 20 K rise in temperature.*

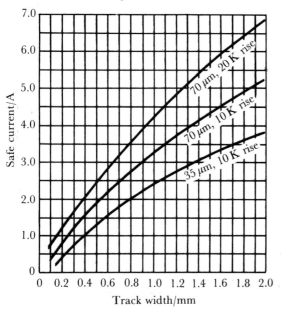

Figure 1.11 *Graphs for copper tracks of thicknesses 35 μm (0.035 mm), 70 μm, and 105 μm. For a given track width, the lines give the resistance of a 10 mm length of track. The data is for tracks at 25 °C, and also at 100 °C for 35 μm thickness.*

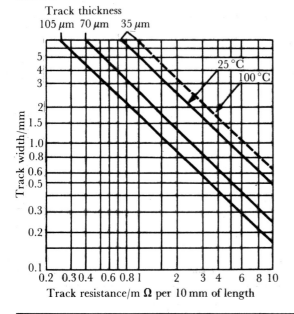

(b) A twin track is 150 mm long. What is its resistance (out and back) at 25 °C?

(c) What is the power loss in the track at 25 °C when it carries the current in (a)?

Voltage drop along a conductor

The nature of voltage drop

If an electric tool is plugged into a 110 V supply, the voltage available for driving the tool is not 110 V. It may be only about 108 V, or perhaps as low as about 106 V. This is because there is a potential drop along the cable. If the voltage at a tool or other electrical machine is significantly below the design voltage, then its performance will be affected and the tool or machine may suffer damage. It is therefore important for engineers to be able to work out the potential drop along a supply cable.

Figure 1.12 shows a uniform bare wire AC of length 1000 mm conducting a current. The potential difference between A and C is 2.0 V. A high resistance voltmeter, M, is connected to A, and its other terminal is connected to a metal knife-edge contact which can be touched on the wire at any point along its length. If contact is made with the wire at B, a distance of 100 mm from A, the meter reading is 0.20 V, being $\frac{1}{10}$ of 2.0 V. The potential difference between A and the contact B will change uniformly down the length of the wire, with the potential difference being proportional to the length AB.

Figure 1.13 shows a conductor carrying a current. For any length of the conductor between two points P and Q, the resistance is given by the definition $R = V/I$, where V is the potential difference between P and Q and I is the current. Thus the potential difference or the potential drop between P and Q is $V = IR$. In the particular instance shown in Figure 1.13, the potential drop $= 3\,A \times 0.2\,\Omega = 0.6\,V$.

Knowing the current in a supply cable, and the resistance of each conductor, we can therefore calculate the potential drop between the supply end and the output end.

Figure 1.12 *The change in potential difference along a uniform wire which is conducting a current.*

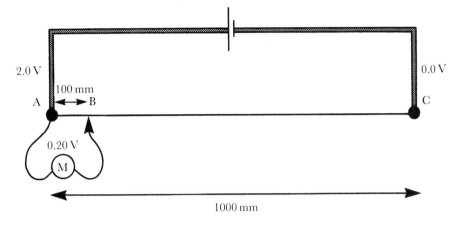

Figure 1.13 *PQ is part of a uniform wire conducting a current. The potential drop between P and Q is V=IR. Therefore V=0.6 volt.*

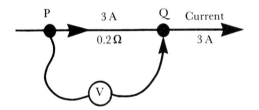

Figure 1.14(a) shows a power socket. The potential difference between its ends is 110 V. Figure 1.14(b) shows about 20 m of cable plugged into the socket at one end, and connected to an electric drill at the other end. The resistance of each conductor is $0.2\,\Omega$ and they are each carrying a current of 10 A.

Let us consider the conductor JK. The potential drop along it is: $pd=IR=10\,\text{A}\times0.2\,\Omega=2\,\text{V}$. The effective supply voltage at K for the tool lead is therefore $+110\,\text{V}-2\,\text{V}=108\,\text{V}$.

Considering the conductor LM, the potential drop between L and M is 2 V, and the effective supply voltage at L for the tool is $+2\,\text{V}$.

Figure 1.14 *(a) M and J are 110 V power supply sockets. (b) Because of the potential drop along the conductor, the voltage available for the tool is not 110 V. It is only 106 V.*

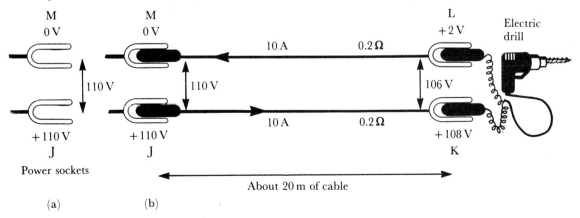

Thus the potential difference across the ends of the tool leads, at L and K, is $+108\,\text{V} - (+2\,\text{V}) = 106\,\text{V}$; and the tool has a pd of 106 V to drive it.

Inevitability of voltage drop, and some effects

An electrical machine or device must have a power supply. Cables and leads have resistance. So there will always be a potential drop between the supply and the machine or device.

If the voltage drop is too great, the machine does not function effectively; heating devices do not rise to their required temperature; fluorescent lights may not light (in a parked caravan with too long a 'jumper lead' to the car and its battery, the internal fluorescent lights will not light); electric motors run too slowly and may overheat, or burn out completely. (An electric motor running at its design speed produces a large, design-level back emf. If the motor runs at below its design speed, the back emf is reduced and the forward current through the coils is above the design level, with consequent overheating.) On a printed circuit board, a device near the end of a track might not have a sufficient potential difference across it for the device to function properly.

Because of the need to avoid such problems, there are regulations which govern the maximum allowable voltage drop along a power supply (Table 1.9). For power supply voltages of under 600 V, the voltage drop must not exceed 2.5% of the supply voltage.

Table 1.9. *Some power supply voltages and their maximum allowable voltage drops*

Supply voltage (V)	120	240	415
Maximum allowable voltage drop (V)	3	6	10

1.23 Figure 1.8 shows a cable supplying an electric machine. The total resistance of the conductors, out and back, at the operating temperature is $0.0493\,\Omega$. The cable is carrying a current of 200 A.
   (a) What is the voltage drop along the cable?
   (b) What is the potential difference across the machine connections?
   (c) Is the voltage drop within the limit of the regulations (a maximum drop of 2.5%)?

1.24 Figure 1.6 shows a small mains distribution unit being set up on a construction site. It contains busbars and circuit breakers. The thick cable can carry a maximum sustained current of 230 A. The cable length is 100 m to a transformer supplying 415 V. The resistance of 100 m of a single conductor at the operating temperature is $0.0493\,\Omega$.
   (a) What would be the voltage drop if the cable carried its full rated current of 230 A?
   (b) Is this within the limit laid down by regulations (a maximum drop of 2.5%)?
   (c) What is the maximum current that the cable may carry without exceeding the maximum allowed voltage drop?

The calculation in Question 1.24 shows that the cable could safely carry a current of over twice the

Figure 1.15 *A 180 V cooling fan is to be run from a 240 V supply. How can this be done simply?*

Cooling fan

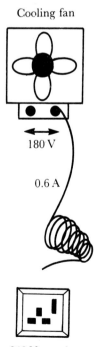

180 V

0.6 A

240 V supply

magnitude that is, in this circumstance, acceptable; the maximum acceptable current is set by voltage drop considerations. The voltage drop, ΔV, is given by $\Delta V = IR$. If the current needed in the circumstances given in Question 1.24 was 230 A, then the only way of reducing ΔV is by reducing R. If the mains distribution unit had to be 100 m from the transformer, then the *length* of conductor in the cable could not be reduced. The only way to reduce the resistance, R, of the conductor is to *increase its cross-section area*.

The cross-section area of the conductors in Question 1.24 and Figure 1.8 was 50 mm^2. The next larger sizes available from cable manufacturers are 70 mm^2 and 95 mm^2; and in fact a 95 mm^2 cross-section area conductor would be needed here.

1.25 Figure 1.15 shows a cooling fan which requires 180 V and a current of 0.6 A. A 240 V supply is available. The 180 V for the fan is to be supplied by placing a resistor in series with the fan and the 240 V supply. The resistance of the supply cable is very small compared with the resistance which will have to be added. What resistance should the resistor have? What power will it dissipate?

Proceed as follows:

(a) Sketch Figure 1.15 and complete the circuit by including a resistor in series.
(b) What voltage drop is necessary between the supply and the fan?
(c) The fan needs a current of 0.6 A, which the resistor will also carry. What resistance value will provide the necessary voltage drop with a current of 6 A?
(d) What power will the resistor dissipate?

1.26 A printed circuit board twin track is 150 mm long. At one end is a 6.0 V supply. At the other end is a device which requires a total current of 2.0 A. The total resistance of the twin track supplying the device is 0.050 Ω.

(a) What is the voltage drop along the track?
(b) What is the potential difference across the device?

Answers to questions

1.1 1.6×10^{-13} A
1.2 8 A
1.3 (1) 11.1×10^{-6} Ω m; (2) same; (3) same
1.4 1.02×10^{-6} Ω m
1.7 (a) (i) 0.023 Ω or 0.024 Ω;
    (ii) 117×10^{-6} Ω K$^{-1} \pm 5\%$; (b) (i) 0.009 Ω or 0.010 Ω; (ii) 47×10^{-6} Ω K$^{-1} \pm 10\%$
1.8 (c) $57 \times 10^{-3} \pm 5\%$; (d) the same as (c)
1.9 360×10^{-6} K$^{-1} \pm 5\%$
1.11 (a) nickel
1.13 13.9 Ω
1.14 0.0493 Ω
1.16 (a) 58.2 K; (b) 80 °C
1.17 (a) 2400 K; (b) about 2400 °C; (c) that the value of α remains constant over the temperature range 20 °C to 2400 °C
1.19 (a) 83.0 kW; (b) 1.97 kW; (c) 2.4%
1.20 (a) 1.37 kW; (b) 1.6%
1.21 25 mm^2
1.22 (a) 4.2 A; (b) 0.051 Ω; (c) 0.90 W
1.23 (a) 9.9 V; (b) 405 V; (c) yes
1.24 (a) 22.7 V; (b) No; (c) 104 A
1.25 (b) 60 V; (c) 100 Ω; (d) 36 W
1.26 (a) 0.10 V; (b) 5.9 V

2. Design and manufacture of some resistors

Power resistors

The nature of power resistors, and some uses

The term 'power resistor' is a loose one, used to indicate a resistor in which a large amount of power has to be dissipated to the environment. That is to say, power resistors tend to be in the range 10 W to 500 W, as contrasted with resistors in electronic circuits where the power dissipation is more of the order of 0.1 W.

A 200 W power resistor has to be able to transfer 200 J of energy to its environment each second, $200\,\mathrm{J\,s^{-1}}$, and in order to do this its temperature may reach values of between 200 °C and 300 °C, and in some circumstances may even approach 400 °C. In contrast, the maximum continuous operating temperature for most types of electronics resistor is around 130 °C.

Figure 2.1 *Three power resistors of differing design for differing functions.* Front: *close wound wire on a cylindrical ceramic former (130 W power);* Centre: *close wound wire on mica sheet (260 W power);* Back: *metal strip element, air separated, on a porcelain former (360 W power). (Designed and manufactured by Claude Lyons Limited, Hertfordshire.)* Reproduced to a larger size on page 114.

Power resistors are used as a means of producing a voltage drop in a power circuit, as potential dividers, and as a means of dissipating energy from a circuit. They are also used as heating elements, for instance in electric furnaces.

The design of a power resistor must be based on its need to *operate at a high temperature*, and on its need to *transfer a large quantity of energy* to its environment *in a short time*.

Some designs and materials

Figure 2.1 shows three different designs of power resistors, using different materials for supporting the resistance elements, and different means of insulating the turns.

A tubular ceramic former, wirewound

The resistor in the foreground has a tubular ceramic former. The resistance material is a nickel copper alloy wire which has been heated in air to form a thin film of metal oxide on the surface of the wire. This metal oxide film is an electrical insulator. The wire is close wound onto the ceramic former, with each turn touching the adjacent one. The metal oxide film on each turn acts as the insulation between one turn and the next. This insulation can withstand a potential difference of 5 V between one turn and the next in contact with it.

A current in the wire raises its temperature; and the resistors are designed to operate with a wire temperature of up to 300 °C when used in free air at a typical room temperature (20 °C). The metal oxide film is very stable at this temperature, and the insulation remains good. The temperature coefficient of resistance of the wire is very low $(\alpha = 0.000\,02\,\mathrm{K^{-1}})$, and the change in resistance of the element between room temperature and 300 °C is, for most purposes, negligible.

The resistor is provided with a moveable tapping band, so that either the full resistance value may be used (from end to end of the winding) or some intermediate value may be chosen by using the moveable band. The tapping in conjunction with the full length of the resistor may also be used as a potential divider.

The company manufactures this type of resistor, with a ceramic former and a close wound wire element, in units from 20 W power dissipation to 180 W.

A mica card former, wirewound

In Figure 2.1, the resistor in the centre is a 'mica card' type. The 'former' is a sheet of the mineral mica. Mica is an excellent insulator, and it is also slightly pliable. The pliability of mica makes these resistors particularly suitable for use in equipment that suffers extreme mechanical vibration and shock.

The resistance element is of nickel copper alloy wire, oxidised, and close wound onto the mica sheet, which is about 2 mm in thickness. The resistor itself is therefore a thin structure.

In whatever function a power resistor is being used, there will be conversion of electrical energy into heat; and a good path for heat escape must be provided if the device is to function effectively. Often natural air cooling is sufficient; air blast cooling, using a fan, is frequently necessary; and sometimes water cooling may have to be used.

Figure 2.2 *Three possible methods of mounting a mica card resistor. Suggest which arrangement would give the best power dissipation in free air.*

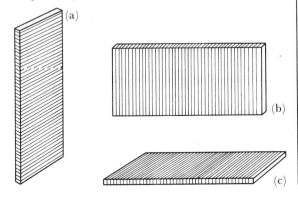

2.1 Figure 2.2 shows mica card resistors arranged (a) with the long axis vertical, (b) with the short axis vertical, and (c) with the main surface horizontal. Only a small part of the heat loss is played by conduction because the cards are supported at the ends of the mica sheet (see Figure 2.1), and mica is a good heat insulator as well as a good electrical insulator.

(a) With a card resistor operating at about 300 °C, suggest whether most of the heat is lost by convection or by radiation.

(b) Suggest which card arrangement given in Figure 2.2 would be most effective.

The manufacturer's *Technical Information Book* includes the following statement: 'All flat mica card resistors should be mounted horizontally on edge so as to obtain the lowest temperature rise. Vertical mounting results in a peak temperature at a point about one third of the resistor length from the top, due to the rising heat from the lower part of the winding. If for some reason the resistor has to be mounted with its long axis vertical, then it should be used to only 70% of its rated wattage.'

In the next section, the *Technical Information Book* states: '*Air blast cooling*. These resistors are ideal for air blast cooling, having a very thin edge section and a large cooling surface. The catalogue wattage of a resistor, for natural air cooling, may be uprated by as much as four times when using suitable air blast cooling. Our engineers will be pleased to give details and to advise.'

In the following section, the *Technical Information Book* states: '*Ratings at high ambient temperatures*. If the ambient temperature (that is the temperature of the environment of the resistor) is higher than 20 °C, then the catalogue wattage rating must be reduced to prevent the final temperature of the resistor from reaching too high a value. Our engineers will be pleased to recommend suitable resistors for use under any working conditions, if the relevant particulars are supplied.'

2.2 The manufacturer's *Technical Information Book* states: '*Mica card resistors mounted in groups*. This form of resistor is particularly suitable for mounting in groups to form units of high wattage dissipation, but when they are so mounted the catalogue rating of each card must be reduced owing to the radiation between adjacent surfaces. The percentage of catalogue watts that the resistors should be allowed to dissipate when mounted in groups a given distance apart are:

Distance between resistors	25 mm	50 mm
Percentage of catalogue watts allowable	80%	90%'

(a) Sketch four mica card resistors arranged in a bank, for normal air cooling. (It is not necessary to show electrical connections in this question.)

(b) If each resistor is rated 100 W for normal, single operation, and if the resistor faces are 25 mm apart, what is the maximum power that the system can be allowed to dissipate?

Users of power resistors need to know the temperature rise produced in the resistor when it is carrying a current and dissipating power. Manufacturers thus provide graphs giving this information. Figure 2.3 illustrates the graphs for four mica card resistors which are designed and manufactured by the company Claude Lyons Limited. The graphs are for resistors in an ambient temperature of 20 °C.

2.3 The mica card resistor shown in Figure 2.1, and card resistors of other sizes, are designed to operate at a maximum wire temperature of 300 °C. The graphs shown in Figure 2.3 are for four different card resistors P, Q, R and S, rated at 45 W, 80 W, 100 W and 140 W, respectively, operating in an ambient temperature of 20 °C in free air.

(a) If a P model resistor is mounted in free air at 20 °C and is carrying its full load current, dissipating 45 W, what is the temperature of the resistor wire?

(b) What is the wire temperature of an R model when fully loaded in free air at 20 °C?

(c) A resistor is needed to operate in free air which is at 70 °C, and the resistor is to dissipate 80 W of power. (i) What would be the wire temperature of a Q model under these conditions? (ii) Is this within the design limit for the resistor? (iii) Suggest a solution. (iv) What would be the wire temperature when using your suggestion?

The company makes mica card resistors in models with ratings from 45 W to 260 W.

Figure 2.3 Graphs for four models of mica card resistors, P, Q, R and S, of different rated power dissipation (45 W, 80 W, 100 W, and 140 W), mounted in free air at a temperature of 20 °C. They show the temperature rise of the resistors at different power loadings. (Source: Claude Lyons Limited.)

Alloy strip, with air insulation, on a porcelain support

In Figure 2.1 the resistor at the back is made from resistance alloy in the form of a strip. The strip is wound into a helix, with an air gap about 5 mm wide between each turn. The helix is supported loosely on a hollow procelain tube made of several loose parts; this is supported by a metal bar which runs axially through the central space, and can be used to secure the whole unit in place. Connections to the resistance strip are made by welding a stainless steel lug onto each end.

Examine the strip resistor in Figure 2.1 and find: the alloy strip helix; two loose porcelain segments of tube; a lug attached to the resistance element; the

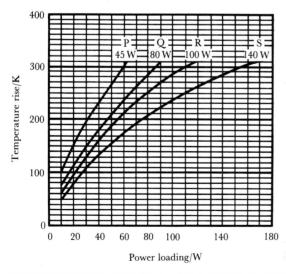

Table 2.1. *The company manufactures 90 different variations of alloy strip helical resistors. The table gives information for some of these resistors. The data is for an approximate temperature rise of 375 K in free air*

Resistor number, and its continuous current rating (maximum) in free air (A)	J1 series of resistors			J9 series of resistors		
	Resistance (Ω)	Power (W)	Element length (m)	Resistance (Ω)	Power (W)	Element length (m)
(1) 85	0.030	220	1.30	0.33	2400	13.8
(6) 36	0.13		1.30	1.4		13.8
(10) 21	0.46		1.30	5.1		13.8

(*Source:* Claude Lyons Limited.)

ends of the axial metal bar (with slots for supporting bolts).

The strip design of the resistance element results in a very large surface area of the material being exposed to cooling air, and this allows very high ratings of power dissipation. The company makes strip resistors with ratings from 200 W to 2400 W (2.4 kW).

Because of the loose nature of the alloy helix and its porcelain support, this type of resistor is very suited to withstanding severe mechanical vibrations and shocks. It is used for heavy industrial duty and in electric traction, such as electric rail locomotives.

The 90 different variations of alloy strip resistors manufactured by the company are in nine series, J1 to J9, ranging from about 200 W to about 2000 W (2 kW). In each series there are ten models, numbered (1) to (10), with maximum allowable current values for continuous use ranging from 85 A to 21 A.

2.4 Table 2.1 gives information about two of the company's series of resistors, J1 and J9. Read the caption, and examine the table.
  (a) From the data in the table, calculate the maximum power dissipation of resistor number (6) in the J1 series, and number (10) in J1; and also (6) J9 and (10) J9.
  (b) When the (1) J1 resistor is carrying its full allowable current, what is the potential difference between its ends?
  (c) When the (1) J9 resistor is carrying its full

allowable current, what is the potential difference between its ends?
  (d) Looking at the J1 series in the table, the resistance increases downwards (resistor (1) to resistor (10)). (i) What happens to the element length? (ii) How will the resistance trend be achieved?

Some design calculations

For these calculations you will need to be familiar with *resistivity* and the *temperature coefficient of resistance*. These were considered in Chapter 1, pages 3–10.

2.5 Calculating the length of wire needed to make the 130 W resistor in Figure 2.1

Look again at Figure 2.1 on page 18 (or page 114) and examine the front resistor. It is made of resistance wire close wound on a ceramic former. The resistor is to have a resistance of $28.5\,\Omega \pm 10\%$ tolerance at 20 °C.

The wire which is recommended has a diameter of 0.60 mm, and is copper nickel alloy with a resistivity of $49 \times 10^{-8}\,\Omega\,\text{m}$ at 20 °C. Its temperature coefficient of resistance is $20 \times 10^{-6}\,\text{K}^{-1}$.
  (a) What length of resistance wire is needed?
  (b) What will be the resistance when the resistor is operating at 300 °C?
  (c) Approximately what percentage difference to the resistance has the temperature change made?
  (d) Is this within the $\pm 10\%$ tolerance allowed?

2.6 Calculating the length of wire needed to make the 260 W resistor in Figure 2.1

Turn back to Figure 2.1 and examine the centre resistor. The resistor is to have a resistance of $68\,\Omega \pm 10\%$ tolerance at $20\,°C$. The wire which is recommended has a diameter of $0.55\,mm$ and is of copper nickel alloy with a resistivity of $49 \times 10^{-8}\,\Omega\,m$ at $20\,°C$. Its temperature coefficient of resistance is $40 \times 10^{-6}\,K^{-1}$.

(a) What length of the wire is needed?
(b) What will be the resistance of the resistor when it is operating at $300\,°C$?
(c) Approximately what percentage change in resistance has been made by the temperature change?
(d) Is this within the tolerance limit?

2.7 Calculating the cross-section area of the resistance strip needed to make the 360 W resistor in Figure 2.1

Look again at Figure 2.1 and examine the rear resistor. It is to have a resistance of $0.50\,\Omega \pm 10\%$ tolerance at $20\,°C$. The resistor is one of a series of ten, each having a power dissipation of about 360 W, and with resistances varying from $0.065\,\Omega$ to $1.05\,\Omega$ at $20\,°C$.

The company wishes to market these resistors on supports, which are all of the same length, and with the length of strip being the same for each, $1.78\,m$. Differences in resistance are achieved by using strips with different cross-section areas.

The strip is made of an alloy of chromium, iron and aluminium, and its resistivity is $135 \times 10^{-8}\,\Omega\,m$ at $20\,°C$.

What cross-section of strip is needed for a $0.50\,\Omega$ resistor?

2.8 Providing a customer with a suitable series resistor

For this question you need to be familiar with the idea of voltage drop along a conductor carrying a current. This was discussed in Chapter 1, pages 14–17.

A customer has a piece of equipment which operates at 12 V and consumes 6.0 W of power. The customer wishes to run this equipment from a 230 V power supply. You recommend placing a power resistor in series with the 12 V equipment and the 230 V power supply.

(a) Sketch the circuit.
(b) Mark in the potential differences across the components.
(c) What current will be required for the 12 V equipment (and therefore also pass through the resistor wire)?
(d) What resistance value does this require for the resistor?
(e) What power will the resistor dissipate?
(f) A mica card resistor would be suitable, with an alloy wire of resistivity $49 \times 10^{-8}\,\Omega\,m$ and a wire diameter of $0.21\,mm$. What length of this wire will be needed to provide the necessary resistance?
(g) You inform the customer that your company makes bulk quantities of a power resistor with a resistance of $487\,\Omega$ and a power dissipation of 140 W, and that it can be supplied with a tapping band. This would be cheaper than making a special resistor with the wire length that was calculated in (f). The wound length of this bulk production resistor is 130 mm. How far from one end must the tapping band be fixed in order to provide the resistance value that is needed for the customer's equipment?

Electronics resistors

Among other functions, resistors in electronics are used to limit current to some desired value, as voltage dividers, and in setting the gain of an amplifier. The power dissipated by a typical resistor in electronics circuits is measured in milliwatts, 100 mW, 200 mW, 300 mW being very common values. The power rarely exceeds 1 W.

There are three principal ways of fabricating resistors for use in electronics. These involve the use of *carbon*; of *metals and alloys* in the form of *wire or thin foil*; and *metals or alloys* in the form of *a film on a ceramic support*.

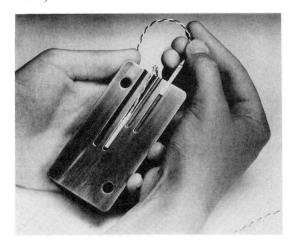

A metal film resistor: a platinum resistance thermometer

The change in electrical resistance of a conductor as its temperature changes can be used to measure temperature. This was discussed in Chapter 1, pages 5–10.

Platinum resistance thermometers form the international reference standard for temperature measurement from −260 °C to +850 °C. There are several reasons for this. The temperature coefficient of resistance, α, for platinum is among the highest available. The relationship between electrical resistance and temperature for pure platinum is well defined. The metal can be refined to a very pure state; and it is very stable chemically, particularly to oxidation. It can readily be formed into thin wire; and temperature determinations using platinum wire resistors are found to have high accuracy and repeatability.

The laboratory platinum resistance thermometer, however, with its partially supported coil of fine platinum wire, is easily damaged by vibration and shock. It is also expensive. For industrial use, a more sturdy design which will stand movement and vibration is needed. It should also be inexpensive.

Figure 2.4 shows two platinum resistance thermometers, each consisting of a platinum film track on a ceramic strip support. The devices are small, robust and reliable. The photograph shows a device being placed into a cut-away specimen of a metal container for lowering into a drilled oil well to determine the temperature at various depths in the well.

In principle *the production process* involves using a metallic 'ink' consisting of very finely divided platinum particles, and laying this down in a track pattern on a ceramic tile as a support. The metallic ink and the ceramic support are then heated in a furnace to fuse the particles of platinum into a continuous metal strip, which will act as the resistance element. The practical steps needed to produce a successful device are much more involved than appears here.

A look at Figure 2.5(a) shows that the entire device is small, measuring 25 mm long by 3 mm wide, and it supports eight tracks, parts of which are in a fairly intricate pattern. Each track is only about 0.15 mm wide, and is separated from the next track by about the same small distance. The problem is how to produce such narrow tracks, with intricate patterns and close proximity to each other, using an ink. A large scale drawing of a mask showing the tracks is drawn, and this is photographed. From the negative are produced emulsion masks, and these are placed over the ceramic strips.

Once the emulsion masks have been produced, the sequence of operations is as follows. An 'ink' is made up consisting of finely divided platinum particles, finely divided glass particles, and an organic fluid. The ink is applied to the ceramic plate by screen printing. The screen used consists of the photographically produced mask attached to the lower surface of a fine metal mesh. 'Ink' is forced through the fine metal mesh and the mask and onto the ceramic tile placed below it by dragging a soft rubber squeegee across the top of the mesh.

The screen is removed, leaving an ink track of platinum and glass particles in the organic binder fluid on the ceramic plate. This is the stage shown in

Figure 2.5 *Stages in the production of an industrial platinum resistance thermometer consisting of a ceramic support and a platinum film track. (a) Actual size, beside a millimetre scale; (b) An enlargement of (a) to twice actual size. Left: bare ceramic plate (0.6 mm thick). Next: 'ink' of finely divided platinum particles and finely divided glass particles printed onto the ceramic. Centre: after firing in an oven at over 1000 °C, giving a continuous platinum track. Next: after applying a protective glass coating, and laser adjustment of track. Right: with leads attached. The resistance is 100.00 Ω ± 0.12 Ω at 0°C. (Samples provided by Matthey Electronics Limited.)*

(a)

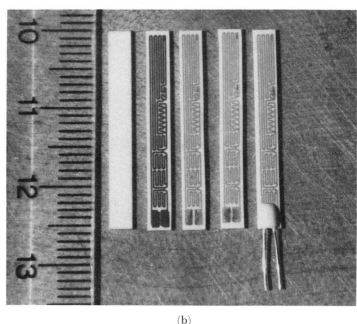

(b)

Figure 2.6(c). It is also shown in the specimens in Figure 2.5 in the second plate counting from the left.

The prints are dried, and a batch of plates is placed in an oven and heated for several hours at a temperature of over 1000 °C. The organic binder is burnt off, the glass particles melt, and the platinum particles soften. The softened platinum particles 'sinter' together to form a continuous metal path, and the molten glass begins bonding onto the ceramic. After cooling, there remains a continuous platinum strip, in the pattern produced by the mask, and this is bonded onto the ceramic by solidified glass.

Next, the platinum track is thoroughly insulated electrically and thoroughly protected from the atmosphere by screen printing a thin layer of glass particles in a fluid over the whole of the upper surface of the ceramic strip (except for the two wide platinum end pieces). This is fired in an oven, resulting in a thin protective covering of glass over the tracks.

A look at Figure 2.5(a) and an examination of the actual track width and track separation will show how technically difficult it is to manufacture such a unit and keep the track width constant at a design value. It is in fact not possible to keep it completely constant, and slight variations in width occur along the length of the track.

Similarly, with an ink and screen printing method of applying the track, it is very difficult to keep the thickness constant at a design value, and slight variations in track thickness do occur. Each of these factors – track width and track thickness – affect the total resistance of the completed unit; even with the best possible control of this part of the process the initial resistors can vary in their resistance by as much as 20% on either side of a design value.

To give some idea of the very small dimensions

Figure 2.6 *These large-scale drawings show how a mask is used to define the track pattern on the ceramic support: (a) a photographically produced mask, negative; (b) a bare ceramic plate; (c) the plate after placing the mask on it, inking over, and removing the mask.*

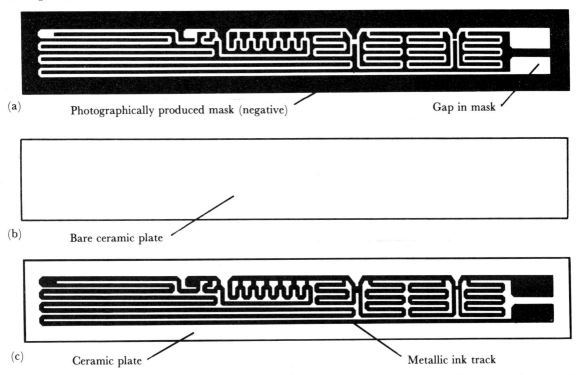

(a)   Photographically produced mask (negative)   Gap in mask

(b)   Bare ceramic plate

(c)   Ceramic plate   Metallic ink track

involved, the screen mesh is made of extremely fine stainless steel with about 16 strands per millimetre. The depth of the track is about $8\,\mu m$, that is, 0.008 mm; and the width of the track is about $150\,\mu m$, that is, 0.15 mm. If in the manufacturing process there is an error of $1\,\mu m$, that is, one thousandth of a millimetre, in the depth of the track along its whole length, what percentage error would this produce in the intended resistance? The tension in the screen and the viscosity of the ink are critical. Under these demanding circumstances, variations of up to about 20% from the desired resistance are inevitable.

The method devised to overcome the problem is to design into the track a series of loops which are in parallel electrically; that is to say, they give two lengths of track which are connected electrically in parallel. Look at Figure 2.6(c) again and find several such loops. Consider how they could be used to alter the resistance of a unit that has been printed and fired.

Each thermometer is to have a resistance of $100.0\,\Omega \pm 0.12\,\Omega$ at 0 °C. The track is designed so that after firing in the oven it has a resistance of between $70\,\Omega$ and $90\,\Omega$ at 0 °C. To bring it up to the needed $100.0\,\Omega$, extra resistance is provided by cutting loops so that the parallel connections are broken.

Examine Figure 2.7(a). At A there are three arrows, each pointing to a loop connected in parallel with a shorter section. If the short section is cut, then the current must follow the longer route of the large loop, and extra resistance amounting to about 9% is added.

Now examine the loops at B, C and D. These become successively smaller, and additional resistance in amounts of about 5%, 1% and 0.5% of the original can be added. At E, cuts in the broad track can provide very small percentages of extra resistance. In this way the resistance can be built up to $100.0\,\Omega \pm 0.12\,\Omega$ at 0 °C.

In Figure 2.5 on page 24, the resistance adjust-

Figure 2.7 *(a) The points at which the looped tracks that are electrically in parallel can be cut (by a laser beam) to add resistance to the overall track. (b) A unit that has had laser cuts made in the looped sections. Make an estimate of the percentage of the original resistance that has been added in. (Source: Matthey Electronics Limited.)*

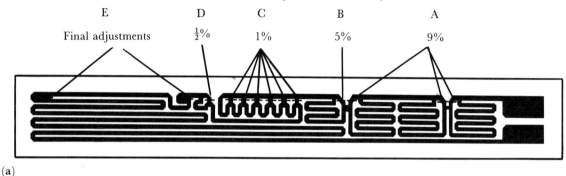

(a)

(b)

ment is done at the second from last stage in the evolving stages shown, that is, sample number 4 from the left. In practice, the adjustment is not done at 0 °C but at room temperature, which is more convenient. The resistance to be adjusted is compared with the resistance of an accurate standard thermometer placed close by, whose resistance would be 100.0 Ω at 0 °C. The cuts in the track are made by a fine laser beam, which can penetrate the thin protective coating of glass covering the track.

2.9 The photograph in Figure 2.7(b) shows a resistance thermometer whose track has been cut. The short black lines on the uppermost track show where cuts have been made by a laser. Using Figure 2.7(a) for information, what extra resistance as a percentage of the original has been cut in (before the final fine adjustments)?

In the final testing, the resistance of each thermometer at 0.00 °C is determined by placing the thermometer in a vessel which contains ice and water at equilibrium (the ice point), and then at

100.0 °C by placing the thermometer in a steam bath (the steam point). These two resistances are recorded for each thermometer, and the record accompanies the thermometer when it is sold to a user.

Following the tests, the thermometers are stored and sold in three grades, as shown in Table 2.2.

Table 2.2. *The three grades of platinum film resistance thermometer produced by the company for industrial use. For very accurate needs, a Grade A thermometer might be required; for very many needs, the Grade C tolerance is entirely adequate*

Grade of thermometer	Tolerance at 0.00 °C	
	Resistance	Temperature
A	100.00 Ω ± 0.06 Ω	± 0.15 °C
B	100.00 Ω ± 0.12 Ω	± 0.30 °C
C	100.00 Ω ± 0.25 Ω	± 0.65 °C

(*Source:* Matthey Electronics Limited.)

2.10 From Table 2.2, what is the percentage resistance tolerance of a Grade A platinum film resistance thermometer?

The temperature coefficient of resistance, α, needed for a resistance thermometer is one with a high value. In Chapter 1, page 7, the temperature coefficient of resistance of a material was defined as the fractional change in the resistance of a sample per unit temperature change.

$$\alpha = \frac{(R_2 - R_1)}{R_1} \times \frac{1}{(\theta_2 - \theta_1)}$$

Rearranging this:

$$\alpha \times R_1(\theta_2 - \theta_1) = (R_2 - R_1)$$

With a resistance thermometer, the largest possible change in resistance $(R_2 - R_1)$ is needed for a given change in temperature $(\theta_2 - \theta_1)$. Therefore, the resistance element of the thermometer should be made from a material with a high value of α. A reference to Table 1.4 on page 9 shows that among pure metals and alloys the highest values of α are possessed by nickel $(6.8 \times 10^{-3} \, \text{K}^{-1})$, copper $(3.9 \times 10^{-3} \, \text{K}^{-1})$, and platinum $(3.9 \times 10^{-3} \, \text{K}^{-1})$, contrasted with resistance alloys such as constantan and manganin (both $0.02 \times 10^{-3} \, \text{K}^{-1}$). Nickel and copper are both used in resistance thermometry.

2.11 For the platinum film resistance thermometers in Table 2.2, find the change in resistance when their temperatures are raised from the ice point $(0.00 \, ^{\circ}\text{C})$ to the steam point $(100.0 \, ^{\circ}\text{C})$. Use the rearranged equation from above, to find $(R_2 - R_1)$. The resistance of the device at $0.00 \, ^{\circ}\text{C}$ is $100.00 \, \Omega$. (For platinum, $\alpha = 3.85 \times 10^{-3} \, \text{K}^{-1}$.)

Uses of platinum film resistance thermometers in industry include temperature monitoring of equipment and of chemical processes, and automatic control of processes. Because they are electrical devices, platinum film resistance thermometers can be used to operate pen and chart recorders, and feedback systems in control.

Resistance thermometry is considered again in the companion volume, *Mechanics and Heat*, Chapter 8.

Metal foil precision resistors: for printed circuit boards

The metal foil precision resistors described in this section are used in precise amplifier circuitry, and

Figure 2.8 (a) This actual size photograph shows two resistors for surface mounting on printed circuit boards. (b) The same photograph enlarged ×2. (c) A plan drawing of the metal foil resistance element for similar resistors. (Specimens and drawing supplied by Rhopoint Limited, Surrey.)

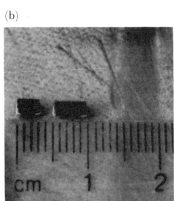
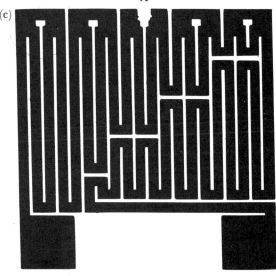

as reference resistances where precise power supplies are needed: for instance in instrumentation and in medical electronic apparatus. They are designed for mounting on printed circuit boards.

Figure 2.8(a) shows two such resistors at actual size. Estimate the length of the left-hand resistor. It is manufactured to provide resistances ranging from $30\,\Omega$ to $100\,\Omega$ with a tolerance of $\pm 0.1\%$, and from $100\,\Omega$ to $30\,000\,\Omega$ with a tolerance of $\pm 0.05\%$. The temperature coefficient of resistance, α, is extremely low at $1 \times 10^{-5}\,\mathrm{K}^{-1}$ (constantan and manganin, $2 \times 10^{-5}\,\mathrm{K}^{-1}$). This is essential for reference resistors, whose resistance must remain as constant as possible even when their temperatures change.

Figure 2.8(b) shows the same photograph enlarged $\times 2$. The shiny strip at each end of a resistor is a metal strip for making contact with a surface mounting fixture on a board.

The resistive element is made from an alloy foil about $3\,\mu\mathrm{m}$ thick ($0.003\,\mathrm{mm}$). The track layout is in principle similar to that which was described for the platinum film resistance thermometer in the preceding section. There is a fixed length of track; and there are loops providing lengths electrically in parallel, which can be cut to add in extra resistance.

2.12 Examine the track layout shown in Figure 2.8(c).
  (a) Find loops with tracks electrically in parallel.
  (b) Are these loops the same in size, or are they variable?
  (c) Can the resistance be increased by successive degrees of fineness?
  (d) Suggest what has been done at the location marked by the letter A.

The manner in which the foil element is mounted on a base, connected, and protected is shown in Figure 2.9. Examine this diagram to see the parts and how they relate to each other.

The manufacturing sequence is shown in Figure 2.10.

The alloy which is used to make the foil is mainly composed of nickel and chromium (together 92%), with copper, aluminium and manganese making

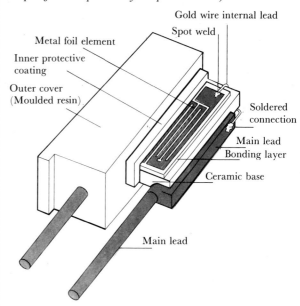

Figure 2.9 *A schematic drawing showing an alloy foil track bonded on to a ceramic base, connected to electrical leads, and surrounded by protective coverings. (These leads are for 'through hole' connection to printed circuit boards.) (Diagram adapted from one provided by Rhopoint Limited.)*

up the remaining 8%. The fine gold wire which is used to connect the track ends to the main leads has a diameter of about $40\,\mu\mathrm{m}$ ($0.04\,\mathrm{mm}$). The electrical tests include 'overload' tests and a determination of the temperature coefficient of resistance. In the overload tests, each resistor is subjected to 2.5 times its rated voltage and six times its rated power in order to ensure that it will withstand these abnormal conditions.

Table 2.3. *Some performance data for ultra-precision chip resistors, Type MP*

Resistance data	
Manufactured range:	$30\,\Omega - 100\,\Omega$
Tolerance:	$\pm 0.1\%$
Temperature coefficient, α:	$10 \times 10^{-6}\,\mathrm{K}^{-1}$
Operating data	
Maximum operating temperature:	$125\,^{\circ}\mathrm{C}$
Rated power at $125\,^{\circ}\mathrm{C}$:	$0.1\,\mathrm{W}$
Maximum working voltage:	$50\,\mathrm{V}$
Maximum working current:	$0.35\,\mathrm{A}$

(*Source:* Rhopoint Limited.)

Figure 2.10 *The main stages in the manufacture of a resistor of the type shown in Figure 2.9. The stages for the surface mount resistors in Figure 2.8(a) and (b) are very similar. Examine the flow chart and work through the stages, relating them to the diagram in Figure 2.9.*

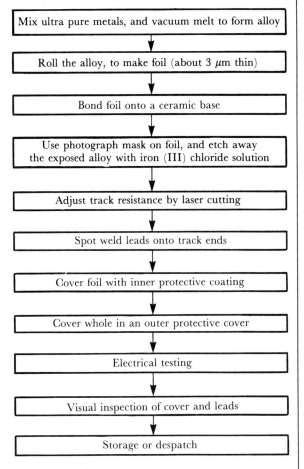

Mix ultra pure metals, and vacuum melt to form alloy

↓

Roll the alloy, to make foil (about 3 μm thin)

↓

Bond foil onto a ceramic base

↓

Use photograph mask on foil, and etch away the exposed alloy with iron (III) chloride solution

↓

Adjust track resistance by laser cutting

↓

Spot weld leads onto track ends

↓

Cover foil with inner protective coating

↓

Cover whole in an outer protective cover

↓

Electrical testing

↓

Visual inspection of cover and leads

↓

Storage or despatch

Figure 2.11 *Graph showing the rise in temperature of the outer surfaces of resistor bodies at various power loadings for the resistors shown in Figure 2.8(a) and (b) and described in Table 2.3 (type MP). (Source: Rhopoint Limited.)*

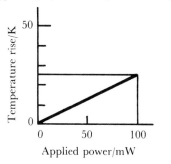

Table 2.3 gives some performance data for the type of surface mount resistor shown in the photograph in Figure 2.8(a) and (b), the left-hand resistor in each instance. The dimensions are 3.2 mm long × 2.5 mm wide × 2 mm deep. Look again at Figure 2.8(a) and (b) and examine the resistors.

The company manufactures this type of resistor with resistance values which can be requested in the range $30\,\Omega$ to $30\,000\,\Omega$. The data given in Table 2.3 is for resistors in the range $30\,\Omega$ to $100\,\Omega$. Examine the Table.

2.13 A manufacturer of precision electronic equipment requests a batch of type MP resistors of resistance value $40\,\Omega$. Within what limits of resistance will each resistor be at 25 °C? (Use Table 2.3.)

2.14 A circuit board with MP-type resistors on it is operating in an enclosure where the ambient temperature is 60 °C. The resistors are on load at their full rated power of 0.1 W. What is the temperature of the outer surface of each resistor case? (Use the graph given in Figure 2.11.)

Answers to questions

2.1 (a) convection; (b) see the paragraph which follows the question
2.2 (b) 320 W
2.3 (a) 270 °C; (b) 305 °C; (c) (i) 355 °C, (ii) No, (iv) the solution which you have probably suggested would give a wire temperature of 275 °C
2.4 (a) J1 (6): 170 W, J1 (10): 200 W, J9 (6): 1800 W, J9 (10): 2200 W; (b) 2.6 V; (c) 28 V
2.5 (a) 16.4 m; (b) $28.8\,\Omega$; (c) 1%; (d) Yes
2.6 (a) 33.0 m; (b) $68.7\,\Omega$; (c) 1%; (d) Yes
2.7 $4.8\,\text{mm}^2$
2.8 (c) 0.50 A; (d) $440\,\Omega$; (e) 110 W; (f) 31 m; (g) 120 mm
2.9 34%
2.10 0.06%
2.11 $38.5\,\Omega$
2.13 $39.96\,\Omega$ to $40.04\,\Omega$
2.14 86 °C

3. Capacitance and capacitors

Capacitance

Figure 3.1 *Two charged metal plates separated by an insulator, air. There is a potential difference V between them; and they are separated by a distance d.*

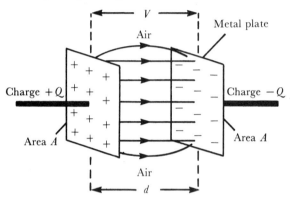

If two conductors are separated by an insulator, the system has *capacitance*. It has the ability to store charge.

In Figure 3.1 a potential difference V has been established between two metal plates; and a flow of electrons has caused one plate to acquire a charge of $-Q$ and the other a charge of $+Q$. The *capacitance of the system, C,* is defined by the ratio Q/V:

$$C = Q/V$$

If Q is in coulombs and V is in volts the capacitance is in *farads*; and the unit of capacitance, the *farad*, is a coulomb per volt.

Expressing the definition $C = Q/V$ in words: the capacitance of a system is the amount of charge that has to be added in order to raise the potential difference between its conductors by 1 volt.

The capacitance of a system is related to its physical dimensions and to the nature of the material which is between the conductors. For a parallel plate capacitor, such as that shown in

Figure 3.1, with two plates each of area A, separated by a distance d, and with a *vacuum* between the plates, the capacitance C is given by

$$C_{vacuum} = \frac{\varepsilon_o A}{d}$$

$$\varepsilon_0 = 8.8 \times 10^{-12} \text{ F m}^{-1}$$

where ε_0 is the *permittivity of free space*.

Thus if a capacitor consists of two metal plates each 1 m × 1 m square separated by a distance of 10 mm in a vacuum, its capacitance is

$$C = \frac{8.8 \times 10^{-12} \times 1 \times 1}{10 \times 10^{-3}} \text{ farad} = 8.8 \times 10^{-10} \text{ F}$$

Thus two sizeable plates, each 1 m square, separated by a distance of 10 mm in vacuum produce a capacitance of only 9×10^{-10} F. Had the material between the plates been air, the capacitance would have been 1.0005 times greater, that is, only very slightly greater. This calculation and information show that the farad is a very large unit; and in practical capacitors the capacitance is usually of the order of picofarads, 10^{-12} F, or microfarads, 10^{-6} F.

In air, each nitrogen molecule has negative charge distributed evenly about its surface, and likewise each oxygen molecule. When air is placed between oppositely charged plates, however, the electron cloud around each molecule is attracted towards the positive plate, causing a separation of charge and resulting in molecules which are distorted in shape. The separation of charge results in molecules with negative and positive ends: *polarised molecules*. The effect is shown in Figure 3.2(b).

The effect is small in the case of air molecules and the resulting effect on the capacitance of the system is also small, only 5 parts in 10 000; but with other materials the effect can be very large, increasing the capacitance many times. The ratio of

Figure 3.2 *A capacitor with a medium, the dielectric, between the plates. In (a) the molecules have their normal charge distribution. In (b) the charges on the plates have induced a charge separation in the molecules.*

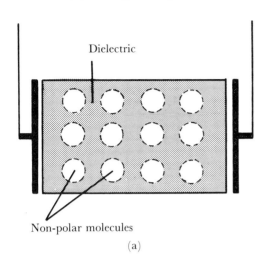

Dielectric

Non-polar molecules

(a)

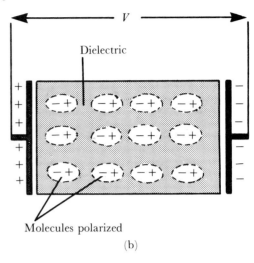

Dielectric

Molecules polarized

(b)

capacitance with dielectric between the conductors to capacitance with a vacuum between the conductors is a measure of the increase in capacitance which is caused by a dielectric, and it is called the *relative permittivity*, ε_r, of the dielectric.

$$\frac{\text{Capacitance with dielectric between conductors}}{\text{Capacitance with vacuum between conductors}}$$

$$= \text{Relative permittivity}, \varepsilon_r$$

The relative permittivity of a dielectric is also called its *dielectric constant*. The values for some materials which are of importance in electric engineering are given in Table 3.1.

Table 3.1. *The relative permittivity (dielectric constant) of some materials that are used in the manufacture of capacitors*

Material	Relative permittivity, ε_r (dielectric constant)
Vacuum	1.0000
Air	1.0005
Polyethylene	2.3
Glass	7
Mica	7
Ceramics containing barium titanate	70 to 20 000

3.1 Does relative permittivity have units or is it a pure number?

From the definition of relative permittivity on page 31 it follows that for a capacitor which has a medium between the plates:

Capacitance =
Capacitance with vacuum between the plates
× Relative permittivity

Thus, from the equation on page 30,

$$C = \frac{\varepsilon_0 A}{d} \times \varepsilon_r$$

and, rearranging

$$C = \frac{\varepsilon_0 \varepsilon_r A}{d}$$

A material cannot stand an indefinitely large potential difference across it. If the potential difference across a material exceeds a certain value, the material will break down and a discharge will take place through it. The *dielectric strength* of a material is the potential gradient through it at which breakdown of the material occurs and a discharge takes place.

Referring back to Figure 3.1: if the metal plates are parallel, then in the central region where the electric field is uniform the potential gradient is equal to V/d:

$$\text{Potential gradient} = \frac{V}{d} \text{ (units, V m}^{-1})$$

The *dielectric strength* of a material is the maximum potential gradient that the material can stand without breakdown. In the manufacture of capacitors it is clearly important to know this quantity so that the dielectric between the plates is designed to withstand the voltages that are to be applied to them (and to have a factor of safety, which is frequently $2\frac{1}{2}$ times the operating voltage).

Table 3.2. *The dielectric strengths of some materials that are used in the manufacture of capacitors (the SI unit is $V m^{-1}$; the practical unit is $kV mm^{-1}$)*

Material	Dielectric strength (kV mm^{-1})
Air	5
Polyethylene	40
Glass	100
Mica	150
Ceramics containing barium titanate	10

Table 3.2 gives the maximum potential gradient that some materials can stand. For instance, a capacitor with plates 1 mm apart and with the space between the plates filled with polyethylene would stand potential differences up to 40 kV (40 000 V) between the plates before the polyethylene started to break down. If a safety factor of 2 were to be used, then the capacitor should not be used above 20 kV.

The manufacture of very small capacitors

Figure 3.3 shows some small capacitors for mounting on printed circuit boards. Examine the photographs and read the caption. In (b), the left-hand

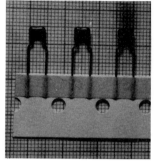
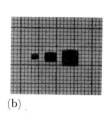

Figure 3.3 *Small capacitors for printed circuit boards (pcbs). They are life size; the small squares are of 1 mm side. (a) Capacitors with wire leads, mounted on tape for automated, robotic insertion into pcbs. Capacitance, 1000 pF; for use up to 100 V. (b) Chip capacitors with metal end-connections, for surface mounting on pcbs. Left: 20 pF, 100 V; centre: 100 000 pF (0.1 μF), 50 V; Right: 47 000 pF, 200 V.*

(a)

(b)

chip capacitor is 2 mm long × 1 mm wide × 0.5 mm deep. It contains several thin metal electrodes (or plates) separated by thin layers of ceramic dielectric; it will be apparent that designing and making such devices poses substantial challenges.

The construction principles

The basic structure of a multilayer ceramic (MLC) capacitor is shown in Figure 3.4. Each capacitor 'plate' consists of a thin film of metal about 4 μm in thickness ($\frac{4}{1000}$ mm). The 'plates' are separated from each other by thin layers of ceramic dielectric, each about 40 μm in thickness ($\frac{40}{1000}$ mm).

Each plate extends fully to one end of its dielectric, but not fully to the other end. Examine this in Figure 3.4. In this way, connection may be made at one end, but the other end is insulated.

The multilayer block is built up from units which each consist of a thin ceramic layer with a metal film deposited on it. This is shown in Figure 3.5(a). There is a ceramic border on three sides to insulate one end and two sides of the metal film from the rest of the final capacitor. The remaining side of the metal film ends at the ceramic edge.

These units are then arranged with the metal edges alternately at one end and then the other end, as shown in Figure 3.5(b). The units are piled in a stack. A protective ceramic layer is added to both

Figure 3.4 *A longitudinal section of a multilayer ceramic capacitor. The diagram is drawn to show the parts and is not to scale.*

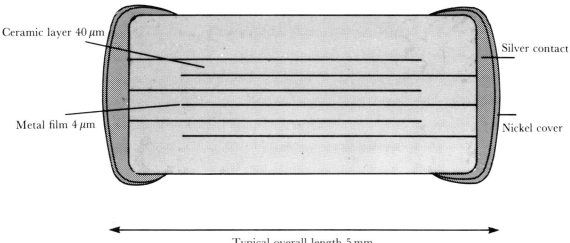

Ceramic layer 40 μm

Silver contact

Metal film 4 μm

Nickel cover

Typical overall length 5 mm

top and bottom. The stack is then heated in an oven, which bonds the layers together, producing a block as shown in Figure 3.5(c). One set of metal film edge remains exposed at each end of the block. (A metal connecting system will later have to be formed over each end.)

The materials

The ceramic is usually made from barium titanate, $BaTiO_3$, which can form 90%–98% of the material. Barium titanate can be produced by mixing together and heating barium carbonate ($BaCO_3$) and titanium dioxide (TiO_2):

$$BaCO_3 + TiO_2 \rightarrow BaTiO_3 + CO_2$$
$$\text{solid} \qquad \text{solid} \qquad \text{solid} \qquad \text{gas}$$

Barium titanate is a solid, which produces a ceramic material on heating it appropriately in a furnace. Its dielectric constant can be varied considerably in two ways. One method is to alter the grain size by altering the heat treatment. Another is to introduce other elements into the initial mixture of chemicals. Strontium (Sr) and zirconium (Zr) are often used; strontium is in the same group of the Periodic Table as is barium (Group II), and zirconium occurs under titanium in the Transition Elements. In these ways, ceramics

with dielectric constants ranging from about 70 to about 20 000 can be formed.

The metal film must be made from a metal that will not react with the ceramic at the furnace temperatures used in the final stages of manufacture. Nor must the metal diffuse into the ceramic at those high temperatures. One of the earliest metals to be used was palladium, and it is still used. It bonds well to the ceramic. Also used are palladium alloys containing platinum, gold and silver.

The manufacturing process

The manufacturing process has to produce very thin layers of ceramic, about 40 μm ($\frac{40}{1000}$ mm) in depth, and very thin films of metal, about 4 μm ($\frac{4}{1000}$ mm) in depth.

The powdered ingredients for the ceramic are weighed very precisely, and then mixed and milled to distribute them evenly and to produce the correct particle size. The milled product is mixed into a binding solution, which consists of an organic chemical solvent and, for instance, an acrylic resin. This results in a viscous suspension. The viscous suspension is 'silk screen printed' onto a flat surface, and this results in a thin fluid layer of *even thickness* and *uniform particle dispersion* in it. The layer is then heated, which causes the solvent to evaporate. The

Figure 3.5 *This shows the principle in making a multilayer ceramic capacitor block: (a) A single layer of ceramic with a metal film deposited on it. There is a ceramic border on three sides. (b) Layers are stacked with the metal edges alternately at opposite ends. (c) The layers have been bonded together by the action of raised temperature and mechanical pressure. Three metal edges are exposed at the right-hand sides.*

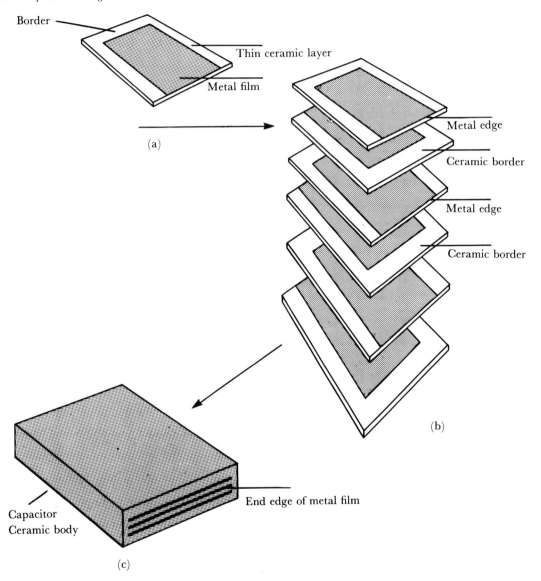

result is a thin plastic tape with a homogeneous mixture of ceramic in it.

The metals which are to be used in the plates are chemically precipitated in a very fine form so that the metal particles are less than 1 μm in size. They are mixed into an organic solvent with an organic binder and a 'metal ink' results.

A template with multiple cut-outs of the shape and size of the required metal film 'plate' is located on each piece of plastic strip. Metal ink is then rolled over the template, leaving a film of metal ink on the plastic. This stage is represented in Figure 3.5(a), which shows the metal film with a border of ceramic on three sides.

Plastic strips with their metal ink layer are then stacked one on top of another, the precise number being determined by the capacitance that is required; and protective plastic top and bottom layers are added. The stack is then integrated into one piece by compressing it mechanically and by raising the temperature.

The chips, while containing the ceramic and the metal particles of the ink, still contain the organic resin, solvent and binders. These are now carefully burned out by slowly raising the temperature to about 500 °C and maintaining that temperature for about 24 hours. The blocks are then transferred to a kiln and heated to a temperature of about 3000 °C, whereupon the ceramic particles fuse together.

When cold, the resulting blocks have the correct plate and dielectric dimensions, but at each end the plates are isolated and unconnected, as in Figure 3.5(c). Connection between the plates is made by means of a metal paint. The paint consists of about 60% silver and palladium particles, 10% of fine glass powder, and 30% of organic binder-solvent. The paint is painted over each end of a capacitor chip, and the chips are then heated in an oven, whereupon the organic solvent evaporates and the silver melts to form a continuous silver/palladium metal contact with the ends of the plates.

A nickel cover is then formed over the end to protect the thin silver/palladium contact layer. The result is shown diagrammatically in Figure 3.4 on page 33.

Typical final products are capacitors with sizes and capacitances such as those shown in Table 3.3.

Table 3.3. *Typical values of dimensions, capacitance range and voltage range for multilayer ceramic capacitors*

Overall dimensions (mm)			Capacitance range	Voltage range
long	wide	deep		
2	1	0.5	1 pF–50 000 pF	Mainly 50 V–100 V
6	5	1	10 000 pF–3 μF	Mainly 50 V–100 V

That such small electrical components, whose parts are only a few thousandths of a millimetre thick, have been devised and are manufactured in bulk as reliable, cheap products is a great achievement requiring imagination and skill. To devise them requires a knowledge of the chemistry and physics of materials, and to make them reliably and economically in large numbers needs on a knowledge of production technology processes.

3.2 What is the capacitance of a multilayer ceramic capacitor similar in design to that in Figure 3.4 if there is a total number of six plates, if each plate has a width of 1.5 mm and an overlap length of 2.0 mm, if the ceramic layers have a thickness of 50 μm (50×10^{-6} m) and if the relative permittivity of the ceramic is 10 000? (In a multiple plate capacitor with N plates, with overlap area A, the effective plate area is $A(N-1)$.)

3.3 The capacitor in Question 3.2 operates with a potential difference of 100 V between its terminals.
  (a) Calculate the dielectric stress, that is, the potential gradient through the dielectric.
  (b) If the dielectric strength of the material is 10 V μm^{-1}, what factor of safety is there?

The manufacture of medium sized capacitors

The following photographs show some stages in a process for making medium sized *single layer* capacitors, of sizes up to about 30 mm diameter and about 5 mm in thickness. You will recognise some of the steps that were described in the process for very small capacitors.

The larger sizes of capacitors, such as those shown in the tunnel furnace in Figure 3.6(c), have capacitances of about 1000 pF and are for use with potential differences of about 8000 V. They have applications in laser systems. The smaller capacitors, such as those on the bench in Figure 3.7(a), are used in making filter assemblies for filtering out unwanted signals. The assembler is making a mains voltage filter; and capacitances of about 500 pF

Figure 3.6 *(a) Mixing barium titanate ceramic powder with additives. (b) Pressing the mixture into discs (rear), and arranging the discs on trays for firing (front). (c) Passing the discs through a tunnel furnace. (d) Screen printing metallic ink onto the discs. (Source: Beck Electronics Limited, Great Yarmouth.)*

(a)

(b)

(c)

(d)

Figure 3.7 *(a) Assembly (ten small capacitors on the bench). (b) Engineers: discussing technical requirements with a customer (rear); order processing by computer (front). (Source: Beck Electronics Limited, Great Yarmouth.)*

(b)

(a)

may be used, with the mains voltage of 240 V. (For unwanted signals and filtering them see Chapter 8 'Interference and filters', pages 85–8.)

The manufacture of power capacitors

Uses of power capacitors

Power capacitors are used to store and release large quantities of electrical energy.

Major fields of use are in the electricity grid and distribution system, in association with electrical machinery that operates by means of electromagnetic induction, such as induction motors and induction furnaces; and in fluorescent lighting systems, which require inductors. All these fields of use involve alternating current.

Other important fields involve direct current and require the production of a burst or pulse of electrical energy. Examples include the testing of high voltage switchgear and high voltage transformers, the pulsing of lasers, and the production of pulses of very large currents for controlling plasma in nuclear energy engineering.

In fluorescent lighting, the capacitors have a capacitance in the region of 10 μF to 50 μF and the voltage of the systems is 240 V.

In the electricity grid system, large numbers of capacitors are connected in parallel to form capacitor banks; for instance, 40 capacitors, each of 100 μF capacity, might be connected in parallel to form a bank with a capacitance of 4000 μF. A large number of these banks might then be connected in series (for instance, about 80 banks in series) for the whole system to operate at a grid voltage of 132 000 V. (How many 100 μF capacitors were used in this system?).

Figure 3.8 shows a bank of capacitors in a part of the grid system.

Figure 3.8   A bank of capacitors in a part of the electricity grid system. (Source: The National Grid Company plc.)

The construction principles

Figure 3.9   The principle on which a capacitor is made. Two metallised plastic films are wound together.

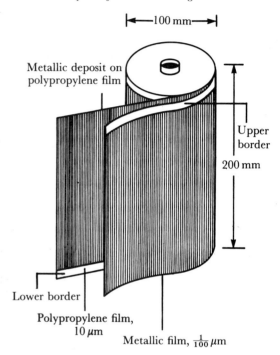

Large power capacitors are manufactured by winding two metallised plastic films together to form a cylindrical capacitor. Figure 3.9 shows typical dimensions for the sheets and how they are wound together. The sheets are very thin indeed. The dielectric sheet is of polypropylene plastic and is about $10 \, \mu m$ thick, that is $\frac{10}{1000}$ mm. A thin film of zinc has been vapourised on to the polypropylene film; and this forms the capacitor 'plate'. It is about $\frac{10}{1000} \, \mu m$ thick, that is, $\frac{10}{1000000}$ mm.

Each sheet has a border of bare polypropylene. One sheet has its border at the base of the roll; the other sheet has its border at the top of the roll.

A typical width of film is about 200 mm; and a typical length of film that has to be wound is about 50 m, depending upon the capacitance required. The more layers that are wound, the greater is the capacitance.

The two plastic sheets are wound slightly offset from each other, as is shown in Figure 3.10. The

Figure 3.10 *The two sheets wound slightly offset from each other. The metal film on one sheet projects beyond the plastic film of the other sheet. The diagram illustrates the scheme and is not to scale.*

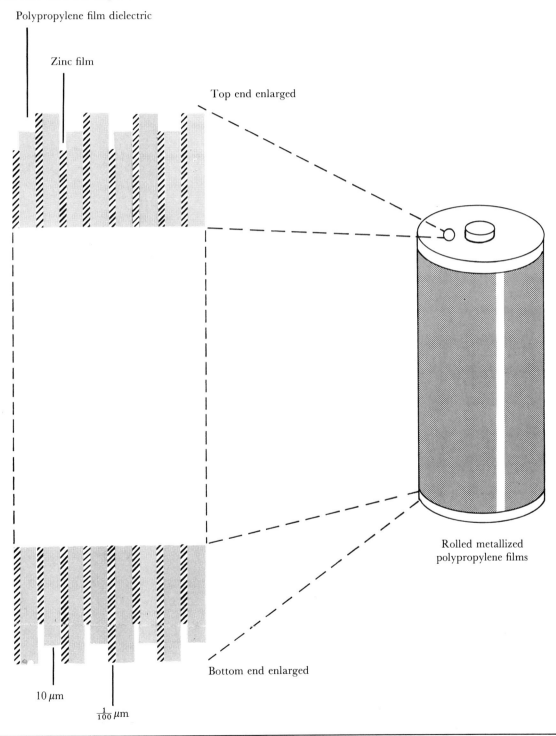

Polypropylene film dielectric

Zinc film

Top end enlarged

Rolled metallized polypropylene films

Bottom end enlarged

$10\,\mu$m

$\frac{1}{100}\,\mu$m

result is that successive turns of metal film on one sheet project above the intervening turns of plastic on the other sheet. This provides a means of making an electrical connection to the metal film of one sheet, at the top end, and to the metal film of the other sheet at the bottom end.

3.4 What practical obstacles do you consider exist to making such connections? (What linear dimensions are involved? What are some of the consequences?).

How would you suggest good connections might be made? Will your method be good electrically, or good mechanically (the connections mustn't break), or both?

Metallising the polypropylene film

The polypropylene sheet is metallised by a beam of zinc vapour striking the plastic sheet and cooling on it, forming a solid film of metal. Figure 3.11 shows the outside of the equipment, and the controller gives an idea of the size. Figure 3.12 represents the

Figure 3.11 *An external view of a metallising machine. (Source: ABB Capacitors Limited.)*

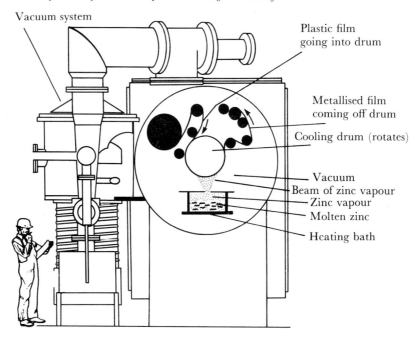

Figure 3.12 *How zinc vapour is deposited on the plastic sheet to form a zinc film.*

Vacuum system

Plastic film going into drum

Metallised film coming off drum

Cooling drum (rotates)

Vacuum
Beam of zinc vapour
Zinc vapour
Molten zinc

Heating bath

inside of a machine. A heating bath containing molten zinc produces zinc vapour, which is constricted to form a beam. Polypropylene sheet is continuously driven round a rotating drum which is positioned over the beam of zinc vapour. Zinc vapour lands on the moving plastic, condenses there and solidifies to form a thin metal film on the plastic.

3.5 The operation is conducted under vacuum. What would you suggest is the main reason for this?

3.6 The rotating drum is cooled by a cooling arrangement. It is labelled a 'cooling drum'.
(a) What is the drum intended to cool?
(b) Why is it necessary to keep this cool?

Winding the metallised plastic film

The winding of the metallised plastic film has to be done in a room with a 'controlled environment'. Dust particles are enormous compared with the thinness of the dielectric, and the air in the room has to be specially filtered. Water molecules in the dielectric would become ionised at large potential gradients, and this could lead to breakdown of the dielectric. The humidity level is therefore carefully controlled; the temperature is also carefully controlled.

In the winding process itself, variations in the film tension can lead to demetallisation of the plastic. Automatic control of film tension and of other parameters is necessary and the machine shown in Figure 3.13 has sensors and feedback arrangements in order to achieve this.

Making electrical contact: end spraying

Another look at Figure 3.10 and examination of the enlarged portion reminds us of the problem of how to make electrical contact with the protruding zinc films. The zinc film is very thin; and the space between a protruding zinc film and the protruding polypropylene opposite it is only about $10\,\mu m$. The method developed is to spray the end of the roll with a very fine spray of molten zinc particles. This

Figure 3.13 An automatic winding machine. With extremely thin film, the winding tension must remain very constant at a set value, and automatic control is essential. (Source: ABB Capacitors Limited.)

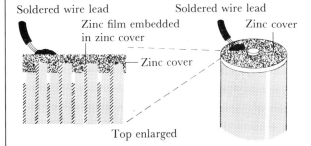

Figure 3.14 The effect of spraying the top end of the rolled films, using a fine spray of molten zinc. A zinc cover forms and makes electrical contact with the protruding zinc films.

fine spray is able to penetrate into the spaces. There it solidifies, making contact with the protruding zinc film. Continuation of spraying leads to a zinc cover which is in contact with the upper part of the rolled metal film. Figure 3.14 shows this. The diagram also shows a terminal soldered to the zinc cap. The lower end of the roll is similarly sprayed

Figure 3.15 *A capacitor roll. A wire end-connection is being soldered on. (Source: ABB Capacitors Limited.)*

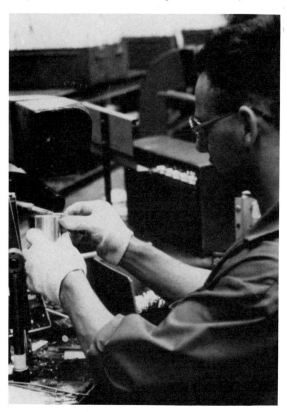

Figure 3.16 *(a) Three capacitors of equal capacitance connected in parallel. (b) Three capacitors of equal capacitance connected in series.*

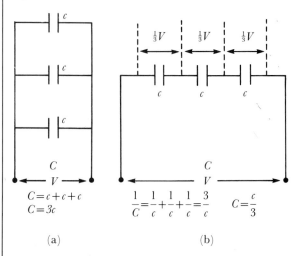

$$C = c + c + c$$
$$C = 3c$$

(a)

$$\frac{1}{C} = \frac{1}{c} + \frac{1}{c} + \frac{1}{c} = \frac{3}{c} \qquad C = \frac{c}{3}$$

(b)

and provided with a solder terminal. The capacitor is now electrically complete. It is then placed in a metal container and the container is filled with a thermosetting resin, to protect the dielectric and the 'plates' from the atmosphere.

Capacitors in parallel and in series

Figure 3.16(a) shows capacitors connected in parallel. If the capacitors have capacitances c_1, c_2 and c_3, then the capacitance of the combination is $C = c_1 + c_2 + c_3$. In Figure 3.16(a) the three capacitors each have the same capacitance, c, and $C = 3c$.

Figure 3.16(b) shows capacitors connected in series. If the capacitors have capacitances c_1, c_2 and c_3, then the combination has a capacitance C which is given by

$$\frac{1}{C} = \frac{1}{c_1} + \frac{1}{c_2} + \frac{1}{c_3}$$

If c_1, c_2 and c_3 are equal, and if each equals c, then $1/C = 3/c$, and hence $C = c/3$.

Figure 3.17 shows a power capacitor unit with part of the outer case cut away so as to show individual capacitors within the unit. The design is for use in high voltage supplies, up to 8000 V. The letter A indicates a stack of ten individual capacitors connected in parallel. The capacitors each have the same capacitance; and typical values used range from about 5 μF to about 15 μF. The letter B indicates another stack of ten individual capacitors in parallel. On the left of the unit are two more stacks C and D, similar to A and B. Thus there are four stacks, A, B, C, and D, each of ten capacitors connected in parallel. Stacks A, B, C, and D are connected in series.

3.7 This question examines the capacitor unit in Figure 3.17:

(a) The letter A indicates a stack of ten individual capacitors connected in parallel. If each capacitor has a capacitance of 8 μF, what is the capacitance of stack A?

Figure 3.17 *A capacitor 'unit' made up of individual capacitors. This is a power capacitor unit for use at voltages up to 8000 V. It is approximately to scale, and the overall height is about 1 m. Labelling code: 1, outer case; 2, mounting bracket; 3, individual capacitors (flattened cylinders); A, a stack of ten capacitors connected in parallel; B, C and D are similar to A.*

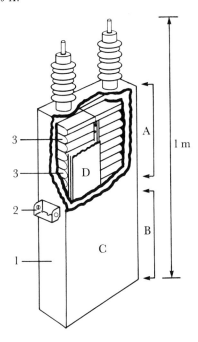

(b) Stack B is identical to stack A and they are connected in series. What is the capacitance of the combination of stack A and stack B?

(c) The complete unit consists of four identical stacks, A, B, C, and D, in series. What is the capacitance of the unit?

(d) How many individual capacitors are there in the unit?

3.8 This question continues the examination of the capacitor unit in Figure 3.17. The unit consists of a stack, A, of ten capacitors in parallel, giving a combination capacitance of $80\,\mu\mathrm{F}$ for the stack. Stack A and three identical stacks, B, C, and D are connected in series. Draw the symbol for a single capacitor to represent stack A and connect stacks B, C and D (similarly drawn) in series with it.

(a) If the whole unit is connected so that there is a potential difference of 8000 V between its

terminals, what is the potential difference across stack A?

(b) What is the potential difference across stack C?

(c) What is the potential difference across each individual capacitor in a stack?

3.9 A capacitor unit similar to the one shown in Figure 3.17 consists of four stacks of capacitors. Each stack consists of eight capacitors, each of $15\,\mu\mathrm{F}$, connected in parallel. The stacks are connected in series with each other. When in use, the potential difference across the terminals of the unit is 6000 V.

(a) What is the capacitance of a stack of capacitors?

(b) What is the capacitance of the unit?

(c) What is the potential difference across a capacitor stack, when the unit is in use?

(d) What is the potential difference across an individual capacitor within a stack, when in use?

3.10 An industrial user needs a $25\,\mu\mathrm{F}$ capacitor unit, to operate at about 11 000 V (12 000 V will not be exceeded). Your company has been asked to make one. Your company makes and has in stock large numbers of individual capacitors of $5\,\mu\mathrm{F}$, $10\,\mu\mathrm{F}$ and $15\,\mu\mathrm{F}$ capacitors, capable of safely operating at up to 2000 V.

Sketch a suitable design for the capacitor unit, labelling it with relevant numerical values. (You could proceed in this way: (a) How many stacks will be needed in the series? (b) What capacitance will be needed for each stack? (c) How should a stack be made up?)

Energy stored in capacitors

Capacitors store charge. By suitably discharging the stored charges, these can be made to do work. Thus capacitors will store electrical energy. Capacitors are used in some applications to supply current for a short time in the event of failure of the normal supply; they are used as the source of energy for pulsing lasers; and they are used to supply pulses of very large current in the production of magnetic fields of very large field strength. The energy, W, stored in a charged capacitor is given by:

$$W = \tfrac{1}{2}CV^2 = \tfrac{1}{2}Q^2/C = \tfrac{1}{2}QV$$

3.11 Let us examine the energy which can be stored in a capacitor unit such as that shown in Figure 3.17:

(a) A unit is made up of individual capacitors, each $8\,\mu\text{F}$. The individual capacitors are operating at 2000 V. How much energy is stored in each capacitor?

(b) A capacitor stack in the unit consists of ten capacitors, each of $8\,\mu\text{F}$ connected in parallel and operating at 2000 V. How much energy is stored in a stack?

(c) The unit consists of four such stacks in series, giving a combined capacitance of $20\,\mu\text{F}$. It is operating at 8000 V across the terminals. How much energy is the unit storing?

Discharge resistors

When a capacitor is disconnected from a working circuit, for instance by opening a switch, *the capacitor*

Figure 3.18 *A capacitor unit with a discharge resistor connected across its terminals. (Source: ABB Capacitors Limited.)*

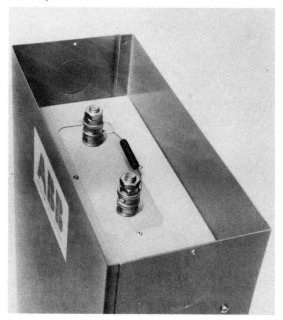

remains charged. Due to the excellent insulating properties of the dielectric and the capacitor cover, the charge will remain stored for a very long time after disconnection. There is thus a substantial risk of electrical shock to anyone handling the circuit or the capacitor. Therefore *a power capacitor must be provided with a discharge resistor.* National and International Standards lay down regulations for the design and use of power capacitors. One such International Standard states:

Every capacitor equipment shall be provided with a directly connected discharge device, unless it is connected directly to other electrical equipment which provides an uninterruptable discharge path.

The discharge device (or the uninterruptable discharge path) shall reduce the voltage across the capacitor from the maximum to 50 V or less within a given time. For capacitors of rated voltage up to 660 V this time is 1 minute. For capacitors of rated voltage above 660 V the time is 5 minutes.

A discharge device is not a substitute for short-circuiting the capacitor terminals together and to earth before handling the capacitor or the circuit.

Figure 3.19 shows a discharge circuit for a capacitor; it shows how the potential difference between the plates changes with time. Let the capacitor of capacitance C be charged with a charge Q_0. With the charges $+Q_0$ and $-Q_0$ on its plates, let the potential difference between its plates by V_0. Let the charged capacitor now discharge through the resistor of resistance R. The charge on the plates decreases exponentially with time; and the potential difference between the plates decreases exponentially with time, t:

$$Q = Q_0 \exp(-t/CR)$$
$$V = V_0 \exp(-t/CR)$$

The product CR is called the *time constant* for the combination of the capacitor and the resistor.

When $t = CR$ we have $V = V_0 \text{e}^{-1}$. Therefore

$$V = \frac{V_0}{\text{e}} = \frac{V_0}{2.7} = 0.37\,V_0$$

Thus the product CR is the time it takes for an initial potential difference across a capacitor to decay to 0.37 of its value, that is, to 37% of its value.

Figure 3.19 *(a) The circuit for a charged capacitor discharging through a resistor in parallel. (b) How the potential difference across the discharging capacitor changes with time. It is an exponential decay.*

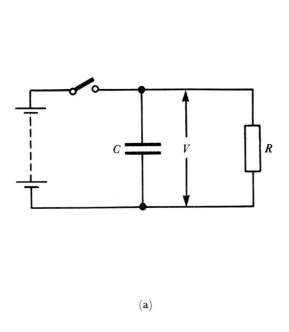

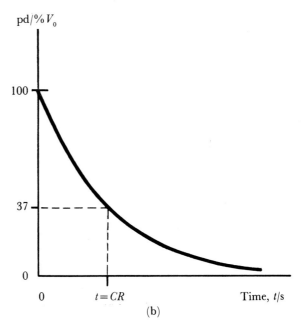

(a)

(b)

The exponential equation provides a means of calculating the value of the discharge resistor needed to meet the International Standards for power capacitors.

We will rearrange the exponential equation to give R:

$$V = V_0 \exp(-t/CR)$$

$$\frac{V}{V_0} = \exp(-t/CR)$$

$$\frac{V_0}{V} = \exp(CR/t)$$

Therefore,

$$\ln\left(\frac{V_0}{V}\right) = \frac{CR}{t}$$

and

$$\ln\left(\frac{V_0}{V}\right) \times \frac{t}{C} = R \qquad (3.1)$$

Let us use this equation in an actual case. An industrial process requires a $100\,\mu\text{F}$ capacitor working at 400 V. What resistance is needed for the discharge resistor in order to meet International Standards for safety? Since the capacitor is operating under 660 V, it must be discharged to 50 V or less in 1 minute.

Using equation (3.1):

$$\ln\left(\frac{400\,\text{V}}{50\,\text{V}}\right) \times \frac{60\,\text{s}}{100 \times 10^{-6}\,\text{F}} = R$$

$$\ln 8 \times 60 \times 10^4\,\text{s}\,\text{F}^{-1} = R$$
$$2.08 \times 60 \times 10^4\,\Omega \quad = R$$
$$1.25 \times 10^6\,\Omega \quad\quad = R$$

So a discharge resistor of value $1.25\,\text{M}\Omega$ would be needed.

3.12 What resistance value would be needed for discharge resistors in the following instances, to meet International Standards for safety?
(a) a $60\,\mu\text{F}$ capacitor charged at 500 V;
(b) a $20\,\mu\text{F}$ capacitor charged at 1000 V;
(c) an $80\,\mu\text{F}$ capacitor charged at 2000 V.

3.13 Show that the product CR has the dimensions of time.

Answers to questions

3.1 A pure number
3.2 27×10^{-9} F
3.3 (a) $2\,V\,\mu m^{-1}$; (b) 5
3.7 (a) $80\,\mu F$; (b) $40\,\mu F$; (c) $20\,\mu F$; (d) 40

3.8 (a) 2000 V; (b) 2000 V; (c) 2000 V
3.9 (a) $120\,\mu F$; (b) $30\,\mu F$; (c) 1500 V; (d) 1500 V
3.10 (a) 6 stacks; (b) $150\,\mu F$; (c) 10 individual capacitors each of $15\,\mu F$, in parallel (or 15 of $10\,\mu F$)
3.11 (a) 16 J; (b) 160 J; (c) 640 J
3.12 (a) $2.3\,M\Omega$; (b) $45\,M\Omega$; (c) $14\,M\Omega$.

4. Inductance and inductors

Inductance

The self-inductance of straight conductors

Figure 4.1 shows a conductor with a potential difference between its ends. In (a), the potential difference V_1 causes a current I_1 and that current is producing a magnetic flux Φ_1 inside the conductor. (It is also producing some flux outside the conductor.) The flux produced is proportional to the current, $\Phi_1 \propto I_1$. In (b), the potential difference has been increased to V_2, causing the current to rise to I_2, and the magnetic flux inside the conductor to Φ_2. By Faraday's law of electromagnetic induction, the change in flux linkage induces an emf in the conductor, and its magnitude equals the rate of change of flux linkage:

Magnitude of induced emf
= Rate of change of flux linkage

$$E = \frac{d\Phi}{dt} \qquad (4.1)$$

But the flux produced is proportional to the current:

$$\Phi_1 \propto I_1 \quad \text{and} \quad \Phi_2 \propto I_2$$

Therefore, the *rate of change of flux linkage* is proportional to the *rate of change of current*:

Rate of change of flux linkage
$\propto$ Rate of change of current

$$\frac{d\Phi}{dt} \propto \frac{dI}{dt}$$

Figure 4.1 *The generation of a back emf when the current changes in a conductor: (a) The current I_1 is producing a magnetic flux Φ_1 in the conductor. (b) In rising to I_2 the current increases the flux in the conductor to Φ_2; the change in flux linkage induces an emf of $-E$.*

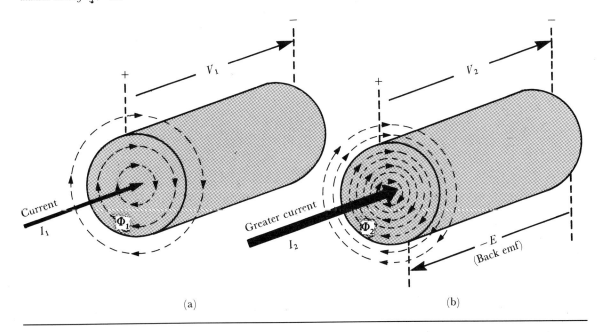

(a)   (b)

Therefore, from equation (4.1),

Induced emf
= a constant × rate of change of current

$E = L \times$ rate of change of current

$$E = L \times \frac{dI}{dt} \qquad (4.2)$$

The *proportionality constant, L*, is called the *self-inductance* of the conductor.

By Lenz's law, the *direction* of the induced emf is such as to oppose the change; that is, *it will oppose the increasing current*. If the direction of the currents I_1 and I_2 are taken as +ve, then the direction of the induced emf is −ve and it is a *back emf*.

Using this sign and equation (4.2) the *magnitude* and *direction* of the induced emf is given by:

$E = -L \times$ the rate of change of current

$$E = -L \times \frac{dI}{dt} \qquad (4.3)$$

The self-inductance of a conductor, or of a system, is a measure of its *opposition to a change of current* in the conductor or system. The unit of inductance is the henry, H.

In a conductor, if a change of current of 1 amp in 1 second produces a back emf of 1 volt, then the inductance of the conductor is 1 henry.

Example. In a conductor, a change of current from 10 A to 20 A in 1 millisecond induced a back emf of 3 mV. What was the self-inductance of the conductor?

From equation (4.3)

$$L = \frac{E}{\text{Rate of change of current}}$$

$$= \frac{3 \times 10^{-3}\,\text{V}}{(20\,\text{A} - 10\,\text{A})/1 \times 10^{-3}\,\text{s}^{-1}}$$

$$= \frac{3 \times 10^{-3}\,\text{V}}{10\,\text{A}} \times 1 \times 10^{3}\,\text{s}^{-1}$$

$$= 3 \times 10^{-1}\,\text{V A}^{-1}\,\text{s}^{-1}$$

$$= 0.3\,\text{H}$$

The henry is a very large unit; and in most practical situations the inductances are of the order of millihenries or microhenries.

The self-inductance of a straight, or uncoiled, conductor of total length l_w is given by

$$L = \frac{\mu_0}{8\pi} \times l_w$$

$$\mu_0 = 4\pi \times 10^{-7}\,\text{H m}^{-1}$$

where μ_0 is the permeability of free space.

4.1 Is the self-inductance of a straight conductor dependent on its cross-section area?

4.2 Obtain a value for the self-inductance of 1 m of a straight conductor.

4.3 What is the self-inductance of 20 m of a straight conductor?

At first sight it may seem from the very small values of the self-inductance of a few metres of a conductor that the quantity is not significant. In long conductors, such as the power lines in the electricity grid system, where the length of the lines may be tens or hundreds of kilometres, the self-inductance of the lines is very significant.

4.4 Obtain a value for the self-inductance of an electricity grid power line between two places which are 100 km apart (two conductors, one out and one back).

The self-inductance of coiled conductors

Figure 4.2 shows the same magnitude of current, I, in (a) a straight conductor, (b) a single turn coil, and (c) a multiturn coil. In the multiturn coil, flux which is produced by one loop is shared by other loops, and the flux linkage is increased.

Study Figure 4.2 and its caption. For a given rate of change of current, the rate of change of flux linkage is greatest in the multiturn coil. Thus the induced back-emf is greatest in the multiturn coil, and its self-inductance is also the greatest.

Figure 4.3 shows two equal lengths of the same type of wire, but one is uncoiled and the other is coiled. We will find the self-inductance of each. The self-inductance of a long thin coil is given by:

$$L = \frac{\mu_0 A N^2}{l} \qquad (4.4)$$

where μ_0 is the permeability of free space, A is the cross-section area of the coil, N is the number of

Figure 4.2 *The effect on flux linkage of coiling the conductor. Flux produced by one loop is shared by other loops.*

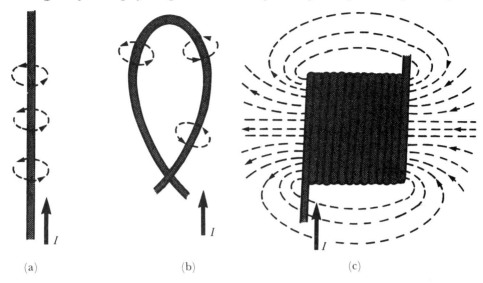

(a)   (b)   (c)

Figure 4.3 *Two equal lengths of the same type of wire. One is uncoiled (a); and the other (b) is in the form of a long thin coil.*

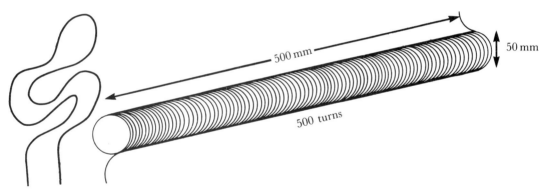

78.5 m of wire, uncoiled

$L = 4 \times 10^{-6}$ H

(a)

78.5 m of wire, wound as a long thin coil

$L = 1 \times 10^{-3}$ H

(b)

turns, and l is the length of the coil. A 'long thin coil' means one whose length is at least ten times its diameter.

4.5 Does the self-inductance of a coil depend upon the thickness or thinness of the wire of which it is made?

4.6 Does the self-inductance of a coil depend upon the current in the coil?

The self-inductance of a coil depends upon its *geometry* – upon its cross-section area, length and number of turns.

The self-inductance of the coil shown in Figure 4.3 is given by

$$L = \frac{(4\pi \times 10^{-7}) \times (\pi \times 0.025^2) \times 500^2}{0.500} \text{ H}$$

$$= 1.23 \times 10^{-3} \text{ H, or } 1.23 \text{ mH}$$

The self-inductance of the uncoiled wire, 78.5 m long, is given by

$$L = \frac{\mu_0}{8} \times l_{\text{w}}$$

$$= \frac{4\pi \times 10^{-7}}{8\pi} \times 78.5 \, \text{H}$$

$$= 3.92 \times 10^{-6} \, \text{H}$$

The ratio of these inductances, coiled wire: uncoiled wire, is $1.23 \times 10^{-3}\,\text{H} : 3.92 \times 10^{-6}\,\text{H}$, which is 314. Thus, coiling the wire into a long thin coil of 500 turns, as shown, has increased its self-inductance by over 300 times.

4.7 Look back to the equation which gives the inductance for a long thin coil (equation (4.4)). In what ways could the geometry of a coil be altered so as to produce a greater inductance?

4.8 If your proposals are carried out more and more extensively, what shape does the coil become?

4.9 Could the coil be described any longer as a 'long thin coil'?

When a coil becomes shorter and wider than the 10:1 length:diameter ratio, its self-inductance becomes less than that predicted by equation (4.4). When the length to the diameter is 1:1, and the coil has a drum-shaped appearance, the self-inductance is about $\frac{3}{4}$ of that predicted by the equation.

4.10 Suggest a way of increasing the number of turns for a coil of fixed length.

In Figure 4.3, wires, each of length 78.5 m, were shown, one uncoiled and the other coiled into a long thin coil. The uncoiled wire has a self-inductance of $4\,\mu\text{H}$, and the coiled wire has a self-inductance of 1 mH. For the same length of wire, 78.5 m, let us find the self-inductance for the two other coil arrangements shown in Figure 4.4.

4.11 By keeping the average diameter of the turns shown in Figure 4.4(a) at 50 mm, as for the long thin coil shown in Figure 4.3, the length of wire

Figure 4.4 *Coils which are modifications of the coil shown in Figure 4.3. Each of the three coils has 500 turns, and in each the length of wire is 78.5 m. In Figure 4.4 (a) and (b) the coils have been shortened to 100 mm and 50 mm by arranging the turns in layers. The average diameter of each coil remains 50 mm.*

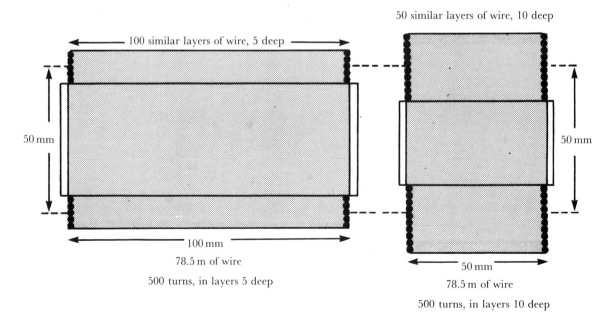

(a)

(b)

used is the same as in the long thin coil, 78.5 m. Find the self-inductance of the 100 mm long coil shown in Figure 4.4(a) using equation (4.4) and a value of 50 mm for the average diameter of the turns. Also, use a correction factor of 0.88 because the coil is no longer long and thin.

4.12 In a similar way, find the self-inductance of the coil shown in Figure 4.4(b) using a correction factor of 0.75 because the coil is no longer long and thin.

An inductor slows down a current rise

The wires used in the coils shown in Figures 4.3 and 4.4 each have the same length and diameter, 78.5 m

of 1 mm diameter copper wire. Each wire has a resistance of 1.72 Ω, at 20 °C.

If a potential difference of 17.2 V is applied across the ends of each wire, the resulting current is

$$I = 17.2\,\text{V}/1.72\,\Omega$$
$$= 10.0\,\text{A}$$

But this current magnitude is not reached instantaneously. In the case of the uncoiled wire, the current rises to 99% of its final value in about 10 μs. But when the same wire is coiled as in our three examples, the corresponding times range from 5 ms to 25 ms. This is shown in the graphs given in Figure 4.5. (The values of the self-inductances of the coil are given to 1 significant figure.) The current growth follows an exponential curve. When a charged capacitor discharges through a

Figure 4.5 *Current rise times for the uncoiled wire and the three coils shown in Figures 4.3 and 4.4. All have the same length of wire and the same resistance; but the current rise times are different. For the uncoiled wire, the current rises to its maximum value almost instantaneously.*

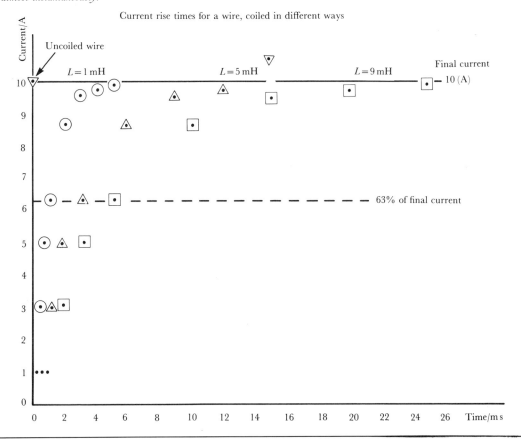

resistor, the decay of charge follows an exponential curve; and the decrease in potential difference across the capacitor also follows an exponential curve. The system has a *time constant*, $T = CR$, in which T is equal to the time that it takes for the potential difference (and the charge) to decrease to 37% of their original values. (See 'Capacitance and capacitors', pages 44–5.)

In the same way, a wire or a coil having self-inductance L and resistance R has a *time constant*, $T = L/R$. For such a system, the time constant is the time it takes for a current to grow from zero to 63% of its final value. This is shown on the graphs given in Figure 4.5.

4.13 The long thin coil shown in Figure 4.3 has a self-inductance of 1.23×10^{-3} H and a resistance of $1.72\,\Omega$. Calculate its time constant.

4.14 If the coil is needed in order to delay the rise of a current for as long as possible, how should it be designed:
(a) with a large or a small time constant?
(b) with a large or a small self-inductance?
(c) with a large or a small resistance?

4.15 The units of self-inductance are $V\,s^{-1}\,A^{-1}$ (see page 48). Show that the time constant, T, has the dimensions of time.

Inductors in power supply

A power transmission circuit contains within it automatically switched circuit breakers in case of a short circuit or similar fault. A circuit breaker has mass and inertia, and a finite time is needed for it to be moved sufficiently far for the circuit to be successfully interrupted. The time needed is between two and four cycles of alternating current. With 50 Hz alternating current, these times are between $\frac{2}{50}$ s and $\frac{4}{50}$ s. The transmission system shown in Figure 4.6 is designed for each of the three lines to carry a normal current of 2000 A; but a short circuit near the transformer could lead to a current of 12 000 A, rising to this level in less than a half-cycle (in less than $\frac{1}{100}$ s).

The need is for a device which will slow down the growth of the fault current; and this is what a large

Figure 4.6 *The location of three large inductors in a power transmission system. On the right of the photograph, large insulated 'bushings' lead to overhead conductors. Inside the rectangular enclosure, they lead to the inductor. Each inductor is part of a 400 000 V power transmission circuit. (Source: GEC Alsthom Transformers Limited.)*

Figure 4.7 *Three inductor coils for a power transmission system. They are current-limiting inductors. Each is designed to carry a normal current of 1500 A and to limit a fault current to 8000 A. The total height of the unit is about 3.4 m. (Source: Brush Transformers Limited.)*

inductance will do. With alternating current, an inductance also has an *impeding effect* on current and it actually 'adds ohms' to the circuit. This reduces the final current, and limits it (this is considered in Chapter 8, pages 88–91). A power transmission line is therefore designed with a large inductor in series. Since its function is to slow down the growth of the current and 'limit' its value until the circuit breaker can operate, it is called a 'current-limiting inductor'.

Figure 4.7 shows current-limiting inductors for a power supply. It is a 'three phase' supply, and current will travel along three shared lines. Three inductors are needed, one in series with each line. These inductors could be made and mounted as separate units; but to design and make them as one unit achieves economy of space, economy in manufacturing, and increased electrical efficiency when in operation. The unit seen in Figure 4.7 is about 3.4 m high, and it has a mass of about 63 tonnes (45 tonnes of steel and 18 tonnes of copper). Examine Figure 4.7; in particular look at one coil and its windings.

Making a large current-limiting inductor

The inductor which is described in this section was required for a power transmission system and was designed and made by the staff of E.B. NITRAN, Transformers and Fusegear, Dundee. (The photographs were taken during visits to the workshops.)

The specifications

Three identical inductors were needed for a power transmission system for alternating current. The maximum current to be maintained along a line and through an inductor over a long period of time would be the equivalent of 437 A of direct current (i.e. alternating current of 437 A rms value; see the section on 'RMS values', pages 81–4).

The potential difference at the sending end of a pair of lines would be 19 000 V. In order to limit any fault current until the circuit breakers could operate, inductors were needed, each with an inductance of 21.5×10^{-3} H.

Figure 4.8 *A longitudinal section through the inductor. The copper conductor is wound in eight layers, and there are 29 rows of such layers down the length of the coil. Between the rows a space is left for cooling oil to circulate. The conductor is rectangular in cross-section. This is a scale diagram, one-sixth actual size.*

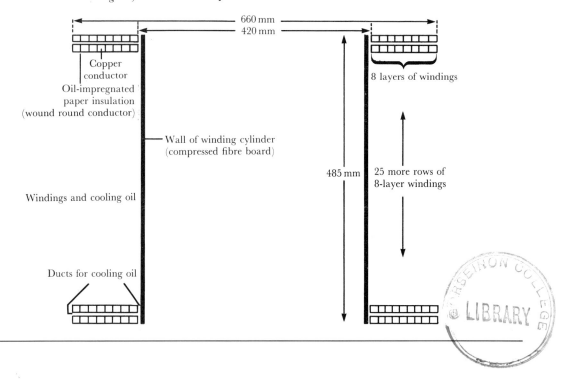

The inductor coil design

Figure 4.8 shows the coil design for the inductor. Four matters are fundamental, and these dominate the design: the conductor must carry the required current safely; the coils must provide the required inductance; the large magnetic flux must be controlled; and the heat produced must be provided with a means of escaping.

The conductor

The conductor must be capable of carrying a current of 437 A continuously, and must also be able to carry larger 'overload' currents for a short period. It must also be able to carry, for at least one-tenth of a second, large short circuit currents of as much as 7000 A. A copper conductor with cross-section area of approximately 140 mm² is needed. Look at Figure 4.8 and note the cross-section shape of the conductor. It is rectangular. The dimensions are approximately 14 mm × 10 mm. Use a millimetre scale to visualise the cross-section. Solid copper of these dimensions would behave as a copper bar and could not be wound round a cylinder to form a coil.

The conductor is therefore made not as one piece but from several ribbons of copper which together give the required cross-section area. The ribbons of copper, insulated with varnish, are placed closely together and are bound with oil-impregnated paper as overall insulation. When a bending force is applied, the ribbons slide over each other and the bundle bends. On Figure 4.8, find the paper insulation which separates one layer of conductor from the next.

The photograph in Figure 4.9 shows a large coil being wound. It is similar to that for the inductor, and the caption to the photograph indicates the features to look at.

The inductance and the magnetic flux

The inductance required is 21.5 mH, and the coil design shown in Figure 4.8 was worked out to provide this value. Examine that diagram again. The coil is clearly not a long thin solenoid.

Figure 4.9 *A large coil, somewhat similar to the inductor coil, being wound. The inner cylinder is of compressed fibre board. The horizontal strips are of compressed fibre board. They separate the coils from the cylinder, and thus create passages along which cooling oil can flow. The spacers which separate the coil layers are of compressed fibre board. The gaps allow cooling oil to flow between the coil layers. (This photograph, and those which follow in this chapter, were taken in the workshops of E. B. Nitran, Transformers and Fusegear, Dundee.)*

4.16 Obtain a value for the inductance of the coil shown in Figure 4.8. Use the long thin solenoid equation and a correction factor of 0.561. For the area A of the coil cross-section use a mean value of the coil radius.

(a) What value could be used for the mean coil radius?

(b) How many turns are there on the coil?

(c) Using the correct factor of 0.561, what value of inductance is obtained?

(d) How does this compare with the required value of 21.5 mH?

Figure 4.10 *This diagram is intended to show: (i) that with a current of 400 A, the magnetic flux density, B, would be very high in the region of the inductor; (ii) that some of the flux can travel considerable distances from the coil by following ferromagnetic routes such as steel beams and supports; (iii) that if alternating current is in use, then neighbouring ferromagnetic materials can become very hot.*

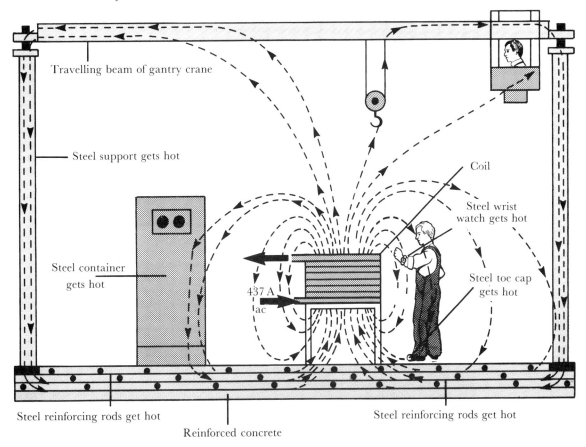

You will have found that the value obtained for the inductance is less than the required value. The reason is that the calculation was done for a coil surrounded by air. The actual inductor, in its completed state, will have a shield of steel laminations around it. The steel shield will increase the inductance of the coil. The reason for having a steel shield will now be examined.

The *magnetic flux density, B,* is very high in the region of a coil which has over 200 turns and which carries a current of 400 A.

Figure 4.10 illustrates two important consequences of this high magnetic flux density. A substantial magnetic field due to the coil exists at considerable distances from it, for instance 15 m to 20 m away. Since it is easier for magnetic flux to pass through ferromagnetic material than through air, some flux becomes diverted into ferromagnetic material such as the surrounding structural steel; and it can travel for considerable distances through this steel. It can be easier for the flux to take a long route through steel than to take a shorter route through air. Examine Figure 4.10 and follow some of the flux routes.

When alternating current is used the magnetic flux grows and then decreases, doing so with twice the frequency of the supply. The changing flux in the steel surroundings induces emfs internally in these surroundings; and internal currents result within the steelwork. These 'eddy currents', like any current in a conductor, result in a loss of energy, which becomes apparent through a rise in the temperature of the conductor.

Examining Figure 4.10 once again, a person standing near the coil when it is operating on ac can feel a steel wrist watch becoming hot; and protective steel toecaps in boots become hot. Surrounding structural steelwork becomes hot; and an isolated container such as a tank or cabinet of thin sheet steel could become red hot.

Clearly, the distribution of magnetic flux must be controlled. A 'flux guide' of magnetically soft steel laminations is built to go around the coil. The magnetic flux will become located almost entirely in the steel, in preference to air. In this way the location of the flux can be controlled.

Figure 4.11 shows the magnetic flux guide and Figure 4.12 shows it with the inductor in position and connected electrically. Examine each photograph and read each caption.

4.17 Having examined the photographs given in Figure 4.11 and 4.12 make a sketch of a longitudinal section through the coil and its flux guide. Also sketch in some flux paths to show the operation of the guide.

Figure 4.11 The magnetic flux guide for the inductor coil. It is made of laminations of magnetically soft steel. Vertical laminations are interleaved with horizontal laminations to form a continuous box. The internal dimensions of the box are almost 1 m wide × about $\frac{3}{4}$ m high. Examine the photograph for laminations.

Figure 4.12 The inductor mounted in its flux guide. An idea of scale is given by the hand and sleeve at the left of the photograph. Examine the photograph and note how the coil is connected. Consider the diameter of the vertical leads.

Figure 4.13 The production of flat laminations from rolls of thin steel sheet. The machine line is computer controlled. For each flux guide unit, the dimensions of the different sized laminations required are entered in the computer. Steel from a roll is fed in at the left-hand end of the machine, which then cuts the sheet to appropriate sizes. Flat laminations emerge at the right-hand end. The photograph shows the Laminations Production Supervisor and an operator at the control console, at E. B. NITRAN, Transformers and Fusegear, Dundee.

The flux guide is very effective; about 98% of the magnetic flux produced by the coil is guided round in the laminations. About 1% of flux escapes at the front and about 1% at the back. Because the flux guide holds the flux within it and prevents flux from reaching nearby objects, it is also known as a 'magnetic shield'.

Figure 4.14 *Flux guides for the three inductors for the transmission system. It is electrically more efficient, and economically more sound, to make one large magnetic shield with shared flux paths than to make three separate smaller ones. The mass of the steel laminations is 6.5 tonnes.*

Making the magnetic shield

Figures 4.13, 4.14 and 4.15 shows a sequence in the manufacture of the magnetic shield and the install-ation of the three inductors which are required for the customer's power transmission system. Examine each photograph and read its caption.

4.18 What is the mass of the assembled unit, inductors and magnetic shield?

4.19 In Figure 4.15, find the electrical connections for the top inductor; similarly, find those for the middle and lower inductors.

4.20 The calculation of the inductance of one isolated coil, using the long solenoid equation and a correction factor, gave a value of 17.9 mH

Figure 4.15 *The three inductors mounted in the magnetic shield and connected electrically. The mass of copper in the windings is 1.5 tonnes (half a tonne in each inductor).*

(Question 4.16). The steel in the flux guide adds about 20% of flux.
(a) Calculate the inductance of a coil in its flux guide.
(b) How does this compare with the required value of 21.5 mH?

4.21 Examine how the coils are supported in the flux guides. Study Figures 4.12 and 4.15 for this purpose.

Each coil is not resting directly on laminations, nor directly on a thick sheet of compressed fibre board (Figure 4.12). It is supported on short pillars of compressed fibre board, thus leaving gaps below the coil.

Suggest the main function of these gaps. (Help will be obtained by examining Figure 4.8, the longitudinal section of the coil and in particular the left-hand side of it. Further help will be obtained from the paragraph that immediately follows this question.)

Energy losses and heat

Heat is produced by a current in a conductor. The lost or waste energy resulting from a current in a conductor causes the temperature of the conductor to rise. If the temperature of the conductor is to be kept to a safe low value, then the lost energy must be conveyed to the atmosphere at a sufficient rate.

The average operating temperature of the inductor coils is 60 K above the temperature of the surrounding atmosphere. Thus if local atmospheric temperature is 25 °C, the average coil temperature is 85 °C, or almost the temperature of boiling water.

What is the rate at which energy is lost in an operating coil? The rate of loss of energy due to a current in a conductor is $P = I^2 R$. The resistance of the coil at the operating temperature is $0.058\,\Omega$, and the current is 437 A:

$$P = I^2 R$$
$$= 437^2 \times 0.058 \text{ J s}^{-1}$$
$$= 11\,100 \text{ J s}^{-1}$$
$$= 11.1 \text{ kW}$$

Thus the rate of loss of energy is just over $11\,000\,\text{J s}^{-1}$, which is a power loss of just over 11 kW. With three inductors operating at their full load currents of 437 A each, the loss for the whole unit is 33 kW.

In addition to energy loss in the copper conductors, energy loss occurs in the steel of the flux guide. This arises from eddy currents in the steel; and the process is the same as was described for steelwork surrounding the unshielded coil, on pages 55–6. The rate of loss of energy as a result of eddy currents is $26\,000\,\text{J s}^{-1}$, which is a power loss of 26 kW.

Thus the power losses are

I^2R loss in the copper conductors = 33 kW
Eddy current loss in the steel   = 26 kW
Total losses   = 59 kW

This is equivalent to the heat produced by 30 domestic electric two-bar radiators, and a special cooling system is essential.

The cooling system: oil and air

The insulation on the copper conductor of the coils is oil-impregnated paper. This is a very satisfactory insulation material provided that the temperature of the copper does not rise so high as to damage the paper. The unit is designed so that when the coils

Figure 4.16 The cooling system. The three inductors and flux guides are inside the metal tank. Panels for cooling circulating oil are attached to the tank. The tank is being filled with oil.

Figure 4.17 *The tank and cooling panels have been filled with oil. The coils have been connected to a high voltage power supply and the whole unit is being tested.*

are carrying the maximum sustained current of 437 A the average temperature of the copper does not rise more than 60 K above the temperature of the surrounding atmosphere.

The copper coils and the steel flux guides are surrounded by oil, which fills the tank. There are gaps between the rows of the eight-layered conductor and there are gaps between the inner turn and the fibre board cylinder on which the coils are wound. The coils heat the oil and this rises up the vertical channels by convection.

Look at Figures 4.8 and 4.9 to find gaps and channels. The temperature rise of the steel of the magnetic shield, due to eddy currents, also causes the steel to heat the oil.

The hot oil rises to the top of the tank. There it meets outlet pipes which lead to cooling panels

consisting of a number of thin hollow rectangular elements, each of which presents a large surface area to the atmosphere. Hot oil entering a panel at the top, at say 60 K above atmospheric temperature, loses energy to the atmosphere; its temperature falls; its density increases; and the oil sinks down the panel, continuing to lose energy and continuing to decrease in temperature as it does so.

At the bottom of the panels are pipes which lead into the lower part of the tank. The cooled oil enters the lower part of the tank and the convection cycle is repeated.

During the passage of the oil down through the panels, its temperature may drop by about 15 K. Thus if the hot oil passes from the top of the tank into the top of a cooling panel at about 85 °C, it passes from the bottom of the panel into the foot of the tank at about 70 °C.

Air between the leaves of the panels becomes heated and rises by convection. Of the energy transfer from the panels to the atmosphere, about 80% takes place by convection and about 20% by radiation.

Answers to questions

4.1 No
4.2 $\frac{1}{2} \times 10^{-7}$ H
4.3 1×10^{-6} H
4.4 1×10^{-2} H
4.5 No
4.6 No
4.7 Increase the cross-section area and shorten the coil length
4.9 No
4.10 By winding it in layers
4.11 5.4×10^{-3} H
4.12 9.3×10^{-3} H
4.13 0.72×10^{-3} s
4.14 (a) large; (b) large; (c) small
4.16 (a) 270 mm; (b) 232; (c) 17.9 mH
4.18 8 t
4.20 (a) 21.5 mH

5. Forces between current-carrying conductors

The equipment shown in this chapter is used for alternating current. In the discussion of forces, however, we will consider direct current flowing in the conductors.

Figure 5.1(a) shows two adjacent conductors, A and B; each is carrying a current. The currents are in the *same* direction, and each conductor experiences an inwards force, F, towards the other.

Figure 5.1 *The directions of the forces experienced by adjacent conductors, each carrying a current.*

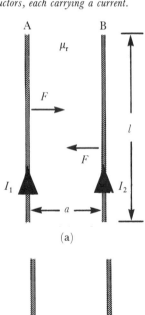

(a)

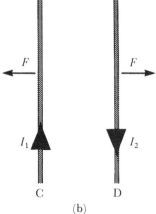

(b)

Conductor A experiences a force towards conductor B; conductor B experiences a force towards conductor A. The magnitude of these forces is the same for each; it is F.

Figure 5.1(b) shows adjacent conductors, C and D, each carrying a current; the currents are in *opposite* directions. Each conductor experiences a force away from the other, outwards.

In Figure 5.1(a), the two conductors are a distance a apart; they are carrying currents of I_1 and I_2. The conductors are each of length l; they are in a medium with a relative permeability of μ_r. If the conductors are *long* and are *parallel to each other*, then the magnitude of the force F experienced by each is given by

$$F = \frac{\mu_0 \mu_r I_1 I_2 l}{2\pi a}$$

and

$$\mu_0 = 4\pi \times 10^{-7}\,\mathrm{H\,m^{-1}}$$

Thus the force on a given conductor in the pair is:
- proportional to the product of the two currents;
- proportional to the length;
- inversely proportional to the distance between the conductors.

Figure 5.2 *A length of domestic two-core cable, approximately actual size. The cable is rated for currents up to 3 A.*

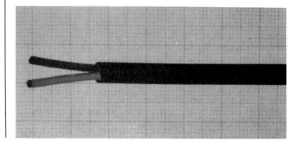

Figure 5.2 shows a two-core domestic cable, approximately actual size, which is rated for currents up to 3 A. The conductors are 2.0 mm apart, centre to centre. For the insulation, being non-magnetic, we will take $\mu_r = 1.0$. Thus if the conductors are carrying their rated current the force on a 1 m length of each conductor is

$$F = \frac{4\pi \times 10^{-7} \times 1.0 \times 3 \times 3 \times 1}{2\pi(2 \times 10^{-3})} N = 9 \times 10^{-4} N$$

So the force on a 1 m length of one conductor is closely equal to 10×10^{-4} N or 1×10^{-3} N, about $\frac{1}{1000}$th of a newton. This may not seem a very significant force. In domestic cables where currents are of a few amps the force is not significant. In industrial distribution systems, however, currents are measured in thousands of amps, and short circuit currents are of the order of tens of thousands of amps. Moreover, the force is proportional to the *product* of the currents in the conductors; thus, where each conductor carries the same current the force is proportional to the *square* of the current. With these large currents, very large forces are experienced by adjacent conductors. In large busbar systems, each busbar must be firmly fixed at regular intervals along its length to prevent bars being blown apart by the effects of fault currents.

In a large block of offices or flats, or in a factory, large currents are not normally distributed by means of insulated power cables. Instead, large cross-section copper bars or aluminium bars are normally used; these are called 'busbars'. Frequently, they are not insulated; but they are enclosed by a box-like structure, or trunking, of metal sheeting. Figure 5.3 shows busbar trunking leaving a transformer. Figure 5.4 shows four bare copper busbars in trunking. Each bar is fixed in a glass reinforced plastic insulator, and the insulators are supported by aluminium cross-pieces.

The copper bars shown in Figure 5.4 have a rectangular cross-section of 200 mm height and 10 mm width. In free air they are rated to carry 3000 A each; in enclosed trunking they are rated to carry 2500 A each. The trunking may be perforated to improve ventilation and cooling. The bars and the trunking have been designed so that when the full rated current is being carried continuously the

Figure 5.3 *A transformer, busbars, and trunking enclosing busbars along their route. The transformer enclosure is about 2.5 m high. (Source: Barduct Limited.)*

Figure 5.4 *Four busbars in trunking. Each is of copper, of rectangular cross-section 200 mm × 10 mm, and each is rated to carry 2500 A. (Source: Barduct Limited.)*

Figure 5.5 *Trunking and tapping boxes for 800 A busbars.*
At this level of distribution, the busbars are insulated.
(Source: Barduct Limited.)

Figure 5.6 *A test rig to demonstrate the effect of short*
circuit electromagnetic forces on busbars. The bars were
straight before the short circuit. (Source: Falcon Testing
Laboratory Limited.)

temperature rise of a bar will not exceed 55 K.
Thus, if the ambient temperature is 20 °C the bars
may be operating at a temperature of about 70 °C.

Figure 5.5 shows trunking for 800 A busbars,
typically for use in hotels, office blocks, hospitals,
machine shops and assembly lines. Attached to the
trunking are two tapping boxes. Inside a box,
power cables can be clamped to the busbars, and
then led out of the box to a nearby distribution
board with fusegear. The two tapping boxes in
Figure 5.5 are for 60 A (a) and 100 A (b)
distribution.

Because of the large forces between the conductors, the busbars must be secured frequently along
their length, and held firmly with regard to
sideways movement. But they must be allowed to
move lengthwise to enable expansion and contrac-

tion to take place with temperature changes. A look at Figure 5.4 shows that the bars are in slots in the lower and upper insulators; and the bars can move lengthways in the slots.

Figure 5.6 shows demonstration busbars. The two bars on the right-hand side formed part of a circuit and carried a short circuit current of 60 000 A. Before the short circuit, the bars were straight; during the short circuit, the forces between the conductors forced them apart, permanently deforming the bars.

Let us calculate the force per metre run of a bar. The current in each bar was 60 000 A; the bar separation was 100 mm; and the length of bar being considered was 1 m. For air, $\mu_r = 1.0$:

$$F = \frac{(4\pi \times 10^{-7}) \times 1.0 \times 60\,000 \times 60\,000 \times 1}{2\pi \times 0.1}\,N$$

$$= 7200\,N$$

A mass of $\frac{3}{4}$ tonne (that is, 750 kg) has a weight of 7500 N; so the force required to hold up a $\frac{3}{4}$ tonne

mass is about the same in magnitude as the sideways force being experienced by each bar.

60 000 A is a typical value for a fault current in a high current distribution system.

5.1 The busbar system in Figure 5.4 has been designed and made for continuous currents of 800 A in the conductors, and to safely withstand a 50 000 A fault current for 1 s (by which time a circuit breaker would operate). The manufacturer recommends a support every 2.5 m along the length of the busbars. The bars are 75 mm apart, centre to centre.

Find the force on each of two adjacent bars, between supports, when they form the out and return paths of a 50 000 A fault current. (For air, $\mu_r = 1.0$.)

Answer to question

5.1 $17 \times 10^3\,N$

6. Phases and phase differences

Some waveforms

When a potential difference across a conductor varies *in magnitude* and *in direction*, then the charge flow in the conductor changes in magnitude and direction. Thus the current changes in magnitude and in direction. This is alternating current. An infinite number of different waveforms can be produced, and Figure 6.1 shows some of these.

Figure 6.1(a) shows a square wave, a type that is important in logic and computer systems; (b) shows the emf being generated in a simple alternator consisting of a single turn of wire rotating between the pole faces of a horseshoe magnet; (c) shows how the current in the *primary* coil of a transformer changes with time when there is no completed circuit on the secondary coil (no load), and the transformer is not delivering power; (d) is a sine curve. The output emf of commercial alternators is very close to being a sine curve.

Of these waveforms, the sine curve is particularly important. Alternating current machines and transformers operate most efficiently on sine waveforms. (Other waveforms result in higher energy losses and lower efficiency.) In electric motors, sinusoidal potential differences and currents produce smoother accelerating torque for the load than do other waveforms. Alternating current machinery and equipment produce stray high frequency electromagnetic fields that can affect other equipment, and can be heard on telephone lines; and sine waveforms result in less interference than do other waveforms.

Mathematically, sine waves are important because all periodic waveforms, that is, repetitive waveforms, no matter how complex they are, can be synthesised by combining a sufficient number of sine waves of different frequencies and amplitudes. A close approximation even to square waves can be made by combining sine waves.

Phase relationships

A busbar short circuit

Conductors in power distribution systems may be carrying currents of hundreds of amps. If a short circuit occurs, the current can rise to many times its initial value and the conductors experience a sudden and very large force of repulsion between them, the force being electromagnetic in origin. The conductors in the supply cable are held together by their outer protective coats of plastic material, and they are not usually damaged.

Figure 6.1 *Some alternating current waveforms: (a) a square wave; (b) the emf from a simple alternator with a single turn rotating loop; (c) the primary coil current of a transformer not delivering power from the secondary coil; (d) a sine wave.*

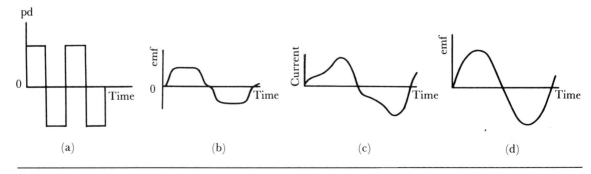

(a) (b) (c) (d)

Figure 6.2 *The cathode ray oscillograph for a short circuit test on busbars, using alternating current from a power transformer. The potential difference across the supply end of the busbars, and the current in the busbars, are shown as they vary with time. (Source: Falcon Testing Laboratories, Loughborough. This figure may be photocopied.)*

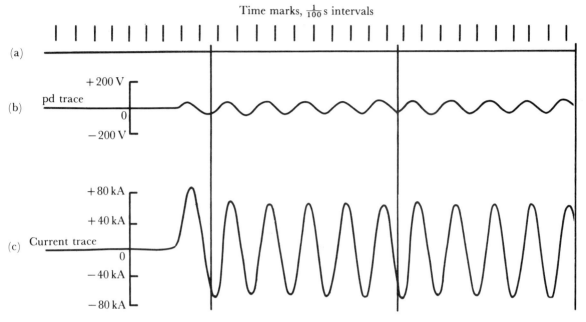

Figure 6.3 *Schematic of the circuit for a short circuit test on busbars. This is the arrangement from which the oscillograph traces in Figure 6.2 were made.*

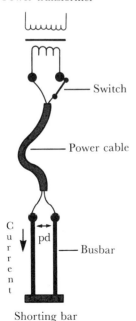

Busbars, however, may be blown apart if their fixings are not adequate. A photograph of this is shown in Figure 5.6.

Manufacturers of busbar systems therefore take a randomly chosen unit from a production run and send it for short circuit testing. Figure 6.2 shows actual oscillograph traces from the test. Figure 6.3 shows a schematic circuit for such a test.

6.1 A photocopy, or other form of copy, of Figure 6.2 may be used for this question. (The diagram in the book should be left unmarked.)

From the oscillograph traces in Figure 6.2:
(a) Approximately what was the peak value of the recurring potential difference across the supply end of the busbars?
(b) Approximately what was the recurring peak value of the current in the busbars?
(c) What was the frequency of the supply?

6.2(a) Examine the positions of the peaks and troughs in the pd trace and the current trace, in Figure 6.2.
(b) Examine the growth and fall of the pd, and the growth and fall of the current. Does the

first current peak appear to occur (i) at the same time as the first pd peak, (ii) after the pd peak in time, or (iii) before the pd peak in time? On your photocopy of Figure 6.2, use a ruler and a pencil to draw a vertical line to help in deciding.

6.3 Look at the first trough in the pd trace and in the current trace.
  (a) Does the current trough occur before, at the same time as or after the pd trough in time?
  (b) Could the current pattern be said to 'be ahead of' or to 'lag behind' the pd pattern in time?

It will have become apparent from studying the traces and from answering Questions 6.2 and 6.3 that the current peaks and the current troughs occur *later in time* than their corresponding pd peaks and troughs. In fact, the whole current pattern *lags behind* the pd pattern in time. *The current is out of phase with the potential difference which produces it.*

The reason for this is that the circuit possesses *inductance*. Most of this is produced by the turns in the secondary coil of the transformer, but a little of it is produced by the conductors themselves. Even a straight conductor possesses some inductance. (Inductance was considered in Chapter 4.)

Figure 6.4 shows diagrammatically how the free, or conduction, electrons behave in a straight metallic conductor when an alternating potential difference with sinusoidal waveform is applied across its ends. It thus shows how the *current* behaves when it is produced by a sinusoidal pd. Study the sequence of events, reading the text which goes with the stages.

Figure 6.5 shows diagrammatically how the charge changes on the plates of a capacitor when there is an alternating potential difference of sinusoidal waveform across the plates. Because the charge Q on a capacitor at any instant is $Q = Cv$, where C is the capacitance and v is the potential difference at that instant, the charge Q is at a maximum when the potential difference, v, between the plates is at a maximum; this is shown on the middle graph in Figure 6.5. Examine this.

Now, a current in a conductor is a rate of flow of charge, dQ/dt coulombs per second. The electrons which flow on to and off the capacitor plates do so along the supply leads. The *rate of change of charge* on the plates, dQ/dt coulombs per second, at a particular moment is given by the *slope* of the *charge against time graph* at that moment. Thus *the slope of the curve* at any instant gives the value of the *current in the supply leads* at that instant, $dQ/dt = i$.

Examine the middle graph in Figure 6.5 and read the accompanying text. See how the slopes relate the *current* and the *potential difference*. The current and the pd can then be plotted on the one graph; this is done on the lower graph.

With a *capacitor* the *pd* and the *current* are *out of phase with each other*; and *the current phase is* **ahead** *of the pd phase* in time by one-quarter of the periodic time, $\frac{1}{4}T$.

Examine the upper diagram in Figure 6.5 again. The capacitor is fully charged at stage c, when the pd across it is a maximum, at c. At that point, the energy stored in the capacitor, in the electric field, is a maximum. Where the peak or maximum potential difference is V_m, and the capacitance is C, the peak energy stored, W_m, is:

$$W_m = \frac{1}{2}CV_m^2$$

Figure 6.6 shows a sinusoidal potential difference and its effect when connected across an inductor. The potential difference, and the current which it creates in the inductor, are out of phase.

6.4 By how much are the pd and current out of phase?

6.5 Is the current phase ahead of or behind the pd phase in time?

Consider the pd curve in Figure 6.6. From A, the pd increases (in the positive direction) to a maximum at C; it then decreases to a zero at E. When the pd is at its maximum the current is zero but increasing (in the positive direction) until it reaches a maximum. The current, rising in the positive direction, has reached its peak *after* the pd (which was also rising in the positive direction) reached its peak. Therefore the current phase is *behind* the pd phase in time.

The magnetic flux density, B, in a coil is directly proportional to the current, i, in the coil:

$$B \propto i$$

Figure 6.4 *A straight metallic conductor with a sinusoidal alternating potential difference across its ends.*

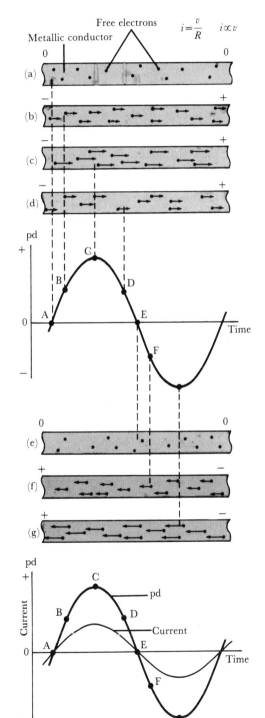

The current is proportional to the potential difference between the ends of the conductor. $i \propto v$

No potential difference; no current. Point A on graph

Potential difference causes drift of electrons; current results. Point B on graph

Doubled pd doubles the drift velocity; current doubled. Point C on graph

pd decreased; current decreased. Point D on graph

The variation of potential difference with time is following a sine curve.

No potential difference; no current. Point E on graph

Direction of pd reversed; current reversed. Point F on graph

Doubled reverse pd doubles the reverse current. Point G on graph

Potential difference and current plotted against time

When the pd was zero, the current was zero: (a) and A When the pd was a maximum, the current was a maximum: (c) and C

When the pd was a maximum in the reverse direction, the current was a maximum in the reverse direction: (g) and G

The pd and the current are *in phase* with each other

Figure 6.5 *A capacitor with a sinusoidal alternating potential difference across its plates.*

The charge on the capacitor is proportional to the pd between its places. $Q=Cv$ $Q\propto v$

Diagram a and point A on the graph: no pd between plates, no charge on plates

Diagram b and point B: pd rises, electrons flow onto left-hand plate, capacitor being charged. Maximum pd, point C, capacitor at maximum charge, c and C. pd decreases, electrons flow off left-hand plate, charge decreases: D and d. At E pd is zero and capacitor is uncharged, e

Direction of pd reversed

Follow the stages of the cycle through E to J, and e to j

From G through H to J are electrons flowing off the left-hand plate or onto it?

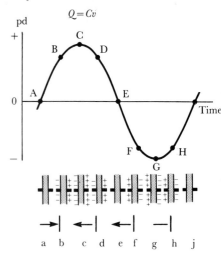

A capacitor in varying stages of charging

Graphs of pd and charge against time
The charge curve (thin line) represents the stages in a to j

Tangents have been drawn to the charge curve at five places. These give the slope, $\frac{dQ}{dt}$, the rate of change of charge

At point A, *the slope of the charge curve* is *greatest*, and positive, but *the pd is zero*. At point C in time, *the pd is a* maximum, but *the slope of the charge curve* is a *minimum* (zero)

Follow the slope of the charge curve as time increases, and find the positions of maximum slope and minimum slope

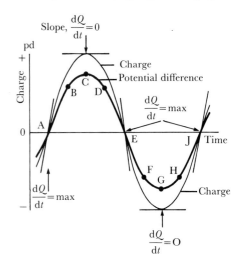

Graphs of pd across the plates and current in the leads, against time.

$\text{Current} = \frac{dQ}{dt} = \text{Slope of charge curve}$

The slope of the charge curve, being a rate of change of charge, gives the current in the supply leads

At A, the charge slope is a maximum and therefore *the current in the supply leads is a maximum*, but *the potential difference is zero*. At the time represented by C, the slope is a minimum (zero) and *the current is zero*, but *the pd is a maximum*

On the middle graph, find the current maxima and zeros; and check their plotting on the bottom graph

The pd and the current are *out of phase*

They are out of phase by *one quarter of the Periodic Time,* $\frac{1}{4}T$

At point A the pd is increasing; but the current has already risen to a maximum and is about to decrease. *In timing*, the *current phase is ahead* of the pd phase

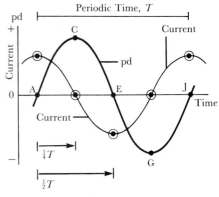

Figure 6.6 *An inductor with a sinusoidal alternating potential difference across it.*

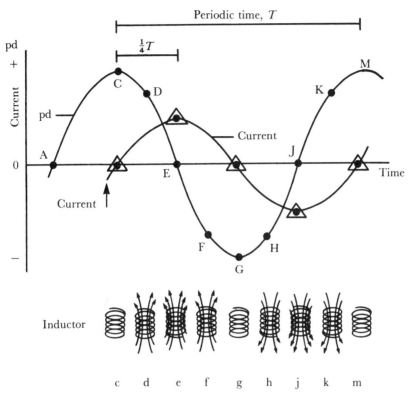

Figure 6.6 shows how the flux density in the inductor changes with time. In the series of diagrams showing the inductor, at the time represented by diagram c there is no current in the coil, and therefore no magnetic flux. As the pd falls to D on the graph, the current rises and the flux grows in the coil, as seen in diagram d.

Follow the change in current with time and the change in flux.

As the magnetic flux grows, the energy stored in the inductor grows. The energy stored in the magnetic field in the inductor at any instant is given by

$$W = \tfrac{1}{2}Li^2$$

and the peak energy stored,

$$W_m = \tfrac{1}{2}LI_m^2$$

where L is the inductance, i is the current at the instant, and I_m is the peak current.

Consider again the relationship in a *capacitor* between pd across the plates and current in the leads; look again at the lower diagram in Figure 6.5. With a *capacitor* the *current leads* the pd by $\tfrac{1}{4}T$.

We have just seen in Figure 6.6 that with an *inductor* the *current lags behind* the pd by $\tfrac{1}{4}T$. Thus if a capacitor and an inductor were connected in parallel with each other, and a pd applied across them, the current in the wires to the capacitor and the current in the inductor would be out of phase with each other by $(\tfrac{1}{4}T + \tfrac{1}{4}T)$ which is $\tfrac{1}{2}T$, *half the periodic time*. That is, they are *out of phase by half a cycle*, which is to say that when the capacitor is fully charged the inductor will have zero magnetic flux in it. Conversely, when the inductor has maximum magnetic flux in it, the capacitor has zero charge on it. The situation is represented in Figure 6.7.

Figure 6.7 *(a) An inductor and a capacitor connected in parallel; (b) how the capacitor charge and the inductor magnetic flux relate as the pd across them changes.*

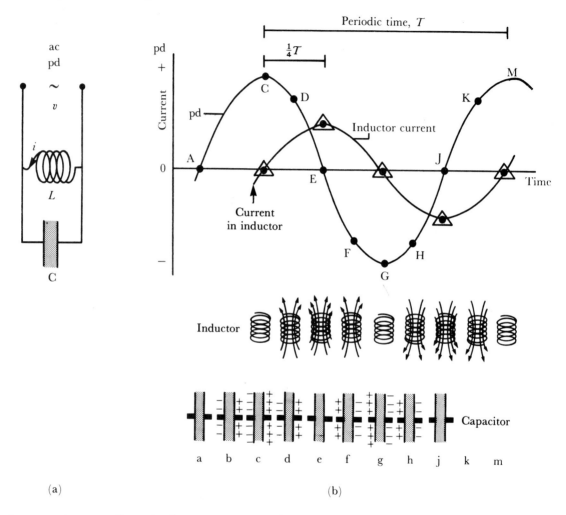

(a)   (b)

A capacitor and an inductor in parallel

Figure 6.7(a) shows an inductor and a capacitor connected in parallel, and Figure 6.7(b) shows how the capacitor charge and the inductor magnetic flux relate to each other as the pd across them changes.

Figure 6.7(b) is formed by putting together the capacitor diagram of Figure 6.5 and the inductor diagram of Figure 6.6. Study Figure 6.7(b). Check that: (1) when the pd is a maximum, the charge on the capacitor is a maximum; (2) when the inductor

current is a maximum, the magnetic flux in the inductor is a maximum; (3) that in stages a to j the capacitor and inductor are in *opposite conditions* with regard to energy storage.

Hence see that with regard to stored energy the capacitor and the inductor are *exactly opposed in phase*; they are half a cycle out of phase with each other. (In angular measure they are 180° or π radians out of phase with each other.)

This is a circumstance of fundamental importance in alternating current applications, because it means that *a capacitor* can be used to *pick up and store energy* that was in an inductor earlier in the cycle; and *an inductor* can be used to *pick up and store energy* that was in a capacitor earlier in the cycle. *The energy can be held in the system*, being transferred backwards and forwards between capacitor and inductor.

6.6 Examine Figure 6.7. Examine the sequence of flux changes in the inductor, stages c to m. Sketch the state of the capacitor at stage k, and also sketch the state at stage m.

Of what use in this phenomenon in industry?

An induction furnace and capacitors

Figure 6.8 shows a sequence of diagrams which build up to give the basic electrical requirements for an induction furnace, for melting metals.

Induction furnaces are particularly suitable for metals and alloys where cleanliness and avoidance of contamination is important. It is relatively easy to provide and maintain an inert atmosphere over the melt. The electrical principles enable furnaces to be built from very small sizes, to take about 5 kg of metal, to very large sizes involving as much as 30 tonnes of metal. They are particularly suited to the processing of special metals and alloys which are used in small quantities.

Figure 6.8(a) shows the basic arrangement at the furnace. A refractory container is surrounded by a coil capable of carrying a large current. Alternating current is supplied which produces changing magnetic flux in the coil; and this induces eddy currents in metal in the container. The eddy currents in the metal cause an energy loss there (I^2R), and the temperature of the metal rises.

The current needed to create the magnetic field pulses forwards and backwards along the supply line; this would happen even if there was no metal at all in the refractory container. Let us call this current I_m, the current needed to make the magnetic flux.

In addition, a current is needed to do the work in heating the metal; let us call this 'working current' I_w.

It is a waste of generator capacity or of transformer capacity to supply a current which simply pulses backwards and forwards along the supply line as the magnetic flux is made and collapses.

The arrangement used is to transfer the energy stored in the coil, $\frac{1}{2}LI_m^2$, to a capacitor so that the capacitor becomes charged up during $\frac{1}{4}$ of a cycle. During the next quarter of a cycle the capacitor discharges, sending the energy back to the coil and

Figure 6.8 *The basic electrical arrangements for an induction furnace, for melting metals.*

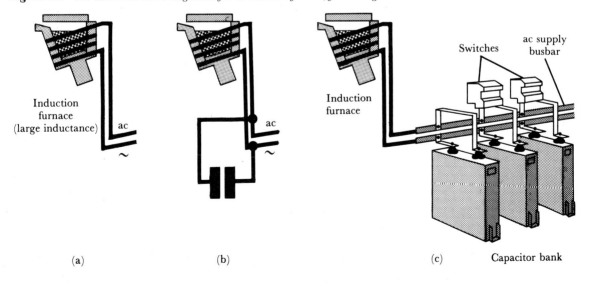

Induction furnace (large inductance)   ac   ~

ac   ~

Switches   ac supply busbar

Induction furnace

(a)   (b)   (c)   Capacitor bank

Figure 6.9 *Molten metal is poured from an induction furnace into moulds, to make castings. The cabinet on the left contains the power supply and the capacitors. (Source: Radyne Limited, Wokingham.)*

remaking the magnetic flux (in the opposite direction). This arrangement is shown in Figure 6.8(b), where a large capacitance is connected in parallel with the furnace coil. This corresponds to the circuit diagram in Figure 6.7(a).

A more developed representation is given in Figure 6.8(c), which shows the alternating current being supplied along busbars. These would be of large cross-section aluminium or copper to carry the necessary large current. Connected to the busbars are capacitor units, forming a capacitor bank. A basic minimum capacitance is always needed, and the left-hand capacitor unit is permanently connected. Other capacitor units can be switched on as necessary. Thus, after start-up and

after reaching a steady state, the supply has to provide the 'working current', I_w. It does not have to supply the main magnetising current, which comes from the capacitors. (As energy losses occur in the inductor–capacitor system, which cannot be 100% efficient, the losses are made up by a small extra current in the supply.)

In this way, smaller cross-section busbars and supply cables can be used, and a smaller capacity supply (alternator or transformer) than if the main inductor current were pulsing forwards and backwards along the whole length of the supply route.

Figure 6.9 shows an induction furnace being tilted over in order to pour the molten metal contents into moulds to make castings. On the left is a large cabinet which contains the power supply, including the capacitors.

Figure 6.10 shows the interior of a power supply cabinet. Power arrives at the cabinet along the 50 Hz ac mains. Units in the cabinet convert the 50 Hz ac to dc (diode rectifier, A), convert the dc to 25 000 Hz ac (inverter, B), and transform the voltage up to 1000 V (transformer, C). Capacitor units provide smoothing for the dc from the rectifier (smoothing capacitors, D), and storage of energy from the furnace inductor (furnace capacitor, E). Other units present are an *inductor*, F, to contribute to the smoothing of the dc from the rectifier; a cooling water supply, G, to cool several of the units; and a printed circuit board, H.

Examine Figure 6.10 and find the various parts. In particular, find the furnace capacitor unit, E.

Answers to questions

6.1 (a) 60 V $\pm$ 6 V; (b) 70 kA $\pm$ 7 kA; (c) 50 Hz
6.2 (b) after the pd peak
6.3 (a) after; (b) lag behind
6.4 $\frac{1}{4}$ of the periodic time
6.5 behind

Figure 6.10 *The interior of a power supply cabinet, similar to the one in Figure 6.9. A, diode bridge rectifier; B, inverter (dc to ac); C, transformer; D, smoothing capacitors; E, furnace capacitor unit; F, inductor; G, cooling water supply; H, a printed circuit board. (Source: Radyne Limited.)*

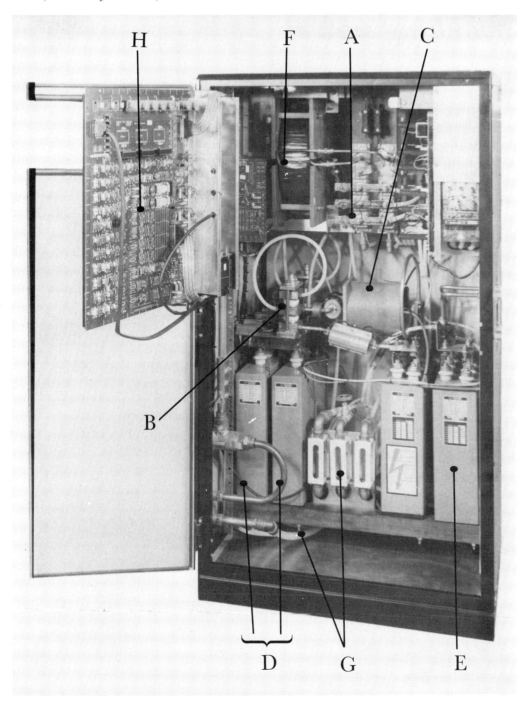

7. Inductive machines: inductive power and working power

AC motors in industry

Figure 7.1 *Over half of the power in industry is used to supply electric motors. The photograph shows electric motors which are driving mixing paddles in reaction vessels in a chemical plant. (Source: Brook Crompton, Huddersfield.)*

Over half of all the power used by industry is used to supply electric motors. An electric motor contains fixed coils (*stator* coils) which are designed to produce magnetic flux; and *through the medium of magnetic flux, power is transferred* to a *rotor* which is fixed on a shaft that can rotate. *The coils possess inductance.* Most electric motors use alternating current. The magnetic flux produced in the coils therefore grows and falls; and as it falls, the energy stored in the flux is released and a current surges back along the supply line. This was described in Chapter 6, Figure 6.6, and page 69.

The photographs in Figure 7.2 show the two main parts of an alternating current induction motor. Figure 7.2(a) shows the stationary (stator) coils, fixed inside the main frame. When an alternating pd is applied to a coil, a magnetic flux grows and falls, and energy is stored and released, the magnitude of the energy depending on the inductance, L, of the coil.

Figure 7.2 *The two main parts of an alternating current induction motor: (a) the stationary coils (stator coils) fixed firmly in the main frame; (b) the rotor, attached to the shaft. (Source: Brook Crompton, Huddersfield.)*

Each coil is made of copper conductor; and while the resistance, R, is low, it nevertheless exists. The current, I, in the coil thus results in a power loss of I^2R, which causes the temperature of the coils to rise. To restrict the temperature rise to a safe value, and to avoid damage to the coil insulation, an adequate route for heat loss is needed. This is provided by a metal outer case, which is deeply ribbed to increase its outer surface area. In the assembled motor there is also a fan attached to the rotor, and this blows or draws cooling air around the coils and the rotor.

When assembled, the rotor occupies the cylindrical space inside the coil groups, and each end of the shaft is mounted on bearings. For the purposes of this chapter, it is not necessary to know the electrical structure of the rotor; briefly, it is in fact a 'squirrel cage' rotor, and it does not need slip rings and brushes. At each end of the rotor are blades which, on rotation, assist the circulation of air and thus aid cooling.

The end of the shaft is coupled to the load, either directly or indirectly, for instance, by a gear system or by a pulley and belt system.

Inductive power and working power

In general, motors do not run continuously at full power. They may run at any point between no load (that is, rotating but not connected to a load and thus not doing any useful work) and full load. When running at no load, a current still rises and falls in the stationary (stator) coils. Even if the rotor were removed altogether this would still be so, because a pd across stator coil ends would result in a current and magnetic flux, and in the storage and return of energy as a consequence of the *inductance* of the coil. So the motor *always* requires *inductive power*.

Figure 7.3 represents a motor which can deliver 90 kW of power to do work, at full load. The diagrams show: in (a), the motor operating at half-rated load (45 kW); in (b), three-quarters rated load (70 kW); and in (c), the full rated load (90 kW).

In (a), when the working power is 45 kW, the inductive power is 70 kVA. (Because the inductive power is not doing work it is not given the unit W, or kW. It *is* still a product of potential difference

Figure 7.3 A representation of an induction motor which can deliver 90 kW of power to do work, at full design power (rated load). At various fractions of rated load, the diagrams show the power needed to produce the magnetic flux, and the power available for work.

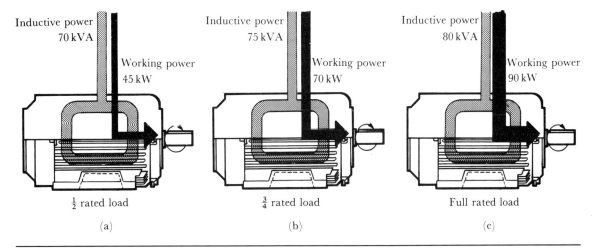

Inductive power
70 kVA

Working power
45 kW

Inductive power
75 kVA

Working power
70 kW

Inductive power
80 kVA

Working power
90 kW

$\frac{1}{2}$ rated load

(a)

$\frac{3}{4}$ rated load

(b)

Full rated load

(c)

Figure 7.4 *Some adverse effects of inductive power required for inductive machinery and equipment.*

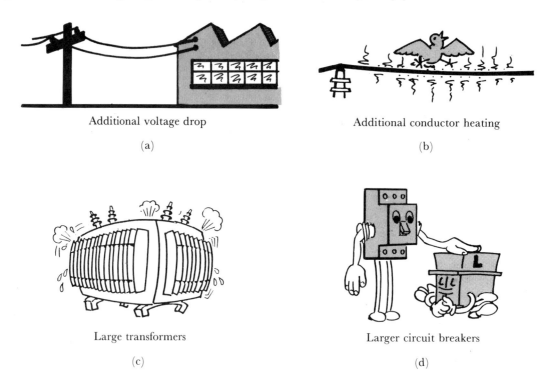

Additional voltage drop

(a)

Additional conductor heating

(b)

Large transformers

(c)

Larger circuit breakers

(d)

Larger switches

(e)

and current, pd × current, and it is given the units VA and kVA).

In (b), at three-quarters rated load the inductive power and the working power are about equal. In (c), at full load the inductive power is only slightly less than the working power.

While the working power changed from 45 kW to 90 kW, the inductive power remained relatively steady and *relatively high* at about 75 kVA. The current for this inductive power would be over 100 A and it would be surging forwards and backwards along the supply lines, *doing no useful work*. It would in fact be *causing adverse effects*.

Adverse effects of inductive power and inductive current

Inductive power and current inside workshops and offices require additional power and current in the supply lines to the works. This causes *additional voltage drop* in the supply lines (Figure 7.4a), and *power loss* in the lines through I^2R heating, (Figure 7.4b). At the works' transformer, there could be overloading; or, in order to avoid overloading, a *larger transformer* would have to be installed than was necessary for the working power alone (Figure 7.4c). *Larger protection devices*, that is, circuit breakers and fuses would be needed (Figure 7.4d); and larger control devices, that is switches, would be needed (Figure 7.4e). Within the works, *larger cross-section* cables would be needed in order to carry both the working current and the inductive current; the inductive current in these cables would produce a further I^2R temperature rise and power loss.

Each of these effects adds to costs.

Electric motors are not the only consumers of inductive power and requirers of inductive current. Figure 7.5 shows some others.

Some resistive and some inductive loads

In Figure 7.5, the two upper loads are almost purely resistive. The left-hand load is made up of the resistance wire in the lamp filament, and the right-hand load consists of resistance wire on ceramic supports in the resistance furnace. Each load has resistance, but such low inductance (approaching zero) that for all practical purposes inductance can be ignored.

The remaining diagrams show machinery and equipment that does have inductance, and in which inductive power is needed to provide a magnetic field. In power transformers, the ratio of inductive power to working power is low, being about 1 : 10. Thus about 10 kVA of inductive power is needed to provide the field for a 100 kW output of power that can do work.

Induction motors on low load, fluorescent lighting systems (with inductors in their lamp circuits), arc welding units, and workshops with motors on low load and fluorescent lighting, all require more inductive power than their working power output.

Induction furnaces are highly inductive, and their requirement for inductive power can be around five times that of their working power.

These inductive loads lead to the adverse operating conditions of additional voltage drop along the supply cables, extra I^2R power loss in the supply cables, extra load on the source of supply (transformer or alternator), and the need for larger circuit breaking and switching equipment which was indicated in Figure 7.4.

In order to avoid these effects, power capacitors can be connected in parallel with the inductive equipment; this is shown in Figure 7.6.

Receiving and returning inductive energy

The current in an inductor lags one-quarter of a period behind the applied pd; and the current to a capacitor is in advance of the applied emf by one-quarter of a period. For an inductor and capacitor in parallel and supplied by an alternating pd, the current in the inductor and the current to the capacitor are therefore *out of phase by half a period*, or half a cycle.

Thus, when the magnetic field in an inductive machine collapses, the energy that was stored in it

Figure 7.5 *Two almost pure resistive loads, and some loads which have resistance and inductance. The diagrams give approximate values for the amount of inductive power (in kVA) needed to provide 10 kW of working power.*

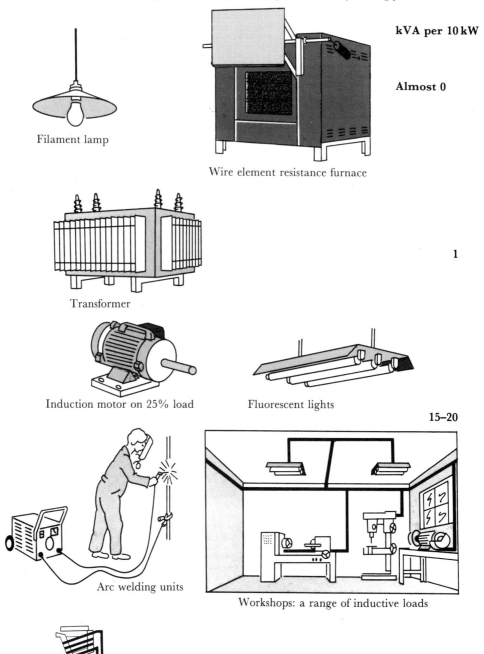

kVA per 10 kW

Almost 0

Filament lamp

Wire element resistance furnace

1

Transformer

Induction motor on 25% load   Fluorescent lights

15–20

Arc welding units

Workshops: a range of inductive loads

50

Induction furnace

Figure 7.6 *This shows how to avoid loading supply cables with inductive power, by using a power capacitor unit: (a) the supply circuit, from a transformer to two induction motors; (b) inductive power and working power being supplied along the line; (c) a power capacitor unit in parallel with each motor, accepting inductive energy, storing energy, and returning energy to the motor.*

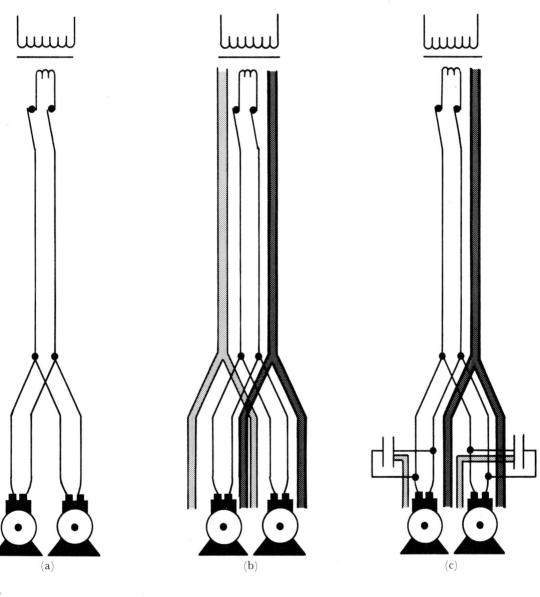

(a)   (b)   (c)

Key

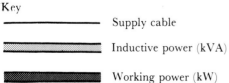

—————————————   Supply cable

▨▨▨▨▨▨▨▨   Inductive power (kVA)

████████   Working power (kW)

Figure 7.7 An induction motor with two capacitors. One is connected in parallel with the stator coils, to accept and return inductive energy. (Source: Brook Crompton, Huddersfield.)

can be passed to a capacitor in order to build up the electric field in the capacitor and be stored there. The reverse can then take place. In this way power surges forwards and backwards between inductor and capacitor, thereby maintaining the fields.

This was described in detail in Chapter 6, pages 70–3, in relation to phase differences and the induction furnace. You should look back to these pages and make sure that you understand the principles. You should then return to Figure 7.6 and examine it, to see how the use of a capacitor unit close to inductive machinery eliminates inductive energy transfer in the supply lines.

7.1 How does the steady state running of an inductive machine and power capacitor system get under way? Consider the diagrams given in Figure 7.6(a) and (c). What happens in the transition from (a) to (c)?

7.2 Once the steady working state shown in Figure 7.6(c) has been reached, is any 'topping up' of the inductor–capacitor energy exchange needed? If so: (a) why is it needed; and (b) how does it come about?

7.3 Is any form of matching needed between the inductance and the capacitance? Suggest what should be matched, and give a formula for each.

Figure 7.7 shows an induction motor with two power capacitors. One is to aid the starting of the motor. The other is to accept inductive energy from the stator coils, and then to return energy to the coils; this capacitor is connected in parallel with the coils.

Let us take an example from the series of motors illustrated in Figure 7.7. A motor with a full load output of 3 kW of working power has a capacitor of 40 μF capacity in parallel with the stator coils; it absorbs and returns energy at the rate of about 2 kVA. Such a motor has an overall length of about 400 mm and an overall diameter of about 200 mm; use a millimetre scale to help to visualise this size. It has a mass of about 30 kg, and is designed to work from the 240 V mains supply.

8. RMS values; reactance and impedance; and losses

RMS values

Figure 8.1 shows a circuit with a resistive load, which has an alternating potential difference across it. The pd is asymmetrical, as can be seen from the graph of pd against time.

The question arises: 'What value of pd should be assigned to the system, with which one could then do calculations?' In reality the question becomes 'What value of *continuous unidirectional pd* would have the same effect as the alternating and variable pd?' That is, 'What would be the equivalent or "effective" dc potential difference?'

The question can only be answered by considering *the power* which is consumed by the circuit, and which becomes apparent as *heat loss*.

The power, P, which is consumed by a circuit is given by

$$P = VI = I^2R = \frac{V^2}{R}$$

In this instance we are provided with values for potential difference and for resistance and will use $P = V^2/R$.

Examine Figure 8.1(b), where the power which is consumed in the positive and negative half cyles is worked out. For the positive half cycle, curve (1), this amounts to 12.5 W; and for the negative half cycle, curve (2), it amounts to 4.5 W. Notice that the *power* has a *positive sign* in each half cycle; whatever the direction of the current, forwards or backwards, work is still done and heat is still lost.

In Figure 8.1(c), the powers for each half cycle are plotted against time, and the power is calculated for one cycle. It turns out to be 8.5 W.

Now,

$$P = \frac{V^2}{R} \quad \text{and} \quad P_{\text{effective}} = \frac{(V_{\text{effective}})^2}{R}$$

Therefore,

$$8.5\,\text{W} = \frac{(V_{\text{eff}})^2}{2\,\Omega}$$

$$8.5\,\text{W} \times 2\,\Omega = (V_{\text{eff}})^2$$

$$V_{\text{eff}} = 4.1\,\text{V}$$

Therefore the *equivalent dc potential difference* (or *effective pd*) is 4.1 V.

From this, the *equivalent direct current* can be found:

$$I = \frac{V}{R} = \frac{4.1\,\text{V}}{2\,\Omega} = 2.05\,\text{A}$$

Thus, although the alternating current changes direction and alters in magnitude it is *equivalent to a steady direct current* of 2.05 A.

A power calculation shows that the power consumed is

$$P = I^2R$$
$$P = 2.05^2 \times 2.0 = 8.4\,\text{W}$$

This correlates with the 8.5 W calculated earlier, the difference being due to the number of significant figures used in the calculation.

We have seen that, for an ac waveform, the equivalent dc pd and current can be calculated by working through the power which is consumed. A quicker method is derived from the power approach. We shall use the pds given in Figure 8.1 as an example. These were $+5$ V and -3 V:

$$\text{Equivalent dc pd} = \sqrt{\left[\frac{5^2 + (-3)^2}{2}\right]}\,\text{V}$$

$$= \sqrt{\left(\frac{25 + 9}{2}\right)}\,\text{V}$$

$$= \sqrt{\left(\frac{34}{2}\right)}\,\text{V} = \sqrt{(17)}\,\text{V}$$

$$= 4.1\,\text{V}$$

Figure 8.1 *Features of a resistive load which has an alternating potential difference across it: (a) the circuit diagram; (b) a graph of the alternating pd against time; (c) a graph of the power developed in the load (and lost as heat) against time.*

(a)

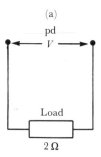

(b)
pd against time for the circuit in (a)

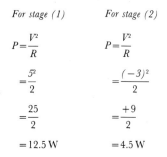

(c)
Power against time for the circuit in (a)

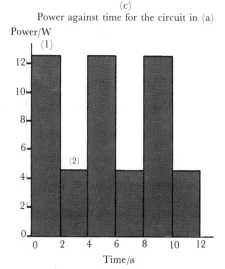

Work done = Power × Time
= Area under graph

Under graph (1)
$W = 12.5 \, \text{J} \, \text{s}^{-1} \times 2 \, \text{s}$
$= 25 \, \text{J}$

Under graph (2)
$W = 4.5 \, \text{J} \, \text{s}^{-1} \times 2 \, \text{S}$
$= 9 \, \text{J}$

∴ Total work done in 1 cycle (4 s) is
Total work done = 25 J + 9 J = 34 J
∴ Effective power = 34 J/4 s = 8.5 W

For stage (1)

$P = \dfrac{V^2}{R}$

$= \dfrac{5^2}{2}$

$= \dfrac{25}{2}$

$= 12.5 \, \text{W}$

For stage (2)

$P = \dfrac{V^2}{R}$

$= \dfrac{(-3)^2}{2}$

$= \dfrac{+9}{2}$

$= 4.5 \, \text{W}$

Figure 8.2 *An alternating pd. What is the value of the equivalent dc pd?*

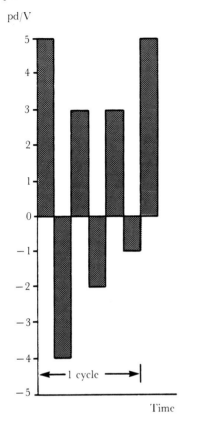

If the pds in the ac cycle had been $+7\,\mathrm{V}$, $-4\,\mathrm{V}$, $+6\,\mathrm{V}$, $-5\,\mathrm{V}$ (followed again by the same sequence) then the equivalent dc pd would be

$$\sqrt{\left[\frac{7^2+(-4)^2+6^2+(-5)^2}{4}\right]}\,\mathrm{V}$$

That is, it is the *square root* of (*the mean* of the *squares of the component pds*). In short, it is called the *root mean square* value or *rms* value.

8.1 Calculating an rms value

Figure 8.2 shows an alternating pd, with three positive pulses and three negative pulses in one cycle.

(a) Calculate the equivalent dc pd, that is, the rms voltage.

(b) If the pds are applied across a $4.0\,\Omega$ resistor, what is the equivalent dc steady current in the circuit?

(c) What power is consumed by the resistor, over a period of several cycles?

Figure 8.3 shows sinusoidal waveforms for potential difference and current.

If the 'power consumed by the circuit' method is applied to *sinusoidal* alternating current, it emerges that the *dc equivalent value*, or effective value, or *rms*

Figure 8.3 *Graphs showing sinusoidal waveforms and their rms values: (a) for potential difference; and (b) for current.*

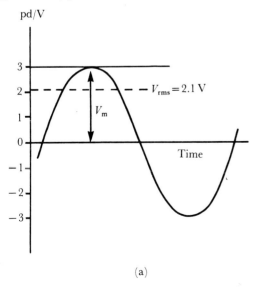

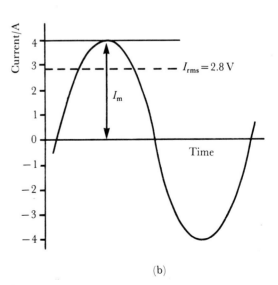

(a)   (b)

value for pd and for current is equal to the *peak value* ÷ $\sqrt{2}$. Thus,

$$\text{rms value} = \frac{\text{peak value}}{\sqrt{2}} = \text{peak value} \times 0.707$$

Let us use this for the sinusoidal waveforms in Figure 8.3:

(a) Potential difference   *(b) Current*

Peak pd, $V_m = 3.0\text{ V}$ Peak current, $I_m = 4.0\text{ A}$

$$V_{rms} = \frac{3.0}{\sqrt{2}}\text{ V}$$ $$I_{rms} = \frac{4.0}{\sqrt{2}}\text{ A}$$

$$= 2.1\text{ V}$$ $$= 2.8\text{ A}$$

Thus the alternating pd in Figure 8.3(a), if applied across a resistor, would produce the same heating effect as a continuous direct pd of 2.1 V across the same resistor.

Similarly, the alternating current in Figure 8.3(b) carried in a resistor would produce the same heating effect as a continuous direct current of 2.8 A in the same resistor.

The alternating supply gives an rms pd of 2.1 V; and there is an rms current of 2.8 A.

8.2 Calculating rms values

Figure 8.4 shows two oscillograph traces, one for pd and one for current. A larger-scale version is given in Figure 6.2. Use a photocopy, or other type of copy, of Figure 6.2 and find:
(a) the peak pd;
(b) the rms pd;

Figure 8.4 *These oscillograph traces are for the pd and current in a busbar short circuit test. The same traces at a much larger scale are shown in Figure 6.2.*

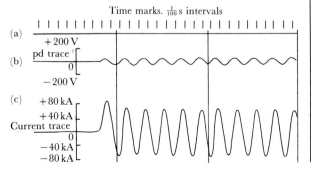

(c) the peak current (ignore the initial single high peak);
(d) the rms current.

8.3 Heat loss from a power inductor

Figure 4.15 shows three inductor coils which form part of a 33 000 V power distribution system. Look at the photograph. When the unit was tested under operating conditions, an oscillograph trace showed the peak current in a coil to be 618 A. The resistance of the coil at the operating temperature was 0.058 Ω. What was the power loss from the coil (appearing as heat loss)?

Reactance and impedance

Capacitive reactance

Look again at Figure 6.5 which shows a capacitor with a sinusoidal pd across it. In the uppermost diagram of Figure 6.5, stages A, B, C, D and E, and a, b, c, d and e represent electrons flowing on to the left plate of the capacitor, and off it. Now use Figure 8.5, which is a reduced copy of Figure 6.5.

The flow of electrons on to and off the capacitor plate constitutes a *current in the leads* to the capacitor; and $Q = Cv$, where v is the instantaneous pd:

Figure 8.5 *A capacitor with a sinusoidal potential difference across it. An enlarged version is given in Figure 6.5.*

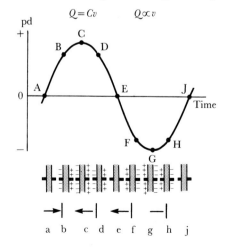

Current, I = rate of change of charge

$$= \frac{dQ}{dt} = \frac{d(Cv)}{dt} = C\frac{dv}{dt}$$

Now, for a sinusoidal pd it can be shown by differentiation that the maximum value for dv/dt is when $dv/dt = 2\pi f V_m$. At this instant, the current, I, will also be a maximum, I_m. Therefore,

$$I_m = C\left(\frac{dv}{dt}\right)_{max} = C\,2\pi f V_m \qquad (8.1)$$

Now, for a *metallic conductor*, potential difference divided by current equals resistance, $V/I = R$. In equation (8.1) we have a potential difference, V_m, and a current, I_m.

Rearranging equation (8.1) to give V_m/I_m we have

$$\frac{V_m}{I_m} = \frac{1}{2\pi f C}$$

Converting to rms values we have

$$\frac{V_m \times 0.707}{I_m \times 0.707} = \frac{V_{rms}}{I_{rms}} = \frac{V}{I} = \frac{1}{2\pi f C} = X_c \qquad (8.2)$$

The quantity $1/(2\pi f C)$ is known as the *capacitive reactance* of the system. It is given the *symbol X_c* and, like resistance, V/I, it is expressed in *ohms*. It is a measure of the extent to which the system *impedes* the flow of electrons, impedes current, in the leads.

The impeding effect produced by capacitive reactance has the characteristics of resistance. In a circuit it produces a similar effect to resistance; but it is a *frequency-dependent quantity*. The capacitive reactance X_c, that is V/I, is inversely proportional to the frequency of the ac supply; refer to equation (8.2).

Figure 8.6 shows a capacitor connected to an alternating potential difference. The capacitance of the capacitor is $1\,\mu F$, and the value of the pd is $240\,V_{rms}$.

When the frequency of the supply is $0\,Hz$ the supply is dc. The capacitor acts as a complete block, and no current flows in the leads.

Let us examine the situation when the supply frequency is $5\,Hz$. The extent to which the capacitor impedes a current in the leads is given by the *capacitive reactance* of the system:

$$X_c = \frac{1}{2\pi f C} = \frac{1}{2\pi \times 5 \times 1 \times 10^{-6}} = 32 \times 10^3\,\Omega$$

So, in terms of limiting the value of the current, the capacitor is behaving like a resistor of $32\,k\Omega$ resistance. Now,

$$X_c = \frac{V_{rms}}{I_{rms}}$$

Thus,

$$I_{rms} = \frac{V_{rms}}{X_c}$$

Therefore

$$I_{rms} = \frac{240\,V_{rms}}{32 \times 10^3\,\Omega} = 7.5 \times 10^{-3}\,A_{rms}$$

Thus the current, I, in the supply leads is $7.5 \times 10^{-3}\,A_{rms}$, or $7.5\,mA$.

8.4 Capacitive reactance and current

The ac source in Figure 8.6 can provide a supply at different frequencies. For UK mains frequency ($50\,Hz$), for USA mains frequency ($60\,Hz$), and for $1000\,Hz$, work out:
(a) the capacitive reactance; and
(b) the current in the leads.
(For each capacitor, $C = 1\,\mu F$.)

Interference and filters

Audio amplifiers can suffer interference from nearby radio and television stations; and television sets can suffer interference from a car's ignition

Figure 8.6 *A capacitor connected to an alternating pd whose frequency can be varied. The extent to which the capacitor impedes a current in the leads depends upon the frequency of the supply.*

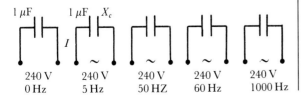

Figure 8.7 *Three major ways in which electrical interference can alter the signal in a line. Interference comes from circuits A and B, and from the power supply, C.*

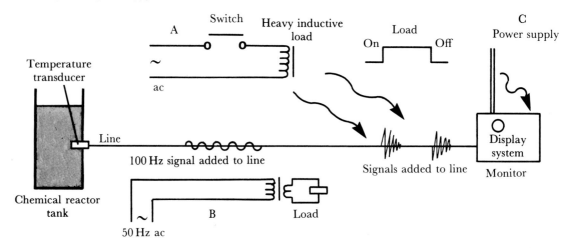

system. In these cases an unwanted signal has been added to the desired signal.

Information for control, say the control of a chemical reactor vessel, is carried along lines; and signals from nearby sources may be picked up by the line. Figure 8.7 shows three very common sources of such interference. In the upper part of the diagram, in circuit A, a heavy inductive load on an ac supply is switched on and an oscillating signal is radiated from it. When the load is switched off a similar signal is produced; each of these signals is being picked up by the line carrying the control signal.

In the lower part of Figure 8.7, in circuit B, a power supply cable runs parallel to and fairly close to the signal line, and the alternating magnetic field from the power cable induces an alternating signal in the control line.

On the right, the power supply to the control system is a source of interference. There can be interference by 50 Hz signals, at the supply frequency, but there can be sources of violent voltage fluctuations with high frequencies in the kHz to MHz range. These are caused by current surges as heavy power circuits are switched on and off; the operation of a floor-to-floor lift near a room which has mains-powered electronic equipment can affect the equipment.

Once an interfering signal has been added to a desired

signal it becomes part of it. The original signal can only be recovered if the interfering signal has some characteristic which allows it to be removed. Now, the reactance of a capacitor is frequency-dependent and this provides a means of removing lower frequencies from higher frequencies, and higher frequencies from lower frequencies. This is termed *filtering*.

Figure 8.8(a) shows a filter circuit. The input signal is across a capacitor and a resistor in series; and the output signal is taken across the resistor. The capacitive reactance of the capacitor, X_c, is

$$X_c = \frac{1}{2\pi f C}$$

X_c is: large for low frequencies
        low for high frequencies

In our example, Figure 8.8(a), the impeding effect of the capacitor at a low frequency is 1000 Ω; at a high frequency it is only 10 Ω.

The circuit is a *potential divider*.

Let us consider the high frequency. The output is taken from across 100 Ω, which is almost the whole of the impeding ohmic values (contributed by 100 Ω due to resistance and 10 Ω due to reactance); V_{out} is almost as great as V_{in}, and the signal passes on little reduced.

For the low frequency, the output is taken again from across 100 Ω; but this is only a small fraction of

Figure 8.8 *A filter circuit, in (a); and its response at different frequencies, in (b). The system allows through high frequencies with little loss of signal, and it tends to block low frequencies.*

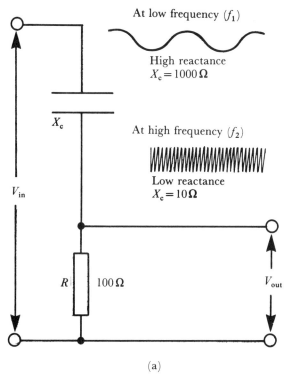

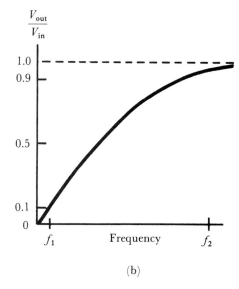

(a)   (b)

the whole of the impeding values (contributed by $100\,\Omega$ due to resistance and $1000\,\Omega$ due to reactance); V_{out} for the low frequency signal is only a small fraction of V_{in}, and the low frequency signal is significantly reduced.

These effects are shown in the graph given in Figure 8.8(b). A high frequency signal, at f_2, is passed on at over 0.9 of its original value. A low frequency signal, at f_1, has been reduced to about 0.1 of its original value.

The circuit is known as a *high pass* filter. It passes on high frequencies.

The filter circuit is a potential divider, and the ratio $V_{out} : V_{in}$ can be calculated. Figure 8.9(a) shows a resistor potential divider and the relationship between the quantities. The denominator is the sum of the resistances, $R_1 + R_2$, in ohms. For the filter circuit, the capacitor pd and capacitor current are out of phase with each other by one-quarter of a period, $\frac{1}{4}T$, and this has to be taken into account. It is taken into account by *phasor addition* of

X_c and R (similar to vector addition), and the denominator becomes $\sqrt{(X_c^2 + R^2)}$.

Just as in Figure 8.9(a), $(R_1 + R_2)$ represents the total *resistance* across V_{in}, so in Figure 8.9(b) the quantity $\sqrt{(X_c^2 + R^2)}$ represents a total 'resistance effect' and is known as the *impedance*. The unit for both resistance and impedance is the ohm.

Example. Let us calculate V_{out}/V_{in} for the low frequency signal given in Figure 8.8(a):

$$\frac{V_{out}}{V_{in}} = \frac{R}{\text{Total impedance for low frequency}}$$

$$= \frac{R}{\sqrt{(X_c^2 + R^2)}}$$

$$= \frac{100}{\sqrt{(1000^2 + 100^2)}} = \frac{100}{1004} = 0.1$$

Thus the low frequency output is only 0.1 of its original value; 0.9, or 90%, of the original low frequency signal has been removed, or filtered out.

Figure 8.9 *The similarity of the circuits (a) for a resistor potential divider, and (b) the filter circuit. They show that the calculations for V_{out}/V_{in} are similar but not identical.*

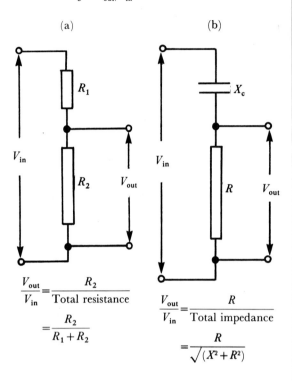

$$\frac{V_{out}}{V_{in}} = \frac{R_2}{\text{Total resistance}}$$

$$= \frac{R_2}{R_1 + R_2}$$

$$\frac{V_{out}}{V_{in}} = \frac{R}{\text{Total impedance}}$$

$$= \frac{R}{\sqrt{(X^2 + R^2)}}$$

A similar calculation for the high frequency signal shows that V_{out}/V_{in} is 0.99. That is, 99% of the high frequency signal passes through.

For this reason, this filter arrangement is known as a 'high pass' filter; it passes high frequency signals and filters out low frequency signals.

8.5 V_{out}/V_{in} for a high frequency

Calculate V_{out}/V_{in} for the high frequency signal in the filter circuit given in Figure 8.8(a).

8.6 A 'low pass' filter circuit

Examine Figure 8.8(a) again. Rewire it so as to take V_{out} from across the capacitor; draw a sketch of this. Show that this rearrangement forms a 'low pass filter'; that is, it will pass low frequency signals, and filter out high frequencies.

Proceed as follows:
(a) What does the equation for V_{out}/V_{in} become?

Figure 8.10 *Part of a power supply unit. The labelled capacitor is part of a filter circuit. (Source: Intelligence Power Technology Limited, Brighton.)*

Filter
capacitor
2nF

(b) Find V_{out}/V_{in} for the low frequency signal, for which $X_c = 1000\,\Omega$.
(c) Find V_{out}/V_{in} for the high frequency signal, for which $X_c = 10\,\Omega$.

Inductive reactance

In Chapter 4 we saw that when a current in an inductor changes, an emf is induced and its value depends on the *rate of change of current*. It also depends upon *the inductance, L*, of the inductor. The emf is a back-emf:

$$E = -L\frac{di}{dt} \tag{8.3}$$

Now, if the current in the inductor changes sinusoidally, as in Figure 8.11, the instantaneous value of the current is given by

$$i = I_m \sin 2\pi f t$$

where I_m is the peak current and f is the frequency.

Figure 8.11 *An inductor with an alternating pd across it.*

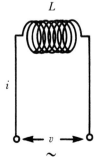

It can be shown by differentiating this equation that

$$\frac{di}{dt} = 2\pi f I_m \cos 2\pi f t$$

This is a maximum when $\cos 2\pi f t = 1$, and at that instant

$$\left(\frac{di}{dt}\right)_{max} = 2\pi f I_m$$

Substituting this in equation (8.3), we get the maximum induced emf, E_{max}:

$$E_{max} = -L\left(\frac{di}{dt}\right)_{max} = -L\,2\pi f I_m$$

If the inductor has an extremely low resistance, the whole of the applied voltage, v, is used in opposing the back emf. Thus when v is a maximum, V_m, $V_m = -E_{max}$. Therefore,

$$V_m = -(-L\,2\pi f I_m) = L\,2\pi f I_m$$

and

$$\frac{V_m}{I_m} = L\,2\pi f$$

Now

$$\frac{V_{rms}}{I_{rms}} = \frac{V_m \times 0.707}{I_m \times 0.707} = L\,2\pi f$$

Now V_{rms}/I_{rms} has the unit ohm and is a measure of the *impeding effect* which the inductor has on sinusoidal alternating current. It is known as the *inductive reactance* of the system, and is given the symbol X_L:

$$\frac{V_{rms}}{I_{rms}} = \frac{V}{I} = 2\pi f L = X_L \tag{8.3}$$

The impeding effect which an inductor has upon alternating current *has the characteristic of resistance*, and its unit is the *ohm*. It is a *frequency-dependent quantity*. The inductive reactance X_L is directly proportional to the frequency of the supply. That is, the higher the frequency, the greater is the impeding effect of an inductor on the alternating current; and its value in ohms increases.

Figure 8.12 An inductor with a 50 Hz ac supply across it.

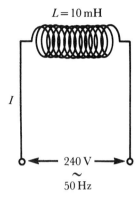

$L = 10\,\text{mH}$

I

$\longleftarrow\; 240\,\text{V} \;\longrightarrow$

$\sim$

$50\,\text{Hz}$

Example. Let us take as an example the inductor shown in Figure 8.12, which has an inductance of 10 mH, and a 240 V_{rms}, 50 Hz ac supply across it. We will find, first, the inductive reactance of the inductor and, second, the rms current, I, in the circuit.

Inductive reactance,

$$X_L = 2\pi f L = 2\pi 50 \times 10 \times 10^{-3} = 3.1\,\Omega$$

Now

$$\frac{V}{I} = X_L$$

$$\frac{240}{I} = 3.1$$

$$I = \frac{240}{3.1} = 77\,\text{A}$$

Thus the inductor has an impeding effect on current equivalent to 3.1 Ω, and the rms current in the circuit is 77 A.

8.7 Inductive reactance and current

For the inductor shown in Figure 8.12, with a 240 V_{rms} supply across it, find the inductive reactance and the rms current in the circuit for

(a) a supply at the USA mains frequency of 60 Hz;

(b) 100 Hz;

(c) 1000 Hz.

Inductors in power transmission

A short circuit in a power line will lead to an abnormally large current in the secondary circuit of the transformer, and also in the primary circuit, which will include the generator. In grid transmission lines and in distribution lines these fault currents are of a magnitude of kiloamps, and in the primary circuit of the transformer they are of a magnitude of tens of kiloamps.

Figure 8.13, upper diagram, shows a line fault; it also shows the normal full load currents and the short circuit fault currents. Power systems are provided with circuit breakers to protect equipment against faults; but a circuit breaker has mass and inertia, and time is needed for it to be moved and to break the circuit. The time required is between two and four cycles, which, with a 50 Hz supply, means between $\frac{2}{50}$ s and $\frac{4}{50}$ s, that is, between $\frac{4}{100}$ s and $\frac{8}{100}$ s. But with a short circuit near to a transformer the current can rise to around ten times its normal value in less than $\frac{1}{2}$ cycle, that is, in less than $\frac{1}{100}$ s.

A device is needed which will slow down the growth of the current, and which will also limit the final magnitude of the current.

An inductor slows down the growth of a current (as was described in Chapter 4, pages 51–2); and it also *'adds ohms'* to the circuit as a result of its *inductive reactance*, X_L. That is, it *increases the impedance of the circuit*. This means a decrease in the maximum value that a current can reach.

The lower diagram in Figure 8.13 shows that an inductor has been placed in series in the primary circuit of the transformer. The inductor's inductive reactance, X_L, is $0.24\,\Omega$. The impedance of the original circuit was:

$$
\begin{aligned}
Z &= Z \text{ generator} + Z \text{ transformer} \\
&= \quad 0.08\,\Omega \quad + \quad 0.16\,\Omega \\
&= \quad 0.24\,\Omega
\end{aligned}
$$

Figure 8.13 *The upper diagram shows a short circuit fault occurring where power lines have fallen and touched; the lower diagram shows how the fault current can be limited by placing an inductor in the primary circuit.*

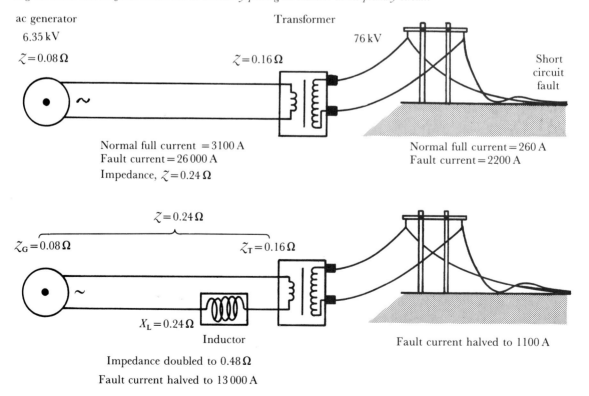

That is, the inclusion of the inductor has doubled the impedance, from $0.24\,\Omega$ to $0.48\,\Omega$; and the fault current has been halved as a result. Because of this effect, the inductor used in this way is known as a *'current-limiting'* inductor.

The coil of the inductor will have to be designed and manufactured so that it has an inductive reactance of $0.24\,\Omega$, and also so that it will carry continuously a normal full load current of $3100\,A$ and a fault current of up to $13\,000\,A$ for a short time. The conductor will therefore have to have a large cross-section area.

Designing and making a current-limiting inductor

The photograph given in Figure 8.14 shows three current-limiting inductors for a power system. Each inductor will be connected in series with a primary coil in a power transformer.

The normal continuous current in the primary circuit, and thus in the inductor, is to be $437\,A_{rms}$; and the function of the inductor will be to limit a fault current to $3000\,A$ in the primary circuit. For this purpose, the inductor will have to have an inductive reactance, X_L, of $6.75\,\Omega$. (This is found by knowing the impedance of the rest of the circuit.)

8.8 The inductive reactance, X_L, and the inductance, L, of the inductor

In order to limit a normal circuit current of $437\,A$ to one of $3000\,A$ on fault, the inductor will need to have an inductive reactance of $X_L = 6.75\,\Omega$. (This is determined from a knowledge of the rest of the circuit.) The supply is $50\,Hz$ ac. Calculate the inductance, L, which the coil must have.

8.9 The impedance, Z, of the inductor

The conductor for the coil is copper strip of cross-section approximately $14\,mm \times 10\,mm$, and length approximately $370\,m$. At the operating temperature it has a resistance, R, of $0.058\,\Omega$. The inductive reactance, X_L, is $6.75\,\Omega$.
 (a) Calculate the impedance, Z, of the inductor, where $Z = \sqrt{(X_L^2 + R^2)}$.
 (b) Does the resistance of the coil make any significant contribution to the impedance?
 (c) What is the reason for this?

Figure 8.14 *Three inductors for a power system. They are current-limiting inductors. A larger photograph is given in Figure 4.15, as part of the series on designing and making the inductors.*

Power losses

Real inductors and real capacitors

It is not possible to have a perfect inductor; and it is not possible to have a perfect capacitor. In real inductors and real capacitors there are always power losses, and efficiencies are less than 100%.

In an inductor, the energy which becomes stored in the magnetic field as the current increases is returned to the rest of the system when the current decreases; but in order to create a magnetic field, a current, I, has to be carried in the conductor coils, which have resistance, R. There is therefore always an I^2R power loss.

8.10 Power loss in a current-limiting inductor

In Figure 8.14, the full load continuous current for an inductor coil is 437 A_{rms}. The inductor's inductive reactance of 6.75 Ω does not lead to a power loss; its resistance of 0.058 Ω does do so.

The temperature of the conductor rises, and power is lost as heat.

(a) Calculate the power loss as heat at the full load current, due to resistance.
(b) Why does the inductance effect not lead to power loss?
(c) In addition to the resistive losses there are losses from eddy currents induced in the silicon alloy steel shield; these equal 79% of the resistive losses. What is the total power loss as heat?

Figure 8.15 The tank and radiators for the cooling oil for the three-inductor unit.

Since the design of the power unit incorporates three inductors, for three circuits, the total power loss as heat is close to 60 kW. To remove energy at this rate, an oil cooling arrangement is needed. Figure 8.15 shows a photograph of the oil tank and oil cooling radiators.

The design of the inductor to produce the inductance of 21.5 mH needed to give an inductive reactance of 6.75 Ω was described in Chapter 4 on pages 53–9.

A capacitor which had a perfect vacuum between its plates would function as a perfect capacitor, and there would be no power losses. But real capacitors have real materials as the dielectric between the plates, and these give rise to power

Figure 8.16 A water cooled power capacitor unit. Cooling water is circulated through the pipes. The unit is about $\frac{3}{4}$ m high, and its capacitance is about 250µF. (Source: ABB Capacitors Limited, Ellesmere Port.)

losses. If the dielectric is non-polar, then the electric field due to the applied pd displaces electrons in the dielectric molecules and creates polar structures. If the dielectric is already polar, then the applied pd causes the randomly oriented polar particles to align in the electric field. In each case, energy is absorbed. When the electric field reduces to zero, the stored energy is released and appears as heat. Polarisation in a capacitor dielectric was described in Figure 3.2, and on pages 30–1; you should re-examine these.

Other sources of power loss exist in a capacitor. For instance, when a capacitor is charged, electrons flow on to one metal plate and off the other. This constitutes a current, I, along the metal of each plate; and each plate has resistance. There is therefore an I^2R power loss because of current in the capacitor plates themselves; this becomes apparent as a rise in temperature.

Capacitors operating on alternating current therefore experience an *internal rise in temperature* due to power losses. If damage to the interior of the capacitor is to be avoided, the capacitor should be well ventilated. It may require forced air cooling; and it may even require water cooling. Figure 8.16 shows a water cooled capacitor unit.

As an example, to indicate the magnitude of power losses, a power capacitor constructed of metallised polypropylene dielectric (such as was described in Chapter 3) with capacitance $1000\,\mu\text{F}$ and operating on 50 Hz ac at 300 V_{rms} would have a *dielectric power loss* of about 3 W. Other losses might be about 7 W, giving total losses of about 10 W.

Answers to questions

8.1 (a) 3.3 V; (b) 0.82 A; (c) 2.7 W

8.2 (a) $60\,\text{V} \pm 6\,\text{V}$; (b) $42\,\text{V} \pm 4\,\text{V}$; (c) $70\,\text{kA} \pm 7\,\text{kA}$; (d) $50\,\text{kA} \pm 5\,\text{kA}$

8.3 11 kW

8.4 (a) 50 Hz, 3.2 kΩ; 60 Hz, 2.7 kΩ; 1000 Hz, 160 Ω. (b) 50 Hz, 75 mA; 60 Hz, 90 mA; 1000 Hz, 1.5 A

8.5 0.99

8.6 (a) $V_{\text{out}}/V_{\text{in}} = X_{\text{c}}/\sqrt{(X_{\text{c}}^2 + R^2)}$; (b) 0.99, or 99%; (c) 0.1, or 10%

8.7 (a) 3.8 Ω, 64 A; (b) 6.3 Ω, 38 A; (c) 63 Ω, 3.8 A

8.8 21.5 mH

8.9 (a) 6.75 Ω; (b) No

8.10 (a) 11 kW; (c) 20 kW

9. AC to DC: rectification

Why rectify?

The most convenient large-scale source of electric power supply is the ac mains. There are, however, many purposes for which alternating current is not suitable and for which direct current is needed.

The *extraction of metals* such as aluminium and magnesium is done electrolytically, using molten materials and direct current, the metal being deposited at the cathode (−ve electrode). For aluminium production, the supply is typically at about 800 V and it provides a direct current of about 70 000 A.

The *large-scale production of many non-metals* such as chlorine, hydrogen, oxygen, and of sodium hydroxide is done electrolytically with direct current. The supply is typically at about 50 V and provides a direct current of about 50 000 A.

Many *metals are refined by electrolysis*, requiring direct current.

Figure 9.1 *An ac bridge rectifier consisting of four power diodes. The unit will provide a direct current of 200 A from an ac power supply. Each diode is mounted on an air cooled heat sink to keep the diode cool. (Source: GD Rectifiers Limited, Burgess Hill.)* Enlarged on page 96.

Many components receive a *surface finish*, such as electroplating or anodising, by electrolysis. The rectifier shown in Figure 9.1, if used at 200 V to provide a 200 A direct current, could supply a small bath for anodising aluminium (power 40 kW).

Where a metal is too hard to machine into shape by normal methods, or where it must not be distorted or stressed during machining, it can sometimes be electrochemically formed. *Electrochemical forming* is the reverse of electroplating. The principle is shown in Figure 9.2. The workpiece which has to be shaped is the anode (+ve electrode). It is placed close to a cathode (tool) which is accurately shaped, the separation being about 0.2 mm. A stream of electrolyte is passed at high speed between the tool and the workpiece; when direct current is being supplied, metal from

Figure 9.2 *The principle of electrochemical forming. Metal from the workpiece goes into solution, and the workpiece surface changes shape to that of the tool.*

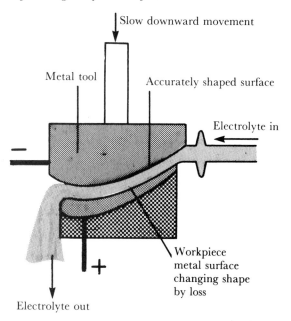

Slow downward movement

Metal tool

Accurately shaped surface

Electrolyte in

Workpiece metal surface changing shape by loss

Electrolyte out

the workpiece goes into solution. The workpiece surface changes its shape to take up the shape of the tool surface opposite it. Metal ions from the workpiece are swept away in the electrolyte stream and are not deposited on the tool, which retains its precise shape. The dc supply is usually at about 20 V, with currents in the kiloamp range.

In these electrochemical processes the power is taken from the ac mains and is rectified to dc using power diodes. Because of the large values of the currents passing through them, and the power losses which result within them, the diodes have to be cooled. Air cooling, oil cooling, and water cooling are used.

Most *electronic devices* require direct current for their operation. In portable equipment, batteries are used, particularly rechargeable ones. In almost all other instances, however, the power is taken from the ac mains, and the supply is rectified to dc using diodes.

Full wave bridge rectifiers

The rectifier circuit

Figure 9.3 shows three ac rectifier circuits. Diagram (a) shows an alternator connected to a transformer which then provides a source of alternating pd.

Circuit (a) contains two diodes in series; the forward pd at the transformer produces a current through the diodes and the load. The oscilloscopes show the variation of pd with time. There is a sine waveform of pd at the transformer output, and pulses of half sine waves at the load. The current through the load therefore also has a waveform which consists of pulses of half sine waves. This is *half-wave rectification*.

The current through the load is direct in the sense that it is in one direction only, but it is discontinuous. It is a series of separate pulses of current, and in this form it is of limited practical use.

Figure 9.3 *Three ac rectifier circuits with oscilloscopes connected. An alternator, shown in (a), is connected to a transformer. This is providing an alternating pd.*

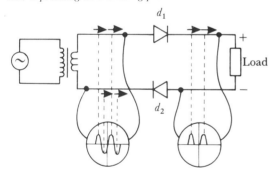

(a) A half-wave rectifier, using the forward pd

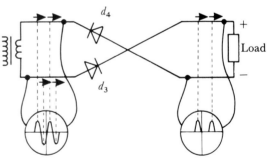

(b) A half-wave rectifier, using the reverse pd

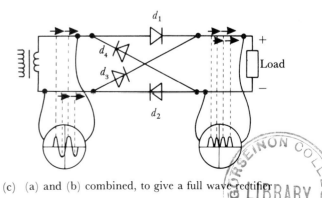

(c) (a) and (b) combined, to give a full wave rectifier

The circuit in diagram (b) also contains two diodes in series; these are forward biased from the *other* terminal of the transformer secondary coil, as compared with circuit (a). It is now the *reverse* pd at the transformer which produces a current; and, by crossing over the leads, this current is fed to the + terminal of the load, as in (a). Examine the circuit and the oscilloscope traces, and see that it is now the reverse pd pulse at the transformer that is producing a forward pd pulse at the load (and therefore a forward current pulse in the load). This is also *half-wave rectification*.

The circuit in (c) combines (a) and (b). The forward and the reverse pds at the transformer each produce a forward pd at the load, and hence a forward current in the load. Examine the circuit in (c), and the oscilloscope traces.

In circuit (c) the pd across the load, and the current through the load, each consist of a series of pulses of half sine waves. Both the forward and the reverse pd at the transformer are being made available at the load, but in one direction. This is *full wave rectification*.

Figure 9.4 *Alternative ways of showing the full wave rectifier circuit of Figure 9.3(c).*

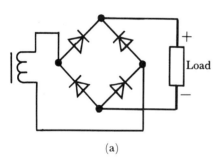

(a)

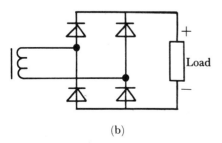

(b)

Figure 9.5 *This photograph is the same as Figure 9.1. The ac and dc terminals are superimposed upon it.*

Examine Figure 9.4: (a) and (b) are the same electrical circuit, drawn differently; each is the same as the full wave rectifier circuit shown in Figure 9.3(c), which is drawn differently again.

The circuit layout in Figure 9.4(b) is the one most widely used in electrical engineering. It is a simple layout to draw; and it can easily be extended to include another pair of diodes (giving three pairs) for a circuit to rectify current which in the national power distribution system is carried along three live lines (and a neutral), that is, a three-phase supply.

Examine Figure 9.5 to see the ac terminals and the dc terminals.

9.1 The full wave bridge rectifier in Figure 9.4(b) is drawn using the circuit diagram that is most widely used in electrical engineering:

(a) Imagine the top connection at the transformer to be alternately +ve and −ve, and see that a *forward pd* is always provided at the +ve terminal of the load.

(b) Select the circuit diagram in either Figure 9.4(a) or Figure 9.3(c), and mentally rearrange it to show that it is the same circuit as given in Figure 9.4(b).

Figure 9.6 *(a) A reservoir capacitor placed between the rectifier and the load. (b) The improved unidirectional waveform.*

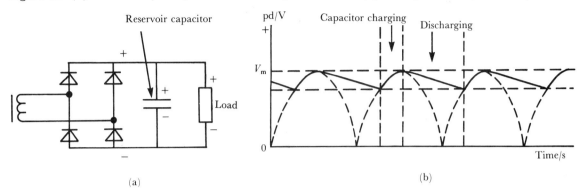

Smoothing

The pd waveform which is produced on the rectified side of a full wave bridge rectifier is a succession of pulses. This was indicated in the right-hand oscilloscope in Figure 9.3(c). When applied across a load, this pd produces current in the load in the form of unidirectional pulses. For most purposes this is not satisfactory. For most purposes, a current which is nearly steady is needed.

A marked improvement to the pd waveform, and thus to the current waveform, can be achieved by placing a capacitor of suitably large capacitance across the rectifier output. It is called a *reservoir capacitor* or *storage capacitor*.

Figure 9.6(a) shows a storage capacitor connected between the rectifier and the load; (b) shows the improved waveform and how the capacitor produces it.

As the output pd from the rectifier rises, it causes the capacitor to charge up, and it also causes a current to pass through the load. The capacitor stores energy, W, to the value of $W = \frac{1}{2}CV_m^2$, where C is the capacitance and V_m is the pd at the maximum of the cycle. When the pd from the rectifier starts dropping after a peak in the cycle, the current through the load would normally drop, but now the capacitor starts *discharging electrons* through the load, and this *maintains the current* at a high value.

If a suitably large value of capacitance, C, is chosen, then before the current has dropped very much, the next pd peak will develop. Then current

will be supplied from the rectifier to the load, and the capacitor will also be recharged.

Figure 9.7 shows part of an advanced form of power supply. It takes a mains ac input at 240 V, 50 Hz, and converts this into an extremely steady dc at 15 V. The first stage is rectification of the ac input, and the bridge rectifier is at the back right-hand corner of the equipment, where the air cooled

Figure 9.7 *Part of a power supply, showing the bridge rectifier cooling device, and two reservoir capacitors. (Approximately half-size. Source: Coden Electronics, Hitchin.)*

Reservoir capacitor 500 μF   ac input 240 V 50 Hz   Bridge rectifier on a heat sink (air cooled)

Figure 9.8 *A smoothed output pd, showing ripple.*

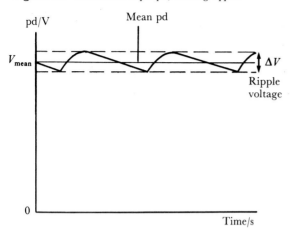

heat sink for the four diodes can be seen. The next stage is the smoothing of the full wave pulses, and a reservoir capacitor of $500\,\mu$F is shown labelled in the photograph. In fact, two capacitors each of $500\,\mu$F connected in parallel are used, giving an effective capacitance of $1000\,\mu$F.

Figure 9.8 shows a smoothed output and that it can be considered to be a steady pd, at the mean pd, V_{mean}, with an alternating pd superimposed on it. This pd alternating about the mean pd has a peak to peak voltage, ΔV, which is called the *ripple voltage*. The smaller the ripple voltage, as a percentage of V_{mean}, the better the smoothing.

With a reservoir capacitor only, the ripple voltage may typically be about 10% of the mean voltage. On a mean output of $20\,$V this gives a ripple of $2\,$V. By adding a good filter circuit, the ripple can then be reduced to about $0.02\,$V ($20\,$mV).

Power loss in a diode: temperature rise

When a diode is conducting a current, there is a potential drop across the diode; Figure 9.10 illustrates this. A potential drop of about $1\,$V is typical for power diodes. This potential drop is a measure of the energy that is required to force electrons through the diode. The energy lost by the electrical system in this way is gained by the diode material,

Figure 9.9 *A power diode, designed and made for the rectification of ac. It will deliver a direct current of up to 380 A, if mounted on a suitably large heat sink. The bridge rectifier shown in Figure 9.1 is fitted with these diodes. (Photograph approximately one-third actual size. Source: GD Rectifiers Limited.)* Enlarged on page 100.

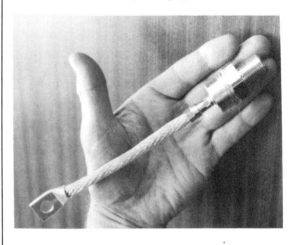

Figure 9.10 *A power diode conducting a current of 100 A. There is a potential drop of about 1 V across it.*

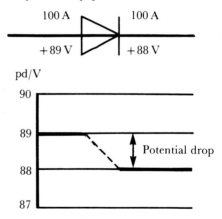

whose internal energy rises, leading to a rise in temperature. Almost the whole of the potential drop occurs in the junction layer, and it is here that the temperature rise is greatest. To project the diode, most manufacturers quote an upper operating temperature of about $160\,^{\circ}$C for silicon diode junctions.

In order to keep the junction of a power diode at a safe operating temperature it is usually necessary to provide a cooling system, the choice of which will depend upon the rate at which energy has to be removed as heat. Thus it is necessary to know the power loss (Js^{-1} or W) in the diode at the operating conditions. Power losses can be found from a diode's forward characteristics, but obtaining values is outside the scope of this book.

The power diode in Figure 9.9, when being used with an ac input to give a dc output of 300 A, has a power loss of about 400 W. That is, about 400 joules per second are being liberated in the junction region, causing its temperature to rise. The diode is used mounted on an air cooled heat sink, such as is shown in Figure 9.1.

A miniature bridge rectifier for electronic equipment

The photograph in Figure 9.11 shows a miniature bridge rectifier, actual size. The manufacturer states that typical applications are: 'Internal power supplies for electronic equipment, control equipment, and TV sets'.

Figure 9.11 A bridge rectifier for electronic circuits. It will provide a direct output current of 2 A. Photograph actual size; scale divisions 1 mm. (Sample provided by Semikron Limited, Hertford.)

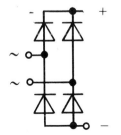

Figure 9.12 The bridge rectifier circuit diagram.

Examine the photograph; find the ac input leads and the +ve and −ve output leads. Also examine the circuit diagram in Figure 9.12; find the input and output leads in relation to the diodes.

The manufacturer gives the following information:

dc output current: 2.0 A maximum

ac input pd:

Type number	Input pd (V_{rms})	Reservoir capacitor (max) (μF)
SKB2/02	60	3000
SKB2/04	125	2200
SKB2/08	250	1000
SKB2/12	500	500

Diode junction temperature (max): 150 °C

Cooling: On printed circuit boards. If the rectifier is not seated directly onto the pcb but is standing 10 mm away from it on its four wire leads, this can improve the cooling by about 15% due to the air cooling of the wires.

9.2 Examine the photograph of the rectifier shown in Figure 9.11, and find its type number. Using the manufacturer's data, in the text:
(a) At what ac input pd is it intended to work?

Figure 9.13 Graph showing the power loss in the rectifier (four diodes) against the dc output current. (Source: Semikron Limited.)

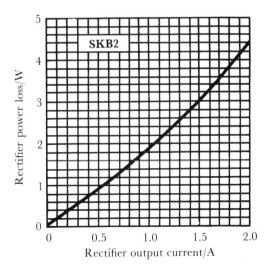

(b) For smoothing the output, what is the recommended maximum capacitance for the reservoir capacitor?

9.3 If the rectifier (Type SKB2) is delivering its full load current of 2.0 A, at its rated pd:
(a) What power is it supplying?
(b) What power loss is occurring in the rectifier? (The circuit being used is the simplest possible one; the rectifier is supplying a resistor as load. There is no smoothing capacitor. Use the graph in Figure 9.13.)

Answers to questions

9.1 (a) 280 W; (b) 370 W
9.2 (a) 60 V$_{rms}$; (b) 3000 μF
9.3 (a) 120 W; (b) 4.4 W

Figure 9.9 reproduced. Approximately two-thirds actual size.

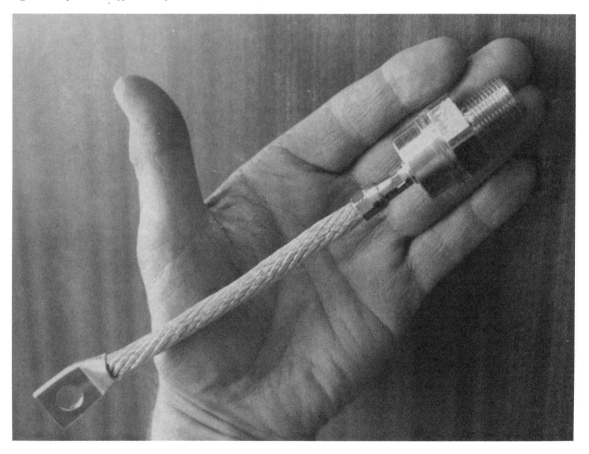

10. Forces between conductors carrying AC

Busbars

Repulsion

A current in a conductor creates a magnetic field around the conductor. When two conductors, each carrying a current, are near to each other the magnetic field around one interacts with the magnetic field around the other, and each experiences a force. If the currents in the conductors are in the *same direction*, the forces are of *attraction*. If the currents are in *opposite directions*, the forces are of *repulsion*. This was described in Chapter 5, pages 60 to 63; you should read this chapter again, paying particular attention to Figures 5.1 and 5.6.

Figure 10.1(a) shows parallel busbars carrying alternating current in the positive, or forward, half of the cycle. The outward current and the return current are in opposite directions and thus the forces on the bars are of repulsion. Figure 10.1(b) shows the negative, or reverse, half of the cycle. The

Figure 10.1 *Alternating current in parallel busbars, and the forces on the bars due to electromagnetic interaction: (a) positive half-cycle; (b) negative half-cycle.*

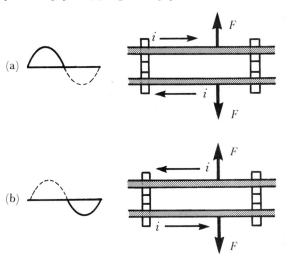

directions of the outward current and the return current have reversed, but they are still opposite to each other, and so the bars still experience forces of repulsion.

Thus, with two busbars in an ac circuit, carrying the outward and return current, the forces experienced are always of repulsion. *Under normal operating conditions the forces are small, but under short circuit conditions they may be very large indeed.* They must be calculated, and taken into account in the design of the insulators for the bars and the supports for the insulators. In a serious short circuit, the bars may be deformed; this is shown in Figure 5.6, page 62.

Vibration

Examine Figure 10.2 and read the caption.

The maximum force on the bars will occur when the current is at its peak value. The bars deform: there is a change in shape, and an increase in total length. When the deforming force is reduced and falls to zero, the elasticity of the metal bar restores the bar to its original shape and length.

Figure 10.2 *(a) An ac waveform. (b) Two busbars with their displacements (greatly exaggerated) in response to repulsion forces at normal current levels.*

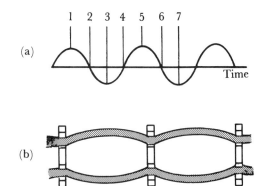

10.1 Figure 10.2(a) shows an ac waveform with peak and zero current values, labelled 1 to 7.

(a) At certain instants in time, the deforming force is zero. List the numbers for these instants.

(b) At certain instants in time, the deforming force is a maximum. List the numbers of these instants.

(c) Describe simply, using between one word and about six words, the nature of the movement of the bars.

(d) How many pulses of deforming force are there per cycle of ac?

(e) If the ac is 50 Hz, what is the frequency of the deforming force?

The vibration of busbars which is produced by the alternating currents they carry must be taken into account in the design of the bars and their supports. A bar secured by two supports has a *natural vibration frequency* (at which it will vibrate if tapped with a hammer). If this natural frequency is the same as the forcing frequency of the vibrations produced by the ac (that is, 100 Hz, for 50 Hz ac), then the amplitude of the bar vibrations builds up rapidly, and could break the supports. The system goes into *resonance*.

The following is an extract from a manual on the design of busbars.

Vibrational Stresses. *Stresses will be created in a conductor by forced vibrations, the amplitude of which determines the value of the stress . . . The conductor should be designed to have a natural frequency which is not within 30% of the vibration frequency produced by the magnetic fields resulting from currents in adjacent conductors.*
(Source: Copper for Busbars. Copper Development Association)

10.2 The frequency of the ac power supply in the United States is 60 Hz. What is the frequency of the forces which cause busbars to vibrate in the United States?

10.3 In order to avoid busbar vibrations going into resonance, what range of natural frequencies for busbars should be avoided in the United Kingdom?

10.4 Similarly, what range of natural frequencies for busbars should be avoided in the United States (60 Hz ac)?

Power transformer windings

The directions of the forces

In power transformers, the primary winding and the secondary winding each carry large currents when the transformer is delivering full power. Each winding is a 'conductor carrying a current', and the

Figure 10.3 *(a) A vertical section through a power transformer, revealing the turns of the windings. (b) A plan view of the transformer, seen from above, revealing one complete turn of each winding. (This figure may be photocopied or otherwise reproduced for class use.)*

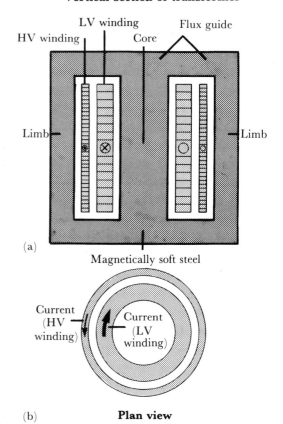

Vertical section of transformer

HV winding LV winding Core Flux guide

Limb   Limb

(a)

Magnetically soft steel

Current (HV winding)   Current (LV winding)

(b)   **Plan view**

windings are close to each other. Therefore *each winding experiences a force on it as a result of the current in the other*. These forces can be very large, particularly if a short circuit fault occurs, and the windings must be designed and made so as to withstand safely these forces. Examine Figure 10.3 and read the caption.

The transformer consists of a central core of magnetically soft steel, with two coils wound around it: the low voltage (LV) winding nearer to the core, and the high voltage (HV) winding farther from it. To provide a complete magnetic pathway, or circuit, for the magnetic flux, the top of the core is made continuous with the bottom of the core by means of a magnetically soft steel top, two limbs and a bottom.

10.5 A study of currents in and forces on windings

For this study, use a photocopy of Figure 10.3, or some other form of copy, or a sketch. The diagram in the book should not be marked.

(a) *Current directions.* The diagram shows the directions of currents in windings at a particular instant. The current in the high voltage winding and the current in the low voltage winding are in *opposite* directions in relation to each other. On your copy, in diagram (a), complete the current direction symbols for the right-hand part of the windings.

(b) *Lenz's law.* If the transformer is a step down one, and if the power input is on the high voltage side, use Lenz's law to show that at all times the current in the low voltage winding will be in the *opposite* direction to the current in the high voltage winding. (The alternating current in the HV coil produces a changing magnetic flux, which is shared by the LV coil; and the changing flux in the LV coil induces an emf in the LV coil, and hence a current in the LV circuit.)

(c) *Directions of the forces.* In diagram (b): (i) Mark in the direction of the forces on the two coils, at the positions of the current arrows. (ii) At the positions of 12 o'clock, 3 o'clock and 6 o'clock, draw in further

current arrows and force arrows. (iii) Describe simply what is happening to each coil, with regard to the forces experienced by them. (iv) In the upper diagram, mark in some force direction arrows on the coils.

(d) *Mechanical consequences for the coils.* Figure 4.9 shows a coil being wound for a transformer. The rectangular section copper conductor is being wound onto a supporting cylinder of compressed fibre board. Look at this diagram again, and read the caption.

When a transformer is on load and is delivering a current: (i) the forces *compress the inner coil* onto the supporting fibre board cylinder; and a cylinder is resistant to compression; (ii) the forces *cause the outer windings to move radially outwards and to stretch.* On a short circuit, the sudden very large outward force could break the winding.

Suggest a means for preventing the outer coils from moving outwards, and breaking, on short circuit. (Look at Figure 4.9 again to see the nature of the structure for which some sort of preventive arrangement is needed.)

Examine Figure 10.4, and read the caption. The photographs show how outwards movement of the outer winding is restrained in a large transformer. The vertical strips are of compressed fibre board, bound tightly over the winding by means of terylene cords. The tight cords, acting on the strips of board, provide an inwards force on the winding; this force opposes the outwards force on the winding which arises from the currents. In Figure 10.4(a), the coil in the background is the inner, or low voltage, coil for the same transformer.

Estimating the magnitude of the forces

The force, F, between two parallel conductors each of length l, and a distance a apart, carrying currents of i_1 and i_2 is given by:

$$F = \frac{\mu_0 \mu_r i_1 i_2 l}{2\pi a}; \quad \text{and} \quad \mu_0 = 4\pi \times 10^{-7}\,\text{Hm}^{-1}$$

This was discussed in Chapter 5, 'Forces between current-carrying conductors', pages 60 to 63.

Figure 10.4 *The outer winding of a large transformer, and the arrangement to restrain the winding from outwards movement. The strips and binding provide inwards forces, which oppose the outwards forces arising from the currents in the conductors. (Photographs taken at E. B. Nitran Limited, Transformers and Fusegear, Dundee.)*

(a)

(b)

If the conductors are in air or in oil (as they would be in a transformer), $\mu_r = 1$; and the force is

$$F = \frac{4\pi \times 10^{-7} \times i_1 i_2 l}{2\pi a} = \frac{2 i_1 i_2 l}{a} \times 10^{-7} \qquad (10.1)$$

We will take the example of a 7500 V/435 V distribution transformer, such as might supply a small group of houses, providing a maximum output power of 600 kVA. Its structure could be very similar to that of the transformer in Figure 10.3. The height of the *coils*, without flux guides, might be about 0.35 m, that is, about one-third of a metre. The outside diameter of the windings might be about 0.4 m. The conductor separation, a, might be about 50 mm.

The high voltage winding might have 380 turns,

and the low voltage winding 22 turns (380 turns: 22 turns = 17.3; and 7500 V:435 V = 17.2).

When delivering full power, of 600 kVA, the current in the high voltage (7500 V) winding would be $I_{HV} = 80$ A (600 000 VA/7500 V = 80 A). Similarly (for a 100% efficient transformer), the current in the low voltage winding would be $I_{LV} = 1380$ A (600 000 VA/435 V = 1380 A).

We need a value for the lengths of the windings. An approximate value may be obtained from the mean diameter of the two sets of windings; this would give a mean *circumference* for the windings, of about 1.25 m.

Summarising this data and using rms values, we have $I_{HV} = 80$ A; $I_{LV} = 1380$ A; conductor separation, $a = 50$ mm; HV turns, 380; LV turns, 22;

average circumference of windings $= 1.25$ m; height of coils $= 0.35$ m.

$$F = \frac{2I_{HV}I_{LV}l}{a} \times 10^{-7}$$

Taking into account the number of turns, we have:

$$F = \frac{2 \times (80 \times 380) \times (1380 \times 22) \times 1.25 \times 10^{-7}\,\text{N}}{0.050}$$
$$= 4600\,\text{N}$$

Thus the outwards force on the whole of the outer winding is 4600 N, and the inwards force on the whole of the inner winding is 4600 N. The outwards force is spread over the outer surface area of the HV windings. This area is (circumference × height) $= (1.25\,\text{m} \times 0.35\,\text{m}) = 0.44\,\text{m}^2$

Therefore, the outwards stress exerted on the HV coils is $4600\,\text{N}/0.44\,\text{m}^2 = 10\,500\,\text{Nm}^{-2}$. One atmosphere pressure $= 101\,000\,\text{Nm}^{-2}$, so the stress on the coils is equivalent to about 0.1 Atm.

This stress would safely be taken up by the mechanical strength of the copper conductors. But the situation is very different under short circuit conditions. Then the HV peak current might be about 4000 A, and the LV peak current about 70 000 A. Under these circumstances, copper strip conductors would not be able to withstand the stress and they would deform, unless restrained by some inwards force such as is provided by the protective strips and cords shown in Figure 10.4.

10.6 Repulsion forces on short circuit

The transformer which has just been described, pages 104 to 105, when short circuited, carries a current of 4070 A in the HV winding and a current of 70 200 A in the LV winding. Calculate:
(a) the outwards force on the whole of the outer winding;
(b) the outwards stress on the outer winding;
(c) the value of (b) in terms of atmospheres pressure.

Answers to questions

10.1 (a) 2, 4, 6; (b) 1, 3, 5, 7; (c) vibratory; undergoes vibrations; (d) 2; (e) 100 Hz
10.2 120 Hz
10.3 70 Hz–130 Hz
10.4 64 Hz–156 Hz
10.5 (c) (iii) The outer coil is being forced radially outwards, and is being stretched; the inner coil is being forced radially inwards, and is being compressed
10.6 (a) 12 000 kN; (b) 27 000 kNm^{-2}; (c) 120 Atm

11. Generating AC

Electromagnetic induction

Charge separation in a moving conductor

Electricity may be generated by *the relative movement of a conductor and a magnetic field*. The field may be stationary, with the conductor moving in it; or the conductor may be stationary, with a moving field affecting it.

When an electric charge moves across a magnetic field, the charge experiences a force on it. For instance, an electron fired across a magnetic field in a vacuum tube experiences a force on it which deflects the electron.

A metallic conductor consists of fixed positive charges in the metal lattice, and mobile electrons. If the conductor moves across a magnetic field, all the charges experience a force on them. The positive charges, being fixed in the lattice, cannot move; but the electrons will move. In Figure 11.1, a conductor is moving upwards, and its electrons are moving upwards with it. This is equivalent to a conventional current moving downwards. The use of Fleming's left-hand rule, or some other suitable

Figure 11.1 *A metallic conductor being moved at right-angles to a magnetic field. A potential difference is developed between the ends of the conductor, due to the force on the electrons.*

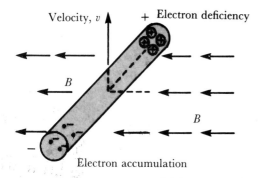

rule, shows that the electrons experience a force on them acting along the axis of the conductor and towards its left-hand end. Mobile electrons thus move along the conductor towards that end, leaving the other end deficient of electrons. A potential difference therefore develops between the two ends of the conductor.

The magnitude of the potential difference can be found either by considering the electrostatic field formed by the charge separation, or it can be found from Faraday's law of electromagnetic induction.

Faraday's law of electromagnetic induction

Faraday's law of electromagnetic induction states that *the emf induced in a conductor is directly proportional to the rate of change of flux linkage.* (In terms of flux cutting, *the emf is directly proportional to the rate of flux cutting.*)

$$E \propto \frac{\mathrm{d}}{\mathrm{d}t}(N\Phi)$$

and

$$E = \text{a constant} \times \frac{\mathrm{d}}{\mathrm{d}t}(N\Phi)$$

$$\left.\rule{0pt}{2.5em}\right\} \quad (11.1)$$

If the unit of magnetic flux, the weber, Wb, is defined as the magnetic flux which in a one-turn coil induces an emf of 1 V when the flux is reduced to zero in 1 s, then the proportionality constant in equation (11.1) is 1. Thus

$$E = \text{rate of change of } (N\Phi) = \frac{\mathrm{d}}{\mathrm{d}t}(N\Phi) = N\frac{\mathrm{d}\Phi}{\mathrm{d}t}$$

E is in volts, $\mathrm{d}\Phi/\mathrm{d}t$ is in webers per second, and N is the number of turns if the situation involves a coil.

The flux density of a magnetic field, B, is defined as the magnetic flux passing through a unit area which is at right-angles to the field. Thus

Figure 11.2 *A conductor of length l moving upwards with a velocity v in a magnetic field of flux density B.*

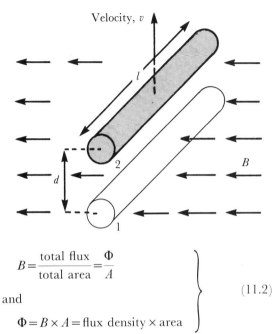

$$B = \frac{\text{total flux}}{\text{total area}} = \frac{\Phi}{A}$$

and

$$\Phi = B \times A = \text{flux density} \times \text{area}$$

(11.2)

Figure 11.2 shows a conductor of length l. It is lying at right-angles to a field of flux density B; and it is moving upwards, at right-angles to the field, with velocity v. If the velocity is 4 m s^{-1}, then in 1 second the conductor will have travelled upwards a distance $d = 4$ m. The area swept out by the conductor in 1 second in moving from position 1 to position 2 is $(4 \times l) \text{ m}^2$.

The flux cut in $1 \text{ s} = $ Area swept out $\times B$
$\qquad\qquad\qquad = 4lB$

Since the distance travelled per second is the velocity, v,

Flux cut per second $= vlB =$ rate of flux cutting
Thus, induced emf $= vlB$

Example. A conductor of length 2 m lies at right-angles to a magnetic field of flux density $B = 3$ Wb, and the conductor is moving mutually at right-angles to its length and to the flux at a speed of 10 m s^{-1}. What is the emf which is induced between its ends?

$E =$ rate of cutting of flux
$\quad = vlB = (10 \times 2 \times 3) \text{ V} = 60 \text{ V}$

Machine elements

An isolated moving conductor, as shown in Figure 11.2, is not a practical arrangement for providing a current. A loop, with some simple means of drawing a current, is needed. A simple form is shown in Figure 11.3. A fixed rectangular conductor, ABCDEF, has a magnet rotating within it. The rotating flux results in a change of flux linkage in the loop; viewed in another way, the loop cuts the rotating flux. The result is that an emf is induced and can be measured across the ends of the loop at A and F. If a circuit is connected, then the potential difference between A and F results in a current in the circuit.

The rotating magnetic field produces a force on the electrons in the loop, and these electrons in moving along the conductor repel others along the circuit, thus producing a movement of electrons in the entire circuit.

Every half-rotation of the magnet produces a reversal of the polarity of the magnetic field at the fixed conductor. The direction of the force on the electrons reverses, the polarity of the emf reverses, and if there is a complete circuit the direction of the

Figure 11.3 *A looped conductor, with a magnet rotating inside it. The changing flux linkage in the coil induces an emf between the ends of the coil.*

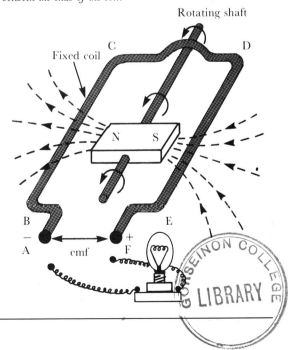

Figure 11.4 *This rotating magnet is provided with a flux guide of magnetically soft steel. Most of the magnetic flux path is in the steel. In Figure 11.3, most of the flux path is in air.*

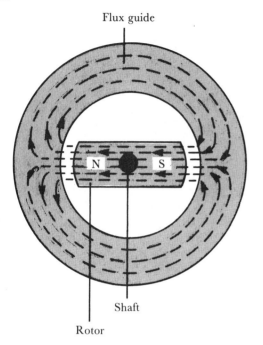

Flux guide

Shaft

Rotor

Figure 11.5 *The stationary conductor has to be fixed so that it does not move. It is fitted into slots in the flux guide.*

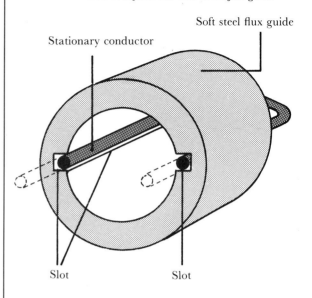

Soft steel flux guide

Stationary conductor

Slot   Slot

Figure 11.6 *The main elements of a simple alternator or ac generator. On the outside is the flux guide; the stationary conductor is located in slots; and the rotating magnetic field in this instance is provided by an electromagnet.*

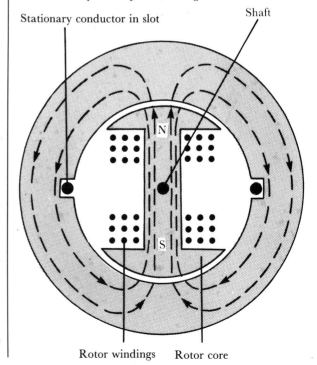

Stationary conductor in slot   Shaft

Rotor windings   Rotor core

current reverses. The system produces an alternating emf, and the device is termed an 'alternator' or 'ac generator'. Figure 6.1(b) shows the waveform for the emf of a simple one-loop device such as we have been considering. Look again at Figure 6.1(b), because the output is not a sine wave: which you might expect.

Since sine wave emfs and currents are particularly desirable for many purposes, practical alternators have to be designed so that their output does have a sine wave.

It is difficult to create magnetic fields in air, and very much easier to create them in a magnetic material. In Figure 11.3, the magnetic flux is almost entirely in air; in Figure 11.4, the magnet has been surrounded by a ring of magnetically soft steel which acts as a flux guide, and the flux is almost entirely in steel. For the same magnet, the flux density in the air near the pole pieces would be much greater with the flux guide arrangement (Figure 11.4) than without it (Figure 11.3). In machinery in which magnetic flux has to travel through air, engineers try to design it so that the air gap is as small as possible: usually just sufficient to allow a safe clearance for moving parts.

The stationary conductor has to be held fixed in relation to the rotating flux. Examine Figure 11.5 and read the caption. Since the steel flux guide is a conductor of electricity, the stationary conductor coil has to be insulated.

These basic elements may now be put together.

In power alternators, even those of just a few kilowatts, the rotating magnetic field is provided by an electromagnet. This enables the output emf to .be adjusted. The current in an electromagnet winding can be increased or decreased, increasing or decreasing the flux produced, and thus increasing or decreasing the emf at the stationary conductor terminals. This is shown in Figure 11.6, where a flux guide, stationary conductor in slots, and rotating electromagnet (or rotor) are assembled together.

A mobile 5 kVA AC generating set

The generating set's main units, and performance

On a large construction site there is a need for electric power on a temporary basis at many different places, and small mobile generating sets meet the need. The photograph in Figure 11.7 shows a generating set which may be pushed along by one person, and which will provide 5 kVA of power. This would typically be used to drive circular saws, band saws, drills and grinders, and also to provide temporary lighting. The tools would typically require about 1.5 kVA of power each, and a floodlight would require about 1.5 kW. (The significance of power quoted in units of VA and of W was discussed in Chapter 7, 'Inductive machines: inductive power and working power'; but it is not necessary to know the details for this chapter.)

An electric generating set consists of two principal units: an *alternator* or *ac generator* which

Figure 11.7 *A mobile generating set which can produce 5 kVA of power, delivered at either 120 V or 240 V. Here it is being used to drive a circular saw, top left, requiring 1.5 kVA of power. On the generating set, the cylindrical alternator occupies the lower left-hand half, and the engine to drive it occupies the whole of the right-hand half.*

produces the emf, and an *engine* which drives the generator. In the photograph given in Figure 11.7, the right-hand half of the generating set is occupied by a petrol engine. On the left, the lower half is occupied by the generator. Above the generator is a selector and distribution box. On its left is a selector switch for selecting an output of 240 V or 120 V. On its right are two sockets with plastic covers.

At full power, the *engine* provides 6.21 kW of mechanical power along the shaft, and the *generator* provides 5.00 kVA of electrical power. Thus there is a loss of 1.21 kW of power in the generator. Most of this is due to energy loss in the conductors (the stationary coils and the rotor coils) as a result of their resistance to the currents in them, and it appears as heat, i.e. as I^2R power losses. In consequence, the temperature of the coils rises; and they may be operating at about 120 °C: well above the boiling temperature of water.

The efficiency of the conversion is given by

$$\text{Efficiency} = \frac{\text{Electrical power out}}{\text{Mechanical power in}}$$

$$= \frac{5.00 \text{ kVA (or kW)}}{6.21 \text{ kW}} = 80\%$$

Figure 11.8 *A sectioned ac generator about $\frac{1}{3}$ m long (320 mm) and 200 mm in diameter. Its total mass is 30 kg. (Source: Markon Division of Newage International Limited, Stamford.)*

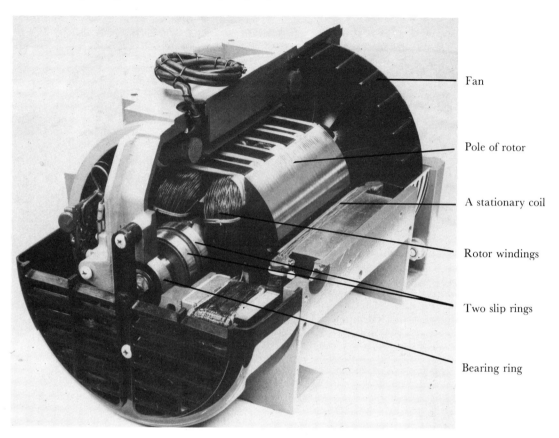

Fan

Pole of rotor

A stationary coil

Rotor windings

Two slip rings

Bearing ring

The main parts of the ac generator

Figure 11.8 shows a sectioned generator. Examine the photograph and read the caption.

If the energy which is released in the generator, and which appears as heat, is not removed then the temperature of the windings will continue to rise. The insulation on the windings will become damaged and the generator will cease to function. At the far end of the generator shown in Figure 11.8 is a fan; at the near end is a series of slatted openings. Cool air from the outside is drawn in by the fan and is drawn over and through the windings. This cools the windings; and warmed air is then passed out of the machine at the fan end into the atmosphere.

The rotating electromagnet, or rotor, occupies the middle portion of the machine. Examine it, and compare its shape and structure with the earlier diagram in Figure 11.6.

In Figure 11.8 find a stationary coil, and part of the flux guide.

The current for the rotor is led in and out by means of two slip rings mounted on the rotor shaft, and by carbon brushes (which are not shown) pressed lightly onto the rotating rings.

The near end of the shaft is supported in a bearing ring which rotates in a ball bearing race.

The rotor

The rotor core and poles are made of steel. Around the core are wound 500 turns of 1 mm diameter copper wire, insulated with varnish. The resistance of the coil when the alternator is cold and not in use is $10\,\Omega$, but when delivering full power the operating temperature of the interior is about $120\,°C$ and the resistance of the coil has risen to about $14\,\Omega$.

11.1 Resistance of the hot, working rotor coil

At $20\,°C$, the rotor coil has a resistance of $10.0\,\Omega$. If the operating temperature of the coil at a particular time was $120\,°C$, and if the temperature coefficient of resistance of the copper winding was $3.73 \times 10^{-3}\,K^{-1}$, what was the operating resistance of the rotor coil?

11.2 Power loss in the rotor, as heat

Find the rate at which energy is lost in the rotor, as heat (I^2R), at full power. Rotor coil current at full power $=5.0\,A$; rotor coil resistance: use the value found in Question 11.1. Give the answer:
(a) in joules per second;
(b) in watts.

11.3 Rotation rate for 50 Hz ac

In order to produce 50 Hz ac, at what rate must the engine rotate the rotor? (Give your answer in revolutions per minute.)

The generator is tested at a higher rotation rate, at $4000\,\text{rev min}^{-1}$, as a safety check. The mass of wire on the rotor is 1 kg, $\frac{1}{2}$ kg at one pole and $\frac{1}{2}$ kg at the other pole. At a rotation speed of $4000\,\text{rev min}^{-1}$ the centripetal force required to hold the wire in and prevent it from flying off the core is a force equivalent to the weight of a mass of about half a tonne.

11.4 The centripetal force required to retain the rotating coils

The average distance of the wire coils from the axis of rotation is approximately 50 mm. Each coil has a mass of approximately 0.5 kg. For the test rotation rate of $4000\,\text{rev min}^{-1}$, obtain an approximate value for the centripetal force required to hold the wire in position.

To provide the centripetal (or retaining) force, the coils could be tied down in some way. The main retention, however, is provided in another manner. Examine Figure 11.8, and also Figure 11.6. The coils are wound *under* the plane surface of the top and bottom projections, or pole pieces, of the rotor

The steel pole pieces and steel core provide the main retention.

In addition, steel bands pass across the coils, from the tip of one pole piece to the tip of the other one. Find these bands in Figure 11.8.

The stator

The stator is the stationary part which is made up of the fixed flux guide, and the stationary windings (in their slots in the flux guide). Each coil can provide an emf of 120 V. The coils may be connected in series, as in Figure 11.9(a), giving an output at 240 V; or they may be connected in parallel, as in Figure 11.9(b), giving an output at 120 V.

The stator coils have to carry large currents.

Figure 11.9 *Our generator has two separate stationary windings, each producing an emf of 120 V. The windings may be connected in series to provide 240 V; or they may be connected in parallel to provide 120 V.*

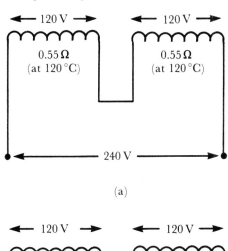

(a)

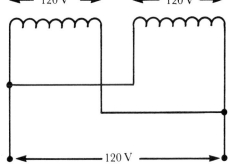

When operating at 240 V the full power current is about 20 A; and when operating at 120 V the full power current is about 40 A. Thick copper conductors are not easily bent and fitted into place. Each winding is therefore made not of a single thick conductor but of several 1 mm diameter copper wires, insulated with varnish and connected together in parallel. Each coil consists of 20 turns of this composite wire. As shown in Figure 11.9(a), the resistance of each stator coil at an operating temperature of 120 °C is 0.55 Ω.

11.5 Full power currents at 240 V and at 120 V

The generator is able to provide 5.0 kVA (or 5.0 kW) of power when operating at full power. Calculate the current delivered at full power:
(a) at 240 V;
(b) at 120 V.

11.6 Stator coil power loss in the form of heat

Find the rate at which energy is lost as heat from the stator coils (the I^2R loss) at full power:
(a) at 240 V output;
(b) at 120 V output. (Use the current values obtained from question 11.5.)

As the magnetic flux rotates, with the rotor, there is a change of flux not only in the stator coils but also in the steel of the flux guide. This change of flux causes emfs to be set up within the steel, and since steel is a conductor the emfs result in currents in the steel. These are known as *eddy currents*. Like other currents in a conductor, they lead to a temperature rise in the conductor and to a loss of energy as heat.

If the flux guide were to be made of a wide piece of solid steel the current values could be large, and thus the heat losses would be large. The flux guide is therefore made of thin sheets, or *laminations*, of steel, each about 1 mm thin. Examine the flux guide in Figure 11.8 and look for laminations. The laminations are made of high resistance steel; and the surfaces of the sheets are lightly insulated. In these ways the eddy currents are kept down to low values and energy losses are kept down.

Obtaining DC for the rotor coil

In order to provide an electromagnet which has fixed polarity, the rotor coil must be supplied with

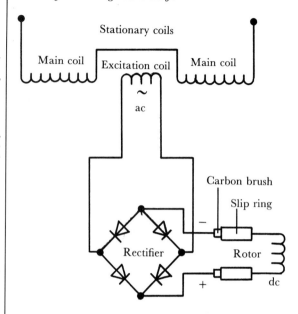

Figure 11.10 *How a direct current for the rotor coil is obtained from the ac generator itself.*

direct current. This is not obtained from an external source such as a battery; it is obtained from within the generator itself. In addition to the two main stationary coils there is a smaller third coil: the 'excitation coil'. Like the main coils, it is wound in the flux guide; examine the upper part of Figure 11.10.

A rotating flux in the excitation coil produces an alternating emf, and an alternating current if there is a completed circuit. The circuit includes a bridge rectifier, and the dc from this is connected to the brushes and thus to the slip rings and the rotor coil; examine the lower part of Figure 11.10.

When the generator is not in use, and the petrol engine is motionless, there is no current in the rotor coil and thus no electromagnetic field. The reader may rightly ask: 'In that case, when the engine is started, how can the generator produce an emf, for there will be no flux to rotate within the fixed coils?' The answer is that the core of the rotor is made of steel which is a weak permanent magnet. On start-up, the weak flux rotating in the excitation coil generates an emf. This produces a weak current in the rectifier circuit and in the rotor coil. This reinforces the rotor field and the flux rapidly builds up to the required value.

The generator's power losses and efficiency

Some of the sources of energy losses which occur have already been mentioned: I^2R losses due to the currents in the rotor coil and in the stationary coils, and due to eddy currents in the magnetically soft steel laminations of the flux guide. In addition, there are mechanical losses: the energy required to drive the fan (and draw air in over the coils), and energy to overcome friction in the bearings. (With ballbearings, this friction loss is usually very low, low enough to be ignored compared with the other losses.)

When the generator is operating at full power output, at 110 V, and at 120 °C, the losses are shown in Table 11.1.

Table 11.1. *Power losses in the main parts of the ac generator, when delivering full power at 110 V.*

Unit	Power loss (W)
Main stationary coils	569
Excitation coil	62
Rotor coil	343
Eddy currents in flux guide	111
Fan, drawing air over coils	97
Stray losses	28
	1210

(*Source:* Newage International Limited.)

The engine input along the shaft is 6210 W, and the output is 5000 W. The efficiency is

$$\frac{\text{Output power}}{\text{Input power}} = \frac{5000\,\text{W}}{6210\,\text{W}} = 80.5\%$$

Answers to questions

11.1 13.7 Ω
11.2 (a) 343 J s^{-1}; (b) 343 W
11.3 3000 rev min^{-1}
11.4 4.4×10^3 N
11.5 (a) 21 A; (b) 42 A
11.6 (a) 477 W; (b) 477 W

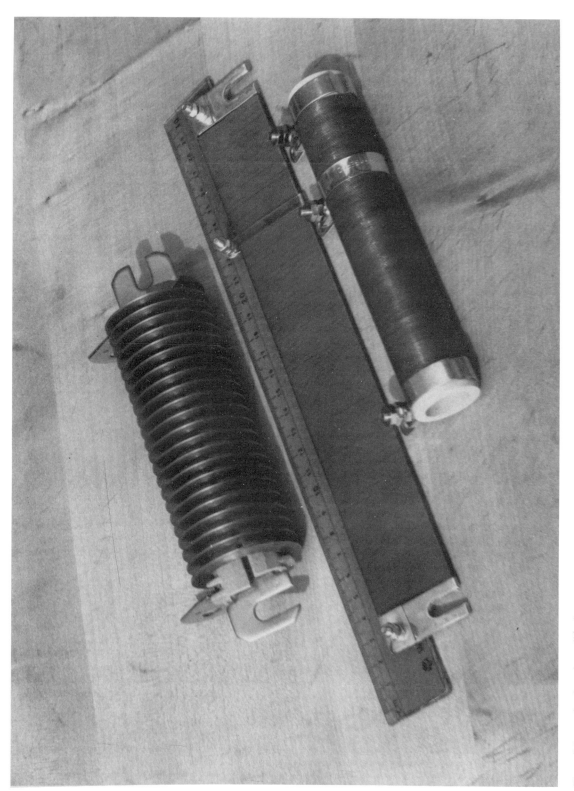

Figure 2.1 reproduced to almost life size.

Index